STUDIES IN ENGLISH LITERATURE

Volume CIV

"Unfinished Replica of Giotto Painting the Portrait of Dante"
Plate 48, vol. ii of Virginia Surtees, *The Paintings and Drawings of Dante Gabriel Rossetti (1828-1882): A Catalogue Raisonné*, Oxford Press, 1971.

THE POETRY OF DANTE G. ROSSETTI:
A CRITICAL READING AND SOURCE STUDY

by

FLORENCE SAUNDERS BOOS

1976
MOUTON
THE HAGUE · PARIS

© Copyright 1976
Mouton & Co. B.V., Publishers, The Hague

No part of this book may be translated or reproduced in any form, by print, photoprint, microfilm, or any other means, without written permission from the publishers.

PR
5247
.B6

ISBN 90 279 3471 1

Printed in the Netherlands

To William Boos

and

To the Memory of

Harry O. Saunders
(1886-1967)

and

Ella R. Saunders
(1875-1973)

TABLE OF CONTENTS

Preface ix

Introduction: Critical Views of Rossetti 1

1. Style in "The House of Life" 18
   A. Is there formal development or change in sonnets of different periods? 20
   B. Characteristics Devices; Resemblances with Other Poets 44
   C. Imagery and Mannerisms of Five Sonnets 76
   D. Sex, Guilt, and Victorian Preoccupations 88
   E. Notes 92

2. Evolution of a Narrative Ballad Style 102
   A. Early Romantic Narrative Ballads 104
   B. Condensed Ballads of Sexual Revenge 141
   C. Final Ballads: Darkened Romanticism 159
   D. Notes 193

3. Reflective and Lyrical Poetry 200
   A. Poetry on Pictures and Statuary 200
   B. Philosophical Poems 232
   C. Romantic and Philosophic Lyrics 245
   D. Political Sonnets 248
   E. Notes 254

Appendix: Sources and Resemblances 259
   1. *The Divine Comedy* 260
   2. Poe 266
   3. Blake 266

4. Lord Houghton's *The Life and Letters of John Keats* . . . 269
5. "No Ship Came Near": A Rejected Echo of Coleridge?. . 272
6. The Nineteenth Century "Literary" Ballad "The Rime" and "The Ballad of Reading Gaol" 273
7. Resemblances to Wordsworth in "On Mary's Portrait" . . 274
8. Leigh Hunt 275
9. Charles Wells 276
10. "Jenny" and W.B. Scott's "Rosabell" 277
11. David Scott 278
12. Elizabeth Barrett Browning 279
13. A Passage from Tennyson and Two Rossetti Lyrics 282
14. "The House of Life" and "Modern Love" 283
15. The French Symbolists and Wilde 285

Selected Bibliography 287
  A. Earlier Drafts and Versions of Rossetti's Poems 287
  B. Works by Rossetti 288
  C. Biographical Materials on Rossetti 289
  D. Works on Rossetti's Poetry and Translations 290
  E. Sources and Influences 293
  F. Related Works 294

Index 299

PREFACE

This work began with many intentions: to understand traits of literary Pre-Raphaelitism; to place Rossetti's woman-motif and use of nature in historical and sociological context; to compare Rossetti with Keats, Coleridge, Morris, Hopkins, and the Decadents; and to make comments on the development, shifts, and qualities of his style. Clearly these cannot all be accomplished at once, and each requires careful fusion with recent analyses of Victorian poetic mannerisms and historical studies. Further problems arise in arrangement: Rossetti's poems can be examined chronologically (pre-1850, 1850-1853, *etc.*), or studied in various dyadic combinations with those of other authors (Rossetti/Poe, Rossetti/Coleridge, Rossetti/Tennyson), or divided into thematic categories. The first method requires that the reader keep in mind the entire range of his poetic types and styles, the second demands a knowledge of both chronology and range, while the third, which I have chosen, permits rather precise comparisons of Rossetti's development within each form. Was Rossetti better at some types of poetry than others, for example? Did he develop or alter more in sonnet writing, ballad writing, philosophic poems, or poems on pictures?

I decided to attempt the following:

(i) A series of formal poetic criticisms designed for internal comparison of Rossetti poems.
(ii) A study of his evolution within each of the nominal categories I have chosen, with emphasis on revisions as indices of development.
(iii) Comment on his rhythms.
(iv) Comparisons with later and contemporary poets (Morris, Tennyson), source studies and speculations (Biblical sources, Elizabeth Barrett Browning, Leigh Hunt), and comments on Rossetti's tastes and reading. As much as possible I have shifted these to the appendix.

I do not wish to argue that increased reading of Rossetti is an improvement over or regression from former tastes, or to enhance or diminish past reputations. I believe that we are all at least partially unconscious of what accidents of tradition and associations cause particular writings to seem important; as soon as one has read anything it becomes a source (beware!). Rossetti understood this cycle of sources, and all his life kept reiterating its message to his world. A description of Dante Gabriel Rossetti's poetic style not only comments on his eclectic tastes or on Victorian characteristics, but on present terminology for reading Victorian poetry.

My allusion in the introduction to the scarcity of criticism on Rossetti's poetry is now less accurate; since then three useful works on Rossetti have appeared: Lionel Stevenson's *The Pre-Raphaelite Poets* (1972), containing a long chapter on Rossetti, Ronnalie Howard's *The Dark Glass: Vision and Technique in the Poetry of Dante Gabriel Rossetti* (1972), and Joseph Vogel's *Dante Gabriel Rossetti's Versecraft* (1971). I have revised the bibliography to include materials through the end of 1972.

It gives me pleasure to record that William Boos read and edited each draft of this manuscript. I would also like to express my gratitude to former professors, especially Morris Greenhut of the University of Michigan, Karl Kroeber, now of Columbia University, and Alvin Whitley of the University of Wisconsin, and to the University of Wisconsin librarians, who were unusually diligent in obtaining materials for me. If Eugene Boos, who entered the world as this book neared completion, cannot exactly be described as an aid to its composition, at least he constituted a cheerful distraction.

Fort Erie, Ontario December, 1972

Florence Saunders Boos

INTRODUCTION: CRITICAL VIEWS OF ROSSETTI

One reads frequently of the need for critical studies of Rossetti's poetry, for example in Howard Jones' and William Fredeman's survey of Pre-Raphaelite criticism (*Victorian Poetry: A Guide to Research*, 1956, 1968), and Fredeman's huge bibliography begins with a lament that scholarship in this field has gathered memorabilia but made few evaluative comments. Yet despite these exhortations little has appeared until recently. Why? Rossetti's works are difficult to obtain, but this may be the result, not the cause, of their neglect.

More imporant, a simplistic view of Rossetti's poetry was prevalent for some time and inhibited poetic curiosity. Early commentators such as Paull Baum, Graham Hough, and George Ford believed that his poetry showed little development or variation; as a result both anthologists and critics felt justified in emphasizing allegedly representative set pieces from his early work. Entire debates over his merits and mannerisms have been conducted with both attackers and defenders quoting chiefly from the early poems, most notably "The Bride's Prelude", "The Woodspurge", "The Blessed Damozel", and "My Sister's Sleep"; naturally these emphasize the Keatsian colorism and abrupt naïveté of Rossetti's early style.[1] These categorizations of him as an art-catholic word-painter deflect interest; if Rossetti's poetry lacks thought, does not develop, and consists of superficially symbolic quasi-medieval pictures, there are other things to read. Besides, better examples of medievalized description and symbols occur in Romantic poets and in the early Tennyson and Browning.

As with Hopkins, the perception of "atypical" and "mannered" traits in Rossetti has separated him from the usual topics of Victorian criticism; like Hopkins he has been long left to cultists. Hopkins' religion and apparent asexuality obscured his resemblances in language and psychology to such contemporaries as Tennyson and Swinburne;

similarly a related prudery and its inversion have caused great preoccupation with the "unVictorian" eroticism of Rossetti's themes. He expressed much Victorian opinion and sentiment in his work, however, and his poetry parallels Tennyson and others in mannerism and in effort to see the infinite foreshadowed in physical experience.

An example of such a distraction is the century-long debate following Rossetti's treatment of passion. Even now virtually all Rossetti commentators add their opinions on whether Rossetti's synthesis of body and soul is possible. Some deny the relevance of "body" and "soul" terminology and dismiss Rossetti's interest as trivial; others, following Pater and also denying body-soul distinctions, see Rossetti as the prophet who abolished such distinctions; others soberly reargue the question of soul vs. sense in Rossetti's own language, oblivious to their legions of predecessors and to their debate's lack of specific application to Rossetti. A catalogue of offspring of "The Fleshly School" controversy would constitute a compendium of much of Rossetti criticism and a history of tastes in sexual expression since 1870. Of course, in contrast to some of Tennyson's and Patmore's didactic incitements to wedded bliss (*e.g.* "L'Envoi" to "The Day-Dream"), Rossetti might seem Los unchained. (Perhaps under such circumstances Hopkins gained from his avoidance of the subject of heterosexuality.)

Yet debate over Rossetti's sexual mysticism is strange, since the effort to pass through physical to metaphysical experience is characteristic of the century. An earlier and more limited expression of beauty as mediatrix occurs in Keats; "Then I should be most enviable — with the yearning passion I have for the Beautiful, connected and made one with the ambition of my intellect."[2] Philosophical idealism came to the Victorians with more difficulty. Rossetti's "The House of Life", showing in how many ways he pursued "Lady Beauty" to gain his soul's peace, is one of several large quest-for-transcendence poems of the period, including "In Memoriam" and "The Wreck of the Deutschland".[3] Each describes the attempt to find an image and confirmation of immortality in some limited physical experience; Tennyson chooses the memory of a dead friend of the same sex, Hopkins the violence and stress of shipwreck, Rossetti moments spent with an etherealized, elusive beloved. Each brings his chief hostage to fortune to the point where it is apparently destroyed; each is anxious, convoluted, self-questioning. As the sexuality of other Victorian poetry is increasingly analyzed and recurrent homosexual expressions throughout the period less ignored, Rossetti's erotic preoccupations come to seem unremarkable, and his resemblances in mannerism and opinion to other much-analyzed Victorian authors self-evident; incidentally, he may appear a less insignificant poet.

The comparative neglect of Rossetti's later poetry has side effects; comparisons of early and late versions reveal how Rossetti altered earlier romantic mannerisms to reflect shifts in his own and contemporary taste. Since so many drafts and versions of his poems exist, it seems interesting to follow Rossetti's development for its own sake. Since Rossetti in his early stages was more Keatsian and pictorially colorful than later, emphasis on early poems has led to disregard of his non-Keatsian sources, for example the extent to which he absorbed and transmitted an interest in Coleridgean rhythms. Even at first he was neither very detailed nor pictorial; yet these myths about his poetry have been repeated constantly in discussions of poetic Pre-Raphaelitism.

If Pre-Raphaelitism in poetry means colorism and presentation of detail to mirror psychic stress, it is a quality present thoughout early Victorian poetry; it enlightens little, then, to say that a minor poet is Pre-Raphaelite or that a major poet had early Pre-Raphaelitic tendencies (*e.g.* Tennyson, Browning, Hopkins). Do commentators mean a Keatsian or Browningesque use of color, the romantic and Victorian tendency towards palpitating diction, the use of a Morrisean lady of fear and wonder, or a Ruskinian interest in Shrubbery? After all, what kind of color did Keats use? What kinds of palpitations are common to all Victorians, not just Rossetti? These are issues of sensibility, revealing the need for closer study of diction and psychology in specific poets. As it is, ignorance of Rossetti's works prevents comparison except on the level of noticing damozel icons or archaisms — if it occurs in friendly green woods with a woman it must be Pre-Raphaelite.

Also, when Rossetti's own best work is neglected it is difficult to perceive his indebtedness to and influence on contemporaries. I feel Rossetti's later work and art ballads may have influenced his successors more than portions of his work now considered Pre-Raphaelite. His resemblances to Poe,[4] Tennyson, Browning, his sister, Patmore, Elizabeth Barrett,[5] Bailey,[6] Dobell, Dixon, William Bell Scott,[7] Symons, the early Swinburne,[8] Meredith,[9] Morris, Wilde and others merit further analysis. He is a central figure for studying minor Victorian poets since he influenced and appreciated several. His critical and literary opinions are also revealing; he belongs in a loose tradition of assumptions and enthusiasms shared by Blake,[10] Keats, (to a lesser degree) Hunt, Poe,

Pater, Swinburne, and Wilde, the latter three of whom he influenced directly or indirectly. His emphatic and idiosyncratic preferences within nineteenth-century literature reveal criteria opposed to later canons; his tolerant if effusive analytical comments on such poets as Dobell and Mrs. Browning are interesting in themselves.

A bias towards the early and painterly Rossetti was inadvertently fostered by George Ford's *Keats and the Victorians*, (1944), one of the best studies of cross-influences within the Victorian period. A contrast between this and other discussions of Rossetti at the time — before the appearance of Lang's thesis (1949), Doughty's biography (1949), Rossetti's letters in four volumes (1965-67), and later criticism — reveals how skillfully Ford associates Keats and Rossetti. Ford defines the early Victorian conception of Keats as of a decorative, sensuous poet devoted to beauty and opposed to formalizations of morality, philosophy, science, and political interest. To Tennyson this attitude was only partially acceptable, Ford argues, but Rossetti was one of the first who admired an exclusive devotion to decorative beauties. Rossetti translated these decorative effects into analogues; Ford documents his care to avoid direct echoes and his insistence on his own originality of invention,[11] the intellectual trait he most valued. Ford finds several interesting parallels in description between the early Rossetti and Keats, and since he accepts the view that Rossetti's poetry did not develop, he cites these as typical. He quotes William Rossetti: "Perhaps, in his last few years, the poetry of Keats was more present to my brother's thoughts than that of anyone else, hardly excepting even Dante." Ford accurately explains Rossetti's strong appreciation for Keats' mystic and sensuous medievalism, his entranced woman figure, his intensity and pictoralism. Also Rossetti saw in Keats, as in Leigh Hunt and William Blake, someone who like himself was concerned with the resemblances between poetry and painting.

On the same page on which he describes Rossetti's love of Keats, however, William Rossetti comments with almost equal emphasis on his brother's response to Coleridge.[12]

Coleridge, in certain of his poems — not many amid the entire number of them[13] — was always most deeply admired by Rossetti, and as years passed, increasingly so. Towards the close of his life he would perhaps have exalted a few of Coleridge's poems above all others produced in that period of our literature.

And in the introduction to the *Works* he notes:

Tennyson reigned along with Keats, and Edgar Poe and Coleridge along with Tennyson. In the long run he perhaps enjoyed and revered Coleridge beyond any other modern poet whatsoever, but Coleridge was not so distinctly or separately in the ascendant, at any particular period of youth, as several of the others.[14]

He then mentions his brother's successive enthusiasm for Blake, Wells,[15] and Browning.

As Ford notices tangentially, several of what he sees as Keats-Rossetti parallels are equally valid parallels with Coleridge. (A counterpart to Ford, entitled *Coleridge and the Victorians*, might document surprising latent influence, especially in metrics.) The essential traits for which Rossetti admired Keats — high coloration, the woman-in-trance motif, medievalism, intensity, use of the dramatic ballad — are also Coleridgean characteristics. Coleridge uses fewer descriptive adjectives in his ballads (the only portion of his work which Rossetti admired) than Keats in his narratives. A simplified use of Keatsian coloration can suggest that of Coleridge:

Within the shadow of the ship
I watched their rich attire:
Blue, glossy green, and velvet black,
They coiled and swam; and every track
Was a flash of golden fire.

 ("The Rime", 277-81.)

There are obvious parallels in Rossetti:

Her fingers let them softly through,
 Smooth polished silent things;
And each one as it falls reflects
 In swift light-shadowings,
Blood-red and purple, green and blue,
 The great eyes of her rings.

 ("The Card-Dealer", st. 4.)

When Rossetti uses Romantic coloration the effect resembles Coleridge as often as Keats.

Rossetti's early writings show parallels with Keats in sensibility and response to light as well as verbal echoes. Ford cites resemblances in "Dante at Verona", "The Blessed Damozel", "My Sister's Sleep", "The Bride's Prelude", "The Burden of Nineveh", a sonnet "Autumn Idleness", "The King's Tragedy", and "Rose Mary". All but the latter two are relatively early works; "Autumn Idleness" is one of the earliest of the sonnets later incorporated into "The House of Life". The echoes in "The King's Tragedy" and "Rose Mary" exist in comparative isolation. This shift away from Keatsian effects is part of the development of Rossetti's style away from the framed pictures of his early narratives. There he imitates some of the Keatsian-Tennysonian associations of weariness, claustrophobia, and titillating richness; later he writes with starkness and dramatic contrast of coloration.

Furthermore, Richard Milnes' biography *The Life and Letters of John Keats*, avidly read by Rossetti in 1848 and shared with Holman Hunt soon after their first acquaintance, is something of a public relations presentation. Perhaps in response to the prejudices which Ford documents, Milnes emphasizes his subject's morality, high aspirations, love of friends and brothers, meditativeness, and increasing concern with philosophy; Fanny Brawne is the subject of moderate interest. The book's chief concern is to impress its reader with Keats' nobility of spirit. One can argue that Milnes was so notorious that pieties from his mouth would seem insincere; but I doubt if they were intended to be or were interpreted this way. I give only samples:

...I believe that you will find in the clear transcript of the poet's mind, conveyed in these familiar letters, ...a character, whose moral purity and nobleness is as significant as its intellectual excellence.

I had to make prominent the brave front he opposed to poverty and pain—to show how love of pleasure was in him continually subordinate to higher aspirations.

As men die, so they walk among posterity; and our impression of Keats can only be that of a noble nature perseveringly testing its own power, of a manly heart bravely surmounting its first hard experience, and of an imagination ready to inundate the world, yet learning to flow within regulated channels....

["Endymion"] ... undertook to ennoble and purify, as far as was consistent with their retention, the instinctive desires of mankind.

... the vulgar great are comprehended and adored, because they are in reality on the same moral plane with those who admire.... The pure and lofty life; the generous and tender use of the rare creative faculty; the brave endurance of neglect and ridicule, the strange and cruel end of so much genius and so much virtue; these are the lessons by which the sympathies of mankind must be interested, and their faculties educated, up to the love of such a character and the comprehension of such an intelligence.[16]

Notice the fusion of ethical and aesthetic language to defend Keats; in his "Author's Preface" Milnes calls his work a "moral history".[17] An outside source of emphatic respectability, Lord Jeffrey, is adduced to comment that "The Eve of St. Agnes"

> ... is chastened and harmonized in the midst of its gorgeous distinctiveness by a pervading grace and purity, that indicate not less clearly the exaltation, than the refinement of the author's fancy.[18]

Milnes tacitly admits his anxiety in the conclusion, "The artistic absence of moral purpose may offend many readers, and the just harmony of the coloring may appear to others a displeasing monotony ...", exactly the view which Ford suggests was then prevalent. The entire biography is designed to place Keats in a context of moral suggestiveness. While Ford presents Rossetti as imitating a poet whom he interpreted as purely decorative and sensuous, it is more likely that Rossetti accepted the revised and then quite new interpretation of Keats offered by Houghton.

Many of Lord Houghton's evaluations as well as his quotations from Keats suggest, not surprisingly, the rhetoric of the early P.R.B.:

> ...Keats, in his intellectual character, reverenced simplicity and truth above all things....
>
> He had yet to learn that art should purify and elevate the Nature that it comprehends, and that the ideal loses nothing of its truth by aiming at perfections of form as well as of idea.[19]

Rossetti could well have responded to Milnes' ethic of poetry and beauty and to his submerged emphasis on proving such an ethic possible even without sharing the heavy emphasis of Holman Hunt, who saw "The Eve of St. Agnes" as revealing "the sacredness of honest responsible love and the weakness of proud intemperance".[20] But Rossetti's tone was closer to Milnes'; his early style, like the *Life and Letters*, uses moral language for situations formerly alien to this terminology. To apply moral-artistic labels to Keats is, perhaps by definition, to Victorianize him. Although Rossetti eschewed interpretive comments in poetry, his narratives moralize Keats. Of his dislike for the didacticism and philosophizing of Wordsworth and Shelley, William Rossetti comments:

> In all poetic literature, anything of a didactic, hortatory, or expressly ethical nature was alien from my brother's liking.

Yet the less quoted continuation of William Rossetti's statement is also significant:[21]

That it should be more or less implied was right, but that it should be pronounced and preached was wrong: such was his view.

Art should dramatize assumptions, not preach them; this is not a denial that art may have moral content. Ford states that "... in his own poetry, Rossetti breaks away from Tennyson's and Arnold's practice of blending Keatsianisms with Victorian themes; he disengages this foreign element from the Keatsian strain and presents it without any admixture from the world of controversy".[22] Rossetti is admittedly somewhat less topical than Arnold and Tennyson, but his "Keatsian strain" is admixed also. In several poems he attempts philosophy, political metaphor, and adumbrations of a possible afterlife. Ironically, Rossetti's reputation now suffers from somewhat the same biases as altered the early Victorians' view of Keats; he is dismissed or admired as sensuous and decorative. To a lesser degree, his poetry too deserves a counterbalancing explication of its progression and range of thought.

Barbara Charlesworth's *Dark Passages: The Decadent Consciousness in Victorian Literature* (1965) is an antidote to Ford; if Ford reads only the early Rossetti, she reads Rossetti backwards according to the interpretations of the Decadents. Yet the statements of Symons, Wilde, Pater, and others concerning Rossetti are as revealing in what they ignore as in what they perceive; for example the content of art seems mere abstraction to them, sources, particularized stimuli for impressions. Beatrice is significant as source for the Beatrice legend. Charlesworth describes the reactions of Symons and Pater:[23]

Arthur Symons thinks of him as one who never cared to leave the dream world of his own imagination, but who lived, wrote, and painted in an interior world "like a perfectly contented prisoner to whom the sense of imprisonment is a joy."

"Here is a fine saying of Keats's in one of his letters", Rossetti wrote to his mother; "I value more the privilege of seeing great things in loneliness than the fame of a prophet." Pater echoes his approval of solitude when he writes of the glimpses of landscape one catches in Rossetti's poems, "not indeed of broad open-air effects, but rather of a painter concentrated upon the picturesque effect of one or two selected objects at a time .... as he sees it from one of the windows, or reflected in one of the mirrors of his 'house of life'."

True, but somewhat prettified; the isolation of his house of life was often horrible to Rossetti, and the few moments within which seemed to indicate union with another person were especially valued. It is misleading to call his effects "picturesque", and he focused upon "selected objects" in their moment of disappearance. To call Rossetti "a perfectly contented prisoner" is unconsciously precious mockery of real frustration. Rossetti desired not only heightened moments but a perception of the object, beloved and transcendental, which these might reveal.

As Charlesworth implies, Rossetti doubted the possibility of social harmony and sympathy. However to Pater or Symons his preoccupation with guilt would have seemed irrelevant, a social and religious emotion. Marius and the *Renaissance* artists express elegiac regret and pain, but they don't feel guilt towards specific persons or for specific acts. Together with ebullient ambition and a love of idealized sexuality in narrative and life, the predominant trait of Rossetti's character was, in my opinion, guilt. He felt little guilt concerning the range of respectabilities and obligations later labeled "bourgeois" or "Victorian"; but towards his own "soul" – his past ambitions and idealized sexual responses – he felt recurring remorse. His art, as that of Houghton's Keats, was associated with a moral imperative; differences in interpretation of "moral" were among the causes of his estrangements from Swinburne, Morris, Tennyson, *et al*. Charlesworth quotes and interprets the angel's message to Chiaro in *Hand and Soul:*

What He hath set in thy heart to do, that do thou, and even though thou do it without thought of Him, it shall be well done.

"It is", she says, "in other words, God's will that the artist work for art's sake".[24] But whether what was in one's heart to do was "art", whether to do it "without thought of Him" was to do it "for art's sake", whether "He" had placed impressions in the heart, and whether "well done" could be an ethical or philosophic or only an aesthetic-formal judgment: these were the points at issue among Romantics and Victorians and Decadents. Charlesworth's discussion of Rossetti as Decadent may counterbalance my view of Rossetti as an altered Romantic, participant in Victorian terminologies and preoccupations, and precursor of Decadents. She fails, however, to state sufficiently her biases and points of origin.

The study of Rossetti has until now been apportioned somewhat artificially between biographers and critics, with the former in ascendance. Perhaps criticism generates itself after its own kind, historical and biographical records producing further background researches. After ascending a purgatorial mountain of memoirs, histories, and biographies each critic is determined to add his own small construct at the top. Or perhaps many lose faith in the possibility of generalization or pattern on that tortuous and detailed journey through multitudinousness. Also this division may result from the low quality and peripheral preoccupations of many Rossetti biographers, including Doughty, whose standard biography editorializes, assigns motives without proof, condescends and praises from Olympus, and lapses into unmarked reconstructions. I cannot see that Rossetti was shiftless or unintellectual, that Lizzie Rossetti's class origins or Rossetti's late hours are subjects for amused contempt. It is easy to fill many pages commenting with approval or disdain that the dead were immature or neurotic or adulterous in their time. To the extent that Rossetti was, as William Rossetti comments, something of a John Bull in sentiment, his conventionalities have been amply recompensed by fate in the choice of Doughty as biographer. William Rossetti himself is the victim of routine depreciation by critics, who probably identify uncomfortably with this ardent collator of sources and composer of accurate, cautious, but in retrospect overformal prose. He has the essential editorial virtue; that is, he documents his reasons for believing in the accuracy of everything he presents, even his own memories and evaluations. I too regret with others that he could not describe his brother's mistress(es) honestly, but few memoirs so openly describe their author's biases and criteria for selection. A recent book on Rossetti, Sonstroem's *Rossetti and the Fair Lady* (1970), follows Doughty but is a more accurate version of biocriticism. A.D. Culler's article, "'The Windy Stair': An Aspect of Rossetti's Poetic Symbolism" (1969), is one of the few examples of an attempt to use Rossetti's life to explicate a particular trait of his poetry, rather than use his poetry to comment on his life or feelings.

Biographical criticism is as potentially useful as any other kind. I am interested in style and language, but these may be explained through biographical accounts of what Rossetti read or how he responded to contemporary authors. I am also aware that no point of view is uniquely objective; although I reprove what I consider anecdotal, derivative, and gossipy approaches to Rossetti, my own judgments accidentally canonized would seem equally censorious in time. Yet biographers tend to take sides without proclaiming that this is what they are doing, or that there are "sides", to silently close what are still open questions and to obscure the extent of hypothesis. Biographical reconstructions argue over whether Rossetti was a "good" or "bad" poet or man, whether Jenny or Lizzie or Fanny was best or intelligent or a proper influence.

Another possible approach is sociological; studies have begun to appear on Victorian child care, sexual, and economic patterns. For example, J.A. Banks' *Prosperity and Parenthood* (1964) describes in almost comic detail the exactness of Anthony Trollope's financial calculations.[25] Among other things, Rossetti was an upper-middle class Victorian gentleman with compulsions and beliefs not dissimilar to those of others of his station. A reading of his letters suggests that a study could be made of his financial and social relations with female models, servants, family, artistic friends, attendants (Dunn, Watts, Hake, Howells, Caine), wife, wives of friends, intellectual women of day (Mrs. Gilchrist, Barbara Leigh-Smith), businessmen, and literary persons. The contrast between Dante and Christina Rossetti in education, freedom of movement, life pattern, writings, formal religiosity, and in their treatment of each other, is in my opinion much more likely the result of Victorian sexual conditioning and mores than of any accident of temperament. Dante Rossetti expected to borrow the emotional and intellectual resources of others; in turn, if they were women, he expected to support them financially whenever possible, and if they were men he expected to aid them in forming artistic or business connections. William Rossetti was nearly an exception; he and his brother formed almost a Jekyll and Hyde of Rossetti family aspiration, the one collecting and expounding, the other condensing and destroying.

If one understands the social assumptions of the Rossetti family, of Rossetti's upper middle class, and of Rossetti himself, the background of his obsessions and guilts becomes clearer. A range of people were available for the artist's exclusive and more or less inconsiderate use, but he was expected to maintain certain patterns of behavior in return. He absorbed his mother, Christ, Dante, Blake, Keats, and other sources which his brother quietly recorded; he was sexist in a sexist era; and he died with little self-pity when he could no longer uphold the grandiose structure of his own mental preoccupations.

Later critics unconsciously retain Rossetti's own assumptions; Doughty especially seems to dislike Rossetti's wife since their relationship was painful and argumentative. Lizzie Siddal seems to me in part the victim of a sophisticated and mannered society; the idea of her death, for example (the death of the female beloved who controls her lover from the spirit world) was suggested many times to her by her husband's art. And her fate and general anonymity may be compared to that of other women associated with Pre-Raphaelite artists who had mild artistic or intellectual interests of their own — Georgiana Burne-

Jones, Effie Ruskin Millais, Lucy Brown Rossetti.

Recently there has been increasing interest in studying Rossetti both as an analyzable poet and as a Victorian. Four recent theses describe Rossetti's poetry; Ronnalie Howard emphasizes the chronology and development of his early poetry,[26] John Hobbs comments on sources (most interestingly the *Vita Nuova*) and general traits; Stephen Spector constructs a series of essays on Rossetti as Victorian, and Michael Greene is something of an eclectic intermediary. All of these render general Rossetti criticism less needed than when I began reading Rossetti and thought to myself of "The Bride's Prelude" and others, "Well, these are certainly odd poems and they have never been formally analyzed." Concurrently books on Victorian thought and poetry are emphasizing Rossetti more than formerly. Miyoshi's *The Divided Self* (1969) describes a pervasive phenomenon, Rossetti's perception of various and dividing selves. Peckham's *Victorian Revolutionaries* (1970), although only tangentially concerned with Victorians (or Revolutionaries, for that matter; the occasional mention of Marx as Hegelian presumably justifies the title), uses the Pre-Raphaelites as pretext for a chapter. The anthologies of Pre-Raphaelitism by Jerome Buckley and Cecil Lang serve separate ends; the first selects in order to present mannered Pre-Raphaelite traits and Pre-Raphaelitism as a movement, the second is more homogeneous, more fully represents each author, and prods the reader towards the assumption that "Pre-Raphaelitism" is synonymous with mid-Victorian poetry (with Tennyson, Browning, and Arnold collected elsewhere for convenience). Meritt's collection reprints some minor Pre-Raphaelite fragments which would otherwise remain only in nineteenth-century editions. Still needed is a collected edition of Dante Rossetti with variants; portions of his work take weeks to obtain because this continues in abeyance.

Other recent Victorian studies relate to Rossetti, his sources and influence; for example the recent interests in Spasmody (Weinstein, *William Edmonstoune Aytoun and the Spasmodic Controversy*, Bryant, *The Spasmodic School: A Study of a Victorian Literary Phenomenon*[27]) and in feminist issues (studies of Mrs. Browning's *Aurora Leigh*, Hayter's *Mrs. Browning, A Poet's Work and Its Setting*) provide parallels and contrasts with the tastes and emphases of Rossetti. I believe he was influenced by both the Spasmodics and Mrs. Browning, but also by public discussions of their faults.[28] Martha Laurent's *Tennyson and the Poetry of the Germ* traces the surprisingly large intermediary influence of Coventry Patmore between these two, and she reprints the

1844 and 1853 editions of Patmore's early poetry.

Lastly Hopkins is presently fathering a critical industry; the prosodic exactness of Elizabeth Schneider may aid in criticisms of Hopkins' predecessors, and W. S. Johnson's *Gerard Manley Hopkins: The Poet as Victorian* begins with a chapter on Victorian traits shared by Hopkins, almost all of which could be used in describing Rossetti as well. A few illustrations:

The whole Romantic landscape has, it seems, been subtly changed in Victorian poetry ... in the mixed, uneasy metaphors ... the Victorian poetic landscape includes mountains that are magnificent but strange or frightening; marvelously attractive whirlwinds and tempests that threaten to destroy men; animals that signify both freedom and mortality; flowers and fruits that are beautiful but morbid and sometimes deadly dangerous; light that is brilliant and often harsh ....

Beasts, half-beasts, man-like beasts, along with the palpable and closely observed setting of land and sea, intrigue Victorian writers, but the fascinating beasts and attractive settings remain divorced, unblessed, and alien.

The question of identity is the beginning of self-consciousness .... a peculiarly Victorian absorption in and questioning of one's own nature are expressed in poses and in partial disguises – and ... they issue, for better or for worse, in ambiguity.

An even more subtle and pervasive effect of this fascination with and uncertainty about oneself is the Victorian form of dramatic verse which Kristian Smidt has described as "diagonal" or oblique .... the effect of his [the poet's] using a dramatic form is sometimes only to disguise personal convictions and even personal experiences ....

The very sunlight that warms the creature and works for fruitfullness evokes a double response in much of Victorian poetry .... The very metaphor and image of life and truth, for Milton, the Augustans, and Wordsworth, can be for the Victorians uncertain, and can invite ambivalent responses.[29]

Rossetti's landscapes, winds, and spirits are attractive and frightening, his beasts frequently woman-like and alien, his preoccupation with identity and disguise obsessive and oblique, his dislike of direct lighting constant. One could also compare Hopkins' and Rossetti's use of ballad, soliloquy and monologue, and the values which they give to landscape and seascape. Each of Johnson's general comments could preface a thematic study of Rossetti. Victorian poetry is now increasingly studied for common patterns, metaphors, and assumptions, shared also by Rossetti.

My approach to the poetry of Rossetti is linguistic, with discursive conclusions on its characteristic Victorian qualities. It could be called a social-historical view of poetic language. Ideological awareness and analytical relativism are essential to this view, also skepticism about the uses of generalization. I have no necessary brief against large-scale *Zeitkritik*, biographies of "great men" or "great works", or even thematic summaries, but believe in a literal and qualified approach to paraphrase. Our words, contexts, and images are emphatically not Rossetti's, and in the effort to define this distinction lies much of the quiet surprise possible in a close reading of his poetry.

NOTES

1   See, for example, the attacks on Rossetti by W.W. Robson, "Pre-Raphaelite Poetry", *The Pelican Guide to English Literature*, vol. 6 (1957), 352-370, and Harold Weatherby, "Problems of Form and Content in the Poetry of Dante Gabriel Rossetti", *VP*, 2 (1964), 11-19. These are answered in later *Victorian Poetry* articles by Jerome McGann, "Rossetti's Significant Details", 7 (1969), 41-54, and Wendell Johnson, "D.G. Rossetti as Painter and Poet", 3 (1965), 9-18.
2   Letter of Keats to brother George, 29 October, 1818, in Lord Houghton (Richard Monckton Milnes), *The Life and Letters of John Keats* (New York: Dutton, 1927), 142.
3   Compare title of William Fredeman, "Rossetti's 'In Memoriam': An Elegiac Reading of 'The House of Life' ", *BJRL*, 47 (1964-65), 298-341. He mentions briefly the parallels with Tennyson, 318-20, and discusses both poems as personal, elegiac, and retrospective sequences.
4   See appendix, part 2, "Rossetti and Poe".
5   See appendix, part 11, "Rossetti and Elizabeth Barrett Browning".
6   Comments on Philip Bailey and Rossetti occur in Alan McKillop, "*Festus* and 'The Blessed Damozel' ". *MLN*, 34 (1919), 93-97, H.B. Bryant, "The Spasmodic School: A Study of a Victorian Literary Phenomenon", Diss. Vanderbilt, 1968, 277-84, and P.F. Baum's introduction to *The Blessed Damozel* (Chapel Hill: University of North Carolina Press, 1937), xxxix-xlvi. Baum cites many interesting verbal resemblances, for all that he finds source studies repellent, mere "crumbs". His conclusions:

> What can be found in *Festus* resembling "The Blessed Damozel" I have tried to set forth: it is not altogether impressive. But if the process is reversed, if after finishing a perusal of *Festus* one reads through "The Blessed Damozel" the result is surprising. Parts of the latter poem seem like a distillation of Bailey's dilute imagery and diffuse visions. It would be bold to say that the one is the quintessence of certain portions of the other, but there would be a kind of truth in the statement. (xlv)

General discussions of Bailey are in Alan McKillop, "A Victorian Faust", *SP*, 29 (1932), 743-768, and H.B. Bryant, Chapter 2; two brief treatments are in Jerome Buckley's *The Victorian Temper* (Cambridge: Harvard University Press, 1951) and Mark Weinstein, *William Edmonstoune Aytoun and the Spasmodic Controversy* (New Haven: Yale University Press, 1968). For a chorus of enthusiastic spirits from Festus, see Chapter 2, footnote 37.
7   For comments on D.G. Rossetti and the author of *Poems by a Painter*, see appendix, part 10.

8   The obviousness of general resemblances makes precise comment difficult. What Swinburne seems to have done is to absorb Rossettian mannerisms and gimmickry into his rapid, coy, and humorous verbosity. Swinburne's "After Death" sounds like a devil's dance of "The White Ship", and one could make similar statements of many others.
9   See appendix, part 13, "The House of Life" and "Modern Love".
10 See appendix, part 3, "Rossetti and Blake".
11 George Ford, *Keats and the Victorians: A Study of His Influence and Rise to Fame 1821-95* (New Haven: Yale University Press, 1944; rpt. Hamden, Conn.: Archon, 1962), 123-6. Rossetti was touchy about ownership and reproved others whom he felt copied significant parts of his designs. Ford cites other examples of his caution. See the introduction to the appendix for more on "originality".
12 *Works*, 671.
13 Four of Rossetti's "five favorite" Coleridge poems were in the magic ballad style: "Kubla Khan", "Love", "Christabel", and "The Ancient Mariner"; the fifth, "Youth and Age", is a lyric with refrain and varied rhythms, similar to some of Rossetti's lyrics.
14 *Works*, xv.
15 For comments on Rossetti's lifelong admiration of Charles Wells, see appendix, part 9.
16 Lord Houghton, *Life and Letters*, 1, 8, 9, 17, 230-31. Although the Everyman edition of the *Life and Letters* describes Milnes as "minor poet, and writer on social and political questions", he was also the wealthy collector of erotica and flagellation literature to whom Rossetti introduced Swinburne. Milnes was undoubtedly conscious of being answerable to some of the same charges of "effeminacy" that were directed at Keats ("lush" tastes in literature associated by the Victorians with sodomy, weakness, secret vice, an escape from life's arena), thus his aggressive defense of the "manly", moral Keats. Rossetti seems to have shared several of Milnes' and Keats' literary biases, and his reading tastes indicate interest in what to him were literary exotica (*Sidonia the Sorceress, Violet the Danseuse,* Wells' *Stories After Nature*).
17 *Ibid.*, 3.
18 *Ibid.*, 171.
19 *Ibid.*, 7, 21. For parallels between Pre-Raphaelite interests and the emphases of Milnes' *Life and Letters*, see appendix, part 4.
20 Hunt quotes himself in *Pre-Raphaelitism and the Pre-Raphaelite Brotherhood* (London: Macmillan, 1905-06), 85, "... the story in Keats' 'The Eve of St. Agnes' illustrates the sacredness of honest, responsible love and the weakness of proud intemperance, and I may practice my new principles to some degree on that subject". Hunt's heavy style has not endeared him to literary critics, but it must be remembered that his apologia-autobiography contains the reactions of his youth as recorded by a very old man. Diana Holman Hunt's *My Grandfather, His Wives and Loves* (London: Hamilton, 1969) reveals that *Pre-Raphaelitism* was partially written and bowdlerized by Hunt's second wife, both with and without his knowledge. George Ford, *Keats and the Victorians*, mentions Hunt's response as representative of the Victorian concern with edification and beauty (100,101). Cecil Lang depreciates Hunt's opinion in his thesis, "Studies in Pre-Raphaelitism", Diss. Harvard, 1949.
21 *Works*, 671.
22 Ford, *Keats and the Victorians*, 110.
23 Barbara Charlesworth, *Dark Passages* ... (Madison and Milwaukee: University of Wisconsin, 1965), 5.
24 *Ibid.*, 4.

25 J.A. Banks, *Prosperity and Parenthood: A Study of Family Planning Among the Victorian Middle Classes* (London: Routledge and Kegan Paul, 1954). Chapter 8 is "A Case-Study – Anthony Trollope", 113-28.
26 Since the writing an altered version of Ms. Howard's thesis has appeared as *The Dark Glass: Vision and Technique in the Poetry of Dante Gabriel Rossetti* (Athens: Ohio University Press, 1972).
27 Mark Weinstein (New Haven: Yale University Press, 1968) and H.B. Bryant, Diss. Vanderbilt, 1968. An earlier description, "The Spasmodic School", appeared in Jerome Buckley, *The Victorian Temper* (Cambridge: Harvard University Press, 1951), 41-65.
28 Weinstein treats the debates over Spasmody in *Aytoun*, " 'The Spasmodic Years' (1850-56)", 63-191. Especially important is his description of the bitter criticisms of the Spasmodics which began after Aytoun's *Firmilian* (1854), 153-91. The Spasmodics had been colorists, image-makers, and skeptics about artistic structure, systematic philosophy, conventional morality, and the unified self. Perhaps Rossetti took note; in 1855 he criticized *Maud*'s story as worthy of Smith (cited in Weinstein, 181; occurs in *Letters*, ii, 267). "In style too these parts are generally quite overloaded and sometimes almost as bad as "Lady Geraldine's Courtship", without so much 'go' in them either".

Weinstein interestingly attributes to Dobell the Pre-Raphaelite technique of fixing on detail during stress (by now the initiation of this trait must have been attributed to almost everyone of the period):

> Dobell introduces one important element of psychological realism into the Spasmodic tradition. At crucial moments in the story, he has his hero examine minutely some extrinsic object .... A student of psychology, Dobell believed that in moments of extreme tension the mind seeks an outlet by fastening its attention upon some unessential aspect of the immediate environment. This technique is burlesqued in *Firmilian*, used and speculated upon in the celebrated shell passage of *Maud*, and employed in much pre-Raphaelite poetry. (97)

Rossetti had felt Dobell's "Keith of Ravelston" to be "... one of the finest, of its length, in any modern poet–ranking with Keats's "La Belle Dame Sans Merci" (*Letters*, ii, 670-71). Rossetti might have been attracted to the background for Dobell's *Roman* (1850), the Italian struggle for independence; amusingly Dobell's plot partially reverses that of Rossetti's "A Last Confession" (1849, 1869-70); in the former a girl sacrifices her life to save the revolutionary monk Santo; in the latter the revolutionary confesses to a priest that he has murdered a young girl.

Bryant, Chap. 5, "Literary Relationships of the Spasmodic School", 254-84, discusses Spasmodic influence, mentioning Rossetti, 277-84.

> In fact, it could be claimed with more validity than in the case of Browning that Rossetti was in many ways a Spasmodic who managed to be a good poet. The tendency toward the pictorial vignette was a problem to Rossetti, and like the Spasmodics he was apt to create "incident not quite amounting to events". ... He was often unable to avoid the danger of formlessness though he was more likely to be aware of this fact than the Spasmodics, and in Rossetti we feel that there was at least an attempt to strike a balance between form and intensity of imagery, whereas with the Spasmodics the image was its own reason for being." (277-78)

Chapter 6, "Aytoun's *Firmilian and the Decline of the Spasmodic School*", 285-

308, is more concerned with *Firmilian* than with other critical attacks. Later Robert Buchanan's *The Fleshly School of Poetry and Other Phenomena of the Day* (London: Strahan, 1872), 39, associated Rossetti and Swinburne with the Spasmodics:

> It is scarcely possible to discuss with any seriousness the pretensions with which foolish friends and small critics have surrounded the fleshly school, which, in spite of its spasmodic ramifications in the erotic direction, is merely one of the many sub-Tennysonian schools expanded to supernatural dimensions.

I confess to a belief that the Spasmodics had much truth on their side and, unlike others, I see neither humor nor moral to the extinction of their school.
29 W.S. Johnson, *Gerard Manley Hopkins* ... (Ithaca: Cornell, 1968), 32, 33, 19, 18, 35-36.

1. STYLE IN "THE HOUSE OF LIFE"

The most ambitious Victorian sonnet sequence and Rossetti's most formal and extended treatment of his idealisms is "The House of Life", a Victorian meditation on work, will, art, metaphysics and time as well as stylized erotic love. Until recently few credited "The House of Life" with enough formal sequence to merit analysis, but several discussions of its psychological progression have appeared in the last decade to redress the imbalance — Peterson, Baker, Fredeman, Robillard, Kendall, Johnston, Hume.[1] These differ in emphasis over whether to consider the poem as a unified love sequence or treatment of various topics, a compilation of loosely arranged descriptions of emotional states or a definable progression of ideas, a descent from love to despair and disintegration or an ascension into qualified resolution and hopefulness.

None of these arguments seem to involve essential contradictions. As Carl Peterson demonstrates in a discussion of Rossetti's methods of composition, Rossetti often constructed sonnets around images or sensations to which he later attached "ideas" or interpretations of their significance. He was capable of explaining an image or association by widely variant "ideas".[2] A paraphrase of the sequence's thought content yields few causal connections, but a careful repetition of assertions and dualities; whether one wishes to call this a formal structure is a matter of taste.[3] Similar debates have occurred over whether "In Memoriam" and "The Wreck of the Deutschland" present formal arguments or merely religious assertions or negations; the label depends on what one will admit as "progression", "argument", or "evidence".[4]

It is usually assumed that Rossetti intended a shift of emphasis between the two portions of "The House of Life", the first entitled "Youth and Change" and the other "Change and Fate". William Fredeman notices that their respective lengths form the ratio of octave to sestet,[5] but since the latter portion is less unified and contains a few nearly miscellaneous works, it does not bear the full climactic emphasis appropriate to the sestet. The original title of the first portion may have been "Love and Change"; Rossetti's shift to "Youth and Change" emphasizes themes of aging and successive periods of life.[6] How much emotional chronology this provides is debatable; the poem does present a sequence from love to loss, but all is foreboded, foreknown, and foreannounced. This early portion of the sequence is presumably devoted to satisfied love, yet it is difficult to find a sonnet unqualified by fear, weariness, painful memories, and thoughts of death. Even possession of the beloved is a ritualistic, heavy, solemn easing of pain. Emphasis is on that from which the beloved must rescue the lover as much as on their affection or passion; nothing is unself-conscious or lighthearted.

SONNET 2: "BRIDAL BIRTH" (1869)

(Of "Love") Till to his song our bodiless souls in turn
  Be born his children, when Death's nuptial change
    Leaves us for light the halo of his hair.

SONNET 3: "LOVE'S TESTAMENT" (1869)

          ...the whole
  Of the deep stair thou tread'st to the dim shoal
And weary water of the place of sighs,
And there dost work deliverance, as thine eyes
  Draw up my prisoned spirit to thy soul!

SONNET 4: "LOVESIGHT" (1869)

O love, my love! if I no more should see
Thyself, nor on the earth the shadow of thee,
  Nor image of thine eyes in any spring, —
How then should sound upon Life's darkening slope
The ground-whirl of the perished leaves of Hope,
  The wind of Death's imperishable wing?

SONNET 7: "SUPREME SURRENDER" (1870)

      Methinks proud Love must weep
  When Fate's control doth from his harvest reap
The sacred hour for which the years did sigh.

SONNET 18: "GENIUS IN BEAUTY" (1871)

So in like wise the envenomed years, whose tooth
Rends shallower grace with ruin void of ruth,
  Upon this beauty's power shall wreak no wrong.[7]

Rossetti is not eager to present surprises or a cumulative plot; instead his predominant sensibility of melancholy hope-fear is demonstrated through successive emphases and angles of observation. He continually presents the union or harmony of emotions, not their divergence — consequently his personifications and binding devices, his deemphasis of narrative and character. Like "In Memoriam" and "The Wreck of the Deutschland" the poem states full assumptions at the beginning and proceeds circularly.

Is the style of "The House of Life" appropriate to its theme? This is a central question for a poem utilizing so many stylistic devices, varying more in manner than content from contemporary norms, and which has been often criticized as overelaborate, convoluted, artificial, and even repellent in manner. What were the psychological effects of the devices Rossetti introduced into "The House of Life", the visual, auditory, and thematic concomitants of love, pain, and fear? A careful stylistic description could emphasize the function of these techniques, the extent of their resemblance to Rossetti's poetic mannerisms elsewhere, and to poetic techniques in other Victorian poems. A complication results from the thirty-four year period over which "The House of Life" was composed, however; any general comments on style should be qualified by a consideration of whether Rossetti developed or altered his sonnet mannerisms over the course of time.

A. IS THERE FORMAL DEVELOPMENT OR CHANGE IN SONNETS OF DIFFERENT PERIODS?

I have divided the chronology of "The House of Life" sonnets into four periods, a period from 1849-1867 during which eighteen sonnets were written, one from 1868-1870 which resulted in approximately forty sonnets, another 1871-1873 which produced thirty-four, and a final period of nine sonnets after 1873. Carl Peterson has been the most careful student of sonnet chronology so far, and he provides distinctions between the two brief middle periods during which almost three-fourths of the sequence was composed. He contrasts the 1871-1873 sonnets with those of the immediately preceding period:

Even though there are no radical stylistic changes in these sonnets of 1871-1873, there is a rather surprising change of emphasis. Most notable is the fact that images of death and expressions of regret for past days in which love had not been realized appear less often in and after 1871. Furthermore, the Dantean attitudes are struck somewhat less frequently, although Love makes his appearance often enough. In these Kelmscott sonnets visual effects of various kinds are introduced, and more emphasis is placed upon particularization of detail and upon color values and light (the earlier sonnets are relatively colorless).

...In the later sonnets Rossetti seldom used archaic words; in their place he tended to use ornate words such as "galiot", "chrysoprase", "euphrasy", and "halcyon". But he did not use such ornate words very often, as even a cursory glance at *The House of Life* will show....

He also used polysyllabic words with increasing frequency — words such as "commemorative", "culminating", "firmamental", "brimming", "murmuring", "remembrancers", "immemorial" (and many others, in all of which "l" and "m" sounds figure prominently).

These compounds he resorted to increasingly to create the effect of incantation, occasionally producing such a clogged spondaic line as "The storm-felled forest trees moss-grown today" (in "The Trees of the Garden", written in 1875).[8]

The sonnets of this five year period of peak interest are virtually all expressions of Rossetti's love-loss-death preoccupation, and in fact, form a clearer unity of sequence than the completed series. Several of the earliest and latest sonnets are occasional or are arranged in paired or tripled set pieces, somewhat tangentially connected with the others. Perhaps Rossetti wished to include more general poems and looked among his earlier sonnets for suitable candidates, or perhaps he widened his stated subject matter in order to encompass more of what he had already written. The period of the 1868-1873 sonnets was the period of "Eden Bower", "Rose Mary" and the plan for "The Orchard Pit", all poems directly preoccupied with treacherous erotic love, and using a more emphatic, bare, dramatic style than had characterized his previous narratives, ballads, and lyrics. The sonnets of course celebrate a limited but not deceptive love, and their heavy baroque imagery is not direct or dramatic in usual senses; Rossetti at his peak was moving simultaneously in two directions.

By contrast the early sonnets show a noticeable parallel with certain early poems in both theme and style. Rossetti wrote a group of seven early sonnets in 1847-1849, between the ages of nineteen and twenty-one. The earliest of these, "Retro me Sathana!" urges renunciation of the devil since his dominion in time is limited.

Get thee behind me. Even as, heavy-curled,
  Stooping against the wind, a charioteer
  Is snatched from out his chariot by the hair,
So shall Time be; and as the void car, hurled
  Abroad by reinless steeds, even so the world:
  Yea, even as chariot-dust upon the air,
  It shall be sought and not found anywhere.

Get thee behind me, Satan. Oft unfurled,
Thy perilous wings can beat and break like lath
  Much mightiness of men to win thee praise.
  Leave these weak feet to tread in narrow ways.

The heavy biblicalese, stiffness of diction, and careful separation of metaphors are characteristic of his earliest style; notice the images of being hurled through space or sucked upward by an overpowering wind, typical of many Rossettian descriptions of sensations of swooning, vertigo, and pressure.[9] The biblical echoes — for example, broad and narrow pathways — are more prominent than in his later style. The speaker is preaching to himself, a little unsure about his own future conduct, and not too clear about what he means by "narrow ways". He is preoccupied with the cessation of time and the need to use it well. A similar moralism, self-doubt, and imprecisely religious tone appear in the early "Jenny", 1848, and "The Card Dealer", 1849; the latter also contains biblical echoes. The rejected good man scorned but treading narrow paths alone suggests "Dante at Verona", begun in 1848.

In this sonnet the defensive identification with unworldly goodness accompanies a quick religious optimism concerning the world's ultimate fate; the poet can afford to mention injustice contemptuously and pass on. A remarkable contrast occurs with a sonnet placed only two sonnets later in the sequence, yet written twenty-two years afterwards. The poet has no metaphysical predictions to offer, and describes the dominion of this world with less brevity:

SONNET 92: "THE SUN'S SHAME" (1869)

Beholding youth and hope in mockery caught
  From life; and mocking pulses that remain
  When the soul's death of bodily death is fain;
Honour unknown, and honour known unsought;
And penury's sedulous self-torturing thought
  On gold, whose master therewith buys his bane;
  And longed-for-woman longing all in vain
For lonely man with love's desire distraught;
And wealth, and strength, and power, and pleasantness,
  Given unto bodies of whose souls men say,
  None poor and weak, slavish and foul, as they: —
Beholding these things, I behold no less
The blushing morn and blushing eve confess
  The shame that loads the intolerable day.

The placement of these two sonnets in close juxtaposition emphasizes a difficulty of the sequence. Rossetti grouped his "love" sonnets together, then arranged his work, art, and regret-for-lost-time sonnets in terminal positions; however much one perceives their thematic similarity the incongruities in style, treatment, and opinion are confusing unless one understands that a chronological jump has occurred.

Two triplets complete the group of earliest sonnets. They are miniaturized sonnet-sequences, indicating Rossetti's early interest in grouping sonnets by topic. "Old and New Art" is a compilation of sentiments on the need for great artistic effort in the present day. The first sonnet praises St. Luke the Evangelist as the legendary originator of that true religious art which sees God's sacramental presence in nature. Although art has since decayed into "talismans, ... and soulless self-reflections of man's skill", now is the time for repentance.

> Yet now, in this the twilight, she might still
>   Kneel in the latter grass to pray again,
> Ere the night cometh and she may not work.

Characteristically it is unclear whether religious, secular, or technical "talismans" are being censured. A moral earnestness is expected to unite the contradictory associations of Holman Hunt-like religious naturalism and stylized medievalising. Notice again the biblical diction, the emphasis on achievement and time passing, the image of art as a praying woman (pious women predominate in Rossetti's early writings, as in "Ave", "The Bride's Prelude", "The Blessed Damozel"), and the image of day declining into night. The latter Rossetti uses incessantly throughout all stages of his poetry, and to the end it retains some of its early moral associations of regret for wasted or ill-spent time.

The next sonnet reminds the poet-painter not to feel superior to the less gifted around him but to remember that he does not yet equal the great persons of the past:

> And say that this is so, what follows it?
>   For were thine eyes set backwards in thine head,
>   Such words were well; but they see on, and far.
> Unto the lights of the great Past, new-lit
>   Fair for the Future's track, look thou instead, –
>   Say thou instead, "I am not as *these* are."

The image of looking backwards forwards requires a little mental adjustment. Both image and statement are more tòrtured than is common in later Rossetti sonnets. The track metaphor is another of the cluster of pathway, racetrack, hill, and day's journey images which Rossetti will continue to use throughout later poems for meditations on life's purpose. To a nineteenth-century Protestant these probably suggested, among other loose associations, some combination of Bunyan, the author of Hebrews' comments on running "the race that is set before us" (12: 1), and pious allegorical literature of the period. "I am not as these are" paraphrases the self-righteous Pharisee whom Christ satirizes in Luke 18: 11, 12:

The Pharisee stood and prayed thus with himself, God, I thank thee, that I am not as other men are, extortioners, unjust, adulterers, or even as this publican. I fast twice in the week, I give tithes of all that I possess.

The publican is commended for his contrasting prayer, "God be merciful to me a sinner", which Rossetti secularizes into the admonition to emulate outstanding models; "the lights of the great Past" are presumably former great artists. The combination of self-injunction, pride, worry, piety, resolution, admiration of selected heroes, and high ambition is by now familiar.

The final sonnet of the triplet continues the same pattern with a retelling of the vineyard owner parable from Matthew 20. The diction is in many places an almost literal transcription of its original, as when "Why stand ye here all the day idle?" becomes "Stand not ye idle in the market place." As previously the inversions and stiffly verbose admonitions render Rossetti's biblicalese more self-consciously proper than its source. The sonnet's concluding analogy is confusing:

Though God has since found none such as these were
To do their work like them: — Because of this
   Stand not ye idle in the market-place.
     Which of ye knoweth *he* is not that last
Who may be first by faith and will? — yea, his
   The hand which after the appointed days
     And hours shall give a Future to their Past?

The original parable compares those who have worked long and short periods of time respectively to enter the "kingdom"; both the self-righteous and the easily righteous are perhaps being debunked. Rossetti by contrast seems to say that contemporary artists or workers, although they cannot imitate their predecessors who were different in kind, may produce work equally meritorious in degree. Those who have come late to art have not been negligent, of course, but were simply born later in time; the comparison seems to blur distinctions between failure and fate. One of the chief characteristics of Rossetti's sense of loss, in fact, is its frequent shifting between remorse for misdeeds and the sense of undeserved misfortune; sometimes guilt and aggrieved innocence fuse in strange ways. At any rate, Rossetti's sense of departed possibilities occurs elsewhere in the sequence with more immediate reference to his own life.

The remaining triplet, "The Choice", is similarly preoccupied with moral decision. Of three approaches to life, each described in a sonnet, the sensual and hedonistic, the saintly and ascetic, and the active and thoughtful, the poet seems to advocate the third. Ironically the first seems most convincing; it is occasionally cited as Rossetti's own opinion, whereas I have seen no independent references to the "Watch thou and fear" sonnet which follows it.

>   Then loose me, love, and hold
> Thy sultry hair up from my face; that I
> May pour for thee this golden wine, brim-high,
>   Till round the glass thy fingers glow like gold.
>   We'll drown all hours: thy song, while hours are toll'd,
> Shall leap, as fountains veil the changing sky.
>
> Now kiss, and think that there are really those,
>   My own high-bosomed beauty, who increase
>   Vain gold, vain lore, and yet might choose our way!
>   Through many years they toil; then on a day
>   They die not, – for their life was death, – but cease;
> And round their narrow lips the mould falls close.

This has an easy, full cadence; I wonder how extensively it was revised.[10] The image of the golden-haired wine-imbibing seductress suggests immediately Rossetti's other golden-haired dancing, singing, whirling, and drinking women of "The Card Dealer" (1849) and the early "Jenny" (1848); significantly the women in both poems also incite him to reflect on physical attractiveness and the need for self-control. In these poems the speaker feels ambivalence and uncertainty regarding his own conduct:

> Golden goblet of poison-wine,
> Trouble of mine, peril of mine?
>   Peril of mine, trouble of mine,
> Thine arms are bare and thy shoulders shine....
> And the gold makes a daylight in thine hair,
> And under the lids thine eyes' wild glee
> Looketh kindly and laughs to me,
> And the air swoons around and over thee.
>
>   ("Jenny", 1847-48, 11. 109-112, 118-121)

Similarly, the first "Choice" sonnet overshadows the others both emotionally and stylistically perhaps more than Rossetti intended.

The third sonnet, "Think thou and act", reveals again Rossetti's tendency to choose an image central to his emotions, then to place upon it an interpretation which, though not impossible, seems adventitious. The poem's opening sentiment could entitle a discussion of Victorian ideas on work and progress; yet to illustrate his conception of thought and action Rossetti produces one of his excellent images of the illimitable and man's aspiration:

Nay, come up hither. From this wave-washed mound
    Unto the furthest flood-brim look with me;
Then reach on with thy thought till it be drown'd.
    Miles and miles distant though the last line be,
And though thy soul sail leagues and leagues beyond, −
    Still, leagues beyond those leagues, there is more sea.

This scarcely seems activism or intellectual assertiveness, but rather the Rossettian benign trance of the dreamer, artist, or yearning soul. Similarly Tennyson's Ulysses speaks of striving, seeking, finding, *et cetera*, but is motivated by hope of viewing "beyond the sunset, and the baths/ Of all the western stars, until I die".

The seven earliest "House of Life" sonnets do show Rossetti's earliest preoccupations and rhetorical manner; a certain earnest anxiety couched in archaising or biblicalising diction repeats itself in images of artistic achievement, passing time, moral decision, permissible and prohibited beauty. Ironically his early style is both simpler and more sententious than his later one; he seeks a direct sternness of tone which is less accessible to him than the images which express or elicit psychological states − the expansive sea, weary hill and path of life, the kneeling maiden, the seductress, the whirlwind. These images will keep recurring when their earlier contexts have largely fallen away. Even in these earliest sonnets the sensations most significant to Rossetti inspire a sonorous cadence of line, the sudden expansion of a single image, the full rising and sustained weariness of rhythm which characterize his most intensely felt manner. That Rossetti is a poet of psychological states is a critical truism; already in the early stages one can see which psychological states these will be − responses of admiration or pleasure to expansive, whirling, overwhelmingly powerful or illimitable or radiant forces, accompanied by anxiety at their destructive possibilities. These early sonnets suggest at least as many affinities with other poems of Rossetti's early period as with middle and later "House of Life" sonnets.

His original thoughts on the subjects treated in his earliest "House of Life" sonnets — religion, art, beauty, temptation, time — will later atrophy and in their place will be less delimited, more hesitant metaphysical assumptions. His later sonnets show less self-doubt, less guilt, less disapprobation of sexual attraction, but ironically a much greater conviction of inevitable loss.

In the second early period, 1850-1862, Rossetti composed only eight sonnets, bunched so that seven occur in the first five years, after which there is a seven-year gap. Remarkably, with only one exception these sonnets are all preoccupied with uncertainty and failure. The first seven were written between the ages of twenty-two and twenty-seven; they are not anxious in the proud, hopeful, and moralistic manner of the earliest sonnets, but at their most sombre are grieving, resigned, and quietly detached in their judgment of the self. Only a few sonnets of 1869 and 1870 ("Newborn Death", "A Superscription", "The Vase of Life") are as grimly disconsolate.

Perhaps it is significant psychologically that what might seem emotions appropriate to a poet's old age were composed by Rossetti before he had experienced the major external losses and failures of his life. Perhaps Rossetti assumed in early youth that he would find one pathway to his moral, romantic, and artistic ambitions; subsequent failure to do so may have been the chief disappointment of early adulthood. His responses are also consistent with the Victorian phenomenon of poets expressing disillusion and detachment through the use of sages as literary personae (Ulysses, Lucretius, the Pope in "The Ring and the Book", Empedocles). Such laments on his own indolence and indecision have been taken with literalistic disapproval by later interpreters such as Doughty and R.D. Cooper,[11] and applied by easy analogy to his art.

A further characteristic of this period is the first limited appearance of love as a theme. Since Rossetti is often associated chiefly with poetry of romantic or erotic love, it is noticeable that in his early reflective sonnets (as opposed to narrative stories or imagined visions) he does not emphasize love themes; during this second period of 1850-1862 these form the basis for only one sonnet and three images. Perhaps he was hesitant for awhile about composing reflections rather than narratives on the subject; in other words he avoided speaking of love in what would seem his own direct voice. The only lengthy love lyric composed during this period, "Love's Nocturne" (1854), is a highly formal and artificial exercise.[12]

The first sonnet in this group, "Autumn Idleness" (1850), is closer to the hyphenate-laden descriptive manner of Rossetti's later style than anything thus far:

> This sunlight shames November where he grieves
>   In dead red leaves, and will not let him shun
>   The day, though bough with bough be over-run.
> But with a blessing every glade receives
> High salutation; while from hillock-eaves
>   The deer gaze calling, dappled white and dun,
>   As if, being foresters of old, the sun
> Had marked them with the shade of forest-leaves.
>
> Here dawn to-day unveiled her magic glass;
>   Here noon now gives the thirst and takes the dew;
> Till eve bring rest when other good things pass.
>   And here the lost hours the lost hours renew
> While I still lead my shadow o'er the grass,
>   Nor know, for longing, that which I should do.

The tendency to see both sombre ("where he grieves / In dead red leaves") and pleasant characteristics within the same setting, as well as the preoccupation with physical and psychological contrast of sun and shadow, day and night, are continuing traits of Rossetti's poetic manner. The octave is somewhat suggestive of Keats' odes, a quality consistent with the poem's early date of composition. As the speaker senses both nature's fullness and its decay, he is conscious of his own hesitation, unfixed desire, and confusion of indentity in the face of "lost hours" passing and to come. His response is similar to that in the sequence's earliest sonnets, and until the last sonnets he will continue to see himself divided into self and shadow, viewing a processional of passing hours. The leafy, shadowed setting and dappled animals suggest the heavy shrubbery and deflected sunlight of Rossetti's paintings. His poetic perceptions of nature seem to become progressively darkened and claustrophobic, in a loose parallel with the darkening of his paintings.

Both sonnets written in 1853, "The Hill Summit" and "Known in Vain", are quiet mournings over faded opportunity. The first, containing one of the fullest developments of the mountain of life metaphor used previously in the third sonnet of "The Choice", regrets that all the poet can do at this stage of life is regress from former perceptions, ideals, or achievements.

SONNET 70: "THE HILL SUMMIT"

This feast-day of the sun, his altar there
    In the broad west has blazed for vesper-song;
    And I have loitered in the vale too long
And gaze now a belated worshipper.
Yet may I not forget that I was 'ware,
    So journeying, of his face at intervals
    Transfigured where the fringed horizon falls, —
A fiery bush with coruscating hair.

And now that I have climbed and won this height,
    I must tread downward through the sloping shade
And travel the bewildered tracks till night.
    Yet for this hour I still may here be stayed
    And see the gold air and the silver fade
And the last bird fly into the last light.

This was written when Rossetti was twenty-five. Previously he had used metaphors of religious worship in contexts closer to conventional orthodoxy; now the sun, source of earthly heat and light and personified as male deity, receives reverence. This is the earliest blend of religious worship and secular object, later characteristic of "Love's Testament", "Lovesight", "Passion and Worship". The poet has again delayed too long in the mountain sun, as the sleeper in "The Choice" had dozed beneath the mountain in the sun. The sun receives a vague personification, the image shifting into another ("A fiery bush with coruscating hair") before it can be quite visualized, a frequent mannerism in Rossetti's use of vaguely spiritual presences.[13] The interpenetration of human emotion and nature continues as the poet must "travel the bewildered tracks till night", tracks perceived not only as bewildering but bewildered. In the final triplet, the juxtapositions of gold and silver air, last bird and twilight, are quite good.

The entire sonnet suggests a personalized and altered version of Dante's first experience in this world's "dark wood", "midway upon the journey of our life", or upon the Purgatorial mountain. In fact the Rossettian conception of day and night measuring precise stages of life's journey is a diffused version of the stringent astronomical literalism and preoccupation with the sun's positions which characterized each portion of Dante's narrative.[14] The one brief biblicalism, the "fiery bush" reference (Exodus 3: 2), is secularized, a characteristic Peterson cites as typical for biblical references in "The House of Life".[15]

Notice that the speaker of "The Hill Summit" has paused midmountain for "this hour", reminiscent of the sequence's stated purpose of commemorating "one dead deathless hour" in each sonnet. Often these single hours occur at a point of stasis and sensory receptiveness from which the poet can consider both past and future time. Here for example he pauses partially up the mountain, and can look both above and beneath himself, contemplate the past afternoon or approaching night. An even more symbolic midpoint is noon, which had been used in "Autumn Idleness" and the 1849 sonnet, "For a Venetian Pastoral, by Giorgione", and will appear later in "Silent Noon".

Another trait of "The Hill Summit" is some adjustment of word length to content; in the sestet the three lines describing climbing and confusion are of a reasonable polysyllabic turgidity, while the poet's last, simple consolation receives quiet emphasis from prolonged monosyllables ("silver" is an exception emphasized by contrast).

>   Yet for this hour I still may here be stayed
>   And see the gold air and the silver fade
> And the last bird fly into the last light.

In "Known in Vain", Work and Will join the other sonnet personae who have slept away the time alloted for life's journey. Like the previous sonnet of the same year, the sestet suggests a dim reference to Dante, and the octave employs a metaphor of religious worship for non-orthodox ends. The two portions of the analogy are apparently united by the act of gazing:

>   SONNET 65: "KNOWN IN VAIN"
>
> As two whose love, first foolish, widening scope,
>   Knows suddenly, to music high and soft,
>   The Holy of holies; who because they scoff'd
> Are now amazed wth shame, nor dare to cope
> With the whole truth aloud, lest heaven should ope;
>   Yet, at their meetings, laugh not as they laugh'd
>   In speech; nor speak, at length; but sitting oft
> Together, within hopeless sight of hope
> For hours are silent: — So it happeneth
>   When Work and Will awake too late, to gaze
> After their life sailed by, and hold their breath.
>   Ah! who shall dare to search through what sad maze
>   Thenceforth their incommunicable ways
> Follow the desultory feet of Death?

The octave contains a small epitome of the love situation for Rossetti, silent communion with the beloved, accompanied with suggestions of music and reverence. This is the first time he mentions love, as he will again in "The Birth-Bond" and "Lost on Both Sides", both sonnets of the succeeding year. The subject seems close to him at this period, and he yokes the octave by sheer obstinacy to its sestet. It is not apparent why the lovers are "within hopeless sight of hope", and it is also unclear why their frustration is equivalent to the remorse for lost opportunities which Work and Will experience. It has been suggested that if the sonnet expresses responses to Jane Burden Morris, the connection between discovered love and lost opportunity would be clearer. Such an explanation would apply also to "Lost on Both Sides", written the next year, whose octave describes a relationship in which two men love one woman, yoked oddly to a sestet discussing the frustration of two separate ambitions within a soul. This and "Known in Vain" are surprisingly parallel sonnets in both technique and psychology, so that it is interesting that a twenty-six sonnet interval occurs between them; perhaps Rossetti sometimes separated thematically similar sonnets to enhance the sense of variety within the sequence. At any rate, if the Burden explanation is correct, Rossetti has been not only unclear but coy in commenting that the lovers kept their silence only "lest heaven should ope". Again, as in the preceding sonnet, the rhythm seems in places especially designed to convey its content:

> Ah! who shall dare to search through what sad maze
> Thenceforth their incommunicable ways
> Follow the desultory feet of Death?

Of the three 1854 sonnets, "The Birth-Bond" contains a directness in expressing love usually absent from the later eulogies of the beloved and their meetings.

> Even so, when I first saw you, seemed it, love
> That among souls allied to mine was yet
> One nearer kindred than life hinted of.
> O born with me somewhere that men forget,
> And though in years of sight and sound unmet,
> Known for my soul's birth-partner well enough!

It is the furthest extension of the previous sonnet's sensation of having known but not recognized the beloved.[16] Now, as in that sonnet, they have for each other "in silence speech, And in a word complete community." Sometimes one marvels not at Rossetti's repetition, but at the variety of disguises with which he cloaks identical emotions.

The other two sonnets continue the sad chronicle of wasted time. "Lost on Both Sides" uses with ease the device of extending contrasts in a series, characteristic of later sonnets such as the introductory sonnet of 1880:

> As when two men have loved a woman well,
>   Each hating each, through Love's and Death's deceit;
>   Since not for either this stark marriage-sheet
> And the long pauses of this wedding-bell;
> Yet o'er her grave the night and day dispel
>   At last their feud forlorn, with cold and heat;
>   Nor other than dear friends to death may fleet
> The two lives left that most of her can tell: – ("Lost on Both Sides")

The two separate hopes roam together in the soul, winding "among / Its bye-streets, knocking at the dusty inns". Besides a staidly incongruous biblical analogy, this constitutes a transferring of previous journey, road, and search imagery to the bleak city night.

Miyoshi comments that this poem and number ninety eight, "He and I", are expressions of the divided self.[17] If this interpretation is correct, the later sonnet (1870) presents a more psychologically complex version of the phenomenon, a confusion and alteration of identity at once:

> Whence came his feet into my field, and why?
>   How is it that he sees it all so drear?
>   How do I see his seeing, and how hear
> The name his bitter silence knows it by?....
>
> Lo! this new Self now wanders round my field,
>   With plaints for every flower, and for each tree
>   A moan, the sighing wind's auxiliary:
> And o'er sweet waters of my life, that yield
> Unto his lips no draught but tears unseal'd,
>   Even in my place he weeps. Even I, not he.

By comparison the separate hopes described in "Lost on Both Sides" are straightforward and understandable enough; they simply war together and frustrate the poet's ambition for Peace. The sonnet "He and I" may have a more literal meaning however; the other Self could be Death, as before it had been Love, also represented as a small male deity.

Whichever is correct, the differences in use of personification reveal a shift between the early and middle periods. In the earliest sonnets, as we have seen, Rossetti developed verbal pictures which produced in him an emotion, then appended statements of his own interpretation and views. By the 1850's he combined pictures and statements into longer metaphors expressing the speaker's inner landscape and emotions. Later his abstractions became even more objectified, and expressed emotions and interactions of their own, as though they were independent entities affecting the speaker. An analogue might be a shift from moral pictures to psychological lyrics to a theatre of abstraction. It is obviously false to assume that an increase in dramatic techniques implies some progressive fragmentation of the self.

"The Landmark", the third sonnet of 1854, describes another journey which must be retraced, very similar to the situation of "The Hill Summit". As in that sonnet, the journey backwards is associated with night, dearth of birds, and blackness. For the first time in the sequence he uses the drinking at a well image, rendered familiar by the Willowwood sonnets of 1869. The image of the poet gazing at his own reflection also first occurs in lyrics of this period. After so many sonnets of remorse for failed achievement, this is the poet's first attempt to justify or give a reason for his inaction:

> Was *that* the landmark? What, – the foolish well
>   Whose wave, low down, I did not stoop to drink,
>   But sat and flung the pebbles from its brink
> In sport to send its imaged skies pell-mell,
> (And mine own image, had I noted well!) –
>   Was that my point of turning? – I had thought
>   The stations of my course should rise unsought,
> As altar-stone or ensigned citadel.

Reasonably enough, he had expected to be able to discern in advance what he should do. He had expected his goal to attract him as sacred or noble, religious or feudal, "as altar-stone or ensigned citadel".

> But lo! the path is missed, I must go back,
>   And thirst to drink when next I reach the spring
> Which once I stained, which since may have grown black.
>   Yet though no light be left nor bird now sing
>   As here I turn, I'll thank God, hastening,
> That the same goal is still on the same track.

The cadences possess a tenderly mournful repetitiousness, as in, "Which once I stained, which since may have grown black." The Shakespearean echo is appropriate, to "Bare ruined choirs, where late the sweet birds sang" (Sonnet 73). The diction is simple, bleak, arranged for both musical and conversational effect. Astoundingly the entire sestet contains only one polysyllable, appropriately "hastening". The monosyllables are even, lingering, emphasized, with an almost singsong concatenation of alliteration and assonance:

> Yet though no light be left nor bird now sing....

There is contrast between the conversational, shifting octave and the direct, unpausing sincerities of the sestet. It is as though the speaker, ruminating almost evasively on an important subject, comes suddenly and totally to the point.

The single 1855 sonnet is "A Dark Day"; the title does not surprise. Affected by gloom, the speaker remembers a past loss and wonders whether the future bodes further loss or perhaps slight consolation. Rossetti may have been incited to present a cheerful alternative by his fondness for balancing pairs in emotion or language; a dark day naturally suggests cheerful ones. Each of the first two quatrains is constructed from paired alternatives:

SONNET 68: "A DARK DAY"

The gloom that breathes upon me with these airs
   Is like the drops which strike the traveller's brow
     Who knows not, darkling, if they bring him now
Fresh storm, or be old rain the covert bears.
Ah! bodes this hour some harvest of new tares,
   Or hath but memory of the day whose plough
     Sowed hunger once, – the night at length when thou,
O prayer found vain, didst fall from out my prayers?

How prickly were the growths which yet how smooth,
   Along the hedgerows of this journey shed,
Lie by Time's grace till night and sleep may soothe!
   Even as the thistledown from pathsides dead
Gleaned by a girl in autumns of her youth,
   Which one new year makes soft her marriage-bed.

There is a careful variation of caesurae within lines, although several lines divide evenly:

> Who knows not, darkling, if they bring him now ....

> Sowed hunger once, – the night at length when thou ....

How prickly were the growths which yet how smooth ....

Marriage is as formerly the metaphor for happy love and sexuality. The traveller, day-night, and harvest metaphors are familiar; mention of harvesting will occur again in the next sonnet. A poet who speaks of a day's plough sowing hunger is striving valiantly to avoid the visualizable. Perhaps the plough was an earlier unhappiness which sowed a crop of bad memories; the poet is afraid that from some future vantage point this day will seem to have inaugurated a train of woes. As before he looks backwards at loss and forwards with pain, resignation, or qualified acceptance, and is anxious that events are uninterpretable or illusive until they have passed.

The last sonnet written before the peak middle periods was composed in 1862, seven years after the preceding sonnet, and it displays the greater objectification of emotions characteristic of the later periods. The middle sonnets achieved their single effects through speaking directly of disappointment; here emotions are disassociated from the self, then responded to dramatically, but the result is equally unified. Notice again the skilled contrast between the two portions of the sonnet, the series of one-line stark images of the octave and the broken-lined reflections of the sestet.

SONNET 86: "LOST DAYS"

The lost days of my life until to-day,
    What were they, could I see them on the street
    Lie as they fell? Would they be ears of wheat
Sown once for food but trodden into clay?
Or golden coins squandered and still to pay?
    Or drops of blood dabbling the guilty feet?
    Or such spilt water as in dreams must cheat
The undying throats of Hell, athirst alway?

I do not see them here; but after death
    God knows I know the faces I shall see,
Each one a murdered self, with low last breath.
    "I am thyself, – what hast thou done to me?"
"And I – and I – thyself," (lo! each one saith,)
    "And thou thyself to all eternity!"

The length of words once more provides emphasis; the only polysyllables in the octave are "trodden", "squandered", "golden", "dabbling", "guilty", "undying", and "athirst". In other words unpleasant or shameful actions or qualities are stressed by prolongation (with "golden" an exception). In the sestet the only polysyllables are "murdered", "thyself" (repeated three times), and "eternity", together conveying its intent. The monosyllabic lines have a mournful directness:

I do not see them here; but after death
    God knows I know the faces I shall see....

This conception of hell suggests Hopkins' sonnet of 1885, "I Wake and Feel the Fell of Dark, Not Day".

                  God's most deep decree
Bitter would have me taste: my taste was me;
Bones built in me, flesh filled, blood brimmed the curse.

Selfyeast of spirit a dull dough sours. I see
The lost are like this, and their scourge to be
As I am mine, their sweating selves; but worse.

They seek opposite goals, however: what Rossetti fears is loss of self; Hopkins fears its utter retention.

    It is difficult to sense poetic development when only a few poems are available for analysis, since early and later sonnets may differ partially by random chance. Yet I think Rossetti did develop during this extended period, and that sub-stages are perceptible. At first he moralizes with a metaphorical and biblical language, later he draws pictures representing various duties and pleasures. When strongly attracted by an image, his language suddenly expands to an uncluttered fullness. As he realizes he can speak directly of his own lapses, instead of preaching defensively, his metaphors take on personal emotion. In language his best effects become no longer beautiful accidents but involve an increasing balancing of lines, arrangement of contrasts in series, alternation of monosyllables and polysyllables, and binding with alliteration and assonance. His rhythms come to be built around longer units — quatrains and triplets rather than single lines. He contrasts octave and sestet to increase intensity and rhythm; his archaisms are shed for a style at once more conversational and weighty. His images throughout the early period concentrate on ambition, guilt, time passing, sense of remorse for wasted opportunity. Love appears as a reverenced communion but is in no way intrusive; journey, mountain, path metaphors predominate over all others. Gradually his use of abstraction and personification extends until the abstractions are elaborated dramatically at considerable length. The sonnets of the 50's are as musical as any later ones, but they are less heavy in rhythm; his later sonnets have an even denser language of ornate polysyllables and abstract nouns.

In my opinion some of these sonnets of the 50's are as fine as anything he wrote later. My response may of course indicate my taste more than Rossetti's qualities, but I believe him less sincere in his love sonnets than in his complaints of a lost life. The singlemindedness of his emotions during this entire fifteen-year period is remarkable. Always he felt the desire to do better, perhaps to experience more fully or more accurately each small quantity of time; always the past seemed as nothing, the future dim. It is almost an agnostic Calvinism. He values love not for the beloved's qualities but for her capacity to raise him to a consciousness of spiritual and bodily communion; in such moments he feels most himself, a condition which immediately suggests death. When this essential emotion is cluttered with romantic adjuncts and conventions, it palls. If what I am saying is merely that Rossetti wrote best and most sincerely when self-preoccupied, this is no unique censure.

It is now only necessary to see if the latest sonnets of the sequence reveal further alterations of manner. Are there qualities which appear in the final additions but not in the main body of "The House of Life"? Rossetti wrote six sonnets after 1877,[18] but these are bunched into the two years 1880 and 1881, when he was preparing to publish the completed sequence. The two 1880 sonnets discuss the nature of the sonnet and poetry; the four 1881 sonnets treat love and female beauty.

Perhaps the two 1880 sonnets are especially formal and contrived in manner because they are self-consciously model poems, illustrating and defining what poetry should be. "The Song-Throe" uses inversions, formal rhetoric, classical allusions, extended personifications, declamation, baroquely inverted metaphors, latinate diction, constant alliteration. If the sonnet is declaring the need for sincere emotion in the poet, its mannerisms constitute almost a solemn parody of its content.

SONNET 61: "THE SONG-THROE"

By thine own tears thy song must tears beget,
    O Singer! Magic mirror thou hast none
    Except thy manifest heart; and save thine own
Anguish or ardour, else no amulet.
Cisterned in Pride, verse is the feathery jet
    Of soulless air-flung fountains; nay, more dry
    Than the Dead Sea for throats that thirst and sigh,
That song o'er which no singer's lids grew wet.

> The Song-god — He the Sun-god — is no slave
>   Of thine: thy Hunter he, who for thy soul
>   Fledges his shaft: to no august control
> Of thy skilled hand his quivered store he gave:
>   But if thy lips' loud cry leap to his smart,
>   The inspir'd recoil shall pierce thy brother's heart.

A pattern of ornate adjective and noun juxtapositions has emerged, "manifest heart", "feathery jet", "soulless air-flung fountains", "august control", "quivered store", "skilled hand", "inspir'd recoil", reminiscent of eighteenth-century poetic diction, certainly retarding to the rhythm. The result is a slow evenness of sound, an appropriate accompaniment of the increasingly aureate language and careful balance of lines.

The images are remote from the bird, journey, love suggestions of an earlier period; usually they are of artificial or talismanic objects, jewelled, hard, or shining — magic mirror, amulet, cistern, air-fountains, Apollo's arrows. The emotive poet is represented grotesquely through disembodied tears, pierced heart, lips, and thirsting throat. An impartially generalized antiquity and homogenous quasi-religious mystery suffuses the allusions, with the Dead Sea vaguely biblical, Apollo the Hunter vaguely Greek, and cisterns and amulets vaguely charmed, ancient objects. The hard, jewelled, rich, stonelike or cutting images are rigidly contrasted with glimpsed human palpitations — the pierced heart, thirsting throat, crying lips, and wet lids. There is a sense of formal artifice and distance emphasizing an almost dehumanized and passive pain, reminiscent of Crashaw's preoccupation with wounds formally contemplated. No magic mirror exists to dispense unearned wisdom; the singer is a hunted victim crying.

In this latest stage Rossetti seems to strive for new verbal devices; by cramming words together less for meaning than for associative fitness he dislocates and combines in what appears mingled incoherence and paradox. Why would the poet's "skilled hand" possess "august control", for example?

> To no august control
> Of thy skilled hand his quivered store he gave....

Yet "august", "skilled", and "quivered" together express the artistic sensibilities Rossetti is describing. Compression can make reading akin to rapid puzzle-solving:

> But if thy lips' loud cry leap to his smart....

The alliterated staccato monosyllables here increase the sense of sharp formality and the conscious strangeness of juxtapositions. Both the musical variations and smoothness of earlier sonnets have been intentionally foregone. The images are designed as nearly independent, contemplable symbols; the magic mirror suggests romance, mystery, art, and the internal divisions of an identity, the cistern suggests deadly qualities of pride, the air-fountains remind of Coleridge's underground caverns, the amulet is perhaps a sorcerer's token. When Rossetti is considered as an early symbolist, usually examples from his later works are adduced as evidence.[19] It is perhaps unfortunate that Rossetti did not live to experiment further with his later convoluted and baroque tendencies; with time he might have perfected extremely idiosyncratic poems and extended his range of symbols.

The "Introductory Sonnet" is clearly a companion to "The Song-Throe"; since I will discuss it later, I will only mention its resemblances to its partner — the underground cavern scenery, imagery of funeral monuments, sense of doom inherent in the creation of art, suggestions of ancient rituals and legend, classical and other generalized allusions to time past, aureate adjectives and slowed, processional rhythm, even the use of the word "august". The image of a poem as a coin foredoomed to be paid as tribute according to chance decree is another of the vaguely sinister art-symbols of this later period. As the singer, victim of fate and artifice, is pierced by the chance arrows of Apollo, so the coin or work of art inevitably is sacrificed and destroyed before powers more significant and ordered than itself. These last sonnets, interestingly, have shifted from dramatizing emotional states to making statements and declarations on life and art, as the earliest "House of Life" sonnets had done, although with increased indirection, a more mannered sophistication, and less tendency to solve problems by optimistic fiat.

The four sonnets of 1881 all describe love, a lover, or a beloved from without; this is consistent with Rossetti's new tendency to dramatize and objectify emotion. In "True Woman: Herself", the images used to describe the woman are not quite the independent symbols of the preceding sonnets but are still a polished series of Rossetti's ideal associations for women — roses, trees, wine, music, the nightingale, flowers, pearls, secrecy. In language and imagery it is similar to two other late sonnets, "Ardour and Memory" and "The Day-Dream".[20] Some of

Rossetti's best natural descriptions occur in images of women or love, as here:

> A bodily beauty more acceptable
> Than the wild rose-tree's arch that crowns the fell; ....
> The wave-bowered pearl, – the heart-shaped seal of green
> That flecks the snowdrop underneath the snow.

In this sonnet, Rossetti especially emphasizes the sheltered and inscrutable nature of woman; compare the late paintings of Jane Morris as "Pandora" and "Astarte Syriaca". In previous periods other female qualities had interested him more, and this new preoccupation is consistent with his increased interest in the artificial and inscrutable qualities in art. Woman is an elaborate and mysterious art object existing in nature, the deity of an art whose exotic nature requires concealment:

> How strange a thing to be what Man can know
>   But as a sacred secret! Heaven's own screen
> Hides her soul's purest depth and loveliest glow;
>   Closely withheld, as all things most unseen, –
> The wave-bowered pearl, – the heart-shaped seal of green
> That flecks the snowdrop underneath the snow.

The images themselves have a certain exoticism of confusion; "wave-bowered pearl" calls up forest as well as sea and jewel, "heart-shaped seal of green" oddly juxtaposes hearts and shrubbery. Philomel is another of the classical allusions of Rossetti's late period, soberly alliterated with "passionate pulse". The basic contrast and paradox underlying the formal structure of this sonnet and the next – the assumption that men and women have antithetical and mutually impenetrable psychologies – is by now dated and contrived, but it provided the basis for an almost metaphysical juxtaposition of opposing images:

> II. HER LOVE
>
> She loves him; for her infinite soul is Love,
>   And he her lodestar. Passion in her is
>   A glass facing his fire, where the bright bliss
> Is mirrored, and the heat returned. Yet move
> That glass, a stranger's amorous flame to prove,
>   And it shall turn, by instant contraries,
>   Ice to the moon; while her pure fire to his
> For whom it burns, clings close i' the heart's alcove.

Once again emotions have become independent symbols, to be dramatically presented and expounded by the poet. The paralleling of astronomy and human psychology suggests Dante as well as Renaissance poets. The images — lodestar, glass, fire, mirror — are of "pure", elemental, and dehumanized qualities; to them is opposed the inner region of the heart. The sestet continues the opposition, his ardour versus her appreciation for the dawn or twilight "hour of sisterly sweet hand-in-hand", extremes which lead to a silent communion.

The third sonnet repeats the polished artifice of preceding ones with slight variation. To love such a heavenly being is itself heaven, a legend is invoked as evidence, and the beloved is described as possessing a "soul's immediate sanctuary". The sestet contains an accurate definition of Rossettian love, unchanged since the sonnet ten years earlier in which he had described it, "Tender as dawn's first hill-fire, and intense / As instantaneous penetrating sense, / In Spring's birth-hour, of other Springs gone by" ("Heart's Hope", 1871):

> The sunrise blooms and withers on the hill
>   Like any hill flower; and the noblest troth
>   Dies here to dust. Yet shall heaven's promise clothe
> Even yet those lovers who have cherished still
> This test for love: — in every kiss sealed fast
> To feel the first kiss and forebode the last.

The essential emotion is perception of one's physical existence in time. One loves because one's physical being and that of others will be annihilated; love is partially a rebellion against time, partially a shared mourning of the futility of rebellion. In the early sonnets Rossetti feared death because it ended work, forced moral reckoning. As the poet ages the sonnets express a more direct physical fear; natural cycles no longer threaten his life work or moral goals, but physical joy and beauty. The contrasts and poised rhetoric of the late sonnets are appropriate for expressing controlled passions — love and unhappiness restrained not because the speaker desires to qualify but because fate itself inevitably curtails them, renders anything but a self-disciplined response to the inevitable excruciatingly painful. The simply worded elegiac comments have some of the elegance and self-pity of "Tithonus":

> The woods decay, the woods decay and fall,
> The vapours weep their burthen to the ground.
> Man comes and tills the field and lies beneath,
> And after many a summer dies the swan ....

> Thou seest all things, thou wilt see my grave:
> Thou wilt renew thy beauty morn by morn;
> I earth in earth forget these empty courts,
> And thee returning on thy silver wheels.

The final late sonnet is "Michelangelo's Kiss", a good paradigm of Rossetti's late manner and interests. Since Michelangelo is both artist and lover, Rossetti can comment on both of his preoccupations at once. With extreme indirection, the sonnet states that only the love of the soul possesses lasting significance.

> Great Michelangelo, with age grown bleak
>   And uttermost labours, having once o'ersaid
>   All grievous memories on his long life shed,
> This worst regret to one true heart could speak: –
> That when, with sorrowing love and reverence meek,
>   He stooped o'er sweet Colonna's dying bed, –
>   His Muse and dominant Lady, spirit-wed, –
> Her hand he kissed, but not her brow or cheek.
> O Buonarruoti, – good at Art's fire-wheels
>   To urge her chariot! – even thus the Soul,
>   Touching at length some sorely-chastened goal,
> Earns oftenest but a little: her appeals
>   Were deep and mute, – lowly her claim. Let be:
>   What holds for her Death's garner? And for thee?

This is the only sonnet in "The House of Life" devoted to a single historical personage, and the style is dramatic, formal and heavily polysyllabic. There is the familiar contrast between the more factual, restrained, explanatory octet and the exclamatory and meditative sestet, also between the octet's turgid first seven lines and the monosyllabic account of failure,

> Her hand he kissed, but not her brow or cheek.

Even the proper names are chosen to provide elegant polysyllables – Michelangelo, Colonna, Buonarruoti. The chariot and fire-wheel allusions are vaguely classical; the final question shrewdly diffuses what might otherwise be a tediously moralistic ending. The sentiment resembles that of "The Song-Throe"; from the painful failures of life must be forced the emotions and powers that engender art or spiritual experience. The Soul's claim was not lowly by accident; any valuable goal by definition must be "sorely chastened". The rhetorical variety and indirection, the sophisticated weariness, limited sentiment, development of one statement through lengthy metaphor, concern with the psychological rather than the moral bases of art — all these differentiate Rossetti's latest sonnets on art from his earlier declarative and moral art sonnets.

What have these sonnet analyses shown? The consistency with which Rossetti's sonnets continued to develop is remarkable; the sequence can be divided chronologically into reasonably accurate subdivisions, each with particular tendencies of image, rhetoric, rhythm, patterns of word length, and position of speaker. Some of Rossetti's best passages occur within every period, and he was still developing at the time of his death. In his youth Rossetti worried over indolence and effort; in the 1850's he lamented failure and described love; towards the end he became definite and unapologetic, but with few personal hopes. At first he preached, then lamented, then declaimed. Gradually he came to dramatize emotions formally separated from his own persona, and to suffuse them not with moral ardour but with ambiguously classical worship and mystery. Such shifts of manner, whether attractive or repellent, do not necessarily indicate any psychic deterioration or disassociation of identity within a poet; it has been too easy to pass judgment on what Rossetti's personal unhappiness should inevitably have done to his psyche or style. After all, Yeats' later manner involved a shift to the dramatic, the rhetorically formal and impersonal, but he is not on this account accused of psychic deterioration or confusion in his late writings.

Stylistic shifts within "The House of Life" form a subtle qualification of almost any general statements concerning the sequence's intention and language. Virtually every stylistic mannerism or theme occurs with more prominence at some period than at others, and it is useful to know whether a device will be increasingly used or gradually eliminated. Also, to know whether any particular passage or expression can be accurately considered "representative", one must sense which sonnets are most likely to be atypical or idiosyncratic, and this often depends on chronology. An emphasis on the sequence's internal homogeneity and unity can obscure comparisons with Rossetti's other, non-"House of Life" poems, significant because Rossetti develops consistently in all categories, with enough internal variety within and cross-similarities between each kind of poetry to render the original distinction between kinds at least indefinite. Furthermore a sonnet sequence written over an extensive period provides ideal contrasts for the study of a poet's development, since form and theme remain by definition relatively constant.

I will next label and discuss psychological functions of some Rossetti mannerisms within "The House of Life", asking whether they are always appropriate, and whether they fit into a recognizable pattern. For examples, I will emphasize the sonnets of the most typical and prolific period, 1869-1871.

B. CHARACTERISTIC DEVICES; RESEMBLANCES WITH OTHER POETS

In the introduction to his edition of "The House of Life", Paull Baum summarizes some qualities of Rossetti's sonnet style: his use of approximate rimes, his tendency to form "long, resonant phrases often ending with a monosyllable", and his variations on common rhythms and word usage. All of these traits create an effect of painful but inevitable consonance — the continual fusing of simultaneous but slightly divergent responses.

Approximate rimes, in an obvious way, provide concurrent consonance and dissonance; since the reader must accept them as rimes, however, consonance prevails by a painful effort.

> ... Thy mastering music walks the sunlit *sea*:
> But where wan water trembles in the *grove*
> And the wan moon is all the light there*of*,
>   This heart still makes my name its volunt*ary*."
>
>   (Sonnet 9: 1870)
>
> ... Creep, as the Spring now thrills through every *spray*,
>   Up your warm throat to your warm lips: for *this*
>   Is even the hour of Love's sworn suitser*vice*,
> With whom cold hearts are counted casta*way*.
>
>   (Sonnet 14: 1870; italics mine)

Neither "vóluntary", "suitsérvice", nor "cástaway" is accented on the syllable which bears the rime. "Grove" and "thereof" are an inexact rime; Rossetti often rimed one of his frequent polysyllables with a monosyllable.[21]

The use of "long resonant phrases" is more complex. Baum cites five:

An instantaneous penetrating sense (Sonnet 5: 1871)

As the cloud-foaming firmamental blue (Sonnet 12: 1871)

Blazed with momentous memorable fire (Sonnet 62: 1873)

Their refuse maidenhood abominable (Sonnet 85: 1869)

Of ultimate things unuttered the frail screen (Sonnet 97: 1869)

Previously there had been polysyllabic phrases in romantic and early Victorian sonnets:

Holds premature and mystic communings;
    Till such unearthly intercourses shed
    A visible halo round his mortal head.

    (Keats, "The Poet", not included in 1848 *Life, Letters, and Literary Remains*)

But no confusion, no disturbance rude ...
So the unnumber'd sounds that evening store; ...

    (Keats, "How Many Bards")

Thy friends are exultations, agonies,
And love, and man's unconquerable mind.

    (Wordsworth, "To Toussaint L'Ouverture")

Armoury of the invincible knights of old: ....

    (Wordsworth, "It Is Not To Be Thought Of That the Flood")

She must espouse the everlasting Sea.

    (Wordsworth, "On the Extinction of the Venetian Republic")

Behold affectionate eternity.

    (Leigh Hunt, "On a Lock of Milton's Hair")

Burst, to illumine our tempestuous day.

    (Shelley, "Sonnet: England in 1819")

Unnumber'd and enormous polypi ....

    (Tennyson, "The Kraken")

In Rossetti's sonnets, however, the polysyllables are by comparison closely packed, latinate, unspecific, sedative rather than dramatic, as in "momentous memorable", "instantaneous penetrating", "consonant interlude", "close-companioned inarticulate hour". The object or idea requires metrically heavy and formal adjectives, and the classical and elevated adds to the sense of abstraction. Appropriately Rossetti admires in everything its sombre, resonant, slow, emphatic, and elegant qualities — in flowers, images, women, poetry. It is not true, however, that "long resonant phrases" always end in monosyllables:

Of its own arduous fulness reverent:

    (Sonnet 1: 1880)

The inmost incense of his sanctuary;

    (Sonnet 3: 1869)

With sweet confederate music favorable.

    (Sonnet 16: 1870)

Not that it matters — the distinctive trait is cadence, not word-divisions.

Although of course latinisms can express thought and sensations, part of Rossetti's achievement is not the precise statement of what a "predominant presence" (Sonnet 16: 1870) or "silent penetrative loveliness" (Sonnet 20: 1871) may be, but a series of syllables almost equally emphasized in speech and accent, whose meanings and effect will blend. Examples of abstract diction have a certain formal and historical resemblance to each other. Also, the emotional subjectiveness of such words as "arduous", "reverent", "inmost", and "confederate" exists independent of any picture or idea to which they can be immediately applied. The result is a "silent penetrative" effect, Rossetti's heavier and latinate equivalent of the evocativeness of Keats' "faery land forlorn". Similar syllables follow each other, equal and distinct yet merging into a mutual resemblence.

Rossetti also carefully places his polysyllables at climatic points; it is easier to accept their piled-up quality when they occur after preparation:

As many men are poets in their youth,
    But for one sweet-strung soul the wires prolong
    Even through all change the indomitable song: ....

    (Sonnet 18: 1871)

On these debateable borders of the year
    Spring's foot half falters; scarce she yet may know
    The leafless blackthorn-blossom from the snow ....

    (Sonnet 14: 1870)

In each of these the third line of a four or six line unit seems a mild climax. In both there is a slight fall at the end of the third line after the polysyllable, on Baum's terminating monosyllable. When the end of the line is less accented an undertow is created, an effect of ambivalence and hesitancy, as though a strong declaration has been narrowly sidestepped. At other times the climax comes at the end. The mediate cases, where the line neither falls nor rises at the end, seem characteristically Rossettian. They are often associated with rimes on polysyllables or unexpected rimes:

Love's very vesture and elect disguise
    Was each fine movement, – wonder new begot
Of lily or swan or swan-stemmed galiot; ...

    (Sonnet 17: 1871)

Is even the hour of Love's sworn suitservice, ...

    (Sonnet 14: 1870)

Even though Rossetti alternates short and long words to build ascents and descents, he seldom creates an emphatic stress or the sense of rolling rhythms. Instead the variations are quiet and create once more an internal binding by resemblances, although in his ballads and tetrameter poems his stresses are more overt. The result of an adjustment of Rossetti's techniques could be dramatic; a similar patterning of many-and few-syllabled words is important in the extremely emphatic effects of Hopkins' rhythms.[22]

It is not coincidental that many of the frequently cited lines from "The House of Life" end in the carefully anticipated and stressed monosyllable which he often placed at a sonnet's conclusion:

So in like wise envenomed years, whose tooth
Rends shallower grace with ruin void of ruth,
    Upon this beauty's power shall wreak no wrong.

    (Sonnet 18: 1871)

Her face is made her shrine. Let all men note
    That in all years (O Love, thy gift is this!)
        They that would look on her must come to me.

    (Sonnet 10: 1868)

Yet even these terminations are not climactic. Like other aspects of his sonnet style, they have a lingering and subliminally tentative effect.

Rossetti has been much attacked for over-ornateness and elaboration in language; perhaps what such critics sense is less a superfluity of art than the use of metrics and diction to qualify all assertion, the blending of even the most forcefully stated perceptions into other similar expressions. Much has been said of Rossetti's preservation of individual moments, the "moment's monument"; rather he preserves repetitive examples of a specific kind of moment. To some extent this is true of every poet; a certain type of moment or experience seems to him epiphanic, and he describes it in progressive contexts and variations. Such resemblance is not necessarily monotonous, and conversely, the creation of extremely divergent centers of interest could seem fragmented.

Rossetti plots his monosyllables skillfully. At times he builds them up into a great unbroken series:

Ne'er notes (as death's dear cup at last you drain),
The hour when you too learn that all is vain
    And that Hope sows what Love shall never reap?

    (Sonnet 44: 1871)

A virtuoso rapid rolling effect can be created by the reeling off of many small words very fast; Swinburne and Hopkins both became masters of the art:

Ah yet would God this flesh of mine
Where air might wash and long leaves cover me....
Or where the wind's feet shine along the sea.

    ("Laus Veneris")

    No, not in all the strange great sins of them
That made the wine-press froth and foam with wine.

    ("Laus Veneris")

    I wake and feel the fell of dark, not day.

    (Hopkins, Sonnet 67)

    And all is seared with trade; bleared, smeared with toil;
    And wears man's smudge and shares man' smell: the soil
Is bare now, nor can foot feel, being shod.

    (God's Grandeur")

On ear and ear two noises too old to end
    Trench-right, the tide that ramps against the shore;
    With a flood or a fall, low lull-off or all roar,
Frequenting there while moon shall wear and wend.

        ("The Sea and the Skylark" — 3 words with more than 1 syllable,
            36 monosyllables)

Although Rossetti often creates a sedate and generalized statement with his small words, Hopkins and Swinburne frequently use them for speed and, at least Hopkins, for masses of precise description. Browning also was skilled at building up monosyllables; perhaps Rossetti noticed this trait in him. There are of course examples in Tennyson, and a lessened concentration of them occurs in romantic poetry; the romantics preferred a more even texture and less dramatic contrast in length and type of words.

Although Rossetti often interrupts his piled monosyllables with longer words, his skillful use of monosyllables in sequence and for contrast is definitely part of his style. Short words balance what otherwise might be an offensive density, and the alteration of a great many small words with a few long ones contributes to the measured, musical quality always ascribed to "The House of Life".

Rossetti also stacks his monosyllables together in hyphenates and compounds, creating unusual polysyllabic effects. These juxtapositions are not designed to clarify or to describe the object more concretely, but to blend and alter expected syntactical associations.

One flame-winged brought a white-winged harp-player .... (Sonnet 9: 1870)

Sweet twining hedgeflowers wind-stirred in no wise .... (Sonnet 12: 1871)

Rossetti uses hyphenates at least as frequently as any previous nineteenth-century poet. Keats, for example, had used only a few:

Before high-piled books, in charactery
    Hold like rich garners the full ripen'd grain ....

        ("When I Have Fears")

Such dim-conceived glories of the brain
    Bring round the heart an undescribable feud....

        ("On Seeing the Elgin Marbles")

Coleridge also uses his hyphenates one at a time. Wordsworth hyphenates even less, usually in situations where the hyphenation is merely conventional, not a grammatical variant or original coinage.

Leigh Hunt was not a great sonneteer, but passages from one of his little-known poems, "The Fish, the Man, and the Spirit", may indicate an increasing tendency towards the use of hyphenates in natural description. A man addresses a fish:

You strange, astonished-looking, angel-faced
    Dreary-mouthed, gaping wretches of the sea,
    Gulping salt-water everlastingly,
Cold-blooded ....

The fish is equally inventive:

Long-useless-finned, haired, upright, unwet, slow!
O breather of unbreathable, sword-sharp air....

The Spirit asserts a conclusion:

Man's life is warm, glad, sad, 'twixt loves and graves,
    Boundless in hope, honoured with pangs austere,
Heaven-gazing: and his angel-wings he craves: —
    The fish is swift, small-needing, vague yet clear,
A cold, sweet, silver life, wrapped in round waves,
    Quickened with touches of transporting fear.[23]

Perhaps the poem's humorous subject has encouraged freedom in style, although Leigh Hunt's poetry is noted for its freedom of diction and versification.[24]

Hyphenated words do not occur frequently in Tennyson's sonnets, but an occasional hyphenated neologism is a general characteristic of Tennyson's style, one which is shared in a lesser degree by Patmore:[25]

Thou art no Sabbath-drawler of old saws,
Distill'd from some worm-canker'd homily; ....

    (Tennyson, "Sonnet to J. M. K.")

    When from crimson-threaded lips
Silver-treble laughter trilleth ....

    (Patmore, "Lilian")

    The forward-flowing tide of time ....
The citron-shadows in the blue ....
Often, where clear-stemm'd platans guard ....
Was damask-work, and deep inlay....
Fall'n silver-chiming, seem'd to shake ....
A walk with vary-colour'd shells ....

    (Tennyson, "Recollections of the Arabian Nights")

The grey-flies hum their weary tune,
    A distant, dream-like sound; ....

    (Patmore, "The River")

Rossetti customarily uses hyphenation when describing natural phenomena, although the result is still generalized description. He presents categories of natural objects, not the unique or atypical.

The leafless blackthorn-blossom from the snow....

    (Sonnet 14: 1870)

What dawn-pulse at the heart of heaven, or last
    Incarnate flower of culminating day, – ....

    (Sonnet 17: 1871)

All round our nest, far as the eye can pass,
    Are golden kingcup fields with silver edge
    Where the cow-parsley skirts the hawthorn-hedge.

    (Sonnet 19: 1871)

O'er water-daisies and wild waifs of Spring,
    There where the iris rears its gold-crowned sheaf
    With flowering rush and sceptred arrow-leaf,....

    (Sonnet 20: 1871)

    ... Some wood-born wonder's sweet simplicity;
    A glance like water brimming with the sky
Or hyacinth-light where forest-shadows fall; ....

    (Sonnet 31: 1871)

Often Rossetti hyphenates where it is grammatically unnecessary, emphasizing auditory blending and his tendency to consider paired adjectives and nouns as one sustained, evenly stressed unit. The second quotation above suggests Hopkins — the "dawn", "pulse", "heart", "heaven", "last", "incarnate", and "flower" could all be his, although they could also be from Tennyson. It is one of Rossetti's more robust, concentrated, and "fully-blooded" passages ("pulse", "heart", "incarnate"), perhaps revealing that if Rossetti had been more impassioned about nature his style might have come to resemble more closely that of Hopkins. The culmination of descriptive hyphenates of course occures in Hopkins, writing in the late 1870's and 1880's:

For skies of couple-colour as a brinded cow;
    For rose-moles all in stipple upon trout that swim;
Fresh-firecoals chestnut-falls; finches' wings ....

    ("Pied Beauty")

... up above, what wind-walks! what lovely behavior
Of silk-sack cloud! has wilder, wilful wavier
Meal-drift moulded ever and melted across skies?

    ("Hurrahing in Harvest")

The heaven-flung, heart-fleshed, maiden-furled
    Miracle-in-Mary-of-flame ....

    ("The Wreck of the Deutschland")

Though it is dangerous to assert specific influences, a definite tendency towards virtuoso monosyllabics and hyphenates does seem to enter sonnet conventions during the century. Rossetti was one of the transmitters of the tradition, using both hyphenates of natural description and hyphenates of psychological states and abstractions — "Love's soul-winnowing hands" (Sonnet 28: 1871); "hour-girt life" (Sonnet 34: 1871). The latter form of hyphenate not only permits more complex verbal acrobatics to convey Rossetti's guiding personifications,[26] but creates more fusings of act, effect, and idea. "Soul-winnowing hands" invokes no physical image except perhaps that of a spirit-like motion, or vaguely, of hands and a threshing-floor with fan separating the chaff and grain. Once again separate suggestions do not contradict or create paradox but combine and harmonize through a common muted tone, limited concreteness, and associated ideation.

Rossetti's internal auditory binding devices are significant in creating the blurred but plotted elegance he desires. Baum describes such devices with the comment, "He plays tricks ..." and lists as examples the phrases "the *lifted shifted steeps*" (Sonnet 79: 1870),

"*Fire* with*in fire, desire in de*ity" (Sonnet 6: 1869), and others:

*L*eaves us for *l*ight the *ha*lo of *h*is *ha*ir

(Sonnet 2: 1870)

*Th*y *m*astering *m*usic walks *th*e *s*unlit *s*ea

(Sonnet 9: 1869; italicized alliterations mine)

What he seems to describe are compound alliterations and internal rimes. More complex effects can be created with linked alliterations:

*Wh*at *wh*ile Love *br*eathed in *s*ighs and *s*ilences
   *Th*rough *tw*o *bl*ent souls *o*ne *r*aptu*r*ous unde*rs*ong.

(Sonnet 13: 1871)

Rossetti is noted for his alliterative strings of "s's", "w's", and "l's"; these are merely instances of his care with assonantal and alliterative patterns. He carefully restrains the variety and vigorousness of the sounds he emphasizes. Also in using many elongated and open vowels he creates some of the full mournful restlessness and seriousness which Tennyson's "In Memoriam" acquires from the same means.

*Sl*eep *s*ank *t*hem *l*ower *t*han *t*he *t*ide of *dr*eams,
   And *t*heir *dr*eams *w*atched *t*hem *s*ink, and *sl*id a*w*ay.
*Sl*owly *t*heir *s*ouls *s*wam up *a*gain, *thr*ough *gl*eams
   Of *w*atered *l*ight and *d*ull *dr*owned *w*aifs of *d*ay,
*T*ill from *s*ome *w*onder of new *w*oods and *str*eams
   He *w*oke, and *w*ondered more: for *th*ere she *l*ay.

(Sonnet 6a: 1869) (italics in preceding passages mine)

All poets use considerable alliteration and assonance; Rossetti's only possible distinction could be in using them more frequently than earlier poets had done. The tendency towards what Baum calls "tricks" seems a pronounced quality in every major Victorian poet except Arnold, first in Tennyson, Browning, and Rossetti, then in Swinburne and Hopkins. Hopkins and Swinburne attempt more massed linked-alliterative effects, more architectonically piled cadences and echoes. Rossetti's "lifted shifted steeps" will become Swinburne's "bright like blood", "thy fleeter feet", and Hopkins' "daylight's dauphin, dapple dawn-drawn Falcon" or "five-livèd and leavèd favor".

Again Rossetti does not choose an emphatic combination of devices but an equal emphasis on and careful resemblance between those he does use.

O love, my love! if I *no mo*re *s*hould *s*ee

(Sonnet 4: 1869)

The vowels are evenly stressed; two "l's" occur at the beginning of the line, two "s's" at the end. The "m's" add to the alliterative pattern; otherwise there would be merely the Anglo-Saxon paired alliteration in each half-line. Frequently Rossetti uses such simple alliterative pairs, or adds an extra linkage:

What *s*mouldering *s*enses in *d*eath's *s*ick *d*elay

(Sonnet 6: 1869) (italics mine)

Often he uses a simple series of three or four alliterations on the same letter. Such patterns create a restrained, careful emphasis, the stateliness and measured joining of similar sounds which I have described. These are excellent mannerisms for a formalizing and muting of self-pity, although they can also form monotonous and repetitious restraints on what otherwise might seem more dramatic and varied responses.

The sonnet rhythms are like the rimes in their imposition of a certain dissonance within regularity. The ability to create very even rhythms seems to have come to Rossetti by the time he was writing most of his "The House of Life" sonnets. He apparently passed through three stages in the creation of rhythms, an early stage during which there were some irregularities, a later period in which the early poems were revised in the interest of greater smoothness, and a final period of more contrived variations from convention. During all periods he was generally regular, however, and in all periods exceptions can be found. Also a poem revised many times should naturally come to seem both more artificial and more regular; and while both his early and middle poems could be subjected to revision, the poems written in the years before his death were obviously not subjected to as many years of afterthought.[27]

Rossetti's irregularities in sonnet rhythm are difficult to particularize and describe since they do not seem merely inversions or occasional additions of syllables. Rather they consist of partial shifts of beat, so that many lines hover between two or more metric patterns. There are extra stresses, not strong, emphatic additional stresses as in Hopkins, but lighter, more uncertain ones which may or may not form spondees, primary stresses, or secondary stresses. I have marked three lines which illustrate this deviation from simple and clearly emphasized iambic:

Of the deep stáir thou tréad'st to the dim shoal

    (Sonnet 3: 1869)

Trúth, with awed líps; and Hópe, with eýes upcást

    (Sonnet 1: 1871)

Where one shorn tréss long stírred the lónging ache

    (Sonnet 7: 1870)

This is how these lines appear with regular stresses, assuming a trochaic foot at the beginning of the second example; initial inversions are frequent in Rossetti's iambic lines. The first line is doggerel as marked, but if I shift the accent to the more important words "deep" and "dim", the result is an odd line indeed:

Of the déep   stáir thou   tréad'st to   the dím   shoal

one anapest, two trochees, one iamb, one uncompleted trochee. There is also the possibility of a light initial stress on "of":

Of the   déep stair   thou tréad'st   to thé   dim shóal
                                or   ᴗ ᴗ | / /

It is still hard to read "déep stair thou tréad'st" without seeking at least a secondary intervening accent. Of course secondary stresses have been devised as a method of indicating imperfectly polarized emphases, and not every line is expected to scan immediately into iamb, trochee, dactyl, anapest, and spondee. Yet is should be possible to separate primary and secondary stresses by some method other than fiat, and in Rossetti's even lines this is difficult. To Rossetti several neighboring words often had the same, not subtly variant, stresses.

    In the line above it is difficult not to keep hearing an "undersong" of accent both on "stair" and "dim" — perhaps a line describing the treading of deep stairs to dim shoals should contain heavy, evenly weighted syllables and few light ones. Likewise in the second line cited, the meter is within an accepted pattern of variation, yet there seems to be extra weight on "awed" and to a lesser extent on "with". The result is a slow equal emphasis on all the initial words, adding seriousness and unity of tone to the personification. "Awed" becomes not only an adjective describing "lips" but part of the concept "awed lips"; "Truth" associates similarly. In the third line the same even stress occurs on "shorn tress". It is easy to scan the line conventionally:

> Where ońe shorn tresś long ....

but I think this violates the actual climax of the words if read aloud (shórn-tréss).

Such double-stress bonding is a quiet, conscious prolonging of emphasis; accents are gathered from surrounding feet and placed on the two words which Rossetti wished to fuse. This is very different from the violent successive stresses of Swinburne and Hopkins:

Our heárts' chárity's heárth's fíre ....,

    ("Wreck")

yet the principle of gathering together stress and meaning onto juxtaposed syllables is the same; Swinburne lets more little syllables get in between his stresses, and both he and Hopkins use stresses as preparation for greater sweeps downward into the unstressed. Rossetti's stresses are like a processional in which there is a slight hastening of step every once in a while.

There is always the possibility of debate over secondary accents on Rossetti's carefully plotted polysyllables. Although Rossetti's irregularities can be described as some variation of regular patterns, they do not fit firmly into these or any other categories but hover simultaneously in and out of several scansion patterns. The reader is expected to hear several rhythms so that none possesses complete authority; sometimes he hears one, sometimes two, sometimes he is uncertain how many he should hear. Hopkins adapted the word "counterpoint" to describe a contrary rhythm running simultaneously; Rossetti writes a partial counterpart with interchanging melodies. He does not want the clear contrasts of metaphysical poetry or oxymoronic imagery, nor the obvious counter rhythms which are Hopkins' idiosyncratic contribution to Victorian metrics. Instead he creates a concentrated and obscure effect of several forces pulling concurrently at each other; within this regularized heavy balance he varies stresses to emphasize particular words and juxtapositions.

The most difficult and most discussed aspect of Rossetti's language, as with most poets, is his imagery. Commonly imagery can be divided into categories — color imagery, imagery of natural description, sea or jewel or star or animal imagery; with Rossetti's poetry these categories are only relevant in a limited way, although he uses many conventional images. Ifor Evans gives an accurate description of the manner of "The House of Life":

> The moment is explored with an intricacy of imagery, whose landscape belongs to intangible, twilight things, waters, and silence, moonlight, and still-half-shadowed shapes. The realistic detail of the earlier Pre-Raphaelite experiment has been exorcised so that these sombre dream shapes may exist unchallenged.[28]

Rossetti's images are of things which could possibly merge (as dream images) under cover of darkness; they are emanations rather than the objects themselves, physical and spiritual elements continually reforming in new ways — waters to clouds to winds to wings to human breath to flames to gems. The images of natural elements — sea, wood, waves, fire — are carefully selected for the quality of revealing an "essence", and their use has an emblematic and Heraclitean quality — everything strains to become not itself, to present its last perceivable quality before becoming another or suffering extinction.

In this way the innumerable hands, tresses of hair, breathings, and glances of the "lady" are explicable — they are the last emanations she would leave behind if, like the Cheshire cat, she suddenly faded away. The Cheshire cat's eyes faded last: eyes → glances → light → golden → fire → passion, and her associated imagery has returned again. Similarly there is a large cluster of images of nature fading, nearly faded, or changing, occuring in sonnets from all periods of composition:

> Of the deep stair thou tread'st to the dim shoal
> And weary water of the place of sighs
>
> > (Sonnet 3: 1869)

Tender as dawn's first hill-fire, and intense

> (Sonnet 5: 1871)

The ground-whirl of the perished leaves of Hope,

> (Sonnet 4: 1869)

Then the dark ripples spread to waving hair,

> (Sonnet 49: 1869)

To be an essence more environing
Than wine's drained juice ....

> (Sonnet 56: 1881)

The sunrise blooms and withers on the hill
Like any hillflower ....

> (Sonnet 58: 1881)

... some dying sun whose pyre
Blazed with momentous memorable fire; ....

> (Sonnet 62: 1873)

This sunlight shames November where he grieves
In dead red leaves, and will not let him shun....

> (Sonnet 69: 1850)

                        God's breath
Even at this moment haply quickeneth
The air to a flame; till spirits, always nigh
Though screened and hid, shall walk the daylight here.

> (Sonnet 72: 1847-1848)

The flame turned cloud, the cloud returned to flame,

> (Sonnet 79: 1870)

    Rossetti is not the first nineteenth — century poet to concentrate on transitional states. In Keats, for example, the listener in "Ode to a Nightingale" imagines dying while the nightingale sings, in "The Eve of St. Agnes" the lovers merge into one another and the night, and in "Isabella" the physical transition between life and death is emphasized both in the living Isabella and the dead Lorenzo:

XXXV

It was a vision. – in the drowsy gloom,
    The dull of midnight, at her couch's foot
Lorenzo stood, and wept: the forest tomb
    Had marred his glossy hair which once could shoot
Lustre into the sun, and put cold doom
    Upon his lips, and taken the soft lute
From his lorn voice, and past his loamèd ears
Had made a miry channel for his tears.

       (Lorenzo to Isabella)
             XL
'That paleness warms my grave, as though I had
'A Seraph chosen from the bright abyss
'To be my spouse: thy paleness makes me glad....

As in Rossetti's sonnets, in Keats visions occur in dim light and at indeterminable stages of human experience; also at such moments the spirit and the body seem to fuse and perception heightens. But in Keats the transitions directly concern human beings, and nature or its memory remains precise and clear – Lorenzo's lustrous hair, even the loamèd ears of his decay, the spices at Porphyro's table, or the nightingale's firm voice. Human consciousness is measured by its ability to perceive these precise phenomena of nature, not by participation in a Rossettian "silent communion". Lorenzo's spirit, for example, has progressively more difficulty hearing "the little sounds of Life" knelling around him (st. 39):

'And glossy bees at noon do fieldward pass,
   'And many a chapel bell the hour is telling,
'Paining me through: those sounds grow strange to me,
   'And thou art distant in Humanity.

There is never any question as to the distinctness and permanent identity of the natural objects in Keats' world; they may blend into the darkness or each other, or undergo the natural cycles of blooming and death, but they remain concrete and minutely describable:

White hawthorn, and the pastoral eglantine;
   Fast fading violets cover'd up in leaves;
      And mid-May's eldest child,
The coming musk-rose, full of dewy wine,
   The murmurous haunt of flies on summer eves.

    ("Ode to a Nightingale", st. 5)

Rossetti's shifts, by contrast, are more ominous and total; they include all degrees of life, not merely the human, and are seldom qualified by an evocation of the minute and specific. Sometimes in "The House of Life" an element turns into another, "the flame turned cloud", a relatively happy occurrence, but more often the sun or leaf or wine merely vanishes, one does not know to where. Other images of nature falling off occur; he frequently returns to the decaying flower:

Nor stay till on the year's last lily-stem
   The white cup shrivels round the golden heart.

     (Sonnet 83: 1870)

Faint as shed flowers ....

     (Sonnet 40: 1871)

The leaves drop loosened where the heart-stain glows ....

     (Sonnet 52: 1869)

or even to the idea of its petals parting:

Their bosoms sundered, with the opening start
   Of married flowers to either side outspread
   From the knit stem ....

     (Sonnet 6a: 1869)

The images of dimness and near silence evoke a double effect; since Rossetti does not wish to see any external objects except the obscure vision, near-negation, darkness, and silence are desired conditions for him. But dark silence can also constitute the expiration of the vision, the lingering impression after "Peace" has descended into "a sunk stream long unmet" (Sonnet 101: 1870) — the twilight can be hideous.

Human presence, the speaker's or the beloved's, is evoked indirectly, as though persons were most alive when nearest to decomposition into physical elements and motions — the wind of breath, the water of tears, the moving of the heart, warmth, heat, and passion perceived as elemental fire. Shadows are also a form of attenuation into elemental forms:

> *Warmed* by her *hand* and *shadowed* by her *hair*
>   As *close* she leaned and *poured* her *heart* through thee,
>   Whereof the articulate *throbs accompany*
> The smooth black *stream* that makes thy whiteness fair, —
> Sweet *fluttering* sheet, even of her *breath* aware, —
>   Oh let thy *silent song* disclose to me
>   That soul wherewith her lips and *eyes agree*
> Like *married* music in Love's *answering* air.
>
>   (Sonnet 11: 1870, "The Love Letter", italics mine)

The hand and hair are not the psychological center of most persons' perceptions of personality, and even these are indirectly conveyed through the media of "warmth" and "shadow". Her heart is "poured" — it becomes liquid and leaves the self; it "throbs", the letter "flutters". The Rossettian lady comes to resemble an elegant and sexualized version of Coleridge's Aeolian harp — not a projecting psyche but an instrument that records and transmits the emotions that play upon her — in breaths, sighs, glances, pourings, throbbings, footprints.

The references to fusion and harmony — "close", "married", "agree", "answering", "accompanying", "song", "music" — encourage the sensation of the blending of successive emanations. Characteristically to Rossetti both music and silence seem most harmonious when just approaching the limits of each other. The description of an ideal moment or experience as one of fusion and synthesis accompanied by "silent song" occurs throughout romantic poetry and into later Victorian romanticism. It is a basic association, for example, in Coleridge:

>   ... and the world so hush'd!
> The stilly murmur of the distant Sea
> Tells us of silence.
>   And in that simplest Lute,
> Placed length-ways in the clasping casement, hark!
> How by the desultory breeze caress'd,
> Like some coy maid half yielding to her lover,
> It pours such sweet upbraiding, as must needs
> Tempt to repeat the wrong!....the mute still air
> Is Music slumbering on her instrument.
>
>   ("The Eolian Harp")

The woman-music-silence configuration is also significant in Shelley and Keats:

> He dreamed a veiled maid
> Sate near him, talking in low solemn tones.
> Her voice was like the voice of his own soul
> Heard in the calm of thought; its music long,
> Like woven sounds of streams and breezes ....
>
> ("Alastor")

> Heard melodies are sweet, but those unheard
>   Are sweeter; therefore, ye soft pipes, play on ....
>
> ("Ode on a Grecian Urn")

> Awakening up, he took her hollow lute, —
> Tumultuous, — and, in chords that tenderest be,
> He play'd an ancient ditty, long since mute,
> In Provence call'd, 'La belle dame sans mercy':
> Close to her ear touching the melody: —
> Wherewith disturb'd, she utter'd a soft moan .
>
> ("The Eve of St. Agnes")

Both experience silence and music as beauties increased by mingling with each other; perhaps the perfect moment is a silence becoming song or a song ceasing on the still air:

> And now 'twas like all instruments,
> Now like a lovely flute;
> And now it is an angel's song,
> That makes the heavens be mute.
>
> ("The Rime of the Ancient Mariner")

Frequently the song-silence-love association also suggests the sea, as in the first two examples and sometimes in Rossetti. After Rossetti, concern with the moment of music and silence becomes partially formalized in Pater's dictum concerning the aspiration of all art to the condition of music, silence and beauty expressing their nature in song.

Rossetti's emphasis on images of merging and fusion also suggests Tennyson. Sometimes the rapidity of Tennyson's images and smooth quickness of his meters give a sense of the constant conjoining of natural and human elements, a more solid and clarified version of the successions of Shelley and Blake.

> The arching limes are tall and shady,
>   And faint, rainy lights are seen,
>   Moving in the leavy beech.

> Rise from the feast of sorrow, lady,
>> Where all day long you sit between
>>> Joy and woe, and whisper each.
>
>> (Tennyson, "Margaret")

> I knew the flowers, I knew the leaves, I knew
>> The tearful glimmer of the languid dawn
> On those long, rank, dark wood-walks drench'd in dew,
>> Leading from lawn to lawn.
>
>> ("A Dream of Fair Women")

> There would be neither moon nor star;
> But the wave would make music above us afar —
> Low thunder and light in the magic night —
>> Neither moon nor star.
> We would call aloud in the dreamy dells ....
>
>> ("The Merman")

Throughout Tennyson's poetry silence and low sounds often accompany this state of peaceful intensity.

There are innumerable other passages in "The House of Life" where human presence — like that of Love, or Death, or the recurrent "child" — is adumbrated or respired or reflected or merely known inwardly through no sensory process:

> How to their father's children they shall be
>> In act and thought of one goodwill; but each
>> Shall for the other have, in silence speech,
> And in a word complete community?
>
>> (Sonnet 15: 1854)

>> O born with me somewhere that men forget,
>> And though in years of sight and sound unmet,
> Known for my soul's birth-partner well enough!
>
>> (Sonnet 15)

>> Her tremulous smiles; her glances' sweet recall
>> Of love; her murmuring sighs memorial;
>
>> (Sonnet 21: 1870)

>> .... whose summoning eyes,
>> Even now for our love-world's new sunrise,
> Shed very dawn; whose voice, attuned above

> All modulation of the deep-bowered dove,
>   Is like a hand laid softly on the soul;
>   Whose hand is like a sweet voice to control....
>
>> (Sonnet 26: 1871)

The spoken words, the voice, and the letter are also indirectly human.

Characteristically Rossetti uses the medieval emblem of the kiss, yet without interest in the person performing the act. Despite Buchanan's rather comic charge that Rossetti dragged his marital bed out into the street, he only adumbrates sexual situations. He is interested in conveying a strange physical and psychological fusion which he images with a kiss. A kiss is not the property of any one person but rather the creation of a shared boundary, and lacks the qualities of color, shape, and definiteness which Rossetti excludes religiously from all his central images.

> And as she kissed, her mouth became her soul.
>
>> (Sonnet 45: 1869)

> At length their long kiss severed, with sweet smart: ....
>
>> (Sonnet 6a: 1869)

> Who kissed his wings which brought him yesterday ....
>
>> (Sonnet 8: 1869)

> Now kiss, and think that there are really those, ...
>
>> (Sonnet 71: 1853)

> Till only woods and waves might hear our kiss, ...
>
>> (Sonnet 100: 1868-1869)

> Close-kissed and eloquent of still replies
>
>> (Sonnet 4: 1869)

> ... in every kiss sealed fast
> To feel the first kiss and forbode the last.
>
>> (Sonnet 58: 1869)

Keats had also seen human sexuality as a gentle elimination and blending of boundaries:

Into her dream he *melted*, as the rose
Blendeth its odour with the violet, –
Solution sweet: ....

They *glide*, like phantoms, into the wide hall;
Like phantoms, to the iron porch they *glide*; ....
      (italics mine)

Likewise Shelley's "Prometheus Unbound" is a virtual communal hymn to the marriage of all personalities and natural elements, the sexualization of the cosmos.

Tears are another emanation, rendered more poetically conventional by their frequent use in Tennyson and Patmore; at the risk of presenting Rossetti as a second Crashaw I will list a few examples (Rossetti is less strong on milk and blood, however). Tears have the advantage of being water in another form, just as sighs are a tamed wind, glances a reflected light, and warmth a muted fire. The elements have been psychologized, but there is always the premonition that they may return to their original form:

With tear-spurge wan....
    (Sonnet 51: 1880)

And the sweet music welled and the sweet tears.
    (Sonnet 47: 1869)[29]

And watered with the wasteful warmth of tears?
    (Sonnet 39: 1869)

By thine own tears thy song must tears beget....
    (Sonnet 61: 1880)

The tendency to blur and exchange human qualities and elemental forces could be almost indefinitely illustrated, even in passages often adduced to show Rossetti's precision of detail. What detail he uses is a blent picture of the human and non-human:

Your hands lie open in the long fresh grass,–
    The finger-points look through like rosy blooms: ....
    (Sonnet 19: 1871)

In a world of essences and dim shoals one does not expect much color. Far from possessing a "painterly" concern with brightness and variety of color in these sonnets, Rossetti carefully mutes his tones. There is consistency between his painting and poetry in this respect, since his later paintings also limit color to certain emblematic uses and dark effects.

A poet might be expected to expend color on natural descriptions. But the forms of non-human life which Rossetti presents are chiefly woods, flowers, and birds; birds in full Keatsian and Shelleyan tradition are noticed primarily for their voices — if not, they are usually light in color or otherwise unobtrusive:

All modulation of the deep-bowered dove....
    (Sonnet 26: 1871)

The cockoo-throb, the heartbeat of the Spring....
    (Sonnet 64: 1873)

The woods form a darkish background, and the flowers, like his women, although noticed for their regal qualities are often lacking in color. For example, he admires lilies and irises:

O'er water-daisies and wild waifs of Spring,
    There where the iris rears its gold-crowned sheaf ....
    (Sonnet 20: 1871)

Are golden kingcup-fields with silver edge ....
    (Sonnet 19: 1871)

That flecks the snowdrop underneath the snow ....
    (Sonnet 56: 1881)

He also mentions roses and once (Sonnet 24: 1871)[30] a corn-poppy; this might seem to contradict assertions about colorless flowers. Rosetti does consistently uses a range of colors which to him express richness — ivory, pearl, gold, colors which suggest metallic or gemlike properties as much as actual color.

Rossetti's admiration of the rich and metallic is another expression of interest in concentrated, intense, non-human images of perfection. Pre-Raphaelite admiration of jewels in turn influenced Pater and the Decadents. A metal or gem seemed a refining of elements, a concentrated essence, the attempt to pass beyond ordinary expressions of material form. Most are formed by violent heat; there is an affinity of ideas with Pater's famous "gem-like flame", a Hericlitean concern with the composing and decomposing of elements expressed in the extremes of jewels and fire.

Rossetti's preference for the imagery of precious metals has appeared in the lines already cited, "silver edge", "gold-crowned sheaf"; he also likes pearled and marbled effects, mentioning "ivory" and "ebony" (introductory sonnet, 1880). He does tolerate a few colors which are not associated with metals, rose and purple, for example — both associated with the regal or artificially elegant. Almost all of his colors seem aligned to his murky and twilight tastes; perhaps the green of his poetry is as dark as that of his paintings, and he is fond of gray, wanness, paleness, the effects of subdued light. All poets use light-dark imagery; since Rossetti desires to mute stark effects it is interesting that both dark and light often become clouded:

Carve it in ivory or in ebony
As Day or Night may rule ....
    (introductory sonnet)

Frequently they blend into each other in quick succession:

Of darkened love once more the light shall gleam ....
    (Sonnet 40: 1871)

Girt in dark growths, yet glimmering with one star ....
    (Sonnet 39: 1869)

We are seldom permitted all light or all darkness, only twilight. The emphasis on jewelled, golden, and silver color images modifies the simplicity of pale primary colors, and the dim wan visages seem to preclude bright whites and shining blacks. All is shadowed, shrouded.

Furthermore the metal, jewels, and heavy draperies serve an emblematic function; they are not pictorially descriptive but invoke an already programmed reaction. For example, we know that things golden are good or desirable, and gold appears everywhere in the sonnets — coins, hair, goblets, sky:

May pour for thee this golden wine, brim-high,
   Till round the glass thy fingers glow like gold.
    (Sonnet 71: 1847-1848)

Or golden coins squandered and still to pay?

    (Sonnet 86: 1862)

Lies all that golden hair undimmed in death.

    (Sonnet 36: 1870)

O'er poet's page gold-shadowed in thy hair?

    (Sonnet 33: 1871)

Visions of golden futures ....

    (Sonnet 62: 1873)

References to the sea are so multitudinous in Victorian literature that their presence scarcely distinguishes Rossetti. For him, as later for Swinburne and Hopkins, it evokes the unconscious, all latent feeling, and unlimitedness of space, destructiveness, or happiness. Rossetti admired the sensations peculiar to enclosed and baroquely decorated places, so it is natural that the enveloping and expansive sea should suggest to him chiefly images of rupture and loss:

Two souls, the shores wave-mocked of sundering seas: —

    (Sonnet 40: 1871)

    ... yet dawn's first light
On ebbing storm and life twice ebb'd must break; ....

    (Sonnet 88: 1875)

Shall birth and death, and all dark names that be
As doors and windows bared to some loud sea,
    Lash deaf mine ears and blind my face with spray;
    And shall my sense pierce love, — the last relay
And ultimate outpost of eternity?

    (Sonnet 34: 1871)

    Yet if you die, can I not follow you,
    Forcing the straits of change? Alas! but who
Shall wrest a bond from night's inveteracy,
Ere yet my hazardous soul put forth, to be
    Her warrant against all her haste might rue? —
    Ah! in your eyes so reached what dumb adieu,
What unsunned gyres of waste eternity?

    (Sonnet 44: 1871)

More often than not the sea is associated with death. Most of the exceptions are sea-images which describe the evocative Lady:

> That he who seeks her beauty's furthest goal,
>   Beyond the light that the sweet glances throw
>   And refluent wave of the sweet smile, may know
> The very sky and sea-line of her soul.
>
>   (Sonnet 10: 1868)

>   Whose passionate hearts lean by Love's high decree
> Together on his heart for ever true,
> As the cloud-foaming firmamental blue
>   Rests on the blue line of a foamless sea.
>
>   (Sonnet 12: 1871)

Fire imagery is perhaps more Rossetti's own characteristic:

> And Fame, whose loud *wings* fan the *ashen* Past
> To signal-*fires*, Oblivion's flight to scare;
>
>   (Sonnet 1: 1871)

> A god when all our life-*breath* met to fan
> Our life-*blood*, till love's emulous ardours ran,
>   *Fire* within *fire*, desire in deity.
>
>   (Sonnet 6: 1869)

> One *flame-winged* brought a white-*winged harp*-player
>
>   (Sonnet 9: 1870)

>   ... lit
> With quivering *fire*, the *words* take *wine* from it;
> As here between our *kisses* we sit thus ....
>
>   (Sonnet 16: 1870)

> Or but discern, through *night's* unfeatured scope,
> Scorn-*fired* at length the illusive eyes of Hope.
>
>   (Sonnet 43: 1871)

> A *glass* facing his *fire*, where the *bright* bliss
> Is *mirrored*, and the *heat* returned. Yet move
> That *glass*, a stranger's amorous *flame* to prove ...
>   *Ice* to the *moon*; while her pure *fire* to his
> For whom it *burns*, clings close i' the heart's alcove.
>
>   (Sonnet 57: 1881)

> Some prisoned *moon* in steep cloud-fastnesses, –
>   Throned queen and thralled; some dying sun whose *pyre*

Blazed with momentous memorable *fire*; —

    (Sonnet 62: 1873)

The summer *clouds* that visit every *wing*
With *fires* of *sunrise* and of *sunsetting;*
   The furtive flickering *streams* to *light* re-born
   'Mid *airs* new fledged and valourous lusts of morn....

    (Sonnet 64: 1873)

A *fiery* bush with coruscating hair.

    (Sonnet 70: 1853)

          God's *breath*
Even at this moment haply quickeneth
The *air* to a *flame* ....

    (Sonnet 72: 1847-1848)

Lo! as that youth's eyes *burned* at thine, so went
Thy spell through him ....

    (Sonnet 78: 1867)

Behold, this crocus is a withering *flame*;
   This snowdrop, *snow* ....

    (Sonnet 83: 1870)

To Anteros its *fireless* lip shall plight.
Aye, waft the unspoken vow: yet dawn's first *light*
   On ebbing *storm* and life twice ebbed must break ....
                  ....
Of a life's love, and bid its *flame* to shine:
Which still may rest *unfir'd* ....

    (Sonnet 88: 1875)

Whose *heart*'s old *fire* in shadow of shame is furl'd ....

    (Sonnet 93: 1869)

Her funeral flowers were *snow*-flakes shed on her
   And the red *wings* of *frost-fire* rent the *sky*.

    (Sonnet 96: 1873)

   Two *glances* which (together) would rejoice
In love, now lost like *stars* beyond *dark trees*;
Two *hands* (apart) whose touch alone gives ease;
   Two bosoms which, *heart*-shrined with (mutual) flame,
     Would, (meeting) in one (clasp), be made the (same);
Two souls, the shores *wave*-mocked of (sundering) *seas*.

    (Sonnet 40: 1871)

    (italics and parentheses mine)

Fire seems especially associated with references to the heart; fire references also call up familiar accompanying presences of wings, air, light, breath, incense, ashes, words, murmuring, glances, floods, waves, seas, streams, flowers, clouds, snow, glass, moon, sunsets — and doubtless more. Notice in the preceding passage from sonnet forty the number of words concerned with closeness and apartness, and throughout, the number of concentrative, evaluative, and binding words — inmost, sanctuary, intense, instantaneous, emulous, desire, sheltered, illusive, amorous, close, momentous, valorous — also the persistence of emanations that cannot be defined in physical terms:

Lo! as that youth's eyes burned at thine, so went
Thy spell through him ....
    (Sonnet 78: 1867)

The blending of sensations, synaesthesia, is a well-established pattern in romantic poetry; although the individual elements of Rossetti's sequence are different — among other divergences, emphasizing the marmoreal, stony, and elegantly static — the pattern of shifting suggestions of different senses and elements is in the manner of Blake's "Book of Thel" or of Shelley:

I am the daughter of Earth and Water,
    And the nursling of the Sky;
I pass through the pores of the ocean and shores;
    I change, but I cannot die.
For after the rain with never a stain
    The pavilion of Heaven is bare,
And the winds and sunbeams with their complex gleams
    Build up the blue dome of air,
I silently laugh at my own cenotaph
    And out of the caverns of rain,
Like a child from the womb, like a ghost from the tomb,
    I arise and unbuild it again.
    ("The Cloud")

Since Rossetti himself enjoyed Keats more than Shelley, a common nineteenth-century preference, and since he also admired Coleridge deeply, it is common to compare Rossetti's imagery with the more pictorially precise exoticism of Coleridge and Keats. An alternate synaesthetic tradition transmitted through Tennyson may also have been important in the development of his images.

Associated with Rossetti's imagery is a type of diction which transmits evaluations through verbal chiaroscuro — words such as "sweet", "anguish", "ardour", "memorable", "lamentable", "weak", "beauty" directly dictate a subjective response to the reader. It is easy to see how language in turn borders on Rossetti's personifications — "terror", "mystery", "genius", "love", "death". An alternation between personification and image characterizes these sonnets, perhaps intended to engender a certain pain of shadow and indefiniteness — neither the clear picture nor the clear abstraction is permitted.

> Ah! who shall dare to search through what sad maze
>   Thenceforth their incommunicable ways
> Follow the desultory feet of Death.
>   (Sonnet 65: 1853)

> Howbeit athwart Death's imminent shade doth soar
>   One Power, than flow of stream or flight of dove
>   Sweeter to glide around, to brood above.
> Tell me, my heart, — what angel-greeted door
> Or threshold of wing-winnowed threshing-floor
>   Hath guest fire-fledged as thine, whose lord is Love?
>   (Sonnet 41: 1871)

Rossetti uses other mannerisms to evade the clear image. He often defines by negatives, stating what a situation or emotion has lost or failed to be. Similarly many of his physical descriptions require the reader to visualize absent qualities:

> Rests on the blue line of a foamless sea.
>   (Sonnet 12: 1871)

> ... hurled
> Abroad by reinless steeds ....
>   (Sonnet 90: 1847)

> Of soulless air-flung fountains ....
>   (Sonnet 61: 1880)

Sometimes a grim shock results from understatement and pointed evasion:

Upon the sight of lidless eyes in Hell.
>   (Sonnet 63: 1869)

Rossetti's various uses of the negative contribute ambivalence in tone and the strained abstractness of things not quite said or described. What objects are not is clearer than what they are.

A related mannerism is the use of loose oxymorons in description, that is, close juxtaposition of adjectives with opposite associations. Their pictorial qualities cancel out each other, and the confusion suggests a psychological state rather than a specific image:

Her funereal flowers were snow-flakes shed on her
>   And the red wings of frost-fire rent the sky.
>>   (Sonnet 96: 1873)

The flame turned cloud, the cloud returned to flame,
>   The lifted shifted steeps and all the way? –
>>   ... this wind-warm space, ...
>>>   (Sonnet 79: 1870)

Than the wild rose tree's arch that crowns the fell;....
The wave-bowered pearl, – the heart-shaped seal of green ....
>   (Sonnet 56: 1881)

The speech-bound sea-shell's low importunate strain, – ....
>   (Sonnet 47: 1869)

Rossetti wishes to describe muted dissonance, not paradox; later in the century the oxymorons become more direct, violent, and contradictory:

A fiery pulse of sin, a splendid shame ...
Which dies through its own sweetness and the stress
>   Of too much pleasure: ....
>>   (Wilde, "Charmides")

>   Burned like the ruby fire set
In the swinging lamp of a crimson shrine ....
>>   (Wilde, "In the Gold Room")

Father and fondler of heart thou hast wrung:
>   (Hopkins, "Wreck")

Sweet-smelling, pale with prison, sanguine-hearted, ...
> (Swinburne, "Ave Atque Vale", 1878)

Rossetti's evocative presences — breaths, tears, music, spells, — can become as repetitious as Morris' narrative situations. Where one element is, there its associates gather. Occasionally they solidify in Victorian sentimentalizations of sexuality or emotion, as repeated hearts, lips, flowers, breathlessness, kisses. His paintings include several women wearing heart lockets and necklaces, even holding artificial heart images in their hands;[31] as with these so also in his poetry the solemn Rossettian significance of erotic love seems to merge with trivial valentine superficialities. At least his preoccupation with female lips, necks, and throats lends credulity to his emphasis on flower imagery; clearly he saw parallels — heads on long stems, *et cetera*. Always he best appreciates the "natural" images of heart and flower in the forms most related to human passion.

Love and the Lady are served by ritualistic images, relics of the Presence, which intentionally render the emotion of love obscure, weighty, and indirect. Chalices, altars, and incense are about as accidental to divinity as hair, plumes, and jewels to human body and personality, constituting not "religious imagery" but the imagery of a certain methodology of worship.

> When do I see thee most, beloved one?
>   When in the light the spirits of mine eyes
>   Before thy face, their altar, solemnize
> The worship of that Love through thee made known?
>   (Sonnet 4: 1869)

The quality of the worship is often ambivalent, directed perhaps to ominous as well as benign powers. Associated with the close atmosphere are suggestions of shrouded evil or guilt. Ifor Evans comments on what he sees as "chaste-corruptness" in Rossetti's mixture of sex and ritual:

> It is not that sensuality is excluded — the 'Nuptial Sleep' sonnet which led to the 'Fleshly School' attack is evidence of that — but that its portrayal has the sombre sobriety of ritual. The effect is as if a chastity or mind has combined with a corruptness in experience, and a gracious idealism of sentiment existed without innocence.[22]

"The House of Life" still assumes the necessity of certain conventional social bonds, in any case, including marriage and the sharing of silent harmony. Later in the century Swinburne and others will set their "moral" less in social bonds than in preference for a certain type of individual character, while the emphasis on corruption will become more self-conscious and plotted, despite lingering ingenuousness.

Perhaps one of the reasons why Rossetti has been so violently liked and disliked is this repeated use of series of images — if they evoke for the reader the same response they did for Rossetti, his poetry seems profoundly subjective; if one's inner correlatives are different, however, as they commonly are for persons living a century after any poet's work, his preferences can seem a series of cheap devices. Why are jewels beautiful? What is love? Why are twilights mysterious? Why bowers, why flames? Why moons?

The answer of course is that during a certain period a large number of sensitive men seemed to respond to certain things as inherently beautiful; the why of that is the fundamental question that all study of literature is asking. We doubtless make similar assumptions at present as the result of equally arbitrary biases. Closely allied with the characterization of Rossetti as a 'psychological' poet is the sense that his poetic world is a closed mind, its laws and visions justified in circularity, its images suggesting and reflecting each other. Although this would seem a weakness, to those with identical subjective correlatives his poetry could properly seem all the more evocative and direct for its avoidance of many less intuitive structures of thought and imagery: "in silence speech, And in a word complete community" (Sonnet 15: 1854).

After such a catalogue of language mannerisms employed in one sonnet sequence, Rossetti might seem a monomaniac of elaboration, a sort of baroque Tennyson disassociated from the natural world. What is most surprising is the consonance between Rossetti's verbal devices and his themes. His style harmonizes with what might seem opposing traits of character: firmness and heaviness of assertion combined with a sense that all emotion must be qualified, indefinite, simultaneously pleasant and unpleasant. His use of emphasis and shifting abstractions produces sensations analogous to his changing projections and quiet declarations of hope and loss.

Neither does an analysis of his techniques reveal them to be especially atypical among Victorian writers. What is unique is their employment in such concentration, so briefly, and with such ambivalence. Without doubt his tendency towards balancing opposed pairs and compressing similar sounds in close proximity influenced later Victorian efforts at stylizing emotion. As Tennyson in "In Memoriam", Rossetti creates an almost stoically balanced language, although he is less diffuse and sedative than Tennyson.

C. IMAGERY AND MANNERISMS OF FIVE SONNETS

I will discuss the "Introductory Sonnet" of 1880 and four others from the period 1869-1871, to demonstrate their use of these devices of blending, muting, enclosed imagery, and indirection. The initial sonnet, added to the 1881 edition of Rossetti's poems, has been much emphasized because it contains one of Rossetti's few poetic comments on poetry. It closely resembles "The Song-Throe" and other late sonnets in manner:

> A Sonnet is a moment's monument,
>   Memorial from the Soul's eternity
>   To one dead deathless hour. Look that it be,
> Whether for lustral rite or dire portent,
> Of its own arduous fulness reverent:
>   Carve it in ivory or in ebony,
>   As Day or Night may rule; and let Time see
> Its flowering crest impearled and orient.
>
> A Sonnet is a coin: its face reveals
>   The soul, – its converse, to what Power 'tis due: –
> Whether for tribute to the august appeals
>   Of Life, or dower in Love's high retinue,
> It serve; or, 'mid the dark wharf's cavernous breath,
> In Charon's palm it pay the toll to Death.

That a sonnet should embody an intense moment is no shatteringly novel declaration; it is kindred to Wordsworth's celebration of "spots of time". The comment in the sestet is more ambiguous. The "face" of the sonnet reveals the psyche, the "converse", perhaps the hinted or implied meanings, reveal the sources of sensation. Since Rossetti is not usually concerned with psychological causation or with distinctions of in- and externality, the sestet may merely state that a sonnet reveals which of three forms of fate – Love, Life, or Death – is influencing the soul at that moment.

This sonnet begins with paradoxes – the moment is eternal and deathless, yet also dead, needing a monument, memorialized. The marmoreal, static images for the intense moment are revealing. The romantic poets more often expressed intensities by images of living creatures — the tree, the skylark, the woman singing in the fields, the nightingale. Rossetti also produces singing birds, but they are more decorative and incidental. Keats' "Ode on a Grecian Urn" concentrates less on the urn than on the processional carved upon it, while Rossetti's urns are strictly funereal, substituting for descriptions of moving figures the blank, formalized stasis of the vase itself.

Since the moment must die to exist, the marble tomb bespeaks death-and-beauty at once; perhaps a suggestion of aesthetic necrophilia, certainly an expression of what Rossetti admired. Rossetti expects the contradictions of life and death, the light, rapid moment and the heavy, enduring monument, to seem minimal and quickly overcome; his oxymorons seem to him almost reflexive. A paradox is a seeming contradiction, but since little emphasis is placed on the opposition, the effect is generally of assonance overcoming a mild undercurrent of dissonance.

The mention of the idea of monument and memorial evokes reverence, memory, ceremony, introduced in the religious categories of rite and portent, the one lustral, the other dire. The lustral rite presumably is positive and the dire portent negative, but Rossetti purposely creates ambiguous associations with "rite". "Lustral" and "dire" are more evaluative than descriptive. Again Rossetti wishes to avoid clear light and dark, sharp oppositions — "lustral" and "dire" are not quite antonyms. There is a further blurring of pleasant and unpleasant associations in "arduous fulness reverent" — "arduous" connotes effort and difficulty and "reverent" an approved piety, so that the richness and completion of the sonnet's "fulness" should be both desirable and painful. The "ivory" and "ebony" are indeed lustrous, marbled, off-white and black; the flowering crest, like the moment's monument, systematizes an expression of life or nature into a formalized pattern of metal or stone. Consistently this flowering crest is "impearled" — its whiteness is murky, expensive, regal, stony — very like the monument. Throughout the sonnet Rossetti has not proceeded by a clear series of definitions or paradoxes but formed images of multiple association, each surrounded by interpretive adjectives but remaining clouded, swirled. The prescribed response — of reverence and fear — is clearer than its object, but this ambiguity never leaves doubt as to the elegance of what is described — it is regal, crested, jewelled, orient, enshrined, commanding, also the characteristics of the queenly mistress. Both Swinburne and, more indirectly, Hopkins appropriate this attraction towards beauty expressing itself in regal power. Rossetti likes to associate his beauty with a general sense of antiquity; the crest is presumably medieval, the monument has existed from the soul's eternity (although that exists also in future time, and perhaps apart from time).

The coin, like the monument, has both ominous and pleasant associations. It is metallic, sovereign, golden, in the tradition of former images of the valuable, yet it is obviously the object of greed, owed to a hovering Power. "Tribute" calls forth ambivalent connotations, the "august appeals" of life seem somewhat fearful, and life a peremptory and domineering ruler (tyrant?), no friendly companion. The "dower in Love's high retinue", like "crest impearled and orient", combines archaism, sovereignty, and objects of economic value ("money", "pearl"). The conventions of courtly love are added to those of generalized worship, and "dower" further implies marriage. "August" is a word directing the reader's subjective response rather than describing an object, and "high" functions similarly. The last image, of the coin paid to Charon, is the final reduction to grimness, meanness, and futility of the original coin image and its associations of pride. "Dark wharf's cavernous breath" is irregular in meter, one of Rossetti's sonorous phrases sounding out its content. Charon's boat and Styx are typical of the classical references Rossetti used increasingly in his late period.[33] He has been criticized for the brevity of his mythological references, but the blurred associations of the hasty reference to Charon increase the sense of murky, commingled, "cavernous" reality. He does not want a carefully structured epic simile.

The introductory sonnet is atypically specific in the content of its first paradox, more ambiguous thereafter. It also contains the sequence's characterisitically subjective diction and imagery of dead elegance. Imagery of elemental nature is here oblique, consisting only of stone, day and night, metal, jewels, underground water (Hades), and breath. Five lines are metrically regular, one, seven, nine, ten, and fourteen, balanced at the beginning and end of octave and sestet. "Memorial", "whether for", "arduous", "ivory", "Flowering", "Whether for", "dower in" and "cavernous" all squeeze in an extra syllable to form anapests, and the imperatives "Look that it be" and "carve it in ivory" contain initial emphatic trochees. Both octave and sestet end with a mild raised climax, one proud, one ominous:

... Its flowering crest impearled and orient.
... In Charon's palm it pay the toll to death.

It is a carefully regular sonnet, with variations at less prominent points contrasting with the even iambics used for declarations at emphatic positions.

Sonnet five, written in 1871, contains elusive suggestions of love — "word", "key", "paths untrod", "soul", "heart", "instantaneous penetrating sense". We are dictated responses — "difficult", "poor", "evidence", "tender", "intense".

HEART'S HOPE

By what word's power, the key of paths untrod,
    Shall I the difficult deeps of Love explore,
    Till parted waves of Song yield up the shore
Even as that sea which Israel crossed dryshod?
For lo! in some poor rhythmic period,
    Lady, I fain would tell how evermore
Thy soul I knew not from the body, nor
Thee from myself, neither our love from God.

Yea, in God's name, and Love's, and thine, would I
    Draw from one loving heart such evidence
As to all hearts all things shall signify;
    Tender as dawn's first hill-fire, and intense
    As instantaneous penetrating sense,
In Spring's birth hour, of other Springs gone by.

Many Rossettian sonnets record past moments whose memory pains and gives significance to present and future, but this is one of his clearest images of the poignancy and fierceness of reverie.

Almost all Victorian poets seem to have felt intense personal pain in the sudden memory of youth; the past seemed further away to them than to the Romantics, and time's progression more bleakly mechanical. The speed of death seemed to increase exponentially as the century wore on. For the Victorians the sweetness of a lost past often associated itself with severed love — and there were sociological as well as more literary reasons for the prevalence and intensity of romantic memory.[34]

One of the most beautiful expressions of the pain of memory is Tennyson's familiar lyric:

'Tears, idle tears, I know not what they mean,
Tears from the depth of some divine despair
Rise in the heart, and gather to the eyes,
In looking on the happy autumn-fields,
And thinking of the days that are no more ....

'Ah, sad and strange, as in dark summer dawns
The earliest pipe of half-awaken'd birds
To dying ears, when unto dying eyes
The casement slowly grows a glimmering square:
So sad, so strange, the days that are no more.

'Dear as remember'd kisses after death,
And sweet as those by hopeless fancy feign'd
On lips that are for others; deep as love,
Deep as first love, and wild with all regret,
O Death in Life, the days that are no more!

(From *The Princess*, 1847)

The second stanza quoted is a Victorianized "Ode to a Nightingale", and its major images also occur in "The House of Life". Tennyson's sudden and unsought perception of an irretrievable past of beauty ("Dear as remembered kisses after death") has its counterpart in the "Instantaneous penetrating sense / In Spring's birth-hour, of other Springs gone by" of Rossetti's poem. Interestingly in "Tears, Idle Tears" Tennyson like Rossetti uses not descriptive detail but subjectivism – "divine", "happy", "sad and strange", "ah", "so sad, so strange", "dear", "sweet". Parallels in statement and manner could be found throughout Victorian literature; it is surprising to see Rossetti, who usually infuses all he writes with his own peculiar delineations of romance, create lines which, apart from the polysyllabic "instantaneous penetrating sense", might have been written partially by Tennyson or another nearly contemporary lyric poet.

The sonnet's first extended image is of the poet exploring (through song) the depths of love as the Israelites had crossed the Red Sea. It would be interesting if the Biblical record described Moses as ordering the parting of the sea by a "word's power", or if "waves of song" had characterized the event, but unfortunately Exodus 14 reads:

And Moses stretched out his hand over the sea; and the Lord caused the sea to go back by a strong east wind all that night ... (v. 22)

So much for mystic words and melody. There is a song celebration in the next chapter, however, which might remotely have influenced Rossetti's associations.

Frequently phrases appear which are incomplete suggestions of something else – "word", "key", "poor rhythmic period", "name", "evidence" – building up to the "instantaneous penetrating sense" which also signifies something beyond itself. Again Rossetti is concerned with parting and merging — of the waves, of himself and the beloved, of past and present, of musical harmony — and again he evokes the elemental properties — sea, waves, dawn, fire — as well as intensities which possess no shape — soul, love, song, rhythmic period, God, instantaneous penetrating sense, heart. Unlike the introductory sonnet, this one contains no colors, stones, or jewels; the archaisms and courtly associations suggest antique or medieval formality, however, and the recitation of names is slightly ritualistic. The tenth line is a general assertion stated evenly and quietly:

As to all hearts all things shall signify ....

As the line progresses the rhythm hastens, adding musicality. The stresses of the sonnet are relatively heavy, emphasizing the serious melodiousness appropriate to its theme. The rime on "dryshod" and "God" adds eccentricity.

Both the octet and sestet end in small climaxes of feeling, the first confident, the second quieter and sadder.

... Thee from myself, neither our love from God.
... In Spring's birth-hour, of other Springs gone by.

Both concluding lines are strictly iambic and simple in diction. Rhythmic variations in the sonnet are the usual anapests with "Lady" and "Tender" emphatic trochees, each beginning a tercet. Three lines in the octave and three in the sestet are completely iambic, so that this 1871 sonnet is more regular than the 1880 one and the nostalgic sestet staider in rhythm than the more energetic octave.

Sonnet seventeen, also written in 1871, is almost a parodic incarnation of the general characteristics of the sequence:

What dawn-pulse at the heart of heaven, or last
    Incarnate flower of culminating day, —
What marshalled marvels on the skirts of May,
Or song full-quired, sweet June's encomiast;
What glory of change by Nature's hand amass'd
    Can vie with all those moods of varying grace
    Which o'er one loveliest woman's form and face
Within this hour, within this room, have passed.
Love's very vesture and elect disguise
    Was each fine movement, — wonder new-begot
    Of lily or swan or swan-stemmed galiot;
Joy to his sight who now the sadlier sighs,
Parted again; and sorrow yet for eyes
    Unborn, that read these words and saw her not.

First there are the words of intensity – "dawn-pulse", "heart of heaven", "incarnate", "culminating", "marvels", "full-quired", "very", "elect", "amass'd", "wonder", "joy" – and of interpretation – "sweet", "sadlier", "sorrow", "loveliest", "grace", "culminating", "glory". The pulsing, sighing, and throbbing are the usual organic palpitations. As before nature is known by a few select and typifying portions, song, swan, and flower, and no colors are mentioned except, by suggestion, the whiteness of swans or golden of sunset. Further the figures evoked are known by limited or distancing characteristics – Nature's hand, woman's form and face, Love's vesture and disguise, the eyes of him of aftertime. Certain elusive qualities, "the glory of change", the "moods of varying grace" are used circularly for definition or exploration of other obscure qualities. Music, psychological responses, passionate movements, and moments of intense beauty merge with each other and with a sense of loss, sorrow, parting. The first few lines of the octet contain what for Rossetti is a massing of descriptive words, emphasized with heavier than usual stresses.

> What dawn-pulse at the heart of heaven, or last

Typically the energetic natural descriptions are to show to what the Lady is superior. There are slight hoverings of rhythms over "pulse" and in the fourth line over "Or song full-quired". Of elements several references to sky and light occur, the swan and ship suggest water, the earth is represented by lily and flower, but there is no reference to fire. Again the archaisms – "very vesture", "galiot" – and the sense that something will be lost; future persons will not have known the past of the hour now celebrated only as swanlike – not rapidity but regality of motion is admired, and not physical substance but movement. There are several suggestions of closeness in the octet – "marshalled", "quired", "amass'd", "within", balanced by exclusions in the sestet – "parted", "unborn".

We have been given much intensity, but little real description – what is a dawn-pulse on the heart of heaven? What appearance is presented by an incarnate flower of culminating day? or what are marshalled marvels on the skirts of May? a glory of change? The first two images are synaesthetic, the two latter merely uninformative. As indefinite and blurred as these sensations, Rossetti is saying, and as unspecific and defined in motion as swan and ship, is the lady's uncorporeal and symbolic quality. Once again she is perceived as a physical presence only indirectly, through her non-corporeal qualities. She is less person than emblem, and the natural world is significant chiefly in providing images for her human perfection. Rossetti once commented that he had no use for the word "anthropomorphic";[35] ironically it characterizes his conception of nature.

Only six lines are totally regular, and not surprisingly, one concludes the octave, one begins the sestet, and another concludes it. Appropriately the passage describing change contains more anapests than the more regular sestet describing love. They are placed on "flower of", "glory of", "varying", "loveliest", and reproduce the unstable grace of these qualities. An interesting series of syncopations begins three successive lines of the sestet:

> Or lily or swan or swan-stemmed galiot;
> Joy to his sight who now the sadlier sighs,
> Parted again; and sorrow yet for eyes ....

If "Joy to his" is a dactyl, not one and a half iambs, then the twelfth line is unusual for having two variations.

Sonnet fifty-four, also from 1871, contains much fire-sea-cloud-sky imagery, imagery of metals associated with imprisonment, and contrasting suggestions of escape.

LOVE'S FATALITY

Sweet Love, – but oh! most dread Desire of Love
    Life-thwarted. Linked in gyves I saw them stand,
    Love-shackled with Vain-longing, hand to hand:
And one was eyed as the blue vault above:
But hope tempetuous like a fire-cloud hove
    I' the other's gaze, even as in his whose wand
    Vainly all night with spell-wrought power has spann'd
The unyielding caves of some deep treasure-trove.

Also his lips, two writhen flakes of flame,
    Made moan: "Alas O Love, thus leashed with me!
    Wing-footed thou, wing-shouldered, once born free:
And I, thy cowering self, in chains grown tame, –
Bound to thy body and soul, named with thy name, –
    Life's iron heart, even Love's Fatality."

There are too many emotive words – "sweet", "oh!", "dread", "desire", "thwarted", "vain", "hope", "love", "tempetuous", "vainly", "unyielding", "deep", "alas", "moan", "cowering", "tame", "fatality". Images of closeness are all too present – linked, shackled, Love, spann'd, caves, leashed, chains, iron — and images merge into images — hand to eye to vault to fire-cloud to wand and caves to lips to name to soul. Rossetti's contrasting personifications are as always unclear to the eye:

> Love shackled with Vain-Longing, hand to hand ....

while places mentioned, the caves and seas, are unspecific psychological references.

The contrasting abstractions are not paradoxically related but merly conjoined inevitably, like the two sides of the coin in the introductory sonnet. The elusive presences of Love and Vain-longing are known only by the poet's responses — "sweet" and "dread" — and by their response to and perceptions of the external world — "eyes", "gaze", "moaning". The gaze of Love is tempestuous, comparable to a magic wand of spell-wrought power, and associated with deep psychological recesses of emotion, "The unyielding caves of some deep treasure trove". As is often the case, Rossetti is concerned with how his personae register physically their emotion,

> Also his lips, two writhen flakes of flame ....

rather than with the body *per se*. The use of words directly expressing physical pain and coercion is not common in Rossetti; their appearance here, as well as the emotive contrasts in description and evocation of elemental violence, suggest the usages of both Swinburne and Hopkins. "Flakes of flame", for example, superimposes different substances in extreme change; presumably the flakes are ashes falling down from the fire, still flaming as they turn to white dust. The sonnet concludes with a similar image of coercion, "Life's iron heart"; the metallic and shackling qualities emphasized throughout the poem contract around the pulsing heart, Rossetti's image for human intensity, sensation, and eroticism. Love or life, Rossetti's "life force", is subject to fatality, death, stoniness, rigidification, a turning to iron.

Again the sonnet rises to an abstraction, the significance of which is not argued or described (love's gaze and moan are rendered obliquely, Fatality is a mere shadow, the *alter ego* of a shadow) but merely asserted in the quiet and latinate climax.

The meter is quite regular, with eight completely iambic lines if the last line is included:

> Life's iron heart, even Love's Fatality."

Line thirteen however is unusually deviant and rhythmic:

> Boúnd to thy bódy and sóul, námed with thy náme,

with alliteration and stresses linking the nouns. Frequent initial trochees (wĭng-footed) create sudden dramatic and emphatic syncopations:

>   Desire of Love
> Life-thwarted ...
>   whose wand
> Vainly all night ....
>   grown tame
> Bound to thy body ....

One more sonnet, "A Superscription", written in 1869 towards the beginning of Rossetti's prolific period, describes one of the last elusive presences of Death.

> Look in my face; My name is Might-have-been;
>   I am also called No-more, Too-late, Farewell;
>   Unto thine ear I hold the dead-sea shell
> Cast up thy Life's foam-fretted feet between;
> Unto thine eyes the glass where that is seen
>   Which had Life's form and Love's, but by my spell
>   Is now a shaken shadow intolerable,
> Of ultimate things unuttered the frail screen.
> Mark me, how still I am! But should there dart
>   One moment through thy soul the soft surprise
>   Of that winged Peace which lulls the breath of sighs –
> Then shalt thou see me smile, and turn apart
> Thy visage to mine ambush at thy heart
>   Sleepless with cold commemorative eyes.

Here the evocations also elude – "Might-have-been" is a carefully enclosed word, from a dead shell, the small messenger of the larger motions of the sea. The self seems to stand upon the sand, foam-fretted; the shell which complexly vibrates a dim sound is like the mirror which pictures, barely, the "shaken shadow intolerable" of guilt and the death of time. The remembrance that a sonnet is a monument to one dead, deathless hour now loses all but ominous associations. Deadly stillness is no longer "silent harmony" but the ease that deceptively lulls. The "presence" has hovered in evasive and hinted forms, never tangible, never confrontable, appearing in disembodied outposts of the physical — face, smile, cold commemorative eyes. The poet's self is somewhat more embodied in ear, feet, eyes, soul, visage, and heart — but it still suffers from similar dissolution. The shaken shadow is definitely no lustral rite but a dire portent casting a spell, creating the "shadow intolerable". The deserted shell of the dead mollusk, the mirror, and the cold visage are all projections outside the self which have become more powerful concentrators of intensity than anything within. It is hard to say whether a shell is a "natural" object or an artifact; like the jewels Rossetti admired it is nature in its form most approaching artifice. The murmuring shell seems a spectral parody of the sequence's lyres, songs, and breathings; it sighs and whispers, but of death.

In "The House of Life" a "frail screen" has hidden all we have observed; according to Rossetti's taste this screen has aided in the imagination of beauty, but now, the screen hiding "ultimate things unuttered" merely renders their suggestions the more horribly inevitable. There is no real doubt left about the quality of what is "intolerable", creates "ambush", and leaves the self "sleepless", however one may refuse to describe its specific methods or attributes. The idea of the monument has reappeared, but in the meantime the coin has reversed. We are in the deep underground caverns, not of human personality, but of Charon's last ride — the last breath, whisper, fire, shadow, jewel, and song. This is noticeably the most regular, as it is the earliest, of the five sonnets, with either ten or eleven lines without anapests.[36] It is appropriate that the two lines of Rossetti's sonorous metric which are least amenable to the iambic pentameter pattern are the two —

   Is now a shaken shadow intolerable,
Of ultimate things unuttered the frail screen.

In the context of Rossetti's usually limited and musically plotted irregularities, "shadow intolerable" seems to reveal some of the inchoate confusion of true pain.

These "House of Life" sonnets are similar to each other in certain significant ways; they express an internal landscape comprised of emotions, shifting spirits and forms, and blurred or intangible objects, not of complete pictures or external referents. The synaesthesia of the early romantics remains, but the shifting forms mirrored are less organic. The medieval and archaic are imported not, as some earlier critics have argued, to evoke religion, love, or certainty, but to emphasize the elegant and statically baroque. They rigidify and distance rather than comfort.

Stasis is important in "The House of Life"; it appears not only in the marble tombs, urns, jewels, and regal stances of the lady but in the psychological configurations of the entire sequence, the contemplations of reverence and fear which precede and follow each suggestion of approach to Death or the Lady. The moments with the beloved or the concrete fears of death come to seem attenuated in themselves, more important for their expansive reverberations in a later contemplation. In Rossetti longing and fear are always extended; love and death are strangely processional events.

Rossetti's lingering vague refusal-to-be satisfied also distinguishes him from the early poetic manner of William Morris. Morris celebrates insatiable longing but yokes it with peaked expressions of physical desire and the sharp violence of death. All is longing and gore, with none of Rossetti's ambiguous contemplations or sedate processionate sounds. Morris admired Rossetti's earlier paintings of medieval narratives — portrayals of longing, frustration, and reunion — not his later erotic, elaborate single female figures; Rossetti's later paintings were in ways analogous to his "House of Life" manner.[37] In Morris' writing human pain seems simpler; war and murder, not psychological confusions, inexplicable retractions and self-denials, are the estrangers of man from woman, self from life. Rossetti's sonnets can seem murky and unexplained, but Morris' condensation of the associated ideas of love-fatality into a swift single projection of sex and violent death can oversimplify and distort by intensification and by the use of violence as a *deus ex machina* for agonized effects.

Rossetti's shifting responses seem inconsistent with his assertions of hope and love. A tentative vison and the mingling of unutterable sensations cannot be codified and, however religions and philosophies have tried, one can make little more than oracular ambiguity from a mist, sensuous feeling, and a hope. Rossetti's poetry of tensely attuned nervous responses would seem appropriate for expression of moods, not the postulation of vision. On the other hand, the presentation of increasingly sombre sensations darkens the context of his vision, and the stony, static images do prepare for some sort of classification. It is nearly impossible to write poetry with considerable formal and abstract language without constructing statements of some kind. Rossetti characteristically leaves his most important expressions tentative in form:

> Ah! let none other alien spell soe'er
> But only the one Hope's one name be there, —
> Not less nor more, but even that word alone.
>
> (Sonnet 101: 1870)

D. SEX, GUILT, AND VICTORIAN PREOCCUPATIONS

"Love" in Rosetti, as in almost all nineteenth-century poets, is a metaphor for all that is best and most concentrated in life — memory, sensuousness, idealism, the aesthetic and the intense. Whereas in Keats' poetry the knowledge of warm human love seemed of greater significance even than death, and to Pater and certain Decadents aesthetic experience or love was the self-expression of a private identity perpetually verging on extinction, Rossetti offered a middle view; private experience must involve some other human being or be a response, even if purely subjective and internal, to a minimally social relation. Yet he considered the possibility that even this experience might be nullified by death or error, or might only be able to exist in painfully uncertain and attenuated forms.

An ambiguity pervades the sequence, however, as the result of Rossetti's unclarified and perhaps inconsistent attitude toward sexual love. In his narratives and ballads sexuality is more frequently and overtly associated with moral guilt, although considered inevitable. "The House of Life", by contrast, has virtually no moral context; whether the love it celebrates is socially appropriate or "caused" is not explained. The relative absence of value judgments in this sequence and in some of the exotic ballads may explain their greater popularity with the Decadents and later Victorian readers. However one of the sequence's principal obsessions is guilt. The cause of this guilt is never stated, but I feel it is some combination of regret for lost time or opportunity and diffused suggestions of an inevitable taint imposed upon all sexual emotion.

This diffused guilt evokes accusing voices or presences imaging one or several "other" selves. At first Rossetti's "other" self had been associated with images of the beloved and the (indirectly, limitedly) attainable; at the end the non-selves have become a hovering dissolution and guilt, and the tiny self in a house of mirrors quivers beneath the toweringly magnified spectres. In my opinion death is covertly associated with guilt throughout the entire sequence. The many shadowed veils, dim reflections, and frail screens could well be coverings for an irrational, nebulous, contextless guilt. Love and the beloved seem always to suggest time passing, death, separation, the highest intensities of a doomed life. Even though only a few sonnets directly interweave the sense of guilt for lost time, death, and romantic love, to Rossetti erotic love is consistently, among other things, the concentrated symbol of the obscenely hastening hour.

In "The House of Life" Rossetti has associated, in the shifting way in which possibly they were experienced, several of the most recurrent Victorian preoccupations and perceptions – the fragmentation of the self through temporality, guilt-in-isolation, and the strangulation of all sex, art, love, and pleasant nature, not only by bourgeois convention, but by the great gray blankness of the cold and faceless world:

Ah, love, let us be true
To one another! for the world, which seems
To lie before us like a land of dreams ....
Hath really neither joy, nor love, nor light,
Nor certitude, nor peace, nor help for pain ....

    (Arnold, "Dover Beach")

He is not here; but far away
   The noise of life begins again,
   And ghastly thro' the drizzling rain
On the bald street breaks the blank day.

    (Tennyson, "In Memoriam", st. 7)

The preoccupation with marriage, evident in the Victorian novel and to a lesser extent also throughout Victorian poetry, seems clearly the attempt to erect a symbolic working agreement between the private self and convention, and between sexuality and the existence of another ego. It was assumed that the feminine ego was to be subsumed into the masculine; at best the married partners provided each other defense against transience, guilt, and confusion of identity, forming together a larger subdivided ego with which to oppose a frigid, hostile world.

Victorian society has been attacked for its doctrinaire exaltation of individualism; it must be remembered that the few educated Victorians who were impelled to record their emotions also found this atomization deeply painful; much of the intensity of Victorian literature comes from this constant sensation of pain. To shore himself against ruin each must emphasize the quality and value of his own "soul", his discrete self – therefore the Rossettian magnifying, cavernous, and inexhaustible horror when the self begins to divide or dissipate or blur.

It has been many times noticed that Victorians struggled to interfuse past and present, and there is no need to belabor Rossetti's concern with memory and "eternal moments". No one can explain why suddenly in the nineteenth century individuals became more aware of history, progression in time, and therefore of their own constant progression, moment by moment, towards death and away from memory.[38] But all poetic evidence testifies to the intense preoccupation with youth and the dawn of consciousness, the intense fear of time; and perhaps Victorian science, historicism, and religious doubt were results as well as causes of this anxiety. History no longer seemed a simple Augustinian progression, but a resurgence before decay; no wonder it was hard to believe that a non-historical heaven would suddenly climax and transform this slow unwinding into a completely different state of existence. Intensity gave man a sense of his own significance, his own ability to unite several levels of time (or cyclic recurrences) at once, or even be "above" time, more complex (and therefore more enduring?) than simple history. Also intensity was "instantaneous" — thus, as nearly as possible, not in time at all.

The connection of the self and sexuality is a more elusive psychological problem, needing more than a knowledge of Victorian literature to explain. It seems to me, though, that parts of the Freudian model serve accurately for at least three poets of the period — Tennyson, Arnold, and Rossetti. All three considered the early poetic or sensitive self to be largely directed towards a sensual or sexual vision (Arnold, "The Strayed Reveller", "A Summer Night"; Tennyson, "A Vison of Sin") and in varying degrees all felt both pride and guilt in these sensations. Several early Tennyson poems present not art (as often claimed) but sloth as the enemy to be overcome — and sloth is allied with sexuality, as it is later in the Idylls. Yet (shallow) visions of women had formed much of Tennyson's early poetic exercises ("Claribel", "Adeline", "Margaret", "The Ballad of Oriana", "Rosalind", "Eleanore", "Lilian", "Kate"). To him duty demanded both that he write and that he exorcise his "libidinous" visions; he did both, but since the visions and his art were the same impulse, much of his later work seems as though something has been drained from it. Arnold also successfully learns to espouse seeing life steadily in a world exorcised of the intense visions of Marguerite and an alter ego of free beauty. (Empedocles, Sohrab, and Rustum seem personae who suffer from emotional atrophy as a result of similar successes).

Rossetti is the only mid-Victorian poet who expresses throughout all his poetry the intuition that love, art, and guilt must be allied. He must be given a certain intellectual credit for not sorting out these inherent confusions in the stringently damaging ways necessary to most other Victorians; he did not immediately set a guard of order and calm on his own psyche's unpleasant multitudinousness; he sensed that art must reflect inner truth whatever the limitations or incompatibilities it recorded. Rossetti's association of love-sex-guilt-art may explain why he was so violently praised by his immediate successors, but also why in this century he has seemed remote to critics until recently. Miyoshi's irritated eruption at Rossetti's confusion of body and spirit[39] is possibly because to him no metaphysical problem surrounds their relation, and he cannot understand Rosset's vague distress. But granted Victorian terminology their relations were inexplicable, and it was necessary to postulate both a merging of spirit and matter and the ability of each to carry what had formerly been the separate values of the other.

Other critics, too, have spoken of Rossettian inconsistency and the insignificance of his themes — for example, Weatherby and Baum. While mid-twentieth-century discussions of Rossetti either tend to repeat and expound his themes directly within their own context (passion and death *ad nauseam*) or dismiss them as inconsistent, Victorians such as Swinburne recognized what to them was the accuracy of linking conscious life to the guilty unconscious. Human beings may still flee a guilty unconscious, but it is not necessarily assumed to be embodied in an idealized / sexual woman image. Portnoy or Herzog seem more concerned about whether they have failed a tradition or denied a series of values; not the love vision but their own sagacity or potency or social awareness has failed. And then there is what I predict will be an ever lengthening line of middle-aged heroes suffering from Liberal Guilt — having denied a fragmentarily glimpsed vision, they meditate on present entropy.

Rossetti's emphasis on the abstraction Love or the Lady can seem too easy a projection of the ideal for the self onto the object desired, an oversimplified dualism. However, it can be placed in an extensive tradition of Victorian preoccupations with the split, twin, and guilty double attempting reunion with the conscious self. Rossetti deserves to be taken seriously on his own terms, though they are difficult to define. One senses that Rossetti is using a psychological language rendered suddenly dated by changes in taste, but not sufficiently dated to grant him the distancing analysis accorded other presumedly more typical Victorians.

NOTES

1 A synopsis of some "House of Life" criticism:
   a. William E. Fredeman, "Rossetti's 'In Memoriam': An Elegiac Reading of *The House of Life*", *BJRL*, 47 (1964-65), 298-341.
This has become an important article because it presents opinions on numerous issues on which Rossetti's critics differ. Fredeman unfairly assumes that what others mean by defining "The House of Life" as a sonnet "cycle" or a sequence possessing "thematic unity" bears no resemblance to his own assumption that it is structurally coherent, though Fredeman's paraphrase does postulate a clearer progression than had been argued in previous summaries (for my qualifications of this position, see footnote 7).
   b. Carl Peterson, "The Poetry and Painting of Dante Gabriel Rossetti", unpublished dissertation, University of Wisconsin, 1961, see footnotes 2 and 15, and Appendix, part 1.
   c. J.L. Kendall, "The Concept of the Infinite Moment in 'the House of Life'", *VN*, 28 (1965), 4-8. An excellent concise summary of Rossetti's thought and style in this poem.
   d. Douglas J. Robillard, "Rossetti's 'Willowwood' Sonnets and the Structure of 'The House of Life'", *VN*, 22 (1962), 5-9.
Robillard also argues that "The House of Life" exhibits a deliberate progression, roughly analogous to the emotional sequence of love, loss, and partial assuagement of grief which characterizes the four "Willowwood" sonnets. One bold statement of Robillard's has been criticized: "If the 1870 version of this second half of the cycle gives us the impression that it is a grab-bag stuffed with leftovers, the additions to the final version can do nothing but reinforce our impression." I think it is unfair to interpret his statement as a denial of all coherence or arrangement in the second portion. Essentially I agree with what I conceive as Robillard's central perception: despite all arguments that the work and will sonnets follow properly after the celebrations of love, the relation between the poet's various preoccupations remains only adumbrated.
   e. Houston Baker, "The Poet's Progress: Rossetti's 'The House of Life'", *VP*, 8 (1970), 1-14.
Baker's article intends to prove that Rossetti was not an "aesthetic" poet, a reasonable thesis, but in so doing he both oversimplifies previous Rossetti criticism and defines the term 'aesthetic" so pejoratively that it could not apply to any serious poet, including those of the decadence. He also interprets "The House of Life" as a progression from a youthful, narrowly physical ecstasy to a solemn recantation and acceptance of a new ideal of dedication to labor. To create this reading he must steadfastly ignore the early poems' constant preoccupation with transience and the mental or spiritual nature of the beloved, the later poems' insistent regret for lost love and tributes to physical beauty, and the ambiguity of the references to "lost time" which may include regret for missed love as well as incompleted work. Worse, Baker must invent constant "new insights" and recantations of former ideas for which there is no evidence. Each time Rossetti makes a statement Baker seems to assume it directly contradicts a supposed former position.
   f. Robert D. Hume, "Inorganic Structure in *The House of Life*", *PLL*, 5 (Winter 1969), 282-295.
This is the most thorough consideration of structure, division of the sonnets into subcategories, and comparison of the sequence's successive versions. Again I cannot see the early sonnets as exclusively positive or limited to the emotions of youth, but Hume qualifies carefully in his general descriptions of the sequence and his paraphrases are uniformly intelligent.

One of the unusual points of Hume's interpretation is his refusal to consider the final sonnet as a muted affirmation; like Baker he feels that "Hope" is an entity disassociated from love. It is difficult to imagine what such a hope would be, if it is not permitted to have an object.

    g. David Sonstroem, *Rossetti and the Fair Lady* (Wesleyan University: Middletown, Connecticut, 1970).
He discusses "The House of Life" 140-153, commenting on Rossetti's shifting definitions of the word "soul" (used 68 times throughout the sequence), his metaphysical emphases and his use of Dante. Sonstroem follows Doughty in ascribing Rossetti's various frustrations to, among other causes, the irrational conduct of Lizzie or Janey. While discussing "The House of Life", for example, he comments offhand:

> When we recall the many partings and reunions in the course of their romance — changes probably instigated by the unstable and self-centered Janey — we can imagine how often Rossetti had to tailor his fantasies of his fate to reconcile them to Janey's latest mood .... Fate's role in these sonnets may be so large partly because he wished to attribute Janey's flights to something other than her own volition. (149, 150)

This is captious; clearly Mrs. Morris left Rossetti to rejoin her husband and children. Divorce was virtually impossible under Victorian law, and William Morris was a paragon of dispassionate objectivity by the standards of his own or our time. One could as justly complain that the unstable and self-centered Rossetti kept leaving Janey to attend to his professional concerns or from a cowardly fear of her husband's presence at Kelmscott. I comment on such remarks not so much because of concern with Rossetti's biography, but because such narrowminded and intrusive comments often replace serious interpretation and are transmitted from critic to critic. If we must mythologize our forbears, at least we can refrain from the mentality of gossip columnists. There is often unheeding cruelty in judging the personal behaviors of persons in a society more rigidly structured and sexually authoritarian than our own; one form of this is a condescension which seems to be applied with special abandon to uneducated wives/mistresses of famous men.
Sonstroem makes a few small errors in his Dante analogies. For instance Beatrice doesn't descend to hell to deliver Dante's spirit (149); she first appears in purgatory. Sonstroem feels the Blessed Damozel is un-Dantean because she speaks and weeps, yet Beatrice talks expansively thoughout the *Paradiso*, and the first female who appears to Dante, when he is frightened and distracted in the dark wood, is the golden-haired, weeping, and sympathetic Lucy (Canto 2, *Inferno*). But Sonstroem's comments on the *Vita Nuova* are the most complete thus far.

    h. Ronnalie Howard, "The Poetic Development of Dante Gabriel Rossetti 1847-1872", unpublished dissertation, Pennsylvania State, 1968. Chapter 10, 282-297, "The House of Life", discusses with clarity and succinctness former criticsm, the early sonnets, the congruence of form, content, and poetic devices within the sequence, and some of Rossetti's devices of fusion. I did not see this thesis before writing my own chapter, but our conclusions seem consonant.

    i. John N. Hobbs, "The Poetry of Dante Gabriel Rossetti", unpublished dissertation, Yale, 1968. Chapter 3, 143-220, "The House of Life", is essentially a lengthy paraphrase of the sonnets in order; this organization precludes the following of particular topics or ideas for an extended period. I think this would confuse anyone not already familiar with virtually every sonnet. Hobbs exhibits an unusual talent for noticing sources and cross-references, however, and his general evaluations of Rossetti seem consistently careful. In fairness, also, it is difficult to say what a close reading should "prove".

2. Carl Peterson, "The Poetry and Painting of Dante Gabriel Rossetti", unpublished dissertation, University of Wisconsin, 1961. One of the best studies of "The House of Life" is Peterson's, 309-321 and 341-397. His method is chronological. He discusses Rossetti's use of analogies in sonnets of the 50's, 313-321, and traces Rossetti's pattern of selecting images, then constructing an appropriate idea to accord with them, 378-381. I have seen no other comments on Rossetti's processes of composition. For Peterson's view on Dantean influence in "The House of Life", see Appendix, part 1, and on Biblical allusions, footnote 15 below.

3. Rossetti did arrange the sonnets into groupings, and there is a partial pattern of return to former emotions to indicate continuity. Also there is descent into deepened, although controlled, unhappiness. Yet those who see the poet as "learning" or progressing to greater wisdom are, I think, more sanguine than Rossetti. Both his initial perceptions of love and the last laments for death are qualified by memory or foreknowledge of each other. Neither can I see evidence that he renounces an earlier, temporal love in favor of work and aspiration. The love sonnets clearly describe the most intense experience of the sequence, nowhere are their perceptions retracted or denied, and the poet accepts love's absence with continuing regret. The sonnets on work do not claim the same epiphanic significance for achievement as the love sonnets had claimed for love; rather they admonish to performance of a failed duty, a far different response. Some sonnets of regret are also ambiguous; they mourn wasted opportunity, but do not say of which kind. One could regret the absence of love as well as failure to perform other labors. Further, the work sonnets form something of an independent grouping in style and tone (for a chronological explanation, see section B. of this chapter). For all these reasons an overly formal division of the sequence will falsify, simplify the fusing, merging, and repetition within the love and death sonnets, and ignore the alien quality of others. Once again a comparison can be made with Mrs. Browning, whose sonnet sequence also exhibits a limited, informal ordering. Also, I cannot avoid the suspicion that Rossetti padded a little in pursuit of the full one hundred and one sonnets. This is understandable, but cannot be analyzed as further structural nuance.

4. A recent article by W. David Shaw, "'In Memoriam' and the Rhetoric of Confession", *ELH* (1971), argues that "In Memoriam" should be classified as a confession, similar in form to Augustine's *Confessions* or Bunyan's *Grace Abounding*, rather than compared with elegiac or philosophic poems. He defines the genre of confession through ten characteristics, all of which he shows to be qualities of "In Memoriam". What Shaw means by a confession, however, seems similar to what previous critics meant by a philosophic autobiography or autopsychological sequence.

There are parallels between "In Memoriam" and "The House of Life" – occasional similarities in idea or statement, their use of personified abstraction (see footnote 27), or most important, the use of common landscape descriptions and isolated imagery – coins, a child, the summit of a hill and a pathway looking back, seasonal changes, veils, reflections, bonds of children in a family, standing at an empty door in a bleak city. Yet these are not a remarkable array of common images for two lengthy poems by authors influenced by a mutual romantic tradition. Perhaps their common sadness, earnestness, metaphysical hesitation, and vocalic sonorousness are the most essential ties.

5. William Fredeman, "Rossetti's 'In Memoriam': An Elegiac Reading of 'The House of Life'", *BJRL*, 47 (1964-65), 308-309.

6. Rossetti seems to have altered titles to create a sense of chronological progression. William Fredeman comments, *ibid.*, 323f, that the first section "Youth and Change" was probably first called "Love and Change".

> That 'Youth' and 'Love' are in fact synonymous can be clearly demonstrated from those sonnets in Part I in which for 'Love' Rossetti substituted 'Youth' in the title .... It would seem that Rossetti must originally have intended to subtitle Part I 'Love and Change'; William Michael Rossetti invariably refers to it by that title, even in the notes to the 1911 *Works* (p. 651).

7. Virtually all divisions of the poem into progressive segments interpret the earlier sonnets as those of fulfillment and peace. These first thirty or so sonnets are admittedly written in the persona of one who possesses "Love". Yet Rossetti could not meditate on any intense experience without calling other, antipodal intensities to mind; the presence of death, foreboding, and a sense of curtailment are noticeably evident throughout the entire early portion of "Youth and Change". Many passages can be cited from the first thirty-five sonnets in addition to those mentioned in the text. Some examples:

Sonnet 6:
What smouldering senses in death's sick delay
    Or seizure of malign vicissitude
    Can rob this body of honour, or denude
This soul ....

The analogy with Orpheus reminds that his also was a "last lay".

Sonnet 24:
Where night-wrack shrouds the Old Love fugitive ....
Alas for hourly change! Alas for all
The loves that from his hand proud Youth lets fall,
    Even as the beads of a told rosary!

Sonnet 25:
What of that hour at last, when for her sake
    No wing may fly to me nor song may flow;
    When, wandering round my life unleaved, I know
The bloodied feathers scattered in the brake,
And think how she, far from me, with like eyes
Sees through the untuneful bough the wingless skies?

Sonnet 34:
Shall birth and death, and all dark names that be
As doors and windows bared to some loud sea,
    Lash deaf mine ears and blind my face with spray;
    And shall my sense pierce love, – the last relay
And ultimate outpost of eternity?

Lo! what am I to Love ....
    One murmuring shell he gathers from the sand ....

Granted such a conception of life as desolate without the beloved, the early sonnets are at best alternately calm and anxious. The calm is often that of partially detached praises of love and the beloved, and these seem often formal celebrations, rather than expressions of personal contentment. There is something ominous about the conception of a single abstract, idealized Lady as the only cheerful or benign presence in the universe. After sonnet 35, at any rate, the poet's unhappiness intensifies steadily.

8   Carl Peterson, "The Poetry and Painting of Dante Gabriel Rossetti", unpublished dissertation, University of Wisconsin, 1961, 376, 387.

9   A. Dwight Culler, "'The Windy Stair': An Aspect of Rossetti's Poetic Symbolism", *Ventures*, 9 (1969), 65-75.

10 William Rossetti comments only that Rossetti later removed "juvenilities of expression" from "The Choice" before publishing it in 1870 (*Works*, 656). Perhaps Rossetti objected to their moralistic tone, as he later objected to the religious sentimentalism of another early poem, "My Sister's Sleep".

11 R.D. Cooper, *Lost on Both Sides. Dante Gabriel Rossetti: Critic and Poet* (Athens: Ohio University Press, 1970).

Cooper generalizes wildly, failing to define his critical categories. He opposes them loosely and vaguely to construct a series of postulated conflicts and dualities within Rossetti, and his judgments at times approach the bigoted.

> The dazzling personality that attracted Morris, Burne-Jones and Swinburne to the twenty-eight year old Rossetti retained enough of its glitter to win the devotion of such literary hopefuls as Watts-Dunton, William Sharp, and Hall Caine twenty and more years later. But Rossetti never grew to be a leader of anything. Intuitive not logical, imaginative not intellectual, given to excesses of rapture over both the monumental and the mediocre – such was the young Rossetti, and he never changed. (231)

> Rossetti was an Italian, immoral and irreligious, arrogant and money-grasping, moody and aloof, and fickle to his friends. As a critic, he was given to wild excess, brooking no opposition to judgements based on intuition and prejudice alone, and heralding the genius of a host of nobodies. He was a painter who toyed with poetry, a leader of a school that scorned the public and prized imagination over intellect, sensation and beauty over sprirituality, and execution over subject matter and meaning. (241)

Cooper prefers Rossetti's earlier works, and argues that he never developed. The bases of judgment are tautological, however:

> Emotion was the predominant wellspring of that poetry, and that emotion, if intense to begin with, can hardly be expected to "develop". (237)

12 "Love's Nocturne" is an atypical Rossetti poem, something of an artificial set piece. Rossetti seldom wrote evocatory odes with long formal introductory digressions. This one contains 22 stanzas rimed ababbab, and is reminiscent of Shelley, perhaps also of E.B.B. or Poe. Only in the most general sense is it a love poem. The dream state rather than a particular beloved is the focus of interest. Rossetti himself explained that it expressed the emotional state of a young man not yet in love:

> The first conception of this poem was of a man not yet in love who dreams vaguely of a woman who he thinks must exist for him. This is not very plainly expressed, and not I think very valuable, and it might be better to refer the love to a known woman whom he wishes to approach.

Perhaps in one of his first long poems dealing with love in the first person, Rossetti felt some desire to maintain distance. Also, since William Rossetti dates the poem 1859 in his *Family Letters, With a Memoir*, 1895, I, 208 (cited in Peterson, 334, 335, 340), it may not even be contemporaneous with the sonnets of the early 50's.

Although "Love's Nocturne" does contain familiar Rossettian imagery and the occasional archaisms of his early period, it exemplifies a style of literary artifice to which he never returned. In his earliest lyric poetry, as in the early sonnets, he seldom spoke directly of passionate love. The references to love in the lyrics of the 1850's are usually regretful and distantly elegiac, not too different in tone from the early, nearly parodic "Autumn Song" (an extreme example of this is "Even So", 1859).

13   It is interesting that Rossetti attempted clarity and had a definite natural effect in mind. There are three versions of the lines:

1. Yet may I not forget that I was ware,
   So journeying, of his face at intervals,,
   Some fiery bush with coruscating hair,
   Where the whole land to its horizon falls.

2. Yet may I not forget that I was 'ware,
   So journeying, of his face at intervals, –
      Where the whole land to its horizon falls,
   Some fiery bush with corruscating [sic] hair.

3. Yet may I not forget that I was 'ware
      So journeying, of his face at intervals,
      Transfigured where the fringed horizon falls, –
   A fiery bush with coruscating hair.

No. 1 was the original version, and Rossetti explains why it was changed to 2 in *Letters*, I, 227, "only the metre forced me to transpose. It is meant to refer to the effect one is nearly sure to see in passing along a road at sunset, when the sun glares in a radiant focus behind some low bush or some hedge on the horizon of the meadows. But it is obscure, I believe .... I'll try to alter it – if worth working at." He then created version 3, only slightly clearer. See also R.D. Cooper, *Dante Gabriel Rossetti*, 205.

14   See Appendix, Part 1, "*The Divine Comedy*".

15   Carl Peterson, "The Poetry and Painting of Dante Gabriel Rossetti", 393, 364-366.

16   This sonnet is the only "House of Life" sonnet which presents the beloved as sister. The romantic motif of incest-with-sister is almost a parody of the aspiration for union with the beloved or wholeness of self. If the total self includes the beloved, the image is hermaphroditic; it is also an image of exclusion – the self wishes to love nothing that is not like the self.

17   Masao Miyoshi, *The Divided Self: A Perspective on the Literature of the Victorians* (New York University Press, 1969), discusses Rossetti 249-259, and the divided self in "The House of Life", 257-275. He cites "Severed Selves" (no. 40: 1871), "Lost Days" (no. 86: 1862), "A Superscription" (no. 97: 1868), "Lost on Both Sides" (no. 91: 1854), and "He and I" (no. 98: 1870). He does not distinguish between the "lost selves" which these present, however, whether another person, a part of the speaker's present self, or his past. Rossetti's efforts cannot be dismissed as merely a failure to unite "man and woman, flesh and spirit", a "war

on the self". Miyoshi oversimplifies and distorts by reading Rossetti's personifications literally and pronouncing moral judgments. In describing psychological states, especially those adduced as 'representative' of a particular period, his condemnation of a "failure to solve problems" seems an evasion of further analysis — why did the problems exist, why should there necessarily be solutions?

18   I use two lists of dates for the composition of "The House of Life" sonnets, William Rossetti's in *Works*, 1911, and William Fredeman's in the appendix to "Rossetti's 'In Memoriam': An Elegiac Reading of The House of Life", *BJRL*, 47 (1964-65), 298-341. Fredeman does not give reasons for his choice of alternate dates. There are twelve small discrepancies between the two lists, three of which affect the earlier and latest periods which I discuss. Fredeman lists 1880 as the date for "Pride of Youth", no. 24 (William Rossetti lists 1871) and 1879 for "Ardour and Memory", no. 64 (William Rossetti lists 1873). In other words he moves two sonnets from the middle to the latest period. He also moves "Broken Music", no. 47, from William Rossetti's early date 1862 to 1869. I have not discussed these sonnets; if Fredeman is correct, however, Rossetti wrote not six but eight sonnets after 1877.

19   On the other hand, the interest in symbolic detail in Rossetti's earliest poems causes these to be cited also. Edward Engelberg's *The Symbolist Poem: The Development of the English Tradition* (Dutton: New York, 1967), lists eleven selections, five of which are sonnets from "The House of Life". Three of his selections were written in the early 50's, "The Mirror", "Words on the Windowpane", and "The Honeysuckle"; the remaining eight were written in 1869 or afterwards. Engelberg's anthology contains unusual selections throughout.

Stanley Holberg's thesis, "Imagery and Symbol in the Poetry and Prose of Dante Gabriel Rossetti", unpublished dissertation, University of Maryland, 1958, is constructed around the assumption that Rossetti was a symbolist poet. Holberg considers "The House of Life" Rossetti's chief work, and in defining Rossetti's principles in Chapter 2, quotes from it exclusively. He does cite several other Rossetti poems, but chiefly from the early period. He can be so inclusive partially because he never defines a symbolist poem, and the label "symbolist" becomes sufficiently expansive to include all poems with dramatic imagery or which concern dream states.

20   Dante Gabriel Rossetti, *The House of Life: A Sonnet Sequence by Dante Gabriel Rossetti*, with an Introduction and Notes by Paull Franklin Baum (Harvard: Cambridge, Massachusetts, 1928), 11, 12.

21   Inexact rimes were not common in serious Victorian poetry until later; they were considered a humor device, as for comic opera. Rossetti may have been influenced towards off-rimes by the uninhibited practices of E.B.B. A later extreme example of the use of inexact rimes occurs throughout Hopkins' "The Loss of the Eurydice", 1878, certainly one of the oddest of Victorian experimental poems:

> This was that fell capsize
> As half she had righted and hoped to rise
>   Death teeming in by her portholes
> Raced down decks, round messes of mortals.

22   Unlike Rossetti, Hopkins seldom relies on length for elegance of formality; his unusual words are often one or two-syllabled. As nearly as any poet Hopkins is able to destroy consciousness of word length through his unusual rhythms and word divisions. He frequently uses long strings of monosyllables, much less often places several polysyllables in close juxtaposition:

> Earnest, earthless, equal, attuneable, vaulty, voluminous, ... stupendous
> Disremembering, dismembering ....
>
> "Spelt from Sibyl's Leaves"

More characteristic are the aggregates of smaller words hyphenated for massed effects. Even when not hyphenated his short words are often so closely bound together by sound that single shorter words lose their separate quality.

> The thunder-purple seabeach plumed purple-of-thunder,
> If a wuthering of his palmy snow-pinions scatter a colossal smile
> Off him, but meaning motion fans fresh our wits with wonder.
>
> "Henry Purcell"

A comparative study of the diction and word length of several Victorian poets might reveal more than the obvious correlations in their rhythmic patterns.

23   The poem is anthologized in *Nineteenth Century Minor Poets*, ed. W.H. Auden, with notes by George R. Creeger (Faber: London, 1966), 76, 77. It appeared originally in *The Poetical Works of Leigh Hunt* (London, 1844).

24   See Appendix, part 8, "Leigh Hunt".

25   Surprisingly Elizabeth Barrett Browning is not among this group. She used hyphenates infrequently, chiefly in her earlier works. I use *The Complete Poetical Works of Elizabeth Barrett Browning* (Houghton Mifflin: Boston, 1900); the introduction does not mention whether the original punctuation has been retained. And of course punctuation may be established by other persons beside an author, which makes it more difficult to compare preferences of various poets.

26   Personification is often associated with metaphysical and eighteenth-century poetry, but the romantic poets had also made use of typifying abstractions and personifications, especially in sonnets. Even the young Tennyson wrote sonnets which spoke in capital letters of "Love" and "Death".

> That Death lent grace to Life and Life to Death
> And in one image Life and Death reposed
> To make my love an Immortality.

(*The Devil and the Lady and Unpublished Early Poems* by Alfred Tennyson, ed. Charles Tennyson, Bloomington: Indiana University Press, 1964, 58). See also "Love and Death", first printed in 1830 (*The Early Poems of Alfred Lord Tennyson*, ed. John Churton Collins, London: Methuen, 1900, 36). It appeared again in the 1842 volume which Rossetti used.

The personifications of "In Memoriam" only occasionally suggest Rossetti, although some of its vague descriptions are akin in method.

> But where the path we walked began
>   To slant the fifth autumnal slope,
>   As we descended following Hope,
> There sat the Shadow feared of man; .... (XXII)
>
>   ... and sigh
> The full new life that feeds thy breath
>   Throughout my frame, till Doubt and Death,
> Ill brethren, let the fancy fly ...
>
>   To where ...
> A hundred spirits whisper 'Peace'. (LXXXVI)

> What find I in the highest place,
> > But mine own phantom chanting hymns?
> > And on the depths of death there swims
> The reflex of a human face. (CVIII)
>
> > Alone, alone, to where he sits,
> > The Shadow cloaked from head to foot .... (XXIII)
>
> I know that this was Life, – the track
> > Whereon with equal feet we fared; ...
>
> Nor could I weary, heart or limb,
> > When mighty Love would cleave in twain
> > The lading of a single pain, ... (XXV)
>
> > If Death were seen
> > At first as Death, Love had not been,
> Or been in narrowest working shut .... (XXXV)
>
> Sleep, Death's twin brother, times my breath;
> Sleep, Death's twin brother, knows not Death .... (LXVIII)

Like Rossetti, Tennyson mentions hearts and tears frequently and describes his own emotions rather than an objective and detailed scene. As in most comparisons of Rossetti's language with that of another poet, Rossetti's expressions are more concentrated and heavy-laden. Tennyson's sentiments are less stoical, more protesting; he requests, instructs, or questions fate and abstract entities in contexts where Rossetti would simply state an unfortunate truth. It is not, of course, that Rossetti is any less dissatisfied with fate, but he adopts a less active psychological position in response to it. Whether this is perceived as more despairing is a subjective evaluation. The extent to which Tennyson's language, like that of Rossetti, consists of abstractions, personifications, or classical allusions and landscape descriptions which embody emotion is surprising.

Another Victorian poet using extensive personification was Mrs. Browning, especially in the "Sonnets From the Portuguese", published 1847 and 1850. For a comparison of her use of personification with that of Rossetti, see Appendix, part 12.

27   Between the 1870 and 1881 versions only fourteen minor changes in text were made (besides additions), three of which occur in the early trilogy "The Choice" (nos. 71-73). Of the sixteen sonnets published in *The Fortnightly Review* in 1869, ten were unchanged in text in the 1870 version. Baum cites variants for eighteen "House of Life" sonnets in "The Bancroft Manuscripts of Dante Gabriel Rossetti", *MP*, 39 (August, 1941), 48-52. Virtually all changes are improvements in precision, sonority, or clarity of effect. Several times he revised titles for a more evocative and general effect, and frequently titles containing "love" were altered, perhaps to deemphasize sameness of topic and call attention to the theme of youth or to the seasons.

28   Ifor Evans, *English Poetry in the Later Nineteenth Century* (London: Methuen, 1933), 39.

29   This is Fredeman's date for "Broken Music"; William Rossetti lists 1852 in the *Works*.

30   1871 is William Rossetti's date in *Works*; Fredeman lists 1880.

31   Several examples are in *Masterpieces of D.G. Rossetti (1828-1882)* (London, 1912). In "Regina Cordium" (1861) Lizzie is painted with heart necklace, "The Dancing Girl" (1861) holds heart-shaped clappers in her hand, the subject of "Regina Cordium" (1866) wears an elaborated, crowned heart pin while a tiny, jewelled heart-shaped heraldic emblem is painted behind her, and in "Joli Coeur"

(1867), a young girl holds a necklace with a heart pendant. All these examples are from the 1860's, however; he seems to have abandoned the mannerism later. There are also many examples of women painted with flowers in their hands.
32   Ifor Evans, *English Poetry in the Later Nineteenth Century*, 39.
33   Classical allusions in "The House of Life":
Cupid or the male deity Love starts appearing in the sonnets around 1869; often it is difficult to tell whether this being is consciously modeled after the classical Cupid or Dante's "beloved guide", or whether it is merely a personification of love. There are no other classical allusions before 1869, when sonnet six mentions Orpheus. After this date several sonnets contain such allusions, with a proportional increase during Rossetti's last two years. If this increasing use of classical references indicates anything, it might be Rossetti's later interest in legends and stories which did not possess a theological or moral motive (in contrast to his earlier Dantesque and Christian preferences). Mythological persons can embody emotions much as the other personified abstractions of Rossetti's later periods, and mythological name-dropping seems consistent with the mannerisms of his ornate, baroque, and dramatic late style.
34   J.A. and Olive Banks, *Feminism and Family Planning in Victorian England* (New York: Schocken, 1964), explicate the great difficulties associated with middle-class marriage and sexuality, especially in relation to what most men could earn. The resulting pressures caused the median age of marriage for an upper-middle class male in 1847 to be 29.9 years (see page 30). Doubtless there were many men whose "first love" had become a decade-old memory by the time of their wedding day.
35   Rossetti to Hall Caine, *Recollections of Dante Gabriel Rossetti* (Boston: Roberts Brothers, 1898), 199, 200. Rossetti could ironically deflate a poetic practice with the label "monumental", yet still rely on it for sometimes lugubriously serious effects. Similarly he commented disparagingly on both sentimentality and gothicism ("Autumn Leaves" a "howling canticle", "Sister Helen" a "ghastly ballad"), while using them heavily.
36   A comparison of five sonnets from each of four periods (1848-1854; 1869-1870; 1870-1871; 1880-1881) reveals increasingly irregular metre. In the earliest period there were some very irregular sonnets, but also nearly regular ones. Afterwards this latter category vanishes.
37   This is not a unique idea; see the discussion of the parallel stages in Rossetti's painting and poetry by Carl Peterson, "The Poetry and Painting of Dante Gabriel Rossetti"; R.L. Mégroz, *Dante Gabriel Rossetti: Painter Poet of Heaven and Earth* (London: Faber and Gwyer, 1928), summarized 293-297; David Sonstroem, *Rossetti and the Fair Lady*. Richard L. Stein, "Dante Gabriel Rossetti and the Problem of Poetic Form", *Studies in Language and Literature*, 10, 775-792, mentions a few additional parallels between the painting and poetry.
38   Both Jerome Buckley's *The Triumph of Time* (Cambridge, Massachusetts: Harvard, 1966) and Barbara Charlesworth's *Dark Passages: The Decadent Consciousness in Victorian Literature* (Madison and Milwaukee: University of Wisconsin, 1965) treat these shifts in time-sense during the Victorian period.
39   Maseo Miyoshi, *The Divided Self*, 252, 253-257.

2. EVOLUTION OF A NARRATIVE BALLAD STYLE

Rossetti's balladic style fuses narrative, ballad, Victorian contemplativeness and Romantic literary mannerisms, and his genuine originality in recombining these elements inhibits strict division into categories. Rather than emphasizing formal discriminations I will consider together the large number of poems loosely resembling the literary ballad.[1] Within this general category appear some of Rossetti's best and some of his most idiosyncratic poems, and in experimenting with romantic ballad forms he showed his greatest variation and progession in style and preoccupation. This development parallels his shifts within the sonnet and other non-balladic forms, and its extent belies both the charge that he altered technically while presenting identical themes or, on the other hand, that he was able to vary his themes but never improved on his early techniques.

Several very familiar Rossetti poems, such as "Sister Helen", "The Blessed Damozel", and "Jenny", were written early and considerably revised. As a result, there has been the double tendency to emphasize the early-middle periods, and, for convenience, to assume that revisions altered little. Both approaches evade a full consideration of development. In several instances revisions did affect poems substantially, and later abilities or responses seem superimposed on earlier ones; neglect of this fact both causes the earlier periods to seem proportionately more significant than the later ones, and obscures the different traits within each period.

Rossetti's several early romantic ballads illustrate sexual idealism, sublimation, and repression; his later lengthy narratives are increasingly obsessed with revenge and violent death. The early narratives espouse a metaphysic of heavenly reunion for virtuous lovers as reparation for the sufferings of earth; by the late "The King's Tragedy" the specific injustices of earth are more fully documented, but the only reparation possible for murder is a bloody revenge; retribution falls alike on the guilty and innocent. The later narratives are simultaneously more complex and unified in form, contain fewer Keatsian and ornamental mannerisms, and exchange the earlier languishing female figures for more aggressively active heroines.

The category of sexual revenge ballad is roughly intermediate in chronology between the early and late romantic narratives, although "Sister Helen", written in 1851 and revised in 1880, overlaps both of the other categories. "Eden Bower" and "Troy Town" were written in 1869, the year of several "House of Life" sonnets on frustrated love. These concentrated ballad narratives of sexual vengeance constitute Rossetti's most unusual achievement; there is nothing quite so cheerfully or aggressively horrible in Victorian literature. Sex emerges from its romanticized disguises, not to render mankind happy but to extinguish totally the human ego. In most early poems he had moralized over seduction, thus preserving conceptions of human will and choice. Here destruction seems both externally inevitable and internally willed; man is fated to destroy himself, as well as to be destroyed by woman from without, and evilly wills his own overthrow. Rossetti preserves considerable impartiality concerning the natures of man and woman, however; neither agent seems the more blameable, although woman is subjectively the more psychologically threatening.

I will discuss each rough category of poem, with attention to stages of composition and chronological progression. This is a compromise between a strictly chronological ordering (virtually impossible, at any rate, because of the layered versions) and division by theme, and an attempt to preserve general chronological sequence while presenting thematic patterns and shifts. I choose more obscure poems whenever possible; some of these, such as "Dante at Verona", "Rose Mary", or "The White Ship", deserve greater comparative emphasis than they have received.

As examples of early romantic narrative ballads, I will analyze "The Bride's Prelude" (1849, 1859, etc.), "The Staff and Scrip" (1851, 1852), and "Dante at Verona" (1848-50, 1869, 1870); as ballads of sexual vengeance, "Sister Helen" (1851, 1880) and "Eden Bower" (1869); as late narrative ballads, "Rose Mary" (1871, 1879), "The White Ship" (1878-80), "The King's Tragedy" (1881), and the anomalous "Jan Van Hunks" (1846 or 1847, 1882), an early ballad revised shortly before Rossetti's death. Two aborted fragments, "God's Graal" (1858) and "Joan of Arc" (1879) indicate further themes which Rossetti considered for narrative ballads; the early fragment was to preface a tale celebrating Lancelot's heroic deeds and long-frustrated love for Guenevere, and the latter presents an aggressively noble heroine.

Conveniently, also, several of the early and late ballads are sufficiently similar in theme and form for useful paired contrast of early and late styles. "The Bride's Prelude" and "Rose Mary" are both lengthy romantic ballads of pious, wronged, "fallen" women; "The Staff and Scrip" and "The White Ship" are two briefer, derivative literary ballads, and both "Dante at Verona" and "The King's Tragedy" present poet lovers who suffer political and personal rejection. The different emphases in character, moral attitude, and dramatic effect illustrate Rossetti's transformation and darkening of early romantic mannerisms.

All of these ballads are concerned with the psychological responses of one person, whether protagonist or observer; narrative plot is significant only as it rationalizes or precipitates this response. In the use of color and detail Rossetti is only minimally a painter-in-words; instead he records the psychology of intense suspension in the presence of an event, image, or tableau. The long narratives seem extensions of his short poems and sonnets on pictures; in the longer poems he reacts to a changing tableau rather than a single picture, but the psychology is not greatly altered. "The Bride's Prelude", for example, is a lengthy tableau / narrative which reenacts a single psychic state.

A. THREE EARLY BALLAD NARRATIVES: ROMANTIC MANNERISMS USED TO EXPRESS SEXUAL SUBLIMATION (MALE) AND REPRESSION (FEMALE)

1. "The Bride's Prelude" (1848, 1859, et cetera): Ornamented Passivity and Stagnation

"The Bride's Prelude" expresses so many Victorian romance mannerisms that it is virtually a parody of that genre. The elaborated narrative romance form is used to portray a situation simultaneously attractive and repellent, sensuous and painful. Since it is both a tableau and narrative, one might expect narrative action to relieve the tableau's static quality, but in fact these reinforce one another. The tableau concentrates on the heroine's ingrown psychology of shame and stagnation, while the narrative interprets and reinforces her misery by listing, simplistically and oppressively, the past and present sensations which cause it.

In some sense all post-romantic art solidifies romantic patterns of growth and movement into slower, more static responses. The lush, vaguely medieval, and repetitive descriptions throughout "The Bride's Prelude" suggest a transmutation of Keatsian norms of beauty into heavier, more consciously artificial mannerisms. They constitute a poetic equivalent of what in art might be a detailed, small-scale baroque, emphasizing many miniscule, elaborated, and decorative motions within a larger stasis. The Pre-Raphaelite paintings of Holman Hunt and the early Rossetti conform to this description; their delicate, ornamental, and romantic details are inserted into a carefully arrested architectural, domestic, or historical frame, causing motions to seem simultaneously intense and slow, passionate and heavy.

For example, one of Holman Hunt's lesser known paintings is of a woman praying by her bed; to me its atmosphere resembles "The Bride's Prelude" in its interfusion of religious associations, brocaded density, and the effect of sunlight striking elaborate ornament within a darkened, rich interior. As the ornament-in-stasis of "The Bride's Prelude" can seem either luxurious or repellent, the convoluted details of many Hunt paintings, to their creator so unambiguously beautiful, have been later described as grotesque portrayals of ingrown tension, elaborations of a psyche in contortion.[2] The harsh light, stifling spherical haloes, and tightly compact, overround infantine bodies of "The Triumph of the Innocents" suggest intensified discomfort; in "The Light of the World" the small beady eyes of Christ peer out strangely, his eyeleted ornamental lamp and garments possess a plotted, lurid triviality, and the heavy detail with sharply contrasting light enforces painful alertness.

Rossetti seldom again used the extensive detail of this early poem; it here functions, like that of Hunt, not to create movement but to curtail it, to intensify emotion by holding the mind fixed on certain objects. Rossetti's early poetic style is not inconsistent with his late, less consciously descriptive manner, although he learns to produce the same effects of doomed elegance and psychological brooding more briefly and less circularly; his elaborations, ironically, become more direct. Here as in "The House of Life", sensuousness is sedate, uncertain, allied with latent guilts.

Stasis within "The Bride's Prelude" is emphasized by the point in time at which the narrative begins – all is almost ended, the narration is painful memory. The bride awaits with complete passivity what to her is ultimate shame and horror, marriage to the murderer of her former betrothed, also previously the father by her of an illegitimate child. The poem focuses intently on repression — the repression of nature, the repression of her past life, her suppressed pain as she narrates the story, and even her sister's effortful self-strangulation of mirroring responses.

One of the oppressive external restraints is time, which both passes inexorably and yet refuses to pass. Thus the great emphasis on stillness, pause, hesitation:

And the noonday stands *still* for heat. (st. 1)

... beyond the arras'd gloom
And the hot window's dull perfume, —
Where day was *stillest* in the room. (st. 16)

She would have pushed the lattice wide
   To gain what breeze might be;
But marking that no leaf once beat
The outside casement, it seemed meet
Not to bring in more scent and heat. (st. 21)

The room lay *still* in dusty glare,
   Having no sound through it
Except the chirp of a caged bird
That came and ceased: and if she stirred,
Amelotte's raiment could be heard. (st. 31)

It seemed to Aloÿse that the whole
   Day's weight lay back on her
Like lead. The hours that did remain
Beat their dry wings upon her brain
Once in mid-flight, and passed again. (st. 152)

The silence lengthened. (st. 102) (italics mine)

This all-absorbing silence is intensified by the constant stifling presence of heat and glare, culminating towards the poem's end in a destructive fire:

And even in shade was gleam enough
   To shut out full repose .... (st. 3)

There hung a cage of burnt perfumes
   In the recess: but these,
For some hours, weak against the sun,
Had simmered in white ash. (st. 153)

The bridesmaid rose. I' the outer glare
   Gleamed her pale cheeks, and eyes .... (st. 166)

     And a day came
When half the wealth that propped our name
Went from us in a wind of flame.

> "Six hours I lay upon the wall
>   And saw it burn. But when
> It clogged the day in a black bed
> Of louring vapour ...." (sts. 122, 123)

Even when shade and water are permitted to occur, they fail to provide relief; sometimes they suggest further ominous associations:

> ... as one who is afraid
> Sat Aloÿse within the shade. (st.2)
>
> Each stalking wave shook like a shroud. (st. 127)
>
> "The year slid like a corpse afloat .... (st. 178)

The other manifestations of nature are uniformly unpleasant or destructive: famine, storm, harsh noises, or the choked and restrained song of a caged bird:

>   From the outside
> By fits there boomed a dull report
> From where i' the hanging tennis-court
> The bridegroom's retinue made sport. (st. 30)
>
>   Having no sound through it
> Except the chirp of a caged bird
> That came and ceased .... (st. 31)

Pleasant sounds occur only to emphasize their cessation:

> A bird had out its song and ceased .... (st. 23)

As the sun's glare was heavy, so other portions of nature seem effortful and over-weighed. The plunge of the hound in the moat, the hoof-beats of the horses, and the beat of leaves fall heavily on taut nerves:

> Some minutes since, two rooks had toiled
>   Home to the nests that crowned
> Ancestral ash-trees. Through the glare
> Beating again, they seemed to tear
> With that thick caw the woof o' the air. (st. 58)

The rooks "toil", they "tear", they "beat". The repetition of variants of "beat" throughout the poem expresses both external oppression and the psychological onus of time. The juxtaposition of heat, drouth, beating sensations, and isolated passive misery suggests the purgative journey of Coleridge's Ancient Mariner, now domesticized, sexualized, and transposed into a Victorian narrative frame.[3]

Within "The Bride's Prelude" all motion is close, crowded, architecturally limited, virtually imprisoned, yet there is an accompanying emphasis on isolation:

All thrust together .... (st. 5)

The bride turned in her chair, and hid
    Her face against the back .... (st. 18)

Sat thus aloof, as if to hide. (st. 8)

She paused then, weary, with dry lips
Apart. (st. 30)

    ... but felt
Between her hands in narrow space
Here own hot breath upon her face,
And kept in silence the same place.

Aloÿse did not hear at all
    The sounds without. She heard
The inward noise (past help obey'd) .... (sts. 59, 60)

And I woke up at night alone. (st. 148)

Not only the bride's chamber but everywhere she has resided — the convent, her former chamber and sick-room, the litter on which she was drawn in flight, her final destination after escape — have all been places of confinement:

    The stark walls
Made chill the mirk: and when
We oped our curtains, to resume
Sun-sickness after long sick gloom,
The withering sea-wind walked the room.

"Through the gaunt windows the great gales
    Bore in the tattered clumps .... (sts. 140, 141)

"But I, a mother even as she,
    Turned shuddering to the wall: .... (st. 147)

Against the background of the chamber's closeness, the disjoint movements of the sisters are sharply emphasized, creating tension between their physical and emotional juxtaposition and separation. Amelotte paces back and forth, both turn towards and away from each other, each moves closer to, then away from, her sister.

In "The House of Life" fire, light, closeness, and stillness are psychic accompaniments of sensuality; it is not surprising that other

Rossettian properties of sensuousness found there are found also in "The Bride's Prelude" – elaborate dress, music, jewels, incense, gold and silver, swans, religious suggestions, female companions to the central lady, preoccupation with female lips, eyes, neck, forehead, hands, even allusions to magic spells, winds, the elements, mirrors, hovering wings.

The sensuousness of "The Bride's Prelude" is not only sick and oppressive, but its dull insistent monotony is identified with shame and sexual guilt. In "The House of Life" the association of guilt and sensuality is more ambiguous; in "The Bride's Chamber", however, sexuality, dizziness, fainting, sexual gratification, and guilt form recurring associations in Rossetti's mind. The bride, sensuously arrayed, nearly swoons from guilt and tension and describes past faintings associated with sexual behavior, pregnancy, and seduction:

... listless Aloÿse .... (st.1)
... but then i' the autumn noon
My feeble brain whirled like a swoon.

"He made me sit. Cousin, I grieve
   Your sickness stays by you.'
'I would', said I, 'that you did err
So grieving. I am wearier
Than death, of the sickening, dying year.'

"He answered: 'If your weariness
   Accepts a remedy,
I hold one and can give it you.' ... (sts. 70, 71)

(on pregnancy)
"I had such yearnings as brought tears,
   And a wan dizziness:
Motion, like feeling, grew intense;
Sight was a haunting evidence
And sound a pang that snatched the sense. (st. 119)

"My shame possessed me in the light
   And pageant, till I swooned. (st. 173)

Sensuality seems to smother and overpower, and its result is psychic pain, reducing the victim to weak helplessness, insensibility, and near death.

In the light of this identification of discomfort, weakness, and sexuality, the character of Rossetti's heroine is interesting. She is incapble of action and her entire experience is consistent in its weakness, passivity, pain, and fear. Even her responses to her sister are governed, not by her own will, but by what she projects as divine causation:

> God would not permit
> That I should change thine eyes with it. (st. 24)
>
> "I knew God's hand and might not speak. (st. 29)

Her experience with her lover is never a source of happiness; she fears deeply her sister's responses; she accepts willingly her brother's threats of murder; she professes love for her child but has made no attempt to regain it or investigate its murder. Her history is a plaintively lisped tale of weakness and woe; even the original hunting excursion (which led to her fall which caused her sickness which led to her transgression) was at her brother's instigation. Despite her extreme guilt over having been seduced she does not disapprove of her own passivity at other points — for example, in permitting her child's death.

Aloÿse is the ultimate embodiment of a particular early Victorian stereotype of the heroine — swooning, hypochrondiac, self-pitying, creatress of an intense, circular emotionality. It is as though someone were heating a small porcelain kettle but closed all the valves. Sometimes the monotony of passive pain seems to parody both Victorian ideals of womanhood and the suffering romantic hero. Coventry Patmore's sentimental narratives of female sexual sin or infidelity and suffering may have constituted a partial precedent for the confessional defeatism of this poem, as well as Elizabeth Barrett Browning's "Bertha in the Lane", although here the despondent and melancholy elder sister has been merely rejected rather than seduced.

Aloÿse's weakness and passivity could be interminably documented:

> ... and my hand
>   Had but the weary skill
> To eke out upon silken cloth
> Christ's visage ....
>
> My limbs, after such lifetime theft
> Of life, could be but little deft ....
>
> "Besides, the daily life i' the sun
>   Made me at first hold back ....
> I am not blithe and strong like thee. (st. 36-40)
>
>   I tossed, and lay
> Sullen with anguish the whole day. (st. 46)
>
> I lay in the same weary stound,
> Therefore, until the night came round. (st. 48)
>
> She stopped, grown fainter. (st. 165)
>
> "Then I fell back from them, and lay
>   Outwearied. (st. 148)

Every event is carefully described to avoid expressions of her own activity or will; instead of "I fell down from my palfrey", she says, "My palfrey threw me", instead of "I escaped to the postern", "I was led down to the postern". Much of her suffering, symbolically, occurs when she is physically prostrate, in bed, drawn on a litter, *et cetera*.

"Six hours I *lay* upon the wall
    And saw it burn. But when
It clogged the day in a black bed
Of louring vapour I was led
Down to the postern, and we fled. (st. 123)

"But if at night he did not come
    I *lay* all deadly cold .... (st. 116)

    In dreams
All was passed through afresh
From end to end. (st. 137)
        (italics mine)

Her internal sufferings also mirror passively the heat and cold, water and drouth, of the outside elements; she is alternately flushed and chilled, states associated with her weariness, dizziness, and disease:

And pent between her hands, the breath
Was damp before her face like death. (st. 81)

    ... but felt
Between her hands in narrow space
Her own hot breath upon her face .... (st. 59)

Even a limited narcissism, the last refuge of the totally repressed and apathetic, seems barely able to creep out of her:

"Yet I grew curious of my shame,
    And sometimes in the church,
Or hearing such a sin rebuked,
Have held my girdle-glass unhooked
To see how such a woman looked. (st. 115)

It is significant that her narcissism is evoked in a religious setting and by the thought of herself as a sinner. Religious guilt and pious emotions are used to induce a lingering contemplation of one's own (presumably gratifying) sins, as well as to aggrandize their uniqueness and importance. Much Victorian art and writing moralizing over the sinner or his/her reform seems to me to appeal to this somewhat hypocritical and dual emotion.[4]

Rossetti, incidentally, considered feminine narcissism a deeply seductive trait; he describes his painting "Lady Lilith" as "a modern Lilith combing out her abundant golden hair and gazing on her self in the glass with that self-absorption by whose strange fascination such natures draw others within their own circle".[5] In few of his portraits of women do the subjects look directly at the viewer or at anything within the picture; instead they have a vague and misty-eyed look, suggesting self-absorption rather than visionary intensity.

Aloÿse's entire narration is buffeted between inner compulsion and severe external restraints;

>   ... then raised
> Her head, with such a gasp .... (st. 11)
>   ... as she pressed
> Her hand against her throat .... (st. 19)
>   At first
> I lay and bit my hair
> For the sore silence thou didst keep .... (st. 27)
> But marked the breath that came in sighs
> And the hall-pausing for replies. (st. 35)
> Her thought, long stagnant, stirred by speech,
>   Gave her a sick recoil; .... (st. 54)
> And trembling between shame and pride
> Said by fierce effort .... (sts. 87, 88)

Aloÿse's passivity is further emphasized by contrast with her sister Amelotte, who exhibits at once greater violence of response and more self-control. The sisters form an interesting antiphony of unhappiness, since the statements of each reverberate painfully in the other:

(Amelotte:)
> She bowed her neck, and having said,
>   Kept on her knees to hear;
> And then, because strained thought demands
> Quiet before it understands,
> Darkened her eyesight with her hands. (st. 34)
>
> Her fingers felt her temples beat;
>   Then came that brain-sickness
> Which thinks to scream, and murmureth
> And pent between her hands, the breath
> Was damp against her face like death.

> Her arms both fell at once; but when
>   She gasped upon the light,
> Her sense returned. She would have pray'd
> To change whatever words still stay'd
> Behind, but felt there was no aid.
>
> So she rose up, and having gone
>   Within the window's arch
> Once more, she sat there .... (sts. 81-83)

Amelotte moves slightly in the chamber, walks to and from the window, kneels and offers Aloÿse a drink, while Aloÿse remains imprisoned and fixed in her chair as if pinioned by guilt. As Aloÿse experiences emotional prostration, Amelotte kneels in prayer, seeks relief at the window, hides her face, and appears to faint, expressing in alternate form what the speaker (and reader) is enduring.

In "The House of Life" Rossetti's persona and mistress are often represented by a few disjoint portions of their bodies, even by mere breathings and emanations; here also hands, eyes, breath, tears, hair, arms, and necks of his heroines function independently:

> She bowed her neck, and having said,
>   Kept on her knees to hear; .... (st. 34)
>
> So when at last her sister spoke,
>   She did not see the pain
> O' the mouth nor the ashamèd eyes,
> But marked the breath that came in sighs
> And the half-pausing for replies. (st. 35)
>
> But Aloÿse threw up her neck
>   And called the name of God: – (st. 85)
>
> Amelotte kept her knees; her face
>   Was shut within her hands,
> As it had been throughout the tale;
> Her forehead's whiteness might avail
> Nothing to say if she were pale. (st. 55)
>
> Her fingers felt her temples beat .... (st. 81)

Rossetti especially emphasizes necks and hands; his later portraits also suggest that for him the neck was an erogenous zone melting amorphously into boneless shoulder.

Frequently in the poem Rossetti mentions unexpectedly an object or part of the body distant from those he has described – the effect is jerky, brittle, sudden, artificial, and eccentric. This sense of disjoint objects around a blurred center may be a part of what is considered a Pre-Raphaelite manner.

> Long sat she silent; and then raised
> > Her head, with such a gasp
> As while she summoned breath to speak
> Fanned high that furnace in the cheek ....
> > ("The Bride's Prelude", st. 11)

Further, the sense that images are broken up into pieces, that different parts of a body or situation are at any time liable to express emotion independently, gives an effect of automation, of forces popping up mysteriously, emphasising again both the external passivity and the deep obsessive roots of the emotions expressed.

The emphasis on disjoint actions and sensations is a characteristic of nineteenth century visionary and dream poetry, beginning with Coleridge. The use of the passive and disparate gives "The Ancient Mariner" much of its characteristic clarity-in-opaqueness:

> He kneels at morn, and noon, and eve —
> He hath a cushion plump.
> It is the moss that wholly hides
> The rotted old oak stump.
> > ("The Rime", 11. 519-522)

Any added clarity which "The Bride's Prelude" might receive from this technique, however, seems obscured by the general atmosphere of hot breathing and faintness.

Although Tennyson imitated these mannerisms to a lesser extent, their most immediate transmitter may well have been Coventry Patmore. He used a Coleridgean "jerkiness" thoughout his early poems (1844), which were much admired by Rossetti, and his "The Seasons", published in *The Germ* the year after Rossetti composed the first portion of "The Bride's Prelude", is a further example. Rossetti described this poem as "stunning".[6]

> Then sleep the seasons, full of might;
> > While slowly swells the pod,
> And rounds the peach, and in the night
> > The mushroom bursts the sod.

Although the "mushroom", "pod", and "peach" are particular objects chosen rather humorously for their rounded and 'sensual' qualities, they are intended to represent entire classes of organic life. Some of

Pre-Raphaelite "simplicity" may consist of this sort of disjointed enumeration combined with a reluctance to use descriptive adjectives.[7]

The atmosphere of hot breath and faintness throughout "The Bride's Prelude" is not merely physical. Here as in "The House of Life" the reader is told carefully what are the emotions he should see within the situation — shame, luxuriousness, and passion. The definitions are partially Aloÿse's, while nothing in the poem indicates that they should be interpreted with reservations or irony. We are expected, for example, to accept her fears with some seriousness:

(Oh gather round her now, all ye
    Past seasons of her fear, —
Sick springs, and summers deadly cold!
To flight your hovering wings unfold,
For now your secret shall be told.
Ye many sunlights, barbed with darts
    Of dread detecting flame, —
Gaunt moonlights that like sentinels
Went past with iron clank of bells, —
Draw round and render up your spells!) (sts. 12, 13)

    ... all intent
On torturing doubts .... (st. 83)

She said: "The name is as the thing: —
Sin hath no second christening,
And shame is all that shame can bring. (st. 23)

    ... heard
Thus in this dreadful history, —
Was dreadful to her; as might be
Thine own voice speaking unto thee. (st. 92)

"Such still were *griefs*: for *grief* was still
    A separate sense, untouched
Of that *despair* which had become
My life. Great *anguish* could benumb
My soul, — my heart was *quarrelsome*. (st. 143)

In the last passage I have emphasized Aloÿse's designations of her emotions; within the repetitions and closed atmosphere of her tale, grief, despair, and anguish come to define one another, so that her pain is self-diagnosed, then intensified by circular restatement. We are expected to feel many of the sisters's subjective emotions and guilts vicariously, but since the dramatic situation fails to explain or justify them further on rational or objective grounds, Aloÿse's narration remains solely a confession.

"The Bride's Prelude", despite a second lengthy addition, remained unfinished. Since the confessional portion terminates at the present ending, completion of the tale would have required shifting to dramatic and active scenes, a difficult break after so long and heavy a prelude. Rossetti left a memorandum concerning his projected conclusion: Urscelyn becomes a successful soldier of fortune, desires to marry her for her family rank, and obtains her brothers' support for the alliance. Meanwhile she has confessed her past to a young knight who loves her, and they are secretly betrothed. Urscelyn treacherously kills her lover, and his wedding to Aloÿse is about to follow. William Rossetti believed the last suggestion of Rossetti's memorandum, "As the bridal procession appears, perhaps it might become apparent that the brothers mean to kill Urscelyn when he has married her", may have been the idea of Swinburne.[8] Again sexuality, female passive pain, and violent death are conjoined — if there are no sexual overtones, why the marriage at all, since Aloÿse is scarcely expected to grieve for her dead husband. But this final episode is unnecessary since no suspense whatsoever remains concerning the heroine's final state. The entire poem has been a weary stone rolling downhill, and although the death of Urscelyn might remove one source of active pain, the throbbing monotony and despair of her life remain unchanging.

2. Keats' Narratives Compared With "The Bride's Prelude": Sexual Love is Victorianized

Since "The Bride's Prelude" shows Keatsian influence both in descriptive mannerisms and plot, it is a useful poem for illustrating some ways in which Rossetti transformed Romantic emphases in theme and landscape. The plot of "The Pride's Prelude" resembles that of "Isabella; Or, The Pot of Basil" in several identifiable ways, and to a lesser extent that of "The Eve of St. Agnes". In both "Isabella" and "The Bride's Prelude", the lover is lowborn, the lady noble, the brothers evil and murderous. In "Isabella", the lovers experience a "malady" and "sick longing" of love, and, as in "The Bride's Prelude", the lover speaks to cure a sickness into which his mistress has fallen:

Until sweet Isabella's untouch'd cheek
   Fell sick within the rose's just domain,
Fell thin as a young mother's, who doth seek
   By every lull to cool her infant's pain:
'How ill she is,' said he, 'I may not speak,
'If looks speak love-laws, I will drink her tears,
'And at the least 'twill startle off her cares. (st. 5)

But while Isabella's sickness is clearly love-longing, the connection between Aloÿse's sickness and her susceptibility to seduction remains subconscious and unexpressed. While Lorenzo is able to restore Isabella's happiness, there is no equivalent resolution for Aloÿse.

Although in both poems the lover is lowborn and the brothers vicious, Keats is interested in the exploitive sources of the brothers' wealth, and their position as master to one far superior in character to themselves:

> For them the Ceylon diver held his breath
>   And went all naked to the hungry shark;
> For them his ears gush'd blood; for them in death
>   The seal on the cold ice with piteous bark
> Lay full of darts .... (st. 15)

By contrast Aloÿse's comments on her family's dispossession are vague and indefinite; it is unclear whether she regrets loss of wealth:

> "It now was hard on that great ill
>   Which lost our wealth from us
> And all our lands. Accursed be
> The peevish fools of liberty
> Who will not let themselves be free! (st. 120)

Her infatuation is in no sense a reflection on her class or family ambitions, for Urcelyn is at least as culpable. Significantly his illegitimate birth is considered a flaw, and lineal respectability thus upheld. And although Amelotte's family are evil, their conventions are at least morally neutral, since the man who opposes their greed is motivated only by greed himself. What he wants can never be his by "right".

> "Not the guilt only made the shame,
>   But he was without land
> And born amiss. (st. 107)

> "Oh! of my brothers, Hugues was mute,
>   And Gilles was wild and loud,
> And Raoul strained abroad his face,
> As if his gnashing wrath could trace
> Even there the prey that it must chase ....

> "But my stern father came to them
>   And quelled them with his look,
> Silent and deadly pale .... (sts. 130, 132)

Keats approves of the lovers' liaison and his lowborn hero is a noble person; Rossetti disapproves of seduction and so the man who commits it must be socially and morally inferior.

It is perhaps indicative of Keats' greater optimism that he describes the brothers as fleeing immediately when their crime is discovered:

> The guerdon of their murder they had got,
>   And so left Florence in a moment's space,
> Never to turn again. `Away they went,
> With blood upon their heads, to banishment. (st. 60)

Evil fades away when revealed. Other differences include Isabella's much greater aggressiveness in love (as compared with Aloÿse), and the openly sexual and physical nature of her response to Lorenzo:

> His image in the dusk she seemed to see,
>   And to the silence made a gentle moan,
> Spreading her perfect arms upon the air,
> And on her couch low murmuring "Where? O where?" (st. 30)

The greatest difference between the poems, however, is simply that in "Isabella" (and "The Eve of St. Agnes"), love is pure, happy, and free from ambivalence; only the outside world introduces pain and evil. Keats discusses the necessary conjunction of pain and love:

> Even bees, the little almsmen of spring bowers,
> Know there is richest juice in passion flowers. (st. 13)

but he concludes, "The little sweet doth kill much bitterness". Instead of compulsive, strangled sensations endured in repressed isolation, Isabella and Lorenzo experience an uninhibited and energetic mutuality that survives even death. In contrast to the drouth and stagnation accompanying the seduction of "The Bride's Prelude", their love has an implicit affinity with nature and growth. Even the basil plant illustrates their continued love, and their story is preserved in memory and song. Keats' images merge pleasurably; the entire poem seems as rapid as Rossetti's is slow:

> X
> Parting they seemed to tread upon the air,
>   Twin roses by the zephyr blown apart
> Only to meet again more close, and share

>   The inward fragrance of each other's heart.
>   She, to her chamber gone, a ditty fair
>   Sang, of delicious love and honey's dart;
>   He with light steps went up a western hill,
>   And bade the sun farewell, and joy'd his fill.

And in "The Eve of St. Agnes" all seems to merge, glide, and swoon:

> Soon, trembling in her soft and chilly nest,
> In sort of wakeful swoon, perplex'd she lay,
> Until the poppied warmth of sleep oppress'd
> Her soothed limbs, and soul fatigued away; ...
> Blissfully haven'd both from joy and pain, ... (st. 27)
>
> Into her dream he melted, as the rose
> Blendeth its odour with the violet, –
> Solution sweet: .... (st. 36)

In Rossetti sensuality has altered its nature, from good to evil, from openness to covertness, from love to guilt and estrangement. In "Isabella" the lovers sacrifice their lives for a worthy end, their love; they are at least freed from "the weariness, the fever, and the fret" of aristocratic and mercantile egotism, the opposition of convention to emotion. In "The Bride's Prelude", by contrast, the pain is monotonous and circular, yet somehow implicit within erotic experience.

Holman Hunt has been criticized for his naive obtuseness in describing "The Eve of St. Agnes" as a tale of the moral superiority of young love over evil;[9] the implied contrast is with Tennyson and Rossetti, who perceived Keats' sensual and amoral purpose. Yet however foreign to Keats' vocabulary and intent are many connotations of the word "moral", he creates a world in which love and sexuality are in harmony with the psychological and material qualities of nature, and in an oblique way Hunt understood this. By contrast Rossetti has inverted the "moral" and reduced many of Keats' patterns to more conventionally censorious stereotypes, a form of alteration certainly as didactic as Hunt's moralistic terminology.

Not only does Rossetti emphasize the external code of marriage rather than the inner bonds of love, but this shift indicates a more significant alteration of Keats' values. Rossetti no longer views sexual and romantic love in isolation but in relation to a domestic, religious, and familial context. Keats presents Isabella and Lorenzo as individual persons, not family members; nothing indicates that the brothers are of significance in Isabella's emotional life, nor would it seem natural for her to feel guilt towards them for anything she has done. This direct and unfamilial treatment of love is common to Keats' other narratives, "Lamia" and "The Eve of St. Agnes".[10]

Aloÿse on the other hand places intense significance on Amelotte's response; in fact, she partially evaluates her own behavior according to her sister's reaction. Much of the poem's intensity consists in her reluctance and inhibitions over confiding in her sister, and the poem's focus is not romantic love but the sisters' shared response to sexual guilt. Aloÿse even bares her breast to her murderous brothers and father, a meaningless action unless she feels her family have some sanction for exercising judgment over her, and her life is saved by her father's memory of her mother. The sexual act produces an infant which conveniently disappears. Rossetti's greater emphasis on illegitimacy and the child reflects his concern with social and domestic results of sexuality; Keats' lovers do not produce offspring, and they do not acknowledge their families as a moral force in their lives. The center of moral judgment has shifted; the narrative celebration of present love between two persons has become a tableau of confession and repentant memory.

There are descriptive echoes of Keats at several points in "The Bride's Prelude", but these similarities are weighted by the heavy restraints and negations inherent in Rossetti's sensual effects. Ford, Shine, Villard, and Lang, for example, correctly cite stanza twenty-four of "The Eve of St. Agnes" as a source of description in "The Bride's Prelude":[11]

XXIV

  A casement high and triple-arch'd there was,
  All garlanded with carven imag'ries
  Of fruits, and flowers, and bunches of knot-grass,
  And diamonded with panes of quaint device,
  Innumerable of stains and splendid dyes,
  As are the tiger-moth's deep-damask'd wings;
  And in the midst, 'mong thousand heraldries,
  And twilight saints, and dim emblazonings,
A shielded scutcheon blush'd with blood of queens and kings.

"The Bride's Prelude", sts. 4, 6, 7:

Within the window's heaped recess
  The light was counterchanged
In blent reflexes manifold
From perfume-caskets of wrought gold
And gems the bride's hair could not hold ....

>
> Against the haloed lattice-panes
>   The bridesmaid sunned her breast;
> Then to the glass turned tall and free,
> And braced and shifted daintily
> Her loin-belt through her côte-hardie.
>
> The belt was silver, and the clasp
>   Of lozenged arm-bearings;
> A world of mirrored tints minute
> The rippling sunshine wrought into 't
> That flushed her hand and warmed her foot.

Keats' descriptions are more diffuse, subtler, softer, more differentiated and commingling; in "The Bride's Prelude" the bridemaid's clasp is silver, but the tiger moth of "The Eve of St. Agnes" possesses "deep-damask'd wings"; Amelotte's hand is "flushed", but Keats' shielded scutcheon "blushed with blood of queens and kings". In both cases the Keatsian description states more than a color or pattern; it conveys a pulsating emotion in the object described, and permits a freedom for the imagination that Rossetti's clearer and simpler descriptions often do not. For example, how exactly does a scutcheon "blush" with blood, or what are panes of "quaint device"? Paradoxically Keats' descriptions are both more attentive to concrete natural properties and more evocative of dim inscrutable imaginings.

Keats also describes a greater range of natural objects; Rossetti confines himself to persons, clothes, domestic interiors, and images of light and reflection (light counterchanged, reflections on gems, halved lattice panes). His use of light is more conscious and plotted than Keats', while gone are the "bunches of knot-grass" and the tiger-moth. As in "The House of Life", only a few green and growing objects accompany Rossetti's portrayal of love. Rossetti's sensuality does not share with Keats an implied analogue and inspiration in springing and organic nature, but on the contrary, is cultivated in careful isolation from it. Another stanza of "The Eve of St. Agnes" epitomizes a characteristic quality of Keats' sensuous imagination:

>
> XXX
>
> And still she slept an azure-lidded sleep,
> In blanched linen, smooth, and lavender'd,
> While he from forth the closet brought a heap
> Of candied apple, quince, and plum, and gourd;
> With jellies soother than the creamy curd,
> And lucent syrops, tinct with cinnamon;
> Manna and dates, in argosy transferr'd

From Fez; and spiced dainties, every one,
From silken Savarcand to cedar'd Lebanon.

Keats likes the round, smooth, jellied, spiced, things that can be pinched, handled, and above all tasted. There are few similar responses in Rossetti, especially to taste. It is hard to imagine Rossetti salivating cheerfully over the "creamy curd". If Rossetti were to use exotic foods for an effect, he would probably choose two or three and emphasize their strangeness and elegance, not spread forth multitudes in an intermingling, variegated, cheerful, gormandizing profusion.

"The Bride's Prelude" is the Rossettian poem which most clearly resembles a Keatsian narrative; Rossetti's alterations in both the spirit and letter of the original reflect a Victorianizing process. Descriptions are simplified, love and nature have become antithetical, sexuality is veiled and becomes both result and cause of human evil, social assumptions concerning marriage and family duty reassert themselves, and Keats' implicit condemnation of social and economic ranks has vanished. What seems to have appeared suddenly is a conviction of original sin, evil not as a flaw in natural processes or the scheme of things, but as an inevitable quality of human nature. Virtually all of Rossetti's poems reinforce a consciousness of inexplicable, uncaused moral evil in individual and corporate man, although exceptional cases of individual virtue appear occasionally, almost always destined to suffer frustration and rejection. It is interesting that even this early poem, with its components of romance, a pious if "fallen" heroine, and sexual idealism, presents a relentlessly negative judgment on human nature, social relations, and destiny. The later literary ballads record very few cheerful events, and Aloÿse is an exceptional protagonist in managing to outlive her poem.

3. *Characteristics of the Early Pre-Raphaelite Idealized Female: Aloÿse and Women in* The Defense of Guenevere

The term "Pre-Raphaelite woman" is frequently mentioned without definition, as though it referred to a single, already well-explicated ideal. Her manifestations occur however over a considerable period, and in the work of several poets, notably Thomas Woolner, R.W. Dixon, William Morris, and Rossetti. The two best known creators of this type, of course, were Morris and Rossetti, and only during their earliest works do they show common tendencies. Since "The Bride's Prelude" is Rossetti's most expansive early romance treatment of a heroine's character, it is useful to compare it with Morris' first volume of poetry, *The Defense of Guenevere*. Traits of the romantic heroine common to both poets should reveal some qualities of the early Victorian Pre-Raphaelite Lady.

Although "The Bride's Prelude" was not published until 1881, Morris could have seen or heard Rossetti read an early version, just as he and Rossetti were a mutual influence on each other's rendering of Malorian and French subject matter in painting and verse during the 1850's.[12] Rossetti's early writings were of course not the only source of Morris' youthful identification of romantic medievalization with art, since Tennsyon, Keats, Ruskin, and Swinburne all represented alternate sensibilities kindred to his own. The parallels between the "lady" of Rossetti and Morris are quite extensive in themselves, however. In both "The Bride's Prelude" and *The Defense of Guenevere* she is endowed with certain similar qualities:

(1) Emphasis on female hair, lips, neck, arms, and forehead, especially in combinations indicating weakness and passivity, as bowed neck, wan lips, or (in Morris) hair which confines and restricts:

Of her long neck what shall I say?
What things about her body's sway,
Like a knight's pennon or slim tree
    – Beata mea Domina! ....

God pity me though if I miss'd
The telling, how along her wrist
The veins creep, dying languidly
    – Beata mea Domina!

Not greatly long my lady's hair,
Nor yet with yellow colour fair,
But thick and crisped wonderfully:
    – Beata mea Domina!

    ("Praise of My Lady")

But, knowing now that they would have her speak,
She threw her wet hair backward from her brow,
Her hand close to her mouth touching her cheek....
She stood, and seemed to think, and wrung her hair....

    "... while I laughed out loud,
And let my lips curl up at false or true ....

    ("The Defense of Guenevere")

And yet – but I am growing old,

For want of love my heart is cold,
Years pass, the while I loose and fold
    The fathoms of my hair.[13]   ("Rapunzel")

(2) The lady is pale unto death, so sad and languishing that she seems scarcely alive:

Heavy to make the pale face sad,
And dark, but dead as though it had
Been forged by God most wonderfully
    — Beata mea Domina! —

(3) Mannerisms expressing female passivity and repressed pain are emphasized — catching of breath, turning away of face, moaning, silence, tears:

Upon her head and heavy hair,
And on her eyelids broad and fair;
The tears and rain ran down her face ....

She sobb'd, made giddy in the head
By the swift riding ....

She laid her hand upon her brow,
Then gazed upon the palm, as though
She thought her forehead bled, and — "No!"
She said, and turned her head away,
As there were nothing else to say....
She shook her head and gazed awhile
At her cold hands with a rueful smile,
As though this thing had made her mad.
        ("The Haystack in the Floods")

Her tired feet look'd cold and thin,
    Her lips were twitch'd and wretched tears,
    Some, as she lay, roll'd past her ears,
Some fell from off her quivering chin.
        ("Golden Wings")

The days pass on, pass on a-pace,
    Sometimes I have a little rest
In fairest dreams, when on thy face
    My lips lie, or thy hands are prest

About my forehead, and thy lips
    Draw near and nearer to my own,
But when the vision from me slips,
    In colourless dawn I lie and moan ....
        ("Spell-Bound", italics in the original)

These examples illustrate another pattern. Like Rossetti's heroines, those of Morris are not permitted to act aggressively.[14] However their imaginations are more heated, and their physical motions more overtly reflect a desire to act and express. Aloÿse collapses in a stupor from pain:

> ... and like stone
> I slept; till something made me moan.... (st. 148)

but Morris' heroines toss restlessly on their beds and sleepwalk:

And when she slipp'd from off the bed,
    Her cramp'd feet would not hold her ....
Therewith she rose upon her feet
    And totter'd ....
        ("Golden Wings")

But when the vision from me slips,
    In colourless dawn I lie and moan,

And wander forth with fever'd blood
    That makes me start at little things ....
        ("Spell-Bound", italics in the original)

(4) Sudden, quick, and violent acts are associated with these repressions:

    At first
I lay and *bit* my hair
For the sore silence thou didst keep: ....
        ("The Bride's Prelude", st. 27)
        (italics mine)

Predictably the violence, self-destructiveness, and quickness of these responses are more emphasized in Morris, and often directly associated with sexuality:

I saw you kissing once, like a *curved sword*
    That *bites* with all its edge, did your lips lie,
Curled gently, slowly, long time could afford
    For caught up breathings; like a *dying* sigh

They gather'd up their lines and went away,
    And still kept *twitching* with a sort of smile...
        ("Concerning Geoffray Teste Noire")

The ladies' names *bite* verily like steel.

They *bite* – *bite* me, Lord God! – I shall go mad,
 Or else *die kissing* him, he is so pale; ....

> ("King Arthur's Tomb")
> (italics mine)

(5) God and Christ are evoked with sudden incongruous intensity; suppressed emotions release themselves in religious feeling:

Quoth Amelotte: ....
 What secret, for Christ's love,
Keep'st thou since then? Mary above!
What thing is this thou speakest of?

"Mary and Christ! Lest when 'tis told
 I should be prone to wrath, –
This prayer beforehand!   (sts. 32, 33)

 ... dost thou reck
"That I am beautiful, Lord, even as you
 And your dear Mother? why did I forget
You were so beautiful, and good, and true,
 That you loved me so, Guenevere? O yet

"If even I go to hell, I cannot choose
 But love you, Christ, yea, though I cannot keep
From loving Launcelot; O Christ! must I lose
 My own heart's love ....

> ("King Arthur's Tomb")

In Morris, Christ sometimes becomes an alternate lover, object of the intense physical craving of love as well as symbol of its imperishable and ultimate quality:

"Speak to me, Christ! I kiss, kiss, kiss your feet; ...."

> ("King Arthur's Tomb")

the Morrisean concrete equivalent of Rossetti's more vague

Lady, I fain would tell how evermore
 Thy soul I know not from thy body, nor
Thee from myself, neither our love from God.
 (Sonnet 5)

(6) Abrupt shifts in narration, starkness – also indicating violent emotion:

> But, knowing now that they would have her speak,
> She threw her wet hair backward from her brow ....
>
> "Listen, suppose your time were come to die,
> And you were quite alone and very weak ....
>
> "Nevertheless you, O Sir Gauwaine, lie,
> Whatever may have happened through these years,
> God knows I speak truth, saying that you lie."
>
> > ("The Defense of Guenevere")

The beginning of "The Defense of Guenevere", created accidentally by the printer's erroneous excising of the first stanzas, is an extreme version of a characteristic Morrisean mannerism, the excision of transitions between statements of passionate emotion. Rossetti does not shift as violently or suddenly in a poem as languid as "The Bride's Prelude", although a diminished version of the same technique is used, with shifts and pauses emphasized.

(7) Emphasis on female dress:

> "Never within a yard of my bright sleeves ....
>
> > ("The Defense of Guenevere", 1. 139)
>
> Little joy she had of it,
> > Of the raiment white and red ....
>
> And when the song was ended, she
> > Rose up and caught her gown and ran ....
>
> > ("Golden Wings", 11. 61, 62, 89, 90)

It is interesting that Morris, Holman Hunt, and Rossetti all designed women's clothes at one time or another. The elaborate female costuming portrayed in the paintings was clearly considered to be worthy of an art in itself.

(8) In contrast with the female stereotypes, masculinity is associated with sudden anger and violence:

> Sir Peter: ... Now sir, get up!
> > And choose again: shall it be head sans ears,
> > Or trunk sans head?
> >
> > > (before killing Peter)
>
> Sir Lambert: And this, my Peter, is a joy so dear,
> > I cannot by all striving tell you how
> > I love it, nor I think, good man, would you
> > Quite understand my great delight therein ....
> >
> > > ("Sir Peter Harpdon's End")

> My hand was steady too, to take
> My axe from round my neck, and break
> John' steel-coat up for my love's sake.
> *Hah! hah! la belle jaune giroflée.*
>
>   ("The Gilliflower of Gold")

In Keats' "Isabella" and the projected ending of "The Bride's Prelude", the wicked brothers murder from personal wrath and greed; in Morris violence occurs within a more general warfare, with knights fighting for either treacherous or "right" causes. However simplistically defined, the purpose of aggression for Morris' knights is political as well as personal; Morris heartily accepts the ethic of "war in a just cause". War and anger had fewer positive associations for Rossetti. In "The Bride's Prelude" only the evil characters are violent; the only Rossetti poem in which a protagonist engages in nondefensive combat is the early "The Staff and Scrip", derivative from Boccaccio, and here of course he is defending a wronged lady. In "The King's Tragedy" occurs his longest description of combat, in which King James struggles vainly to defend himself against armed assassins.

(9) Emphasis on dreams, association of sexuality with swooning:

And I fall in a dream that I walk'd with her on the side of a hill ....
    ("The Wind")

To kneel before her; as for me,
I choke and grow quite faint to see
My lady moving graciously.
    Beata mea Domina!
    ("Praise of My Lady")

Lady Alice de la Barde:
    I cannot hear much noise now, and I think
    That I will go to sleep: it all sounds dim
    And faint, and I shall soon forget most things
            ....
        Lying so, one kiss,
    And I should be in Avalon asleep,
    Among the poppies, and the yellow flowers;
    And they should brush my cheek ....
        ("Sir Peter Harpdon's End")

In "King's Arthur's Tomb" Launcelot swoons as he hears Guenevere repent of disloyalty to her dead husband. Morris' more active characters fall into total unconsciousness less frequently, however; instead they experience trances or restless states in which they long for their absent beloved. We have seen that in "The Bride's Prelude" everything related to sexuality causes Aloÿse to experience dizziness, near total memory-block, unconsciousness, or the self-conscious discomfort of prolonged guilt.

(10) Repetition of emotive and interpretive words — "pride", "shame", "sin", "love" (Morris frequently also uses "strange"):

As though she had had there a shameful blow,
And feeling it shameful to feel ought but shame
All through her heart, yet felt her cheek burned so ....
    ("The Defense of Guenevere")

Been forged by God most wonderfully ....
Of some strange metal, thread by thread ....
    ("Praise of My Lady")

"Yet am I very sorry for my sin ...."
    ("King Arthur's Tomb")

Besides similarities in their women figures, there are other obvious parallels in the medievalism of the two poets. Both use the motif of ladies singing sadly to convey intensified pain ("The Bride's Prelude", st. 140; "The Blue Closet"). Both use medievalized backgrounds of chambers, draperies, and castles, although Morris more often identifies his personae as members of courts or factions. Morris preferred French medieval literature, Rossetti Italian, and this divergence caused Morris' poetry to reflect to a greater degree the chivalric themes of *Morte d'Arthur* and Froissart's *Chronicles*, while Rossetti emphasized Italian courtly-mystical themes.[15]

Frequently Morris' dramatic poems are more ambivalent and oblique in interpretation than Rossetti's narratives; Morris is more interested in the oddities of point of view. Many evaluations come indirectly through stark descriptions of pleasure and pain, others are spoken with irony of bitterness:

"God wot I ought to say, I have done ill,
And pray you all forgiveness, heartily!
Because you must be right, such great lords — still ....
    ("The Defense of Guenevere")

At times such indirect can evaluations can occur with great swiftness:

By Arthur's great name and his little love ....
   ("The Defense of Guenevere")

In *The Defense of Guenevere* abruptness, suddenness, and violence are all intensified. Morris' longer narratives not only recount dreary frustration or infidelity but also violent death; sexuality is frustrated not through emotional attrition but murder. Moreover, Morris is not at all domestic or concerned with conflicts of legitimacy, filiality, offspring, religious strictures, and marriage; in this respect Morris is an exception among Victorian poets and more closely allied with the interests of his Romantic predecessors. As in Keats' psychic world, in that of Morris there are only adults and lovers.

In Morris' early poetry pleasure and pain are more clearly recognizable and separable from each other than in Rossetti's poems. Morris' response to the lady stereotype is frequently more intense, sudden, affirmative, and individualized. To Morris, for example, belong such perceptions as "crisped hair" and the description of veins creeping along his lady's arm, expressing the minuteness and strangeness of his delight. Since Rossetti later repudiated "The Bride's Prelude", describing its story as "unelevated and repulsive",[16] it cannot be used indiscriminately as the embodiment of a Rossettian ideal. Still, throughout his poetry Rossetti continued to blend sensual effects with diffuse heavy mannerisms that were foreign to Morris' more violent presentation of personal and political ironies. A comparison of the Pre-Raphaelite Lady archetype in Rossetti's and Morris' earliest poems emphasizes the considerable divergence in their conceptions of an ideal sensuousness in man and woman.

4. "The Staff and Scrip": An Ideal Chivalric Love Rewarded

"The Staff and Scrip" is Rossetti's closest approximation to a cheerful and romanticized idealization of sexual love, as well as his only poem mentioning chivalric combat. Perhaps indicatively, it is a brief and derivative effort. Both lovers are virtuous and faithful (this occurs elsewhere in Rossetti only in "The King's Tragedy"), and although frustrated on earth will receive a heavenly reward. The poem openly expresses the metaphysic of a heaven for true lovers which in varying forms underlies all the early romance narratives, although some cases, such as "The Bride's Prelude" or "Sister Helen", embody the inverse, that faithless lovers do not unite in heaven.

Rossetti's early romantic writings tended to idealize the passive, beautiful, golden-haired woman, often an inspiration to male virtue; the Queen of "The Staff and Scrip" exhibits all of these characteristics. Of such early heroines only the Blessed Damozel survives this stereotyping process with any individual traits. Rossetti's other heroines divide roughly into three categories: the virtuous but wronged heroines Aloÿse and Rose Mary are also "fallen" women, the aggressive and interesting Helen and Lilith are evil, and Beatrice and King James' wife are noble and beautiful but totally without character or distinctiveness. The Queen in "The Staff and Scrip" most resembles the flaccid ladies of the last category. It is significant that two out of three such embodiments are found in the early romances.

According to William Rossetti's dating, "The Staff and Scrip" was written in 1851, 1852; if so, it reveals Rossetti's handling of a chivalric theme (from the *Gesta Romanorum*) before his encounter with Morris — complete with Queen, just war, death in battle, attendant ladies, emphasis on heraldic colors, banner, shield, and sword. It is characteristic of Rossetti, however, to be attracted to the pilgrim as his warrior-protagonist, a religious man and an alien within society.

"The Staff and Scrip" was first published in Morris' and Jones' *Oxford and Cambridge Magazine* in 1856, and aside from the omission of two stanzas, the substitution of one, the addition of two more, and minor verbal changes, chiefly to increase clarity, it remained unchanged. "The Staff and Scrip" is partially dramatic and includes dialogue until near the end, when the Queen's grief and later life are simply described. The dialogue, however, concerns external, public matters and, in contrast with Morris' chivalric dramas, nearly all passionate acts are seen from without:

She sent him a sharp sword, whose belt
    About his body there
As sweet as her own arms he felt.
    He kissed its blade, all bare,
        Instead of her. (st. 16)

The close identification of the agent of violence with passion, however, does suggest Morris. The scene containing the poem's most direct expression of emotion, the Queen's lament over the dead pilgrim, resembles roughly a Morrisean tableau, although no situations are exactly parallel.

Within the poem Rossetti attempted to reproduce old balladic effects in several ways. "The Bride's Prelude"'s monotonously regular stanza, with the last three lines rimed and of even length, had been designed to drag each stanza to a heavy pause. By contrast, "The Staff and Scrip" uses its brief fifth line to create a syncopated, jerking effect, probably designed to seem simple and archaic:

"Who rules these lands?" the Pilgrim said.
   "Stranger, Queen Blanchelys."
"And who has harried them?" he said.
   "It was Duke Luke did this:
     God's ban be his!" (st. 1)

The emphasis on older names, "Duke Luke", "Blanchelys", the semi-archaisms, "harried", "ban", the attempt at direct dialogue, and the use of irregularities and roughness in meter —

And you'll see it over the hill .... (st. 2, 1. 4)

are all intended to create a balladic effect. Further syncopations are created by initial trochees, as in line two, where the effect seems appropriate to the meaning. Combinations such as "Duke Luke", in which a stress seems shared or arbitrarily placed, are intended as primitivisms or archaisms. Rossetti's use of piled monosyllables is perhaps also designed as a simplistic ballad device, although it is his own characteristic elsewhere as well. The third from last stanza, for example, contains only two bisyllabic words (excluding the hyphenated to-day), one of them in the last and shortened line:

Stand up to-day, still armed, with her,
   Good knight, before his brow
Who then as now was here and there,
   Who had in mind thy vow
     Then even as now.

"The Staff and Scrip" is useful for comparisons with other early Rossetti poems. As the imagery and situation of the early "The Bride's Prelude" faintly echoes the purgative journey of Coleridge's mariner, several elements of "The Staff and Scrip" seem to recombine or suggest that journey — the hill, heat, fire, setting and rising sun, tribulations, and verbal echoes ("God keep your head", "He passed the hill-side slow"). This is not to argue that Rossetti consciously had Coleridge in mind when writing "The Staff and Scrip", merely that for several decades after "The Rime" it was difficult to write a poem concerning an extended and painful moral/redemptive process without some memories of Coleridge.

While "The Bride's Prelude" had suppressed most water-images, "The Staff and Scrip" has a healthy impartiality of water, fire, sun, air, dust, wasteland, and flower references:

> For him, the stream had never well'd
>   In desert tracts malign
> So sweet; nor had he ever felt
>   So faint in the sunshine
>   Of Palestine. (st. 8)

The Queen of "The Staff and Scrip", another listless, saddened heroine resembling Aloÿse, is similarly placed in Keatsian chambers;

> The Queen sat idle by her loom;
>   She heard the arras stir,
> And looked up sadly: through the room
>   The sweetness sickened her
>   Of musk and myrrh ....
>
> Her eyes were like the wave within;
>   Like water-reed the pose
> Of her soft body, dainty thin;
>   And like the water's noise
>   Her plaintive voice. (sts. 5, 7)

The description of her eyes directly echoes that of "The Blessed Damozel", which in the 1847 version read:

> Her eyes knew more of rest and shade
>   Than a deep water, even.[17]

Thus Rossetti early exhibits a liking for words such as "even", with their uncertain metrical quality, their capacity of wavering on the brink of becoming monosyllables. In "The Staff and Scrip", as in "The Blessed Damozel", Rossetti emphasizes the lovers' reunion in heaven, while the mention of courtly games and sport in "The Staff and Scrip" suggests Aloÿse's experiences. The use of a conventional pseudo-medieval religious framework is common to much of Rossetti's earlier poetry, but here "The Blessed Damozel"'s ambiguities of faith and evil are absent, as well as "The Bride's Prelude"'s theme of treacherous love. Another romantic motif which Rossetti will later rework appears briefly here, that of the beloved known in the unconscious before first seen with physical eyes:

> Right so, he knew that he saw weep
>   Each night through every dream
> The Queen's own face, confused in sleep
>   With visages supreme
>   Not known to him. (st. 9)

This idea, originally Platonic, frequently appealed to the romantics. Among many convergent antecedents, for example, is Charles Wells' "Zara, the Rich Man's Daughter" in *Stories After Nature*, a work which Rossetti intensely admired.[18] Rossetti's Sonnet 15 of "The House of Life" and his early lyric "Sudden Light" (both written 1854) also mention this sensation.

"The Staff and Scrip" is seldom considered one of Rossetti's more skillful or original poems, although Paull Baum found it admirable.[19] However it is interesting as an early romantic literary ballad with few metaphysical complexities, faithful if separated lovers, and a partially happy ending. Also, with a certain evenhanded monotony and unambiguity it collects usefully Rossettian mannerisms and preoccupations expressed elsewhere, especially in other early ballads.

5. "Dante at Verona" (1848-1850; 1869, 1870): The Poet-Lover Suffers Exile and Rejection

"Dante at Verona" is Rossetti's only early narrative ballad which combines political and love themes; it is similar to "The King's Tragedy", his last lengthy narrative, in its definitions of political and personal virtue and its assumption that corruption inevitably prevails in high places. Dante Alighieri was an excellent protagonist for a Rossettian narrative: Rossetti identified strongly with several aspects of Dante's sensibility; the historical sources provided a partial plot, useful to an author who had difficulty in constructing plots for himself; also, as a literary personage, Dante supported more appropriately the pathetic and reverential emotions which seemed only sentimental when expended on other early protagonists. In this way the protagonist's significance was largely imported from historical and literary associations; once given a dignified character and situation, Rossetti was able to exploit his facility at interpreting emotion. Only once again, in "The King's Tragedy", did Rossetti choose a historical and literary personage as protagonist; interestingly these two are also his most directly political narratives.

Unfortunately there are no early drafts of this poem for which the date is known, so that it is impossible to know how much was altered after 1850. William Rossetti emphasizes its early composition, but seems to be speaking partially from surmise:

> The commencement of this poem dates very early, perhaps even before 1848. It may have been substantially completed towards 1852; but was modified in various regards prior to 1870 ....[20]

Also, in 1861 Rossetti first advertised his projected volume of poems as *Dante at Verona and Other Poems*, so he must have considered it one of his most successful and complete efforts by that date. The six line tetrameter abbacc produces a smoother, less jerkily artificial effect than the five line combinations of "The Bride's Prelude" and "The Staff and Scrip" (another excellent early poem, "The Blessed Damozel", begun 1847, is also in six line tetrameter, with the last line trimeter).

The poem reveals its kinship with the other early narratives, however, in its imagery, piety, moralizing tone, its long-suffering, passive protagonist, and its idealized golden-haired woman figures. As the pilgrim chivalrically rescued the Lady Queen Blanchelys from attack, Dante desires to rescue Florence from her evil rulers and moneychangers:

> How would his Florence lead them forth,
>   Her bridle ringing as she went;
>   And at the last within her tent,
> 'Neath golden lilies worship-worth,
>   How queenly would she bend the while
>   And thank the victors with her smile! (st. 24)

Somewhat incongruously the poem contains two idealized woman figures, necessary since the "Lady Florence" scarcely substitutes for a real person. The descriptions of Beatrice suggest the emotions and wording of "The Blessed Damozel"; like the damozel, Beatrice appears in memory to a bereaved and outcast lover, painfully reviving the past in the present:

> At such times, Dante, thou has set
>   Thy forehead to the painted pane
>   Full oft, I know; and if the rain
> Smote it outside, her fingers met
>   Thy brow; and if the sun fell there,
>   Her breath was on thy face and hair. (st. 33)

"The Blessed Damozel", sts. 4, 11:

> (To one, it is ten years of years.
>   ... Yet now, and in this place,
> Surely she leaned o'er me — her hair
>   Fell all about my face ...
> Nothing: the autumn-fall of leaves.
>   The whole year sets apace.)
>
> (Ah sweet! Even now, in that bird's song,
>   Strove not her accents there,
> Fain to be hearkened? When those bells
>   Possessed the mid-day air,
> Strove not her steps to reach my side
>   Down all the echoing stair?)

The mourning lover pressing his face against the pane also suggests the situation of "The Portrait", written at the time "Dante at Verona" was revised. The brief passages of the poem which express the poet's pained and dignified longing for Beatrice are among its best, as well as closest to Rossetti's preoccupations elsewhere.

Further parallels, strangely enough, are with "The Bride's Prelude", for Dante experiences a long series of fatiguing and frustrating sensations in the course of his exile:

>   Like noon-flies
> They vexed him in the ears and eyes. (st. 16)
>
>   And the rusk-strown accustomed stairs
>   Each day were steeper to his feet;
> And when the night-vigil was done,
>   His brows would ache to feel the sun. (st. 55)
>
> So the day came, after a space,
>   When Dante felt assured that there
>   The sunshine must lie sicklier
> Even than in any other place,
>   Save only Florence. (st. 81)

Like Aloÿse, he is repelled by the frivolous amusements of an aristocratic society, and like Aloÿse, he seeks solitude apart in his arrased chambers:

> Till having reached his room, apart
>   Beyond vast lengths of palace-floor,
>   He drew the arras round his door. (st. 31)

However the despair which seems mock-heroic when expended on an unwanted pregnancy becomes more reasonable when describing the life-long frustration of Dante's emotional and political hopes. Further, since Rossetti is able to document the external circumstances attending Dante's unhappy exile, he is not reduced to "The Bride's Prelude"'s constant repetitive descriptions of hot sun, stagnant air, and constricting walls. Mercifully also, "Dante at Verona" is only eighty-five stanzas in length, less than half the length of "The Bride's Prelude"; this provides a more bearable duration for a tale of unvarying woe.

Rossetti's desire to heavily emphasize Dante's rejection is shown by his interpretation of certain historical facts of Dante's life. Dante Alighieri finished the *Paradiso* of *The Divine Comedy* in Verona, dedicating it to Can Grande della Scala; there is no evidence that he was mistreated there, although after 1319 he left to live with Count Guido da Polenta at Ravenna, and was able to reject a Bolognese offer to become the poet laureate of that city. When he died of a fever in 1321 Count Guido planned to raise a large tomb over his remains, although this was not completed until later.[21] Moreover, Dante's excommunication from Florence resulted from his open letters to Henry VI of Germany advocating the invasion of his native city and the reestablishment of the Holy Roman Empire's hegemony throughout Italy. The entire emphasis of "Dante at Verona", on the scorn and rejection heaped by the frivolous Veronese upon the visionary and public-spirited exile, if not necessarily contradictory to the known circumstances of Dante's life, is at least irrelevant and peripheral to them.

Rossetti's complaints concerning the treatment of Dante are somewhat strained in tone. He emphasizes heavily how those at court disliked Dante's austere character, how his duties as a judge distracted him from nobler thoughts, and how the Veronese neglected Dante's desire for a Florentine seige. If Dante was fed and housed at court and sinecured aristocratically as a judge, he was a comparatively fortunate exile; if his preoccupations lay elsewhere, it would not have mattered to him that several irrelevant citizens of Verona disliked him. His desire for war was, after all, motivated by his own factional interest rather than a con-

cern for Veronese prosperity. Rossetti assumes the absolute justice of
Dante's political biases:

>   And as he spared not to rebuke
>   The mirth, so oft in council he
>   To bitter truth bore testimony:
>   And when the crafty balance shook
>   Well poised to make the wrong prevail,
>   Then Dante's hand would turn the scale. (st. 43)

Considering the tangled factionalism of White/Black struggles, this assumption requires a substantial leap of faith.

As further evidence for his claim that Dante suffered persecution, Rossetti invents a series of obnoxious or immoral persons who actively rejoice at the removal of Dante's virtuous presence:

>   No book keeps record how the Prince
>   Sunned himself out of Dante's reach,
>   Nor how the Jester stank in speech:
>   While courtiers, used to cringe and wince,
>   Poets and harlots, all the throng,
>   Let loose their scandal and their song.
>
>   No book keeps record if the seat
>   Which Dante held at his host's board
>   Were sat in next by clerk or lord, –
>   If leman lolled with dainty feet
>   At ease, or hostage brooded there,
>   Or priest lacked silence for his prayer. (sts. 83, 84)

By implication, Dante suffers from a motiveless and petty spite universally accorded the just man. Besides a sentimentalization of a sense of persecution, these passages reveal ignorance of the actual methods by which such persecution is carried out.

"Dante at Verona" is noticeably consistent in moral tone with other early Rossetti poems. Sexual license is condemned (Can Grande's amours, dainty-footed lemans), the nobly aspiring leave sordid, worldly details and affairs for the pursuit of art, and the greedy and unjust dominate and ostracize the worthy. In "'Retro Me, Sathana!'", 1847, for example, the righteous walk lowly ways while Satan's minions travel broad highways; in "The Choice" sexual hedonism and total asceticism must be renounced for aspiration, reflection, and work; in "Old and New Art" the desire for artistic achievement, external fame, and the re-establishment of morality are assumed synonymous. In all cases outward neglect and inward melancholy or hesitation retard the artist's progress.

Rossetti's conceptions of political justice are direct applications of his code of personal morality, although some of his later more skeptical and undogmatic responses to moral evil do not seem paralleled by an equivalent evolution in political views. All of his political expressions assume an absolute and discernible dichotomy between right and wrong, with man committing social evil because of lapses in personal morality and good intentions. Of especial significance is the morality of the king or ruler; in other words, Rossetti believes loosely in an ethic of *noblesse oblige*, a sort of stringent otherworldly toryism, respect for the self-disciplined and self-sacrificing aristocrat. This was not an implausible series of associations for someone with a religious, inward temperament and contempt for politics, or for a poet reaching adolescence in the decade of Carlyle's *On Heroes and Hero-Worship*. And if Rossetti's medievalized toryism lacked all possibility of application to Victorian society, it at least refrained from the grossest implications of Carlyle's more pragmatically formulated ascriptions of morality to power and success.

Not surprisingly for a sexual moralist, Rossetti used rape as a metaphor for aggression throughout his early political sonnets, and "Dante at Verona" parallels political corruption with harlotry:

> (Respublica – a public thing;
>   A shameful, shameless prostitute,
>   Whose lust with one lord may not suit,
> So takes by turns its revelling
>   A night with each, till each at morn
>   Is stripped and beaten forth forlorn,
>
> And leaves her, cursing her. If she
>   Indeed, have not some spice-draught, hid
>   In scent under a silver lid,
> To drench his open throat with – he
>   Once hard asleep; and thrust him not
>   At dawn beneath the stairs to rot.   (sts. 65, 66)

It is the poem's third woman image, a brutalization of his several early siren-figures. In "Jenny" the siren-figure, tamed and rendered pathetic, represents one individual of the aggregate social problem created by male sexual license. In "The Burden of Nineveh" civilizations decay because individual men reject Christ's "lowly ways" for vanity and material gain. Dante and King James are both men of personal honor; King

James redresses the wronged poor and leads a blameless domestic life, while Dante faithfully mourns his early love and desires to rescue his city from moneychangers. In general, the presence or absence of social justice depends on the self-control and rectitude of individual persons. Yet there is some shift between the two political narratives; the moralistically aggrieved tone of "Dante at Verona" differs from the more laconic pathos with which the king's murder is described. Rossetti's early instinctive, vaguely documented pessimism and his fear that the noble must suffer is replaced by a more concrete imagination of political evil. There is less need to exaggerate or plead the malicious intent of what is self-evidently horrible.

a. General Traits of Early Ballads

Rossetti's early ballads manifest several common characteristics of his early style, belief, and expectations. Several narratives describe the trials of unhappy protagonists, ending in death or emotional deprivation. Both male and female personae possess intense emotions; to attain happiness women must divorce these from sexuality and embrace love and religion, while men must channel them into romantic, chivalric, or patriotic behavior. They must deserve their ideal love in order to unite with her in heaven; for the early lovers, then, the real world is of little direct significance except as a place within which they must suffer to earn love. Ironically it is here that Rossetti comes closest to the Morrisean ideal of active chivalric love, although Rossetti's protagonists display long-suffering rather than aggressive virtue.

Throughout the early ballads earthly sexuality is invariably frustrated; the actively sexual are evil. Each ballad contains at least one idealized heroine, who is pious, restrained, and totally lacking in aggressiveness or vigor. Society invariably defeats or victimizes the worthy individual – the rejected poet and statesman, the virtuous if violated heroine, the chivalrous pilgrim. The only female protagonist is identified with sexual transgression, a consistent pattern in Rossetti's narratives, while male protagonists are associated with political and poetic as well as romantic endeavor.

The early ballads are generally somewhat anecdotal. Only "The Blessed Damozel" avoids the effect of running incidents and images arranged without climax, and even the shortest, "The Staff and Scrip", is marred by sudden gaps and pauses in narrative. Yet in spite of these traits, which suggest the rough transitions, disparate images and disconnected moralizing of Rossetti's early sonnets, the early diffuse, romantic ballads have an attractive freshness of open statement and self-revelatory emotion. Although in these early ballads Rossetti is not as skilled as he later will become in altering or embodying point of view, the early poems are at least important in considering his private emotions and poetic development, and some of his early images are bright and memorable in a manner interestingly variant from his later more shrouded, dark effects. Two of the early ballads, "The Blessed Damozel" and "Dante at Verona", are excellent, unusual works, and both reveal qualities characteristic of their early period of composition.

B. CONDENSED BALLADS OF SEXUAL REVENGE: AGGRIEVED WOMAN DESTROYS MAN

The sexual vengeance ballads are a tiny, significant category, consisting of "Sister Helen", "Eden Bower", and "Troy Town". Two out of three were written in 1869, Rossetti's most prolific year, and he considered both among his best.[21] These ballads are the extreme and idiosyncratic expression of one of his chief interests, maleficent sexuality. In the early romantic narratives fatality and women are loosely related, but here he conjoins them suddenly with fierce concentration. The female becomes a more active force, sexual, vengeful; in contrast to the quietist, masochistic Aloÿse, she responds to rejection with destructive rage. The lovers' heaven disappears, and evil is simultaneously contemplated and dramatized.

Rossetti was extremely interested in the motif of the sexually aggressive female. Swinburne reports his fascination with tales of aggressive women, and throughout his life he admired literature concerning the active seductress.[22] Only great interest in Sidonia's aberrant character, for example, could have caused him to consider *Sidonia the Sorceress* a work of high literary merit. The sexually aggressive woman motif may have attracted him because it violated the convention of the Victorian female ideal, but perhaps it also appealed to a certain rapturous passivity in his sexual character. Also the projection of guilt onto the object of temptation is a Freudian commonplace. Yet granted Rossetti's narrow interpretation of the female character — she was formed for love alone — Rossetti is impartial; he considers the two sexes equally 'powerful', and judges them similarly for similar acts ("Jenny", his only direct treatment of sexuality in Victorian society, is a significant exception).

Both the heroines of "Sister Helen" and "Eden Bower" are sinned against as well as sinning; in both poems their revenge is motivated by scorned love, and their lovers are not especially sympathetic persons. Rossetti even altered "Sister Helen" after the 1854 version to render Helen's behavior more defensible, if still malicious. Although in these ballads human sexuality has become a completely destructive force, unproductive of ultimate good or happiness, man and woman are mutually enchained. As inhuman abstractions the destructive women may seem repellent, but they illustrate a certain psychological truth, sex viewed in a state of terror, a puritanised libido arising to protest its discomfort. It is unfortunate that Rossetti was unable to fuse more of this concentration and interest in sexual passion into his later narrative ballads. Perhaps after the Buchanan attack (1871) sexuality was too painful a subject for more direct treatment.

1. *"Sister Helen" (1851, 1880)*

Of forty-two stanzas in the completed version of "Sister Helen", only thirty were published in the *Düsseldorf's Artist's Album* in 1854.[24] According to William Rossetti the poem was first written in 1851, although there is no manuscript of this version. The alterations in the thirty original stanzas produce a clearer and more emotional effect; also they alter the plot from a vague tale of hate and unmotivated love to one in which Sister Helen's vengeance is more credible.

For example, in both versions Keith of Ewern has commited some undefined wrong against Sister Helen:

"He yields you these and craves full fain,
    Sister Helen,
You pardon him in his mortal pain."
What else he took will he give again,
    Little Brother?"
    (O Mother Mary, Mother,
O shame and love between Hell and Heaven.)
       (st. 23, 1854 version)

Except for the refrain this stanza remains constant. The earlier plot, however, included an offer of marriage which Sister Helen inexplicably rejects:

> "O his son is lost, the priest has said,
>   Sister Helen,
> If he die ere you and he be wed."
> I'll be his bride in a warmer bed,
>   Little Brother." (st. 27)

If Sister Helen has been Keith of Ewern's lover, presumably marriage constitutes some reparation; her desire to murder him instead is therefore inscrutable as well as vicious. Interestingly this is one of Rossetti's few poems in which each of a pair of lovers harms the other, in contrast with "Rose Mary" and "The Bride's Prelude", which both contain an "innocent party", in each case female. In the revised version both lovers suffer more complexly and neither seems quite as motiveless and petty in his opposition. Keith of Ewern has a new love, his bride, to whom he presumably owes a counterallegiance. She becomes an innocently wronged female figure in the poem, pleading with Sister Helen for her husband's soul. While the early version at no point indicates that the witch as well as Keith of Ewern endures pain, an 1870 alteration of the line "But he they mourn is sadder still", to "But he and I are sadder still", emphasizes Helen's suffering. By implication the lovers' souls have been in some way united, although damned. The theme is, of course, an inverted version of "The Blessed Damozel", with the woman drawing her lover with her into damnation rather than blessedness.

An example of the minor word changes Rossetti made in later versions occurs in what was originally stanza one:

D. A. A.[25]: "And if ye have melted your wax aright, Sister Helen,
Ye'll let me play, for ye said I might!"
...
(O Mother Mary, Mother,[26]
Dark night and loud between Hell and Heaven!)

1881: "But if you have done your work aright,
    Sister Helen,
You'll let me play, for you said I might."
...
O Mother, Mary Mother,
Third night, to-night, between Hell and Heaven!

"But" is more specific and in context more negative than "and". The substitution of "you" for "ye" might seem to lessen the poem's medievalized tone, but ironically it seems to heighten the reality of the sorcery by rendering it more directly. The refrain repeats the earlier reference to the three days since Keith's marriage, except that here the emphasis is specifically on the night, the time when Keith must die.

Twenty-seven out of thirty of the refrains are altered between the first and final versions.

D. A. A. (5): What ails her heart between Hell and Heaven?)
Works (6):   What rest to-night, between Hell and Heaven?)
D. A. A. (10): Why smiles she thus between Hell and Heaven?
Works (12):   Why laughs she thus, between Hell and Heaven?)
D. A. A. (24): Has she no fear between Hell and Heaven?)
Works (27):   As she forgives, between Hell and Heaven!)
D. A. A. (30): O purge their souls between Hell and Heaven!)
Works (42):   Lost, lost, all lost between Hell and Heaven!)

The refrains of the final version are more carefully patterned to form a sequence with each other, as for example:

What rest to-night, between Hell and Heaven?....
What sight to-night, between Hell and Heaven?....
What sound to-night, between Hell and Heaven?....
Whence should they come, between Hell and Heaven?
Who should they be, between Hell and Heaven? (sts. 6-10)

Of the twelve stanzas which Rossetti added to the poem, one forms an introduction explaining Sister Helen's action, two add single images of the flying moon and heart burning before a flame, one provides the poem's only personifications, "Love" and "Hate", and eight, all written in 1879, introduce the marriage and bride plot.

The extended picture of the lady in distress fills seven of these eight stanzas, forming one of the poem's starker and more elaborated scenes, the ultimate contrast to that of Sister Helen burning her waxen man:

"A lady's here, by a dark steed brought,
    Sister Helen,
So darkly clad, I saw her not," ....
"Her hood falls back, and the moon shines fair,
    Sister Helen,
On the Lady of Ewern's golden hair." ....
"Pale, pale her cheeks, that in pride did glow,
    Sister Helen,
'Neath the bridal-wreath three days ago." ....
"Her clasped hands stretch from her bending head,
    Sister Helen;
With the loud wind's wail her sobs are wed." ....

"She may not speak, she sinks in a swoon,
        Sister Helen, –
She lifts her lips and gasps on the moon." ....
"They've caught her to Westholm's saddle-bow,
        Sister Helen,
And her moonlit hair gleams white in its flow." ....
"Flank to flank are the three steeds gone,
        Sister Helen,
But the lady's dark steed goes alone." (sts. 30-35, 39)

    The plot's time sequence is also tightened in the later version. Sister Helen's sorcery occupies exactly the three days after Keith of Ewern's marriage, a period of time perhaps loosely and ironically suggestive of Christ's harrowing of hell, and Keith of Ewern dies directly after the bride turns away from Sister Helen's door, rejected. Since the poem's most complicating incident and the final climactic confrontation were added in 1879, it is highly inaccurate to consider "Sister Helen" as commonly printed an early dramatic ballad. Rossetti's additions to "Sister Helen" have greatly improved the poem's narrative quality, again illustrating the significance of his revisions and progression in narrative ability from his earlier to later period.

    R.D. Johnston comments inaccurately that in Rossetti's early narrative poems the woman frequently suffers from rejected love but in his later poems she becomes the agent of man's distress.[27] But in the 1854 version Helen is an early agent of distress, while she is presented as more rather than less sympathetic in the 1881 version. Another exception to Johnston's postulated progression is "Rose Mary"; it is the only one of the three later major ballads to deal with unfaithful love, and in it fidelity is still feminine and treachery masculine. Rossetti never presents an unmitigatedly criminal woman in any of his major poems; even Lilith has a certain cause for grievance against God and the Adam who deserted her. However sinning or related to evil forces, all of Rossetti's women of evil deed, and many of his virtuous heroines, have been betrayed by the lust or vice of men.

    The poem contains another one of Rossetti's domestic situations, sister conversing with little brother, used with great irony; amusingly this poem also parallels the other narratives in which a young woman confides a sin to a member of her immediate family. The sister-younger brother situation is not common in poetry, and the religious connotations of "Sister Helen" weirdly belie her actual witch nature.

    The meter and rhythm of the poem are intricately appropriate to the subject, with four of seven lines designed as echo or refrain to comment mournfully on the brother's questions and Helen's answers. In each stanza he speaks two varying lines and she one grimly emphatic one, until her final climactic statement.

"A soul that's lost as mine is lost, ..." (st. 42)

Three of the lines, "Sister Helen", "Little Brother", and "O Mother, Mary Mother", are constant throughout, and of these the first two are trochaic dimeter with feminine endings, with "brother" a weak rhyme to "mother" (!), while the "O Mother, Mary Mother" is not really a firm iambic trimeter because of the caesurae and the tendency to place some accent on the second syllable of Mary. Likewise the "between Hell and Heaven", which also occurs forty-two times within the refrain, is uncertain in accent. In order to avoid an extra syllable at the end of the line, it is necessary to scan the last three measures as trochaic:

between Héll and Héaven

which sounds ludicrous — also this phrase is usually preceded by another stressed syllable; of the other alternatives, the first is improbable:

bétweén Hĕll ănd Héavĕn
bétweén Hĕll ănd Héavĕn
bĕtweĕn Héll ănd Héavĕn,

the last two are better, and the accent may alternate or fall somewhere between them. Otherwise the speakers use iambic, usually varied with anapests, whose absence can provide a metrically stark line:

   ... I heár him crý
That Keíth of Éwern's líke to díe.
...
'And hé and thóu, and thóu and Í,
   Líttle bróther.' (st. 13)
'A sóul that's lóst as míne is lóst .... (st. 42)

Notice the repeated syncopations as two stresses follow each other from lines one to two and four to five. Also the same off-rimes of Helen/Heaven, brother/Mother form an incremental repetition of their own, with the brevity of the short lines adding a strange jerkiness. Under the stress of deep emotions an accent or partial accent may be added, as in the ejaculations of the final stanza:

Ah! whát white thíng at the doór has cróss'd?
...
Ah! whát is thís that sighs in the frost?"

The ah!'s here have a semi-autonomous accent: "what white thing" is a good example of nearly equal stresses, which always add rough syncopation to a line rather than the smoothness one might expect; when a pattern of stress-unstress is established, any deviation seems like hopping spliced into a walk. The last line is granted an extra emphatic beat:

Lost, lost, all lost, between Hell and Heaven!

Also each stanza contains a single new rhyme, repeated in three stressed terminal syllables, creating a single emphatic, evenly echoing effect.

The images are simple, starkly presented, and repeated. Frequently occurring are the moon, wind, chill (cold, ice), and fire:

She lifts her lips and gasps on the moon." (st. 34)
The moon flies face to face with me." (st. 7)
"Her hood falls back, and the moon shines fair,.... (st. 31)
"Oh tell him I fear the frozen dew, ... (st. 12)
Ah! what is this that sighs in the frost?" (st. 42)
"Oh the wind is sad in the iron chill, ... (st. 40)
But his words are drowned in the wind's course." (st. 20)
With the loud wind's wail her sobs are wed." (st. 33)
"Fire shall forgive me as I forgive, ... (st. 27)
And the flames are winning up apace!" (st. 41)
Fire at the heart, between Hell and Heaven!) (st. 18)

Sounds also are important; there are the loud wind, the cries of the first three supplicants, the crying of Keith of Ewern, the "heavy sound" of the knell, the "woe's dumb cry" of the bride and her weeping. Keith of Ewern alone is mentioned as crying or calling five times, with the last four "cries" at three-stanza intervals.

"But he has not ceased to cry to-day, ... (st. 16)

"But he calls for ever on your name, ... (st. 18)
"Oh he says that Keith of Ewern's cry, ... (st. 21)
"He calls your name in an agony, ... (st. 24)
"Oh his son still cries, if you forgive, ... (st. 27)

The number three of course functions as a symbol itself, of magic, and perhaps even the seven-line stanza (seven is a traditional number of completion) has some numerological significance. There are three colors which occur throughout "Sister Helen"; almost everything is white/pale, black/dark, or blood/red.

Shines through the thinned wax *red* as blood!" (st. 5)
"A lady's here, by a *dark* steed brought, ...
So *darkly* clad, I saw her not." (st. 30)
"*Pale, pale* her cheeks, that in pride did *glow*, ... (st. 32) (italics mine)

And all three Keiths are recognized by a white sign, "white mane", "white plume", and "white hair". The bride alters from the "glow" of red cheeks to the paleness of fear. Gold might seem to be another color within the poem, since

> ... the moon shines fair,
> Sister Helen,
> On the Lady of Ewern's golden hair." (st. 31)

But immediately this is diluted to white:

And her moonlit hair gleams white in its flow." (st. 35)
Woe-withered gold, between Hell and Heaven!) (st. 35)

The hyphenated adjective "woe-withered" is worthy of Hopkins. The final picture left by "Sister Helen" is admirably stark — the red fire glowing in the black night, the pale faces, hair, and plumes of the visitants, the "white" soul crossing the door. More than is usual in Rossetti's poems, this one both narrates a story and yet conveys a pictorial effect.

Several of Rossetti's other familiar mannerisms are present. The bride swoons, gasps, spreads out her hands, is unable to speak from anguish, and her paleness and hair are emphasized. Her emotions are rendered more dramatic, however, by the refrains which echo her unhappiness:

What strain but death's, between Hell and Heaven?)
Her woe's dumb cry, between Hell and Heaven!)
Woe-withered gold, between Hell and Heaven!)

Rossetti typically also finds something which scintillates, shakes, or trembles within nature:

In the shaken trees the chill stars shake .... (st. 8)

a complex image. As usual persons are experienced indirectly or through certain discrete, suddenly emphasized features; Sister Helen is perceived only through her voice and the knowledge of her single murderous deed, the brother through his questioning voice. Keith of Ewern "sends a ring and a broken coin" to represent him, and the bride is described by cheeks, hair and dark clothing. "Sister Helen" is certainly no poem of detailed description; all is known by the presence of elemental forces, shapes, contrasts of color, voices, and sounds of pain. In place of description are direct interpretations of the emotions felt by the characters:

"And *lonely* her bridegroom's soul hath flown, ... (st. 39)
And *weary sad* they look by the hill."
"But he and I are *sadder* still ..., (st. 40)
       (italics mine)

Yet the action has given sufficient cause for these reactions; they seem an obvious response rather than an intrusion on the reader's judgment.

"Sister Helen" contains few overt echoes of Romantic poets and is dissimilar to anything in Tennyson, Browning, or Morris. The soul as a "white thing" crossing at the door is similar to "The Blessed Damozel", in which "souls mounting up to God / Went by her like thin flames" (st.7); both reflect legend and perhaps, as Routh points out,[28] a similar literalism in Coleridge:

The souls did from their bodies fly, –
They fled to bliss or woe!
And every soul, it passed me by,
Like the whizz of my cross-bow!
     ("The Rime", 11. 220-223)

The moon/wind/blood/pale-lady-at-night patterns might reflect long reading of Coleridge as well.

The strong colors, emphatic rhythms, and lurid scenes of "Sister Helen" also create an eccentrically humorous and self-parodying effect, incongruous but interesting.[29] Whether or not this was intended by Rossetti, he was probably at least aware of the mock-solemn qualities inherent in a horror narrative of effigy-burning; his first reference to "Sister Helen" in his letters calls it a "ghastly ballad".[30] "Sister Helen" has perhaps appropriately become a Rossettian set-piece, since it is original and direct in stanza form, imagery, and theme. To the extent that "originality" can mean the crafted use of the ballad's potentiality for combining the passionate, symbolic, incantatory, and parodic, this is one of Rossetti's most individualistic and carefully wrought poems.[31]

2. "Eden Bower" (1869): A Subhuman Temptress Revenges Herself on Man

"Eden Bower" was written in 1869, ten years before the major revisions of "Sister Helen", and its triangle love plot (good woman, evil rejected woman, man) may even have influenced his interpolations in the latter. It was one of Rossetti's favorites; writing in 1870 he comments that the four works he would like to be known by are "Eden Bower", "Jenny", "A Last Confession", and "The House of Life".[32] Interestingly he omits both "The Blessed Damozel" and "Sister Helen"; he seems to have preferred his own later poetry. "Eden Bower" is the only balladic narrative or refrain poem which he mentions in this list; he had not yet experienced the late surge of ballad-narrative composition before his death.

"Eden Bower" is that rarity, a long poem intended to be trochaic. Rossetti himself defined the rhythm in a letter:[33]

It rather troubles me that the first verse is readable in an inflexion not intended and may set the reader on a false tack of sound — i.e. he does not at once emphasize the first *it*.

I interpret this as a direction to emphasize "It":
It was Lílith the wífe of Ádam:
    (*Sing Eden Bower!*)
Nót a dróp of her blóod was húman, ...
(Alas the hour!)
Lílith stoód on the skírts of Éden
Shé was the first that thénce was dríven; .... (sts. 1, 2)

If one accepts Rossetti's insistence on a trochaic reading, this becomes easily his most syncopated rhythm. Trochees and dactyls are difficult to use consistently, and the poem's metrical effects result from syllables jumping out of and into the formalized pattern. If the trochaic structure is easily imposed, as in the third example quoted, the result is a very strong, jerked stress pronounced on the first beat, almost a dance rhythm. If it is not, both the artificial rhythm and an opposing one coexist, forming an example of what Hopkins will later call counterpoint. Since inaccurate rhythms seem feeble, both the prevailing rhythm and its opposition must be emphatic; sometimes even the pronounced eccentricity of the patterns makes them easier to hear.

Despite Rossetti's comment on scansion it is uncertain how consistently he wanted the poem read as trochaic, and where he positioned other stresses beyond the first. For example, if "Síng Éden Bówer!" begins with a trochee as marked, it lacks a syllable or caesura; if parallel with "Alás the hoúr!" it loses the emphatic quality of "Sing ...!" And for "Sing Eden" to be dactyllic requires a very conscious non-stress on "Eden". Again in a third line preceding a line which probably begins in iambic, the rhythm pulls in different directions:

"Woúldst thou knów the heárt's hope of Lílith?
    (*Sing Eden Bower!*)
Then bring thou clóse thine heád till it glisten
Alóng my breast and líp me and lísten. (st. 19)

In line three the stress would fall naturally on "bring" had an alternate expectation not been set up; the iambic foot shifts the line into iambic-anapest until the last awkwardly hanging syllable. It is possible that most of "Eden Bower"'s fourth lines are also intended to carry initial stresses, but the variable possibilities are what is noticeable. Even the first lines could be read in different ways, as Rossetti realized, causing congestion at the end:

"Wouldst thóu know thé heart's hópe of Lílith?
"Then Éve shall eát and gíve unto Ádam; ....
"I wás the faírest snáke in Éden: ....

or even

"What greát joýs had Ádam and Lílith! —

"What bríght bábes had Lilíth and Ádam!

which require only minimal inversions. The inherent uncertainty of the rhythm contrasts with its heaviness, producing a certain thudding eccentricity of effect. The quavering of the poem's rhythm is also complemented by the feminine endings of all lines including those of the refrain, a pattern as difficult to continue as the use of trochaic feet. As in "Sister Helen" only one new rime enters each stanza, but it receives two rather than three repetitions, and in the third line the names "Adam", "Eden", and "Lilith" alternate as terminal endings, unrimed but emphatic. They function in a manner similar to that of the second refrain in "Sister Helen". In fact "Eden Bower" successfully condenses several devices of the latter poem, for example, the shorter and alternating first refrain. The occasional off-rimes combine with the feminine endings to emphasize the slight flutters which end each line:

Not a drop of her blood was húman,
But she was made like a soft sweet wóman. (st. 1)
All save one I give to thy freéwill, –
The Tree of the Knowledge of Good and Evil.' (st. 22)

Much ingenuity is expended on the nearly exact double-syllabled rimes; ironically if such rimes are too perfect they will constitute the same word. Often the rhythm seems especially appropriate to the words emphasized:

All the day and the night togéther
My breath could shake his soul like a feáther. (st. 7)
Shapes that coiled in the winds and wáters,
Glittering sons and radiant daúghters. (st. 9)
Lo! with care like a shadow shaken,
He tills the hard earth whence he was táken. (st. 44)

The metrics, refrain, and sound effects of "Eden Bower" seem as consciously and tightly constructed as in any Rossetti work, and perhaps more so than in any other ballad (even its companion piece, "Troy Town", has a monotonously unchanging three-line refrain). As in "Sister Helen" the artifice can seem humorous and self-mocking, but here I think it undercuts Rossetti's intention severely and produces lugubriousness instead of horror. Perhaps Lilith is too simple-mindedly malicious to create much interest or sympathy.

Like "Sister Helen", "Eden Bower" is a narrative conversation preceded by an introduction. Lilith has been evicted from Eden by God; in two introductory stanzas she is defined and located:

Lilith stood on the skirts of Eden;.... (st. 2)

The conversation-seduction begins abruptly:

In the ear of the snake said Lilith: – ....

and the succeeding first lines of each stanza largely carry the poem's narration. Lilith wishes the snake to be her lover, that in his embrace she may be able to tempt Eve and indirectly Adam. How Lilith could actually assume the serpent's shape is never clarified, despite suggestions of the grotesque nature of snake love:

In thy sweet folds bind me and bend me,
And let me feel the shape thou shalt lend me. (st. 23)
Grip and lip my limbs as I tell thee! (st. 47)

A portion of the poem's intended horror lies in the indefinite nature of the relationships to which it alludes, a statement true of much Rossettian sensuality.

Lilith first recounts her past dominance over Adam, her eviction from Eden by God, and then anticipates her future beguilement of Eve and the banishment of Adam and Eve. She reveals near the end of the poem the extent of the revenge which she seeks:

"O bright Snake, the Death-worm of Adam! (st. 35)

Like Sister Helen, she desires not merely to punish but to kill her former lover. Like Helen she turns to strange arts to effect her will, but unlike Helen she cannot suffer damnation or supra-earthly loss, and unlike Helen she turns to an alternate, bestial lover. The final stanza embodies her last wishes:

The soul of one shall be made thy brother,
And thy tongue shall lap the blood of the other." (st. 49)

Lilith's vengefulness is unrelieved by the pathos that had characterized

Sister Helen's and Keith of Ewern's pain; there is only one reference to
Lilith's suffering:

And their hearts ache as my heart hath ached. (st. 28)

Adam and Eve are also presented too externally to reinforce sympathy,
so that neither aggressor nor victims are as appealing as their counter-
parts in "Sister Helen". With the reader's interest alienated from the
central characters, the poem becomes as much a contrived set-piece of
allegorical effects as a dramatic narrative.

As in "Sister Helen" and "The Blessed Damozel", the cosmology
of heaven and hell is rapidly defined:

With her was hell and with Eve was heaven. (st. 2)

In these other poems the complete antithesis between heaven and hell
does not reflect the reader's divided ethical and emotional evaluations;
the same internal tension occurs here. Lilith is both attractive and repellent, the proximate cause of the world's evil, yet herself unexplained:

By the earth's will, new form and feature
Made me a wife for the earth's new creature. (st. 4)

The limitations postulated in Lilith's definition at least prevent false expectations. She is sensual, able to assume many shapes, capable of love
and hate, yet essentially subhuman. Although an active agent in evil,
she has been formed by greater forces than herself and is in that respect
passive; by contrast her definition of love is to subdue:

Once again shall my love subdue thee; .... (st. 5)
And there in a net his heart was holden. (st. 6)

Unlike Rossetti's other lovers, she seeks no reunion with her former
lover either in heaven or earth, only simple revenge. The biblical cosmology places her in context; she is more limited in character than the
humans she affects, yet able to pervert their destiny and happiness.
Trivial in her motives, she is the Rossettian evil/seductive life force –
amoral sexuality – both less human and closer to abstraction than
Sister Helen.

The images of "Eden Bower" are direct and render immediately the poem's psychological content. The picture of the once serpentine temptress seducing the serpent while discussing her last lover presents both her character and a part of Adam's; the coiling serpent is the poem's central image. According to Lilith, serpents and half-serpents are beautiful and brightly colored:

Shapes that coiled in the woods and waters,
Glittering sons and radiant daughters. (st. 9)

She emphasizes her own golden hair, fair body, and red lips, later repeated ironically in the colors of the flaming sword, shed blood, and the unhappy couple's naked bodies:

All her blood as food to its fire! (st. 25)
And stretch this crowned head forth by the apple. (st. 24)
By the sword that for ever is flaming. (st. 32)

The fallen garden is one of hard earth, thorns, thistles, drought, and the absence of birds. To the elements of fire, breath, and blood has been added dust, both in external nature and in the composition of man:

'Dust he is and to dust returneth!' (st. 39)
The springs shall dry and the soil shall harden. (st. 41)

Strangely there are few other repeated images; instead emphasis is on the repetition of serpentine sounds, motions, and sensations, and on Lilith's simple but relatively accurate narration. It is she who provides much of the poem's evaluation and theological exposition:

God shall walk without pity or pardon. (st. 29)
To Eve's womb, from our sweet to-morrow,
God shall greatly multiply sorrow. (st. 46)

Here as in other Rossetti poems the personae are known only indirectly or limitedly, Adam by his cowardly words, the snake by its coiling, glistening, *et cetera*, Lilith by her hair, lips, limbs, breath, heart, and words.

"Eden Bower" suggests immediately comparison with Keats' "Lamia" and Coleridge's "Christabel"; notice that in these earlier romantic poems, however, the serpent maiden does not desire the death of others or seek revenge — Geraldine wishes to treat Christabel well and Lamia does not will the extinction of herself and Lycius. Like "The Rime of the Ancient Mariner", "Eden Bower" ostensibly expresses the theme of the temptation of archetypal man; Rossetti sexualizes the temptation, however, minimizes the Adam figure, and concerns himself with the psychology of the temptress, a female who opposes the poem's cosmological order.

3. "Jenny" (1848, mostly 1858-69): A Contemporary 'Evil Woman' Rendered Trivial and Pathetic

Whatever the repellent qualities of Sister Helen and Lilith, they are vigorous and passionate women. When in "Jenny" Rossetti transfers the pattern of destructive sexuality and the sexually free or "wronged" woman to contemporary England, he becomes noticeably more squeamish, sentimental, and indirect in treating female character. His lengthy pieties on man as the cause of sexual evil might seem to refute this:

What has man done here? How atone,
Great God, for this which man has done?   (st. 21)

    Like a toad within a stone
Seated while Time crumbles on...
Even so within the world is Lust.   (st. 25)

However Rossetti is unable to ascribe to Jenny any of the positive emotions or strength of will which he postulates for his exotically distant or extra-natural heroines, in most cases also "fallen". Jenny is a weak, trivial person, attracted solely to money, personal finery, and gaudy luxuries, at best innocent of her own deeds and oblivious to her sordid future:

Whose person or whose purse may be
The lodestar of your reverie?   (11. 20, **21**)

The narrator solemnly disserts on her prospects, omitting to reflect that she may have thought of these things herself.

    So nought save foolish foulness may
Watch with hard eyes the sure decay.   (st. 23)

And most remarkably, though he compares her lengthily with Cousin Nell, he neglects the obvious contrast between his own future fate and hers, and the relative price each will pay for knowledge of the demimonde.

Baum prints an early manuscript of "Jenny",[34] which is chiefly concerned with the narrator's distress at his own intense response to Jenny; he comments lengthily on how she represents Sensuality, a force that as a philosophical person he should be able to overcome. The moralizations concerning Jenny's future, his meditation in her room, her sleeping, and his leaving gold, the comparisons between Jenny and Cousin Nell, and his own apologies and withdrawal are all absent from the early version. The slight interest which he shows in her as a person is friendly and not especially pitying. Instead he emphasizes his own problem, her seductiveness:

> Peril of mine, trouble of mine,
> Thine arms are bare and thy shoulders shine,
> And through the kerchief and through the vest
> Strikes the white of each breathing breast,
> And the down is warm on thy velvet cheek,
> And the thigh from thy rich side slopes oblique,
> And thy lips are full, and thy brows are fair,
> And the gold makes a daylight in thine hair,
> And under the lids thine eyes' wild glee
> Looketh kindly and laughs to me,
> And the air swoons around and over thee.

Again the swooning response at the approach of sexuality. Thus in its original 1848 form "Jenny" was very similar to "The Card Dealer" written a year later. The speaker sees an "evil woman" and comments on the attractiveness of the sight.

Rossetti's final "Jenny", by contrast, distances the young man greatly from the supposed object of his meditations, and makes her sins rather than his the focus of emphasis. No internal ironies check the narrator's lugubrious manner, while Jenny is carefully altered to lessen the sense of her seductiveness, and her "prettiness" is emphasized to condescension. Her behavior is defended only at the expense of denigrating totally her character and will; she is forgivable because too feeble and inconsequential to have done much else.

It has been pointed out that Rossetti himself is not the persona of the narrator; nonetheless I feel some of the latter's moral anemia was not unrelated to his creator's discomfort at his closest approach to modernity and realism ("A Last Confession" dealt with crime in Italy, a more remote subject). In writing his aunt concerning the published version, Rossetti states that he considers the poem a moral one and recounts his mother's approval, but does not indicate that the narrator's reflections are not to be accepted. Or again, he writes Allingham for an opinion concerning "Jenny", which he considers "the most serious thing I have written", wanting to know "whether there is any objection you see in the subject, or any side of the subject left untouched which ought to be included?"[35] Such comments indicate that Rossetti considered the narrator's reflections worthy projections of at least some of his own opinions on the matter.

Although Rossetti differed from contemporary poets in his somewhat more overt discussions of a self-conscious and intelligent sexuality, his assumptions were not especially deviant. For all his pieties concerning fallen women, the ironies of causation, and so forth, it does not occur to him that acts which the prostitute commits may be morally neutral, or the result of economic coercion rather than choice.[36] He argues for pity, perhaps, or interest in the prostitute's condition, but never for unjudging neutrality or practical aid.

Despite individual compromises, exceptions, and happy accidents, the Victorian code underlined deeply for every middle-class male the notion of original sin. It meant that every sexual act he committed was the degradation of another human being (herself incapable of feeling similar impulses). How horrible if that person were also a beloved, idealized, and respected wife, if one's instinctive affections were of necessity selfish and destructive. This, as well as economic motivations, encouraged the Victorian tolerance of and obsession with prostitution. The consequences of a sexist puritanism appear throughout Victorian literature in endless presentations of seduction, the fallen woman, the debates and redebates over how much evil was evil, how much forgiveness was possible, how much dignity should be granted the morally damaged, who was victimized and who victimizer. Reformers tried to assert that social circumstance and bad training rather than individual error was a source of crime, but virtually all left publically unquestioned the essential Victorian belief that the sexual object was in some way subhuman.

Rossetti's treatment of prostitution expresses these attitudes to an unusual degree. Since he was atypically undomestic and bohemian in contexts he associated with sexuality, he could not retreat into sublimation or the descriptions of domestic attachment which other Victorian poets emphasized. While Tennyson proclaimed feminine sweetness and goodness, Patmore eulogized the home, and the Brownings glorified the selfless-mother icon, Rossetti's artistic interest lay closer to the great Victorian taboos. It is perhaps the more ironic therefore that he was unable to avoid emphasizing many of the presuppositions of his period concerning an economically as well as 'morally' degraded class of persons.

4. Summary on Sexual Revenge Ballads and "Jenny": Fate Expressed Through Sexual Destructiveness and Human Evil

In "Jenny", as in the revenge ballads, human sexuality and attendant jealousy destroy life. Yet the narrator of "Jenny" avoids expressing his own emotional responses directly and severely condescends to those of Jenny. Ironically, in his exotic, supernatural ballads Rossetti represents more clearly his age's preoccupation with sublimation, its conception of women as passive yet secretly demanding.

Rossetti's evil or partially evil heroines are attractive not so much because they incarnate evil passion but because they are assumed to be at least to some degree active agents in their fate. However revengeful Sister Helen may be, she is presented as suffering a long mental trial. She is one of Rossetti's heroines who is simultaneously active and passive, the inflicting force and the afflicted. Lilith is more vicious, less comprehensible, but also vigorous, strikingly colorful, passionate, and peripheral to human moral judgments.

Rossetti's sexual vengeance ballads show great improvement over former works in dramatic concentration, starkness of imagery, and contrived verbal effects. For the revenge ballads he creates his idiosyncratic refrains, and their fusion of narrative and psychological allegory seems as congenial to Rossetti's temperament as any poetic form which he attempted. They parallel the increasingly dramatic, condensed, and consciously rhetorical later sonnets, and their virtues of concentration, symbolic vividness, diminished prudery, and dramatic impartiality were in lessened form transferable to Rossetti's later lengthy narratives.

C. FINAL BALLADS: DARKENED ROMANTICISM

In his last narratives Rossetti experienced a partial return to the early extended ballad, creating his most complex poems and some of the finest examples of a very strange genre, the Victorian tragic narrative ballad. His later narratives reveal increased concentration of form, less emphasis on romantic love and more on death and revenge. What had always been a dark view of the world alters its focus and deepens; the sexual impulse still leads to sin and death, although its victims may be good people, and the external world can only neglect and crucify its noble men. As Rossetti ages, he becomes less eager to condemn human sexual behavior, less preoccupied with the inequities of artistic fame, but more pessimistic concerning the eventual results of sexuality and artistic endeavor.

1. *"Rose Mary" (1871, 1879): Female Sexual Guilt, Death, and Redemption*

"Rose Mary" was begun in 1871, during the spurt of poetic energy which preceded and directly followed Rossetti's publication of the *Poems* (1870). It was completed in 1879, during the period in which Rossetti was writing "The White Ship" (1878-80) and two years before he wrote "The King's Tragedy" (1881). It is Rossetti's most elaborate ballad and romantic narrative, and his longest poem aside from "The House of Life" and "The Bride's Prelude". Also it is one of his most ornately exotic, consisting of a trilogy of situations each surrounding a reflecting image, combining narration, mystery-symbology, and Coleridgean rhythms into an artfully dissonant music.

"Rose Mary" is an intermediary between Coleridge's mystery/sorcery poems and the conscious nightmare imagery of Decadent poetry, as exemplified in Wilde or James Thompson, or even later in Yeats' Byzantium.[37] Since Rossetti has been often described as a symbolist and precursor of end-of-century mannerisms, it is surprising that "Rose Mary" has not received more emphasis than Rossetti's earlier poems, which are frequently less symbolic and more transparent. Only one article, Clyde Hyder's "Rossetti's 'Rose Mary': A Study in the Occult", recounts beryl lore and finds parallels between "Rose Mary" and Dante, "The Rime of the Ancient Mariner", and Tennyson's "The Kraken".[38]

"Rose Mary" is superior to Rossetti's earlier romantic narrative "The Bride's Prelude", and his simple ballad "The Staff and Scrip"; it combines ballad directness with the elaborate plotting and imagery of romantic narrative. Like "The Bride's Prelude" it begins near the end of the action and is presented in tableau; also like "The Bride's Prelude" it contains the gradual uncovering of past treachery and error, and is the unhappy story of a "sinning" woman and faithless lover narrated in a domestic context — here to Rose Mary's mother. Rossetti has managed several improvements since "The Bride's Prelude", however; he conveys weariness and pain without producing those same effects in the reader:

> Rose Mary sank with a broken moan,
> And lay in the chair and slept alone,
> > Weary, lifeless, heavy as lead:
> > Long it was ere she raised her head
> > And rose up all discomforted. (st. 52)

She turns more swiftly to action than Aloÿse; the narrative is climaxed by her resolute breaking of the beryl stone, knowing that she and the spirits will be destroyed. Her emotions shift also from fear to hope to fear throughout the poem, creating suspense; "The Bride's Prelude" has all the suspense of a clock winding down, from slow predictability to slower predictability.

The plot is constructed so that the revelations seem both more elaborate and more direct; instead of a single tableau with linear narration, "Rose Mary" is a series of three tableaux, each containing its own discovery. In the first portion Rose Mary looks in the beryl stone and is able to discern images; however her reading is false because, as she conceals from her mother, she is not a "maiden pure" (st. 56) and is therefore ineligible to read the glass. In the second portion the mother reveals to Rose Mary that she knows of her concealment, then the way in which she has learned — through Sir James of Heronhaye's death; later in examining the corpse the mother learns that Sir James has died intending elopement with a woman other than her daughter, and predicts that her daughter's heart will be broken. In the third portion Rose Mary confronts the deluding beryl; she is innocent of her lover's defection and expects to meet him in death, but instead a clear voice pronounces that she is cleansed of his memory and will be led to heaven, "where the hearts of stedfast lovers are". The first and third portions center around the beryl, the first presenting the beryl's interior and the third its elaborate occult throne and symbolic accompaniments; in some sense the first portion presents a positive vision of the beryl and the third a negative vision. The center tableau is interesting; in the second part the mother examines the corpse, but at its beginning she and the daughter are shown shaking together in a locked embrace:

> Closely locked, they clung without speech,
> And the mirrored souls shook each to each,

> As the cloud-moon and the water-moon
> Shake face to face when the dim stars swoon
> In stormy bowers of the night's mid-noon.
>
> They swayed together, shuddering sore,
> Till the mother's heart could bear no more.
> 'Twas death to feel her own breast shake
> Even to the very throb and ache
> Of the burdened heart she still must break.
>
> (II: sts. 12, 13)

They are alter-egos, even more than Aloÿse and Amelotte, yet the expression of this relationship is more concentrated, less drawn out than the slow complementary hand and body motions of the sisters. Rossetti likes shaking, shuddering, fluttering words to express the tremulous fragility of psychological states; as in the diction of "The House of Life", they emphasize life as a subtle emanation, not a measurable substance:

> And the souls mounting up to God
>   Went by her like thin flames ....
> From the fixed place of Heaven she saw
>   Time like a pulse shake fierce
> Through all the worlds.
>
> ("The Blessed Damozel", sts. 7, 9)

Perhaps this trait is related to his preference for words with lightly or indefinitely stressed extra syllables; they seem to waver and flutter.

The beryl stone is the ultimate form of Rossetti's preoccupation with reflective images. In "The Bride's Prelude" the reflecting jewels and mirror are fortuitous except for their addition to the sense of circularly oppressive heat and narcissism; here the beryl reflects the theme and action and is therefore less extraneous and decorative. Attending the beryl are many incidental reflecting and sphere images, mirroring natural elements and associating the beryl not only with particular events but with a cosmogony:

> The altar-cell was a dome low-lit,
> And a veil hung in the midst of it:
> At the pole-points of its circling girth
> Four symbols stood of the world's first birth, –
> Air and water and fire and earth.
>
> (III: st. 15)

Although both this and "The Bride's Prelude" attempt directness in exclamation and narrative, in "Rose Mary" Rossetti manages simultaneously an additional artifice and obliqueness. In Part II, when Rose Mary's mother wants to tell her daughter that she has learned of her deception, she begins:

"Pale Rose Mary, what shall be done
With a rose that Mary weeps upon?" ....
"Sad Rose Mary, what shall be done
With a cankered flower beneath the sun?" ....
"Lost Rose Mary, what shall be done
With a heart that is but a broken one?"
   (II: sts. 1-3)

The use of incremental repetition seems simplistic, yet this is scarcely a transcription of what might actually have been said; rather it is an evocation of the emotions appropriate to the situation. As in "The Bride's Prelude", Rossetti permits his personae to interpret their own story, but here the interpretation is less heavy-handed and repetitious. The evil of Rose Mary's action is assumed automatically by both characters but not dwelt upon.

This shift in manner is related to another thematic circumstance, ambiguity in the moral nature of the beryl stone and Rose Mary's actions. At first the beryl is presented as the associate of purity and orthodoxy; with apparent approval Rose Mary's mother relates its history:

A thousand years it lay in the sea
With a treasure wrecked from Thessaly;
Deep it lay 'mid the coiled sea-wrack,
But the ocean-spirits found the track:
A soul was lost to bring it back.

The lady upheld the wondrous thing: –
"Ill fare" (she said) "with a fiend's-fairing:
But Moslem blood poured forth like wine
Can hallow Hell, 'neath the Sacred Sign;
And my lord brought this from Palestine.

"Spirits who fear the Blessed Rood
Drove forth the accursed multitude
That heathen worship housed herein, –
Never again such home to win,
Save only by a Christian's sin.
   (I: sts. 10-12)

The purity of the stone has been purchased with the death of wicked men; presumably the stone advocated goodness and can only again be purged by the death of sinners. In their eccentric interludes, the "fire-spirits of dread-desire" reveal that by Rose Mary's secret sin they have entered the stone, "'Gainst whom all powers that strive with ours are sterile". The death of Rose Mary, the source of sin, should purge the stone; instead she feels compelled to destroy the stone in an act of expiation. She herself now has the moral virtue to destroy evil (Why? are not "all powers that strive with ours ... sterile"?), while the stone's power of foretelling has become implicated with evil:

"O ye, three times accurst," she said,
"By whom this stone is tenanted!
Lo! here ye came by a strong sin's might;
Yet a sinner's hand that's weak to smite
Shall send you hence ere the day be night.

"This hour a clear voice bade me know
My hand shall work your overthrow: ....

"And he Thy heavenly minister
Who swayed erewhile this spell-bound sphere, – ....

    (III: st. 31-33)

The beryl is an image of Rose Mary, a beautiful object destroyed by sin, yet since Rose Mary is also the agent of destruction she is granted a final apotheosis. Unlike Aloÿse she possesses an active moral self which can destroy another portion of herself of which she disapproves. Yet why the "fire-spirits of dread desire" should be vanquished by the splitting of the stone is unclear; presumably they had a prior independent existence before entering it. It is also obscure why the stone shouldn't be commended for punishing Rose Mary according to the laws of its nature. The entire idea of sin is either nullified or transformed into suggestions of mystery and fate.

Something of the metaphysic of "Sister Helen" remains here, with the faithless lover burning in hell (though Helen also burned, and she was faithful in her perverted manner):

For under all deeps, all heights above, –
So wide the gulf in the midst thereof, –
Are Hell of Treason and Heaven of Love.

    (III: st. 49)

This is the morality of love and of "The Blessed Damozel" – they who are faithful to love are redeemed – and it conveys more conviction than

Rossetti's more orthodox pieties. It is possible to extract from "The Bride's Prelude" explicit disapproval of Urscelyn's infidelity, but Aloÿse condemns herself as well, so the 'moral' is equivocal and rather banal. Rossetti is at his best when projecting his sense of religion into completely artificial, amoral dichotomies, not describing characters who conform to religious precepts. The blessed damozel is not blessed because she is religious in act but because she is pure in love; to the extent that Rose Mary can also be so described, she embodies Rossetti's ideal of the singlemindedly passionate person (almost invariably female) who will die for love. Rose Mary's story, like Aloÿse's, could be read as a gloss on the theme "sin brings punishment", but since her sin is merely stated rather than elaborated, it becomes less a Victorian disgrace than a mysterious psychological fact with which she must reckon.

There is direct paradox in Rossetti's interpenetration of piety and occultism throughout the poem:

Never again such home to win,
Save only by a Christian's sin.

"All last night at an altar fair
I burnt strange fires and strove with prayer;
Till the flame paled to the red sunrise,
All rites I then did solemnize;
And the spell lacks nothing but your eyes."

      (I: sts. 12-13)

The altar stood from its curved recess
In a coiling serpent's life-likeness:
Even such a serpent evermore
Lies deep asleep at the world's dark core
Till the last Voice shake the sea and shore.

      (III: st. 19)

Both Christianity and sorcery are orthodoxies, religious and anti-religious, and they seem interchangeable here. In "Rose Mary" the sense of mundane reality is lessened by the presence of both world and anti-world; all is mystery, sacred and profane. The identification of the traditional extremes of religion and sorcery divorces the poem's imagery and plot from expected standards of judgment, and responses become personal, arbitrary, and preordained.

"Behold the end of the heavy doom.
O come, – for thy bitter love's sake blest; ....

      (III: st. 47)

The combination of mystery and religion carries conviction, but one is not quite sure of what — the deep, the unfathomable, sudden shocks of "good" and "evil". States of mind and body, such as the trance and swoon, are used not only to convey emotion but to express a relationship to strange cosmic forces:

A swoon that breaks is the whelming wave
When help comes late but still can save.
With all blind throes is the instant rife, —
Hurtling clangour and clouds at strife, —
The breath of death, but the kiss of life....

From the drained heart's fount there rose no cry,
There sprang no tears, for the source was dry.
Held in the hand of some heavy law,
Her eyes she might not once withdraw,
Nor shrink away from the thing she saw.

Even as she gazed, through all her blood
The flame was quenched in a coming flood:
Out of the depth of the hollow gloom
On her soul's bare sands she felt it boom, —
The measured tide of a sea of doom.

      (III: sts. 1, 25-26)

The elemental imagery makes it possible for Rose Mary's trances to convey a sense of struggle, revelation, and motion, and the poem has the sincerity of an artifice which at least clearly defines its referents, however exotic or remote. Rossetti has projected the staid Victorian morality of domestic sexual sin onto an unscrutable theurgy in which good and evil reflect arbitrary fate, not human social categories.

One of the most important characteristics of "Rose Mary" is its variety of rhythm. While Rossetti's early works, "Dante at Verona", "The Bride's Prelude", and "The Blessed Damozel", were regular metrically, here all ten initial stanzas contain irregularities — a considerable departure from Rossetti's early practice.[39] The alterations are generally in the addition of anapests and an initial trochee or dactyl; the increased syncopation and speed combined with heavy stresses increases the sense of emotion and foreboding. "The Bride's Prelude" rimes the last three lines of a five line stanza; in "Rose Mary" the first two also rime, binding the lines more closely together and providing additional locations for emphasis. This increased stress and binding alters the ratio of sound to sense towards the former; of course this also reinforces the poem's theme of inexplicable and elemental mystery:

Round the Béryl's sphére she sáw them páss
And mock her eyes from the fated glass:
One by one in a fiery train
The dead hours seemed to wax and wane,
And burned till all was known again.

    (III: st. 24)

The irregularities are in the first lines in which the spirits move past, presumably in jerking rhythms; although it is possible to argue for direct correlations between the significance and rhythm of particular lines, it is safer merely to recognize a more general appropriateness of rhythm to matter than in previous works.

a. *"Rose Mary" and Coleridge's Mystery Poems*

Another quality of "Rose Mary"'s rhythms is their striking resemblance to those of Coleridge's "Christabel", also a poem of varied meter within four-stress lines. As Ada Shell explains in a carefully worked article,[40] its rhythms are modulated to create subtle analogies with the verbal content. Hyder cites two small parallels between "The Rime of the Ancient Mariner" and "Rose Mary":

> As in "The Ancient Mariner", in which the sailors' look of hate remained after their death ("the curse in a dead man's eye"), hatred of his slayer is seen in the eyes of Sir James after his death; and just as the Ancient Mariner was for a time unable to pray and unable to withdraw his gaze from the dead sailors,
>
> > From the drained heart's font there rose no cry.
> > There sprang no tears, for the source was dry.
> > Held in the hand of some heavy law,
> > Her eyes she might not once withdraw,
> > Nor shrink away from the thing she saw.[41]
> >
> >   (III: st. 25)

There are other possible Coleridgean echoes:

Even as she spoke, they two were 'ware
Of music-notes that fell through the air;
A chiming shower of strange device,
Drop echoing drop, once, twice, and thrice,
As rain may fall in Paradise.

    (I: st. 16)

Around, around, flew each sweet sound,
Then darted to the Sun;

Slowly the sounds came back again,
Now mixed, now one by one.
> ("The Ancient Mariner", 11. 354-59)

Sometimes a-dropping from the sky
I heard the sky-lark sing ....

It was a miracle of rare device ....
And drunk the milk of Paradise.
> ("Kubla Khan", 11. 34, 54)

And as night through which no moon may dart
Lies on a pool in the woods apart,
So lay the swoon on the weary heart.
> (II: st. 25)

For the sea and the sky and the sea and the sky
Lay like a load on the weary eye,
And the dead were at my feet.
> ("The Rime of the Ancient Mariner", 11. 250-52)

The closest resemblance is to "Christabel", however, not only in meter but in narrative and theme. Each is the story of a young and good woman who experiences evil associated with sexuality and separation from a lover. Each heroine endures trances waking and sleeping, encounters snake figures, has (had) a pious mother, and exists in a medieval ambience which includes elaborate castles with chambers, stairways and priests who enter or are mentioned briefly. In both poems wildness of emotion is stressed:

"Christabel":
And wildly glittered here and there (1. 64)
My mother made it of wild-flowers (1. 193)
And slowly rolled her eyes around (1. 246)
Whereat the knight turned wildly round (1. 460)
He spake: his eye in lightning rolls! (1. 444)
She rolled her large bright eyes divine
Wildly on Sir Leoline (11. 595, 596)
His cheeks they quivered, his eyes were wild (1. 641)
Why is thy cheek so wan and wild (1. 621)
He rolled his eyes with stern regard (1. 648)
At each wild word to feel within (1. 691)
"Rose Mary":
Then wildly at length the pent tears came; ....
> (II: st. 11)

And wildly kissed and called on her; ....
        (II: st. 26)

Giddiness, dizziness, shuddering, and fluttering are common states and sensations in "Christabel"; compare the shaking, shuddering, and swooning of "Rose Mary". Ornate interiors are usually associated with Keats, but "Christabel" contains some elaborate ones which are vaguely analogous to those in "Rose Mary":

"Christabel":
The rushes of the chamber floor (1. 173)
"Rose Mary":
As the lady crossed the rush-strewn floor, ...
        (II: st. 31)
"Christabel":
But they without its light can see
The chamber carved so curiously,
Carved with figures strange and sweet,
All made out of the carver's brain,
For a lady's chamber meet:
The lamp with twofold silver chain
Is fastened to an angel's feet.
The silver lamp burns dead and dim;... (11. 177-184)

Rose Mary, like Christabel, climbs a staircase — in fact, the secret staircase occupies portions of six stanzas (II: sts. 26, 59; III: sts. 10-13) — until she reaches a chamber with carved images, although the figures in "Rose Mary" are "strange" but not sweet.

It seemed in sooth that her gaze alone
Had turned the carven shapes to stone.
        (III: st. 28)

    More striking is the centrality of the snake image to both poems; it is continually present throughout "Christabel". In "Rose Mary" her mother is the first to perceive the nature of the opponent, appearing in Jocelyn's "long bright tress of golden hair". The gold tress of hair, one of Rossetti's favorite images of female beauty, is similarly associated with serpentine evil in "Eden Bower".

Even as she looked, she saw again
That dark-haired face in its swoon of pain:

> It seemed a snake with a golden sheath
> Crept near, as a slow flame flickereth,
> And stung her daughter's heart to death.
>
> She loosed the tress, but her hand did shake
> As though indeed she had touched a snake; ....
>   (II: sts. 49-50)

The vision of the snake next comes to Rose Mary:

> The altar stood from its curved recess
> In a coiling serpent's life-likeness:
> Even such a serpent evermore
> Lies deep asleep at the world's dark core
> Till the last Voice shake the sea and shore.
>   (III: st. 19)

"Christabel" and "Rose Mary" are both tales of two women (notice that men are extraneous, evil, or treacherous), with one acting as explicator or foil to the other. Both poems not only vary greatly an essential tetrameter pattern but occasionally introduce a completely alien, more anapestic stanza. In the chief example of this in "Christabel", Geraldine pronounces her spell in a violent departure from previous rhythms:

> 'In the touch of this bosom there worketh a spell,
> Which is lord of thy utterance, Christabel!
> Thou knowest to-night, and will know tomorrow,
> This mark of my shame, this seal of my sorrow;
>   But vainly thou warrest,
>   For this is alone in
>   Thy power to declare
>   That in the dim forest
>   Thou heards't a low moaning,
> And found'st a bright lady, surpassingly fair;
> And did'st bring her home with thee in love and in charity,
> To shield her and shelter her from the damp air. (11. 267-278)

Rossetti's beryl songs, introduced systematically at the end of each section, are also incantations of evil spirits.[42] They form a perhaps intended trinity of evil; when combined with the other stanzas they bring the poem to a total of one hundred and sixty nine stanzas (thirteen times thirteen), the number of ill-fate times itself. The poems have been much criticized; they have the weird interest of the unique, revealing that among the few words riming with "beryl" are "sterile", "imperil", and "apparel". They also provide an interesting miniature catalogue of slant and internal rimes:

> *We cry, – O desolate daughter!*
> *Thou and thy mother share newer shame with each other*
> *Than last night's slaughter.*
> *Awake and tremble, for our curses assemble!*
>
> *(Beryl-Song II)*

and render indirect testimony to the skill of Hopkins in using similar odic rhythms and massed internal rimes to much better effect.

It is possible to see many of these qualities, of course, in "The Rime of the Ancient Mariner" – the varied rhythms and syncopation, the serpent, the priest, the evil woman – and both Coleridgean poems contain descriptions of frenzy, moon imagery associated with madness, trances, and exotic desolation. Coleridge's description of Geraldine beneath the tree suggests the women of both Morris and Rossetti:

There she sees a damsel bright
Drest in a silken robe of white,
That shadowy in the moonlight shone:
The neck that made that white robe wan,
Her stately neck, and arms were bare;
Her blue-veined feet unsandal'd were,
And wildly glittered here and there
The gems entangled in her hair.
I guess, 'twas frightful there to see
A lady so richly clad as she –
Beautiful exceedingly!

Mary mother, save me now!
Said Christabel, And who art thou? (11. 58-70)

The emphasis on the lady's neck, strange manner, hair, arms, gems, and paleness, and the use of religious interjections, could all be Rossettian or Morrisean. The last three lines of the first stanza are echoed in the emotions and rhythm of "Praise of My Lady", with the "blue-veined" quality transferred from feet to wrist. Morris' persona responds with faintness to the lady's appearance, while Coleridge also describes her as "frightful" and the gems as glittering "wildly". In Morris the terrifying and negative qualities of the woman-figure have departed, while in Rossetti they are partially retained.

b. *Language in "Rose Mary"*

Although the imagery and diction of "Rose Mary" display more variety than that of Rossetti's earlier narratives and ballads, the categories have all appeared before. There are archaisms, hyphenated adjectives, and -eth endings. Although some of the descriptions may remotely suggest Keats in concern with jewels, nature, and costume, the direct echoes which occurred in "The Bride's Prelude" are absent. Again as in "The House of Life" there are few colors, aside from white, red, and the metallic colors gold and silver, but there are gems and stones; the crystal, the central image, is both pale and clouded, an association Rossetti liked. One and three are much repeated numbers, linked with religious and mystical references which proliferate – "Sacred Sign", "Palestine", "Altar", "spell-bound", "doom", "curse", "ransoming", "blessed", "Hell", "Heaven", "paradise", "talisman", "Blessed Mary", and so forth. Typically Rossetti is concerned with architectural descriptions of interiors, altars, and niches. He frequently mentions music, and he invokes life, death, and love as direct abstractions, as in "The House of Life". Often he speaks of emotions through their associated emanations – sighs, tears, crying, laughter – and usually describes persons indirectly, mentioning parts of the body or motions which reveal passions but seem detached. Rose Mary herself is merely described as "pale", "fair", "tall", grey-eyed and dark-haired, but Rossetti conveys her actions and those of others in terms of blood, hearts, eyes, the ear, tongue, hands, breath, gaze, lips, steps, bended knee, arms, forehead, brow, and neck. Almost everything is metonymized, and the metonymy involves agencies of perception or emotion. In Rossetti's poetry "blood" and "heart" are not physiological but passional characteristics; in general his descriptive diction has more psychological than physical reference.

There are many flower and garden references, appropriately for a poem about a woman named Rose Mary, yet these are generalized and used more for incantation than description:

But rent rose-flower and rosemary."
    (III: st. 51)

Gardens and flowers are conventional and unelaborated; also these natural forms are rapidly associated with non-organic elements – air, wind, water, moon, sun, and stars:

"Mary mine that art Mary's Rose,
Come in to me from the garden-close.
The sun sinks fast with the rising dew,
And we marked not how the faint moon grew;
But the hidden stars are calling you.

    (I: st. 1)

"Mother, let it fall from the tree,
And never walk where the strewn leaves be
Till winds have passed and the path is free."
"Sad Rose Mary, what shall be done
With a cankered flower beneath the sun?"
"Mother, let it wait for the night;
But sure its shame shall be out of sight
Ere the moon pale or the east grow light."

    (II: sts. 1, 2)

Except for flowers and generic references to fruits and trees, there is virtually no mention of things that grow. References to water are especially frequent – fountains, drops, rain, sea, tide, flood, snows, dew. The earth and dust become almost Heraclitean first properties –

Four symbols stood of the world's first birth, –
Air and water and fire and earth.

    (III: st. 15)

As in all Rossetti's poetry, there are continual references to fire, heat, flame, and warmth, many references to night and dark, few to cold. Nature does not seem to have many isolated qualities that receive detailed description; instead everything is reduced quickly to more generalized qualities and forces.

    A list of Rossettian words for natural objects reveals how large and indefinite are the subjects they categorize – "beast", "earth", "fountain", "tree", "flood", "sands", "cloud", "rain", "brine", "air", "whirlwinds", "tide", "sea", "meteor", "wings", "stone", "shore". He often uses words of distance or separation – "deep", "high", "depth", "deeps", "heights", "poles" – descriptions both intensifying and attenuating. Many words describe the cloudy, murky, or unclear; the stone is "stirred and strewn" with "shuddering light", a "cloud-nest", "freaked", and "rainbow-hued through a misty pall", while hours "whirr" by Rose Mary in a "swarm". Shadowing and blurring result from Rossetti's desire to present objects in generalized terms, reduced to "essential" qualities. He suggests remoteness from the measurable and physical in images of non-color, non-size, and non-shape — clouds, mist, breath, sighs, shadows, secrets. Throughout "Rose Mary" Rossetti predetermines the reader's response through evaluative words, limiting the data with which he can check their accuracy. In the last six stanzas alone are the following evaluations or abstractions — "soft", "sweet", "gentle", "gracious", "bitter", "sweet", "sore", "glory", "Treason", "love", "death", "Love", "true", "blessed", "sweet", "steadfast", "poor".

In "Rose Mary" Rossetti transforms the passive verbs and manner of "The Bride's Prelude" and other early narratives. The verbs become direct, pointed, and dramatic:

the poles throb	(III: st. 22)
They stung her heart	(III: st. 23)
And mock her eyes	(III: st. 24)
the blade flashed high	(III: st. 38),

although many intransitive verbs and indirect expressions remain — not "it boomed", but "she felt it boom", not "she beheld" but "her hate beheld".

More than Rossetti's earlier narratives, "Rose Mary"'s language and imagery suggest "The House of Life". Since "Rose Mary" is the only long romantic ballad whose first draft was composed during the 1869-1873 period when most of "The House of Life" was written, some overlapping of mannerisms is predictable. Both long poems express perceptions of love, mystery, and fate; both treat human emotions indirectly, emphasizing non-living objects, gems, metals, armor, and Heraclitean forces, and use nature in an emblematic, unparticularized manner. The dark spirits peopling the stone resemble the shadowy negative presences that increasingly hover as the sonnet-sequence reaches its close.

c. *Rose Mary's Mystic Vision of Spirits*

"Rose Mary" differs from earlier poems in its complexly interrelated symbology of mysteries, ordering themes which otherwise might seem vague and emotive. The swirling-together of objects reduced nearly to abstractions produces mystical impressions, redeemed from imprecision only by the careful use of a mystic symbology. For example, the rose combines associations of nature, religion, and passion; the sword those of antiquity, time, metallic, flashing qualities, and pain; the crystal, associations of water, clouds, air, light, moon-and-sun shapes, mysticism, gems, reflections, and purity. The snake associates with the mythology of both sorcery and orthodox religion; the architectural projections suggest both the unpleasant tomb and attractive ritual. Virtually all these symbols gather into one description, that of the altar which Rose Mary approaches to confront the beryl stone and to destroy and be destroyed by its evil:

The altar-cell was a dome low-lit,
And a veil hung in the midst of it:
At the pole-points of its circling girth
Four symbols stood of the world's first birth, –
Air and water and fire and earth.

To the north, a fountain glittered free;
To the south, there glowed a red fruit-tree;
To the east, a lamp flamed high and fair;
To the west, a crystal casket rare
Held fast a cloud of the fields of air.

The painted walls were a mystic show
Of time's ebb-tide and overflow;
His hoards long-locked and conquering key,
His service-fires that in heaven be,
And earth-wheels whirled perpetually.
.....
The altar stood from its curved recess
In a coiling serpent's life-likeness:
Even such a serpent evermore
Lies deep asleep at the world's dark core
Till the last Voice shake the sea and shore.

From the altar-cloth a book rose spread
And tapers burned at the altar-head;
And there in the altar-midst alone,
'Twixt wings of a sculptured beast unknown.
Rose Mary saw the Beryl-stone.

   (III: 15-17, 19-20)

  The entire passage is somewhat Biblical, and in turn the Biblical associations reinforce other patterns of imagery. The Biblical passage most similar to "Rose Mary"'s altar passage is Ezekiel 1:

4 And I looked, and, behold a whirlwind came out of the north, a great cloud, and a fire infolding itself, and a brightness was about it, and out of the midst thereof is the colour of amber, out of the midst of the fire.

5 Also out of the midst thereof came the likeness of four living creatures. And this was their appearance; they had the likeness of a man.

13 As for the likeness of the living creatures, their appearance was like burning

coals of fire, and like the appearance of lamps it went up and down among the living creatures; and the fire was bright, and out of the fire went forth lightning.

16   The appearance of the wheels and their work was like unto the colour of a beryl: and they four had one likeness: and their appearance and work was as a wheel in the midst of a wheel.

22   And the likeness of the firmament upon the heads of the living creature was as the colour of the terrible crystal, stretched forth over their heads above.

The fire-spirits, four divisions, lamp-like appearance, whirring wheels, use of circles and fires, and single converging image are all present — also descriptions employing indefinite colors and forms. The descriptions of Solomon's temple in II Chronicles mention winged cherubim above the altar, a veil in front, twelve oxen holding a brazen sea, and emphasize the four points of the temple. One passage even uses the "toward the north .... toward the west, toward the south ... toward the south ... toward the east" format. Rossetti probably did not use such descriptions directly, but he may have been influenced by the Biblical tendency to describe the four sides of everything.

Other Biblical visions are similar; in Revelations the final vision of the throne of God includes a river "pure as crystal" and a tree of life bearing fruit; earlier "a sea of glass like unto crystal" appears, again associated with winged beasts. Although direct reference to fountains is absent from these crystal sea visions, rivers appear to be generally associated with temples and last things, and fountain imagery occurs directly before the vision of Jerusalem in the Apocalypse: "I will give to him that is athirst of the fountain of the water of life freely" (21: 6). Unpleasant visions also occur; one given to Ezekiel includes the examination of an interior alcove with wall paintings:

8: 9-11   And he said unto me, Go in, and behold the wicked abominations that they do here. So I went in and saw; and behold every form of creeping things, and abominable beasts, and all the idols of the house of Israel, portrayed upon the wall round about .... and a thick cloud of incense went up.

Clearly a tradition of descriptions of the ineffable exists, with several prophets finding images for their visitations in the configurations of tabernacle and temple.[43] Imagery of wheels, veils, gems, garden, fruit-tree, crystal, glass, fires, beasts, and the summation of time all form a related complex which would have rested in the consciousness of Rossetti's readers; the seemingly non-descriptive nature of Rossetti's language might have been exactly what they would most associate with these symbols. Other Rossettian images — of clouds, metals, serpents —

seem linked with such scenes, since they too occur in contiguous Biblical passages. Rossetti's use of this tradition of specific indefiniteness adds coherence to the poem's climactic passage as well as fusing what in his other poems are often less clearly related images; here all converge in the beryl vision of fate.

Furthermore Rossetti's usage of Biblical referents includes a definite shift towards the sinister, so that the beryl scene conveys some of the jarring effect of parody, simultaneously suggesting religion and black magic. Whether or not Rossetti associated the painted-walls-and-beasts passage with the other temple visions, he has consciously demonized the rites of the God of Israel. It is not necessary to link Rossetti's beasts with any particular Biblical passage or type of vision, although beasts occur throughout the Old Testament (the brazen calf, idols). After seeing an Assyrian winged bull carried into the British Museum, Rossetti had used the winged beast of Nineveh as the central figure of "The Burden of Nineveh"; the image combined associations of religion and idolatry with the quality of an artifact.

Rossetti adds to traditional mystical visions another element, the dancing of evil spirits.

The hours and minutes seemed to whirr
In a clanging swarm that deafened her;
They stung her heart to a writhing flame,
And marshalled past in its glare they came, –
Death and sorrow and sin and shame.

Round the Beryl's sphere she saw them pass
And mock her eyes from the fated glass:
One by one in a fiery train
The dead hours seemed to wax and wane,
And burned till all was known again.

       (III: sts. 23, 24)

Coleridge had previously presented both dancing death-fires and evil spirits (Death and Death-in-Life) on the sea in "The Rime". Later Oscar Wilde would extend the dancing evil spirits into a six stanza motif in his "Ballad of Reading Gaol"; consistently Wilde demonizes or renders morbid the content of his many Coleridgean borrowings.

About, about, in reel and rout
The death-fires danced at night;
The water, like a witch's oils,
Burnt green, and blue, and white.
      ("The Rime", 11. 127-30)

> A speck, a mist, a shape, I wist!
> And still it neared and neared:
> As if it dodged a water-sprite,
> It plunged and tacked and veered.
>   ("The Rime", 11. 153-56)
>
> They glided past, they glided fast,
>   Like travellers through a mist:
> They mocked the moon in a rigadoon
>   Of delicate turn and twist,
> And with formal pace and loathsome grace
>   The phantoms kept their tryst.
>   ("The Ballad of Reading Gaol", st. 49)
>
> Around, around, they waltzed and wound;
>   Some wheeled in smirking pairs;
> With the mincing step of a demirep
>   Some sidled up the stairs;
> And with subtle sneer, and fawning leer,
>   Each helped us at our prayers.
>   ("Reading Gaol", st. 5)[44]

Although Rossetti was not necessarily an intermediary between Coleridge's dark presences and those of Wilde, nonetheless Rossetti also emphasized the macabre or unpleasant in his Coleridgean borrowings, using muted Coleridgean mannerisms in some of his poems treating mysterious evil. In Rossetti, as well as Wilde, the presence of dark and writhing shapes is not as quickly superseded by heavenly spirits or the process of redemption. To the extent that they deal with similar content, Rossetti and Wilde are Coleridge darkened, Wilde to a greater degree. In *The English Renaissance of Art* Wilde credited his Pre-Raphaelite predecessors with much influence on later poetry,[45] and among many other influences, especially from French poetry, Rossetti's treatment of nightmare visions may have encouraged Wilde in codifying his own.

2. "The White Ship" (1878-1880): Death Destroys the Guilty

"The White Ship", another carefully literary ballad revealing strong Coleridgean influence, presents something as close to a just world as occurs in Rossetti's canon. Complete with refrain and repetition of the same line in different contexts, it resembles the conventional ballad more than do the longer narratives. Both devices are English ballad traits, but the care with which the new juxtapositions are made suggests French exact ballad forms; Omans find echoes of Morris' use of French medievalisms not only in "The White Ship" but in "Rose Mary", "The

King's Tragedy", and other refrain poems.⁴⁶

The rhythm is one of the poem's best qualities, more skillfully varied and heavier than in "The Staff and Scrip". For example the longest stanza, repeated at the beginning, mid-way, and end, contains no completely iambic line:

By nóne but mé căn thĕ tále be tóld,
The bútchĕr ŏf Rouen, poor Berold.
    (Lánds are swáyed bў ă kíng ŏn ă thróne.)
'Twăs ă roýal traín put fóṙth to séa,
Yet the tále can be tóld by nóne but mé.
(The seá hăṫh nŏ́ Kíng but Gód alóne.)

Partial accents give the lines a rolling emphasis (line 4, "'Twas"), and many unaccented syllables are very distinct. The shifting of anapests from middle to end to beginning of the line is carefully patterned, as in the single trochaic initial foot in the first refrain, "Lands are swayed by a King on a throne." Rossetti also plays with his shifts from two to three line stanzas. There are twenty-two three-line stanzas and one hundred two-line ones; twice two three-line stanzas occur in succession, but otherwise they are separated unevenly except in one passage of eight successive alternating stanzas of two and three lines, describing the aftermath of shipwreck (sts. 90-97), and a long stretch of two-line stanzas (sts. 102-118) building suspense until the king learns of his son's death. Appropriately the poem's only one-line stanza is the stark line preceding the final refrain:

But this King never smiled again.

Both of Rossetti's late medieval ballads, "The White Ship" and "The King's Tragedy" notice in passing whether the governance of their medieval kingdoms is for good or evil, Rossetti's closest approach to Morris' political interpretations of the period. The king and son of "The White Ship" are notorious exploiters, so their mutual fate is an earned retribution.

And when to the chase his court would crowd,
The poor flung ploughshares on his road,
And shrieked: "Our cry is from King to God!"
    ("The White Ship", st. 7)

He was a Prince of lust and pride;
He showed no grace till the hour he died. (st. 62)

When he should be King, he oft would vow,
He'd yoke the peasant to his own plough.
O'er him the ships score their furrows now. (st. 63)

A moral import attaches to both the lone survivor's low social position and to the refrain. *The sea hath no King but God alone*". But the emphasis on the victims' evil character is partially counterbalanced by the Prince's self-sacrifice in attempting to save his sister and the king's own death at the shock of hearing of his son's. If cruel to outsiders, they at least show nobility in caring for each other. Once again a Rossettian poem reduces largely to domestic melodrama.

Expiation and a lone-survivor of shipwreck automatically suggest Coleridge. There are several direct echoes or semi-echoes, as in the ship's three hundred "living souls" (Coleridge: two hundred "living men"), the ship's flying through water, the pilot's boat into which the young Prince leaps, mention of prayer after escape, the sole survivor's shrift after reaching shore. It is possible to hear many resemblances in rime and rhythm without finding direct parallels; doubtless Rossetti had memorized the rhythms of "The Rime of the Ancient Mariner" and took care not to transcribe.

Alone, alone, all, all alone
Alone on a wide wide sea!
And never a saint took pity on
My soul in agony.
    ("The Rime", 11. 232-35)

Three hundred souls were all lost but one,
And I drifted over the sea alone.
    ("The White Ship", st. 89)

"The White Ship" has simplified the psychology of Coleridge's poem, however. The Ancient Mariner's becalmed stage occupies only three of seven parts of "The Rime", and each part deals with some aspect of his psychic voyage. In Rossetti the narrator's inner responses are not significant; he only witnesses. The story emphasizes plot and narrative rather than inner states, and reduces to a simple tale of death, suspense, and retribution. While Coleridge's hero achieves an ambiguous life-in-death and a qualified redemption, Rossetti's heroes simply die, an abrupt ending which adds conclusiveness to his poems but also permits evident simplification of the issues.

"The White Ship" uses obvious devices carefully. Colors form simple contrasts or are used in unexpected ways:

"O wherefore black, O king, ye may say,
For white is the hue of death to-day.
"Your son and all his fellowship
Lie low in the sea with the White Ship." (sts. 117, 118)
And under the winter stars' still throng,
From brown throats, white throats, merry and strong,
The knights and ladies raised a song. (st. 37)

The images are clear and brief; terminal accents cause each stanza to seem discrete and suddenly chopped off at the end.

And back with the current's force they reel
Like a leaf that's drawn to a water-wheel. (st. 54)
At last the morning rose on the sea
Like an angel's wing that beat tow'rds me. (st. 90)

The Prince's entourage dances on the deck before they drown; in "The Bride's Prelude", "Dante at Verona" and elsewhere dancing is a sign of foolish or wicked frivolity. Like Morris, Rossetti is able to effectively suggest a great crime by one detail:

And his elder brother's eyes were gone. (st. 6)

Rossetti reaches a central emotion more quickly than he was able to in "The Staff and Scrip". After the introductory refrain he begins the narration:

King Henry held it as life's whole gain
That after his death his son should reign.

The pervasive alliteration and assonance are predictable enough but sometimes complex:

*Sw*if*t*er and *sw*ifter *the* White *Sh*ip sp*ed*
T*i*ll *sh*e *fl*ew as *the* spirit *fl*ies *f*rom *the* d*ead*. (st. 34) (italics mine)

More distinctive is the use of words with ambiguous or doubtful connotations, and unusual or archaic rimes and diction.

"Liege Lord! my father guided the ship
From whose boat your father's foot did *slip*
When he caught the English soil in his *grip*,

"And cried: 'By this *clasp* I claim command
O'er every rood of English land!' (sts. 15, 16)

And I Berold was the meanest *hind*
In all that train to the Prince *assign'd*. (st. 26)

And like the *moil* round a sinking cup
The waters against her crowded up. (st. 44)

       (italics mine)

Compare "The Rime of the Ancient Mariner":

We listened and looked sideways up!
Fear at my heart, as at a cup,
My life-blood seemed to sip! (11. 203-5)

Many active verbs describe the violence of the elements and personae; these often are heavily accented monosyllables:

Which the gulf grapples and the waves *strip*,
They *struck* with the strained oars' flash and dip. (st. 48)
To the toppling decks *clave* one and all (st. 51)
And back with the current's force they *reel* (st. 54)
The sister *toiled* to the brother's side. (st. 56)

       (italics mine)

Rossetti liked "grip"; it occurs twice here (predictably to rime with "ship") and had appeared earlier in "Eden Bower", "Grip and lip my limbs as I tell thee." Seldom is Rossetti both dramatically forceful and condensed, but here he sometimes presents an entire action very briefly:

He clung, and "What of the Prince?" quoth he.
"Lost, lost!" we cried. He cried, "Woe on me!"
And loosed his hold and sank through the sea. (st. 83)

"The White Ship" has some of the abrupt force of Morris' early dramatic poems. Morris' ballads are usually briefer and closer to lyric than narrative (for example, "The Sailing of the Sword"); they more often concern romantic achievement or loss rather than death, magic, or other asexual themes.[47] By contrast, Rossetti's "The White Ship" is one of series of nineteenth-century rhythmical ballads of mystery, the supernatural, darkness, or crime which begins with "The Rime" and continues through W.B. Scott's "The Witch's Ballad" and Wilde's "The Ballad of Reading Gaol".

3. "The King's Tragedy": The Guiltless Poet-Lover is Murdered and Revenged

"The King's Tragedy" is Rossetti's last ballad narrative except the comic moral tale "Jan Van Hunks", and is anthologized and commended with some frequency.[48] As in "The White Ship", the narrator is not the center of interest; the story is told from without. The domestic plot, of the love between husband and wife, seems less strained than some other relationships Rossetti postulates, and the interpolation of King James' songs presents well his inner emotions. The king is characterized more fully than most Rossetti personae, rendering his death significant. Much is made of his justice to the poor, and of the fact that he is first a man and poet, then a king.

> For he had tamed the nobles' lust
>   And curbed their power and pride,
> And reached an arm to right the poor
>   Through Scotland far and wide;
> And many a lordly wrong-doer
>   By the headsman's axe had died. (st. 23)

> "I have held my people in sacred charge,
>   And have not feared the sting
> Of proud men's hate, – to His will resign'd
> Who has but one same death for a hind
>   And one same death for a King. (st. 49)

> With the crown, the King was stript away, –
> The knight was 'reft of his battle-array, –
>   But still the Man was there. (st. 146)

>   "Alas for the woeful thing,
> That a poet true and a friend of man,
> In desperate days of bale and ban,
>   Should needs be born a King!" (st. 180)

Several images continue through the poem. The king's song and his love are compared to a bird and the Queen to a lily, and the king passes from an early imprisonment to his final death immured in a small hole beneath his bedchamber. The piety of the poem is associated naturally with the king's egalitarianism (see stanza 49 above).

Almost every stage of the narrative contains a clear, unpleasant picture – the treasonous pledging of the Voidee-cup in the merry feast, the metaphor of death as a shadow-plant towering into a black yew-tree. One of the most appropriate occurs after the narrative of the king's murder:

> But ere they came, to the black death-gap
>   Somewise did I creep and steal;
> And lo! or ever I swooned away,
> Through the dusk I saw where the white face lay
>   In the Pit of Fortune's Wheel. (st. 162)

The image of the white face barely discernible in the dusk is a typical Rossettian presentation of things half-seen, accompanied by swooning; the "Pit of Fortune's Wheel" is here remarkably precise. In both descriptions of the two women, the old prophetess and the Queen, he emphasizes the fire of passion. With the Queen this contrasts with earlier descriptions of whiteness and pallor:

> (Old Woman):
> But it seemed as though by a fire within
> Her writhen limbs were wrung; .... (st. 37)

> (Queen):
> And still as I told her day by day,
>   Her pallor changed to sight,
> And the frost grew to a furnace-flame
>   That burnt her visage white. (st. 172)

> And now of their dooms dread tidings came,
>   And of torments fierce and dire;
> And nought she spake, – she had ceased to speak, –
>   But her eyes were a soul on fire. (st. 176)

Not surprisingly "The King's Tragedy", like "Eden Bower" and "Rose Mary", contains a snake image (wine-poison-apple-adder, stanza 61); it is only remarkable that "The White Ship" lacked one, perhaps because it dealt not with treachery but death.

Rossetti uses ambiguity well; for example, the prophetess creates necessary suspense and terror, while her uncertain sources of information add the possibility of mysterious, supernatural intervention, satanic or divine. Her form of knowledge is never explained, while the king's reaction is mixed; although presumably he believes her warning, he accuses her of sorcery:

> "What man can say but the Fiend hath set
>   Thy sorcery on my path,
> My heart with the fear of death to fill, ... (st. 51)

Neither does she suggest a plan of escape, so that it is permanently unclear whether or not the king chooses his death. All signs imply that she was the inspired prophetess of inevitable doom, but some realistic restraint is preserved by the uncertainty. The flat declaratives of the early ballads have yielded to obliqueness in presenting the supernatural.

Rossetti's natural descriptions express inner psychology with something of the expertise of Coleridge. Before the old woman first heralds the king's fate, for example, the narrator observes:

'Twas then the moon sailed clear of the rack
    On high in her hollow dome;
And still as aloft with hoary crest
    Each clamorous wave rang home,
Like fire in snow the moonlight blazed
    Amid the champing foam. (st. 38)

A legalistic archaism, Catherine's concern with the etiquette of fighting between knights, functions as a primitive aside:

Ah! well might the people sing and say,
    As oft ye have heard aright; –
"O Robert Graeme, O Robert Graeme,
Who slew our king, God give thee shame!"
    For he slew him not as a knight.) (st. 154)

Rossetti even inserts his love-death personifications into this ballad; personification seems an ultimate device for rendering the ballad "literary". The dark hovering wings and piteous child are reminiscent of "The House of Life".

But Love was weeping outside the house,
    A child in the piteous rain;
And as he watched the arrow of Death,
He wailed for his own shafts close in the sheath
    That never should fly again. (st. 100)

But Death even then took aim as he sang
    With an arrow deadly bright;
And the grinning skull lurked grimly aloof,
And the wings were spread far over the roof
    More dark than the winter night. (st. 79)

The poem's conclusion is noticeable for its insistence on revenge; the flowerlike Queen suddenly becomes insatiable and waits tensely for months to whisper to her husband's corpse,

"James, James, they suffered more!" (stanza 178)

One wonders if the spirit of the kindly king rejoiced at this.

The rhythms of "The King's Tragedy" strikingly resemble those of "The Rime". Coleridge's poem contains three basic stanzas, a six-line stanza with alternating iambic tetrameter and trimeter, occurring sixteen times; a five-line stanza with the first, third, and fourth lines tetrameter, the second and fifth trimeter, occurring fifteen times; and the common four-line stanza, with tetrameter first and third lines, trimeter second and fourth lines. These three stanza forms are each duplicated in "The King's Tragedy", although Rossetti used the longer stanzas more than Coleridge; they constitute over one-third of his poem. The longer stanzas carry the same psychological surges and extended metaphors in "The King's Tragedy" as in "The Rime", although Rossetti frequently also used this six-line stanza for narration:

Like one, that on a lonesome road
Doth walk in fear and dred,
And having once turned round walks on
And turns no more his head;
Because he knows a fearful fiend
Doth close behind him tread.
    ("The Rime", 446-551)

But then a great wind swept up the skies
  And the climbing moon fell back;
And the royal blazon fled from the floor,
  And nought remained on its track;
And high in the darkened window-pane
  The shield and the crown were black.
    ("The King's Tragedy", st. 140)

Notice how attenuatated and external the Keatsian echoes in this stanza have become (if they exist; Lang includes them in his appendix of Keatsian echoes).[49] Rossetti adds frequent anapests to Coleridge's basic iambic pattern, both in the quatrains and longer stanzas. While this gives a more robustly balladic effect to the narrative, it also adds a "sing-song" quality.

As in other late ballads, there are possible echoes of Coleridge in imagery and diction:

Her lips were red, her looks were free,
Her locks were yellow as gold: ...

> The Nightmare Life-in-Death was she ....
> > ("The Rime", ll. 190, 191, 193)
>
> And the apples still are red on the tree
> Within whose shade may the adder be
> > That shall turn thy life to death. (st. 61)
>
> They groaned, they stirred, they all uprose,
> Nor spake, nor moved their eyes: ....
> > ("The Rime", ll. 331, 332)
>
> The woman stood as the train rode past,
> > And moved nor limb nor eye, ... (st. 52)

The sinking sun, moon, wind, and storm of "The Rime" appear in "The King's Tragedy", but not Coleridge's joyful and direct responses to nature:

> The sun came up upon the left,
> Out of the sea came he! (ll. 25, 26)

"Life-in-Death" and "Death" are the only personifications within "The Rime", and "Life" and "Death" are two of the primary personifications used by Rossetti. Both poems seem appropriate predecessors for "The Ballad of Reading Gaol", in which all men are grimly trapped in the hideous nature of their minds, deeds, and society. Finally all three ballads, similar in rhythm and loosely similar in imagery, deal with periods of extended psychological and external trial, although "The King's Tragedy" is the least descriptive of internal sensations and the most simplistic in treating evil, sin, and choice.

4. "Jan Van Hunks" (1847?, 1882): A Comic "Ghastly Ballad"

Seldom is a poem one of the earliest and latest works of its author. Rossetti wrote a first draft of "Jan Van Hunks" when about nineteen, added a couple of stanzas in the early seventies, and revised it on his deathbed. The alterations once more reveal the severe accuracy and directness of Rossetti's later style, with eccentric, active verbs and lurid, unpleasant, at times lugubrious detail. Only a few stanzas of the first version still exist, rendering uncertain the extent to which the sequence of incidents was present from the first.[50] "Sister Helen" is also a tale of suppliants begging a cruel if damned destroyer, and some of the dramatic intercessions were added later. The six-line ballad stanza of "Jan Van Hunks" was used for other early ballads, "Dante at Verona", "The

Blessed Damozel", and "The Card Dealer", more ballads than were written in any other single stanza form.

Several of "Jan Van Hunks"'s qualities are similar to those of "The Card Dealer" — moral allegory, interest in death, emphasis on shimmering bright colors, Coleridgean dancing and writhing shapes, punishment for sins. Compare, for example, the simple, emphasized colors associated with evil in both poems:

Her fingers let them softly through,
    Smooth polished silent things;
And each one as it falls reflects
    In swift light-shadowings,
Blood-red and purple, green and blue,
    The great eyes of her rings.
        ("The Card Dealer")

The bearer shook his burthen off
    As he reached his retinue:
He's flung his into a knot of fiends
    Red, yellow, green, and blue: —
"I've brought a pipe for private use, —
    Go trim it, some of you!"
        ("Jan Van Hunks")

Surprisingly, "Jan Van Hunks" is a good poem; what in the serious ballads seems unconscious self-parody is here intentional; both the mock solemn comic narrative and straightforward moral are planned and complementary. The suggestions of grim humor in "Sister Helen" are made more obvious.

To his moral fable Rossetti added a thorough documentation of Jan Van Hunks' crimes:

A woman's voice came next to the wall: —
    "Father, my mother died:
'Twas three months since that you drove her forth
    At bitter Christmastide:
How could I care for your proffered gold
    And quit my mother's side.

"For two months now I have begged my bread;
    Father, I can no more: ....
Van Hunks laughed up at the scudding smoke:
    "Ay, go what way you will!
Of folly and pride, in life and death,
    Let a woman take her fill!
Mad girl, even choose this road
    So we be asunder still!" (stanzas 24-26)

Rossetti enjoys describing the dense and circling smoke:

"Gossip, well done!" the old man shrieked,
   "And mark how the words come true!"
The smoke soared wildly around his head
   In smoke of knotted blue;
And ever at heart of the inmost coil
   Two fiery eyes shot through. (st. 27)

Smoke is a good image for the indolent and self-enclosed character of Hunks. The devil and Hunks appropriately smoke together in a small, mirror-lined room. The seven mirrors reflect his guilty eyes and pictures of the sufferings he has caused; they become a projection of Hunks' mean and suffocating spirit:

Above the hearth was a carven frame
   Where seven small mirrors shone; ...
And ever the reflex image dwelt
   Alike in every one. (st. 28)
And there the smoker beheld once more
   Seven times his own hard face;
Half-dazed it seemed with the sudden sights,
   But it showed no sign of grace;
And seven times flashed two fiery eyes
   In the mirror's narrow space. (st. 31)

A sly humor results from Van Hunks' ignorance of his visitor's identity. The devil comments with bland, laconic understatement on his career:

The stranger laughed: "I most have watched
   The dire extremes of heat,
Ay, more than you, I have seen men quail,
   And found their sufferings sweet.
Fit gossips, you and I! But hark!
   What sound comes from the street?" (st. 18)

The periodic suggestions of Coleridge in "Jan Van Hunks" can be identified either with the imagery and rhythms of the earlier ballads or with the fatalism and Coleridgean influence of the last narratives. The comic ballad is certainly a very rare species, but appropriate to Rossetti's essentially flat moral divisions, zest for grotesquerie, and exaggeration of formal mannerisms into the obvious. Rossetti enjoys the cheerful totality of Van Hunks' misanthropy. The darkened world of the late revenge ballads has been simplified for amusement, but its preoccupations and imagery remain. It is remarkable that Rossetti revised on his deathbed a poem begun at nineteen with no strain or incongruity between first and last intentions.

5. Two Narrative Fragments: "God's Graal" and "Joan of Arc"

"God's Graal" (1858) and "Joan of Arc" (1879) are fragments of narrative ballads on Arthurian and French medieval themes. "God's Graal", begun during his Arthurian period in watercolors, might have combined the story of Lancelot's heroic adventures and persevering love with a sympathetic treatment of the adulterous, actively passionate Guenevere. The suffering hero ("Dante at Verona"), active warrior ("The Staff and Scrip"), and fallen heroine motifs of other poems might have been fused in a completed version. Rossetti was at his best when using historical sources and when treating of love as fatality.

With both Morris and Rossetti, the use of Arthurian themes is unavoidably a comment on Tennyson's early Arthurian poetry. In 1869, after the publication of the second series of Tennyson's *Idylls* Rosetti wrote that after reading them he would proceed with greater zest to writing "God's Graal", "wherein God and Guenevere will be weighed against each other by another table of weights and measures".[51] Interestingly, this revived enthusiasm appeared in 1869, the year of many poems and fragments on the destructiveness of sexuality. Yet the prose paraphrase which Rossetti prepared is disappointingly dry, mentioning many peripheral details and failing to emphasize or elaborate the plot's central emotional tensions. Some sample stanza plans:

75.   They go down to meet in battle at Salisbury, but afterwards a peace is proposed, and both sides agree to it, but each privily resolves to set on if a single sword is drawn for fear of treason. An adder appearing, a knight of Arthur's draws his sword to kill it, and Mordred's party set on and commence the final battle in which Arthur and Mordred slay each other. (xxi, ii, iv)

79.   A vision comes 3 times in a night to Sir L. and bids him go to Almesbury where he will find Guenevere dead. (xxi, x)[52]

Perhaps Rossetti was hesitant about directly weighing God and Guenevere after all.

The fragments are also interesting for comparison with Morris' less supernaturalized treatment of the worlds of Malory and Froissart. Morris' medieval poems use Christian cosmology chiefly to reflect and enlarge the painful intensities of earthly life. In Rossetti's most structured poems the religious or metaphysical allusions imply the existence of an entire world transcending the one in which the narrative occurs.

In the "God's Graal" fragment, for example, the Lord, cherubim, ark, tabernacle, and tent manifest divine significance before Lancelot is even introduced.

> The ark of the Lord of Hosts
> Whose name is called by the name of Him.
> Who dwelleth between the Cherubim.
> O Thou that in no house dost dwell,
> But walk'st in tent and tabernacle.
> For God of all strokes will have one
> In every battle that is done.   (11. 1-7)

The images of cup, shrine, apple, and wine also appear in "Troy Town" (1869).

"Joan of Arc" (1879) was begun late in Rossetti's life. Joan had been one of Rossetti's lifelong heroines, first mentioned as one of three women in his youthful list of "immortals" (along with the Virgin Mary and Elizabeth Barrett Browning), then twice painted, in an earlier decoratively sensuous portrait in 1862 with Joan's lips puckered to kiss her sword, and in a comparatively simple one completed the year of his death. Had he completed this ballad Joan might have been his only actively heroic virtuous woman, a fusion of his historical, political, and metaphysical interests with romantic idealism, and her crusade and martyrdom might have provided a simple, unified action for concentration of plot. Unfortunately the obstacle seems to have been again a tedious factuality of narrative, though doubtless he would have repressed the following stanza before publishing:

> And where Domremy, by Burgundy,
>   Sits crowned with its oakenshaw,
> Even there Joan d'Arc, the Maid of God's Ark,
>   The light of the day first saw.

In contrast to Morris, Rossetti frequently postulated supra- or sub-human traits for his heroines. Rose Mary has psychic powers, Sister Helen is a witch, Helen of "Troy Town" is "Heavenborn Helen", and Lilith is demonic. Joan's presentation as a subsidiary incarnation of divine qualities reinforces the poem's introductory metaphysical frame:

> This word had Merlin said from of old: – ...
>   God's hand should send a Maid.   (st. 1)
> That, when Time is o'er and all hath sufficed,
> Shall the world's chief Christ-fire rise to Christ
>   From the ashes of Joan the Maid.   (11. 11-13)

It is unfortunate that Rossetti failed to complete fragments which might have added interestingly to his poetry's thematic range. The characters of Guenevere and Joan might have seemed less caricature than those of Sister Helen or Lilith.

6. Conclusion on Ballad Development

In relation to the number of ballads Rossetti produced, he did experiment with a fairly wide range of themes and mannerisms. The later ballads show improvement over their predecessors in heightened incidents, imagery, and subtlety of point of view. In his late narratives Rossetti was more careful to define and qualify perceptions of sexual and political evil, and his early moralistic romantic pessimism became more somberly dramatic. Simultaneously he improved his mixture of the parodic and the simple, the artificial and direct, to produce the incongruous grim cheerfulness of "The White Ship" and "Jan Van Hunks". Since Rossetti's final narratives were his psychological counterpart to Coleridge's mystery poems, it is appropriate that these show more direct use of Coleridge's rhythm and imagery, especially to emphasize descriptions of the weird and inscrutable, than had most of his previous ballads. And because this stage of Rossetti's writing was the most familiar to his immediate successors, their criticisms emphasize the heavy rhythms and enclosed, mysterious qualities of his poetry.

The ballads are often the most admired of Rossetti's works by those who find the moralizing of his sonnets and lyrics trivial, or who feel little empathy for the diffuse melancholia of his reverie poems. They are a fuller ballad corpus than produced by any other major Victorian except Swinburne, whose literary archaic ballads are looser, less symbolic, and more simplistic than Rossetti's. Combining the ballad and narrative cut some of the monotony of successive Victorian blank verse narratives with Wordsworthian and Miltonic echoes, and removed the primitive ballad's reliance on literalism and narrative excisions. "Rose Mary" is Rossetti's final apolitical romantic ballad, "The King's Tragedy" and "The White Ship" poems of nobility, evil, and revenge; had the sexual revenge themes of Rossetti's dramatic "Sister Helen" and "Lilith" been extended into longer narratives such as these, further unusual poems might have resulted, but in his latest period Rossetti avoided directly sexual themes.

More than any other Rossetti poems except the sonnets, the ballads foreshadow effects which will be applied by Wilde and the Decadents.

The resemblance between Coleridge and Wilde, for example, has been often noticed, but Rossetti and even perhaps Patmore may constitute a small intermediary link. Though it is necessary to consider Baudelaire and the French symbolists in discussing what influenced Wilde, there are native as well as French precedents for *fin de siècle* characteristics of English poetry. The reading of Rossetti and Swinburne may also have increased the appreciation of later authors for the characteristics of French symbolism.

Rossetti's romantic narratives seem almost an historical anomaly, successors of Keatsian romance and Tennysonian domestic sentiment but less prophetic of what was to come. "Rose Mary", the final example, seems virtually the last appearance of a contrived and complex literary form. While Rossetti's early ballads could arguably have influenced Morris' *The Defense of Guenevere*, the final ones appeared after Morris had carried an independent tradition of the romantic narrative into a wide range of "matters" — French, classical, Icelandic, and utopian. Morris' romances rather than Rossetti's were the chief influence on the next great practitioner of the romantic narrative, Yeats. Other minor adherents both in the Victorian period and later — R.W. Dixon (*Mano*), Williams, C.S. Lewis, Tolkien — seem to follow Morris more extensively than Rossetti and to be uninfluenced by the longer Rossettian romantic ballads. "Rose Mary" approaches a baroque parody of both ballad and narrative, yet ironically Rossetti's romantic narratives are also among his most eclectic and careful works, fusing lushness and mystery in a way he never quite achieved elsewhere. While "The Bride's Prelude", an early romance, looks backward to Keats, Coleridge, Patmore, and Tennyson, "Rose Mary" echoes only the first two of these poets obliquely, and foreshadows the symbolism of the late century and Yeats. Since Rossetti excelled in artificial, syncretic, complex, and exotic poetry, it is unfortunate that he was unable to complete more works of this kind.

NOTES

1   A strict division of ballads, contemplative poems, and narratives is impossible; some of Rossetti's ballad-like poems are reflective or point a moral, others merely narrate, some attempt contemplation and narration, and at least one reflective narrative, "Jenny", is not balladic. The relation of these components changes literally from poem to poem, augmenting the difficulty of commenting simultaneously on the traits of more than a very few.
For example, "The Blessed Damozel" is partly a narrative, partly the narrator's

response to a picture; both lyrical and ballad-like, it also states the metaphysical assumptions behind several of the early poems. Should it be labelled a "picture poem" and compared with "The Portrait" or the moralistic "The Card-Dealer", identified with narratives such as "Dante at Verona" which emphasize similar woman-icons and romantic archetypes, or classified with the more ballad-like poems, which it resembles in form? If "The Bride's Prelude" or "The King's Tragedy" with their extended narratives are considered literary ballads, what about the similar but mundane "Dante at Verona"? Surely whether a poem is a ballad or not doesn't depend on the existence of dramatic heightening, since many primitive ballads are insufferably dull.

2 William Holman Hunt, *Pre-Raphaelitism and the Pre-Raphaelite Brotherhood* (New York, 1905), i, facing p. 60. Hunt never felt impelled to defend his taste in beauty or to construct a theory of selection. Whatever his comments concerning fidelity to nature (what is fidelity and what is nature?), questions of perception and choice remain.

Admittedly Hunt's pictures often resemble what other persons see when looking at, for example, sheep, goats, or green meadows ("Strayed Sheep", "The Hireling Shepherd", "The Scapegoat") and his figures are drawn with excellent care and solidity. His work suggests photography, although it is more stereoscopic than photographic. His tendency to "see " solidity in everything, to dress persons more heavily and to make their features larger than the norm, constitutes an interpretation of nature. Compare Rossetti's baroque thickening of female garments, ornament, and body.

3 See Appendix, part 5, "No Ship Came Near": A Rejected Coleridge Echo?

4 For an interesting, brief treatment of "woman's role" throughout the Victorian period, see Ronald V. Sampson, *The Psychology of Power* (New York: Random, 1965), chapter 3. He describes specific responses of men and women (John Stuart Mill, Elizabeth Barrett Browning) to the subjection of women in their society. Although several books describe the 19th century woman's movement and document female economic status, there is as of yet no psychological history of the Victorian woman, and very few studies of the literature and education designed especially for women. Victorian children's literature also revealed an extremely strict interpretation of the roles appropriate to each sex. Even the exotic Pre-Raphaelite lady fulfills conventional Victorian expectations that women be spriritualized, idealized, helpless in a world of male practicality, apart, silent, narcissistic, and viewed as objects of male admiration. The aspects of Victorian sexual sentimentality which Rossetti and Hunt reject in their painting are its domesticity, its child-centeredness, and to some extent its prudery.

5 *Letters*, ii, 850.

6 *Letters*, i, 57.

7 The most formal attempt to study the adjectives of poets writing in English is that of Josephine Miles. In Table I to *Eras and Modes in English Poetry* (Berkeley: University of California, 1964), 257, Keats is listed as using 1,470 adjectives in a sample of 9,040 words, while Rossetti used 450 adjectives in a sample of 5,210 words, less than two-thirds Keats' proportion. The Rossetti sample used is from his early poems, however, and he later became more adjectival. In her Table 2 she indicates words used with extreme frequency; common Keatsian adjectives are "bright, deep, divine, fair, full, golden, happy, little, old, pale, sad, silent, silver, soft, sweet, wide, wing'd", while the only adjectives used commonly by Rossetti are "golden" and "sweet". Keats also commonly used a greater range of both nouns and verbs (273, 274).

8 *Works*, 648.

9 See footnote 20 to "Introduction", 15 above.

10   For a study of Keats' interpretation of love consistent with these remarks, see Gerald E. Enscoe, *Eros and the Romantics: Sexual Love as a Theme in Coleridge, Shelley, and Keats* (Mouton: The Hague and Paris, 1967). For example, he argues with traditional interpretations of "Lamia" and "La Belle Dame Sans Merci" which see Lamia and La Belle Dame as evil enchantresses.
11   Cecil Lang's "Studies in Pre-Raphaelitism", unpublished dissertation, Harvard, 1949, has a thorough appendix listing previously cited parallels between Rossetti and Keats along with those he has found. It is unfortunate that this useful appendix, bound in a Harvard thesis and therefore not microfilmed, is not more generally available.
12   See Glen Allen Omans, "Medieval French Poetic Forms in Victorian Poetry", unpublished dissertation, University of Minnesota, 1963, for Morris' introduction of Rossetti to medieval French literature. He also discusses Rossetti's few translations from the medieval French.
13   Echoes "The Lady of Shalott"; Tennysonisms appear throughout *The Defense of Guenevere and Other Poems*.
14   The heroine of Rossetti's early "Henry the Leper" tears her own hair; she is another extreme example of the heroine whose mental sufferings are lengthily chronicled.
15   See again Omans, note 12 above.
16   *Letters*, iv, 1861, March 1881.
17   Rossetti, *The Blessed Damozel: The Unpublished Manuscript, Texts and Collation*, with an introduction by Paull Franklin Baum (Chapel Hill: University of North Carolina, 1937), 5.

1850:   Her blue grave eyes were deeper much
        Than a deep water, even.

1856:   Her eyes knew more of rest and shade
        Than waters still'd at even; ....

1881:   Her eyes were deeper than the depth
        Of waters stilled at even; ....

18   See Appendix, part 9, "Charles Wells".
19   See his footnote to "The Staff and Scrip" in Baum, ed. *Poems, Ballads and Sonnets* (New York: Doubleday, 1937).
20   *Works*, 647.
21   Will Durant, *The Age of Faith* (New York: Simon and Shuster, 1950), 1065. Michele Barbi's *Life of Dante*, translated for the University of California Press, 1954, comments on Dante's final years:

> What seems certain is that Dante sought and found a relative security and peace in the last years of his life. He was able to have his children with him, and whatever may be thought to the contrary, probably even his wife. There is also the question of whether he held a lectureship on poetry and rhetoric in Ravenna for a time.... (28)

22   *Letters*, ii, 746, 747, 770.
23   See footnote 18 above. He also considered Wilhelm Meinhold's *Sidonia the Sorceress* a great work; its chief interest lies in the character of Sidonia, a sadistic temptress who actively enjoyed tormenting those attracted to her physical beauty (for the latter, see Chapter 3, 201).
24   Janet Camp Troxell, ed. *Rossetti's Sister Helen* (New Haven: Yale, 1938), 4.
25   *Ibid.*, 20. All the following texts are from Troxell's edition, in which the poem is printed pp. 18-95.

26   A printer's error which Rossetti corrected by hand in pencil on his copy of the periodical, see *ibid.*, 20, 3, 4.
27   Robert D. Johnston, *Dante Gabriel Rossetti* (New York: Twayne, 1969), 115.
28   James Routh, "Parallels in Coleridge, Keats, and Rossetti", *MLN*, 21 (1910), 33-37. This is the earliest and one of very few attempts to discuss Rossetti's use of Coleridge. Routh is the unfortunate author of the statement, "I have been unable to find between Keats and Rossetti a single specific parallel, in rhythm, in subject matter or in sentiment" (36), which George Ford uses in introducing his long and excellent discussion of Rossetti's use of Keats. Routh's article has consequently been discredited, but I believe he is essentially correct in emphasizing parallels with Coleridge over those with Keats, although he finds only a few of the former. Routh notices that "Jan Van Hunks" is in one of Coleridge's ballad stanzas, a point later observed by Elizabeth Jackson in her thorough and interesting "Notes on the Stanza of Rossetti's 'The Blessed Damozel'", *PMLA*, 58 (1943), 1050-56. In one of the few specific comments on Rossetti's relation to Coleridge in print, she traces the resemblance between this 6-line ballad stanza and that of "The Blessed Damozel".
29   Several Rossetti parodies exist, but to my surprise I can find none which directly parodies "Sister Helen". The closest is Charles Caverley's parody of the refrain ballad, entitled "Ballad" (1872):

The farmer's daughter hath soft brown hair;
   (Butter and eggs and a pound of cheese)
And I met with a ballad, I can't say where,
   Which wholly consisted of lines like these.

Printed in *The Victorian Age: Prose, Poetry, and Drama*, ed. John Bowyer and John Brooks (New York: Appleton-Century-Crofts, 1954), 710, 711.
30   *Letters*, i, 160 (letter to Mrs. Gabriele Rossetti, Autumn, 1853): "For the same collection she asked me to contribute some thing, and I gave a ghastly ballad called Sister Helen" (sic).
31   For comments on Rossetti's concern with originality, see the introduction to the Appendix.
32   *Letters*, ii, 850.
33   *Letters*, ii, 807.
34   Paull F. Baum, "The Bancroft Manuscripts of Dante Gabriel Rossetti", *MP*, 39 (1941), 47-68.
35   *Letters*, i, 384 (postmark 29 November 1860).
36   Rossetti's blandness should be contrasted with the stringently economic view of prostitution developed by his contemporary, Josephine Butler, the campaigner against inspection of and "regulation" (often involving incarceration) of prostitutes. She consistently defined prostitution as the economic-sexual exploitation of lower-class women by wealthy men, supported the right of prostitutes to live independently, not as legal dependents in brothels (with no right to own even minor personal property such as clothing, they could not escape without being subject to arrest as thieves), and exposed hypocrisies in the laws designed chiefly to protect wealthy clients (not the women themselves or their children) from venereal disease.
Rossetti knew George and Josephine Butler peripherally; they visited his studio occasionally and Mrs. Butler admired his work during his earlier, less popular period. He submitted his translations of the *Vita Nuovo* and Cavalcanti's sonnets to her for correction. (The most recent biography of Mrs. Butler is Glen Petrie, *A Singular Iniquity: The Campaigns of Josephine Butler* (London: Macmillan, 1971).)

Other Pre-Raphaelites were also preoccupied with the need for sexual and social consistency; Holman Hunt attempted to educate and marry the prostitute Annie Miller, who married more advantageously elsewhere, Ford Madox Brown married the "fallen woman" with whom he lived after his first wife's death, and William Morris chose as wife a stableman's daughter. All three of the women to whom Rossetti was attracted came from non-bourgeois backgrounds, and one was a prostitute. His delay in marrying Elizabeth Siddal may have resulted from consciousness of family disapproval, and he would have felt intense revulsion at the thought of legalizing his union with Fanny Cornforth.

For a comparison of "Jenny" and W.B. Scott's "Rosabell", see Appendix, part 10.

37 For another possible source of Yeats' Byzantium descriptions, see Ruskin's *The Stones of Venice* (St. Mark's Edition, n.d.), ii, 74, 75, where he describes the Gothic designs of St. Mark in what approaches a phantasmagoric symbolism:

Under foot and over head, a continual succession of crowded imagery,
one picture passing into another, as in a dream;
forms beautiful and terrible mixed together;
dragons and serpents, and ravening beasts of prey,
and graceful birds that in the midst of them
drink from running fountains and feed from vases of crystal;
the passions and the pleasures of human life symbolized together,
and the mystery of its redemption ....

38 *VP*, I (1963), 197-207. Also Peterson, ii, 423-29, discusses "Rose Mary", considering it Rossetti's "one success at composing a long narrative" (423). Other treatments include Howard, 256-272, who contrasts "The Bride's Prelude" and "Rose Mary"; Spector, 117-122; and Sonstroem, 101-103, 164-165. Howard's summary of ballad development, 272-277, is excellent.

39 Four contain five irregularites, and four more contain four. The best treatment of Rossetti's rhythms and meter is in James F. Vogel's *Dante Gabriel Rossetti's Versecraft* (Gainesville: University of Florida Press, 1971), "Meter", 6-40, and "Structure and Rhythm in Stanzas", 50-70. Unfortunately I came across it after completing my own comments, so that I have not been able to utilize it as I would have liked. Vogel explains some of the metrical qualities of "Rose Mary":

Another unusual metrical trait appears in "Rose Mary" – numerous lines that are trochaic through their first half or three-fourths of their length but that return to iambic before the end .... In "Rose Mary" they are remarkably frequent, averaging one line in ten, and sometimes two occur in a single stanza: .... At the point where these lines return from trochaic to iambic the two unstressed syllables before a stressed syllable ("to my sight") produce an anapestic effect appropriate to the poem. What is more, the frequent brief changes in meter create a shifting, elusive quality that accords well with "Rose Mary's" theme of deception. (35, 36)

40 "The Meter of Christabel", *The Fred Newton Scott Anniversary Papers*, ed. C. DeWitt Thrope and Charles Whitman (Chicago: University of Chicago, 1929).
41 Hyder, 206.
42 Rossetti intensely admired Philip Bailey's *Festus*, which contains choruses of spirits who express themselves enthusiastically (Boston, 1856, 2, 3):

Seraphim:
    God! God! God!
    As flames in skies
    We burn and rise

> And lose ourselves in Thee!
> Years on years!
> And nought appears
> Save God to be.
> God! God! God!
> To us no thought
> Hath Being brought
> Towards Thee that doth not move!
> Years on Years!
> And what appears
> Save God to love?
> God! God! God! ....
> Seraphim and Cherubim:
> God ! God! God!
> Thou fill'st our eyes
> As were the skies
> One burning, boundless sun!
> While creature mind,
> In path confined,
> Passeth a spot thereon.
> God! God! God!

Also the choruses and speeches of Elizabeth Barrett's "The Seraphim" (published 1838) present a similar effect, especially those of Jerah, which vary from columns of excited short lines to passages of longer irregular ones. There seems to have been a general tradition of spirits rhapsodizing in irregular, excited choruses. Loose, emotional statement and short, uneven lines apparently were considered appropriate characteristics of minor supernatural beings.

43   I have only recorded those portions of the central vision similar to Rossetti's images, but associated with fires and jewels is an image of God himself upon a throne, appearing in various alterations to Ezekiel, Daniel, and John on Patmos.

44   See Appendix, part 6,'"The Nineteenth-Century Literary Ballad: 'The Rime and 'The Ballad of Reading Gaol'".

45   "The English Renaissance of Art", *Essays and Lectures* (London, 1908), 119-125. It is indicative of a common intellectual tradition that Wilde shares many of Rossetti's artistic tastes — for Blake, Michelangelo, Poe, Keats. Many of their mutual sensibilities were possibly transferred via Pater — Wilde's comments on the Pre-Raphaelites are often Paterian, as are the cadences of his descriptions.

46   Omans, 39.

47   "Rapunzel" contains a witch who is associated with the imprisonment of Rapunzel, but she is easily ignored by the lovers who leave the tower for the palace.

48   Several anthologies manage to exclude all of the three important late ballads, including Arthur Carr, *Victorian Poetry: Clough to Kipling* (New York: Rinehardt, 1959); James Merritt, *The Pre-Raphaelite Poem* (New York: Dutton, 1966): Cecil Lang, *The Pre-Raphaelites and Their Circle* (New York: Houghton Mifflin, 1968); Walter Houghton and G. Robert Stange, *Victorian Poetry and Poetics* (New York: Houghton Mifflin, 1968); John Bowyer and John Brooks, *The Victorian Age: Prose, Poetry, and Drama* (New York: Appleton-Century-Crofts, 1934), John Hayward, *The Oxford Book of Nineteenth Century Verse* (New York: Oxford, 1964), corrections 1965 (he includes "Chimes" from the 1881 volume, however, which is unusual), James Stephens, Edwin Beck, and Royal Snow, eds. *Victorian and Later English Poets* (New York: American Book Co., 1934).

Only two of the four anthologies described as good student texts by Jerome Buckley in the "General Materials" section of *The Victorian Poets: A Guide to Research*, ed. Frederic Faverty (Cambridge, Mass.: Harvard, 1968) — Woods and Buckley, Stephens *et al*, Brown, and Houghton and Stange — contain any of the later ballads at all, and all but Woods and Buckley and Buckley's *The Pre-Raphaelites*, a specialized anthology, show a pointed neglect of the later Rossetti. No wonder so little commentary has been written on the late poems, and so few seem to be aware of Rossetti's development, his late ballad successes, or the equal influence of Coleridge with Keats in the shaping of his mannerisms.

49 Cecil Lang's "Studies in Pre-Raphaelitism", unpublished dissertation, Harvard University, 1949.

50 Rossetti, *Jan Van Hunks, Edited From the Original Manuscripts by John Robert Wahl* (New York: New York Public Library, 1952), 33-37.

51 *Letters*, ii, 779. He describes the poem as "Lancelot losing the Sancgrail"; thus Lancelot and not Guenevere seems intended to be the protagonist.

52 Paull Franklin Baum, ed., *An Analytical List of Manuscrips in the Duke University Library* .... (Durham: Duke, 1931), 92, 93.

3. REFLECTIVE AND LYRICAL POETRY

Since Rossetti was gifted at reproducing trance and reverie, and believed himself able to interpret an inner psychology of paintings, it is not surprising that many of his poems are meditations on pictures "observantly or thoughtfully treated". He also wrote several "songs" or dramatic lyrics, philosophic poems, quasi-balladic meditations, and political sonnets. The longer reflective poems are perhaps less read than the narratives because they seem less "Pre-Raphaelite": contemporary taste vigorously eschews the Victorian philosophical poem unless it can defend itself through use of striking or specific images. Yet at each period of his writing Rossetti wrote a noticeable variety of non-narrative works. They represent a quieter, less consciously dramatic range of his sensibility, often removed from the metaphysic of erotic love with which his name is associated.

A. POETRY ON PICTURES AND STATUARY

1. "The Card Dealer" (1849): An Early Moralistic Picture Poem

William Rossetti lists "The Card Dealer" as written in 1849, appearing in an early form in the *Athenaeum* of October, 1852, and published in final form in 1870.[1] Its inspiration was a painting by von Holst of a female figure dealing out cards;[2] the vaguely evil but beautiful single female figure who personifies fatality is almost a Rossettian icon.

Among other precedents "The Card Dealer" resembles the descriptions of the portrait and appearances of Sidonia in Meinhold's *Sidonia the Sorceress*, a work which Rossetti considered one of the greatest he had read.[3] Doubtless Rossetti was attracted not only by the description of the wicked Sidonia's beauty, but by the emphasis on her portrait:

Sidonia is here represented in the prime of mature beauty – a gold net is drawn over her almost golden yellow hair, and her neck, arms, and hands are profusely covered with jewels. Her bodice of bright purple is trimmed with costly fur, and the robe is of azure velvet .... Her eyes and mouth are not pleasing, not-withstanding their great beauty – in the mouth, particularly, one can discover an expression of cold malignity.

The painting is beautifully executed, and is evidently of the school of Louis Kranach. (ix)

Throughout *Sidonia* descriptions of her in various costumes constitute virtual set-pieces, always emphasizing her hair, jewels, and cruelty. There are other works Rossetti admired chiefly for their treatment of the evil, beautiful woman, among them Charles Wells' *Joseph and his Brethren*, which he frequently praised; in a later reprinting with an introduction by Watts-Dunton, Watts-Dunton describes his conversations with Rossetti concerning the play, and they seem chiefly to have concerned the figure of Potiphar's wife, a type of portrayal, that of the sexually aggressive woman, often suppressed in Victorian literature.[4]

As with the other early poems, "The Card Dealer"'s rhythm and diction are reminiscent of "The Rime of the Ancient Mariner", and the female figure of Coleridge's "Nightmare Life-in-Death":

"The Rime":
Her lips were red, her looks were free,
Her locks were yellow as gold:
Her skin was white as leprosy,
The Night-mare LIFE-IN-DEATH was she,
Who thicks man's blood with cold.

The naked hulk alongside came,
And the twain were casting dice;
The game is done! I've won! I've won!'
Quoth she, and whistles thrice. (11. 190-198)

"The Card Dealer":
Thou seest the card that falls, – she knows
   The card that followeth:
Her game in thy tongue is called Life,
   As ebbs thy daily breath:
When she shall speak, thou'lt learn her tongue
   And know she calls it Death. (st. 9)

"The Rime":
I closed my lids, and kept them close,
And the balls like pulses beat;
For the sky and the sea, and the sea and the sky
Lay like a load on my weary eye,
And the dead were at my feet. (11. 248-252)

"The Card Dealer":
>Around her, where she sits, the dance
>>Now breathes its eager heat;
>And not more lightly or more true
>>Fall there the dancers' feet
>Than fall her cards on the bright board
>>As 'twere a heart that beat. (st. 3)

Of course there are only a limited number of rimes in the language, especially of triple rimes on monosyllables, so that the repetition of similar rimes could be fortuitous, just as the six line tetrameter-trimeter stanza was passing into currency via Patmore and Miss Barrett's Tennysonian-Coleridgean poetry. And, as already mentioned, the woman-card motif was suggested directly by the von Holst painting, one which Rossetti significantly kept in his room. Still the association of the golden-haired card-player with Life-Death seems similar to Coleridge's Life-in-Death, and the fevered atmosphere, "beating", moon, stars, sun, and vivid colors are common to both poems. Rossetti adds his own emphases, as in the first stanza, on gazing, swooning, and languidness, and the silence is associated with wine and music. He speaks of the merging of presences and elements; one can "drink her gaze", yet the splendor of that gaze itself is swooning "into the silence languidly", and the comparison is drawn, "as a tune into a tune". She is known, predictably, through her eyes, hands, brow, and hair, and not even directly through her gaze but through its "spendour"; also one does not perceive it but "drinks" it, a mingling of sensory experiences. The mutual associations of music and silence, night and noon, is a pattern found in "The House of Life"; the cancelling of opposites or their point of merger was always especially attractive to Rossetti. A certain conceit and formal paradox occurs in the lines:

>Those eyes unravel the coiled night
>>And know the stars at noon.

The night is mysterious and must be uncoiled, perhaps as a snake. The "stars at noon" suggest Rossetti's "Dantis Amor" (1859)[5] and his attraction to emblems; the simultaneous presence of woman, sun, moon, and stars is a familiar motif from the Apocalypse,

And there appeared a great wonder in heaven; a woman clothed with the sun, and the moon under her feet, and upon her head, a crown of twelve stars. (Revelation 12:1)

It is not surprising that William Rossetti records the Apocalypse as Rossetti's favorite portion of the New Testament,[6] since it is the most filled with signs and symbols, the least concerned with ethics, the most mysterious.

The second stanza turns on the repetition of the word "rich" and the quality of "golden"; the woman is both rich in coloration and appearance and the hoarder of great material wealth:

The gold that's heaped beside her hand,
    In truth rich prize it were;
And rich the dreams that wreathe her brows
    With magic stillness there;
And he were rich who should unwind
    That woven golden hair.

Again the unwinding and weaving images; stillness here evokes dreams and magic, as formerly the night had associated itself with mysteries and swooning. The wreathing of the brows suggests a crown, another image of gold; there are few descriptions besides the words "golden", but evaluations are repeated, "in truth rich prize", "rich", "magic", "rich". In the next stanza the dance is described as breathing "its eager heat", another description in terms of heat and breath rather than sight; the board is "bright", an adjective used frequently by Coleridge:

His great bright eye most silently (1. 416)
Rested the broad bright Sun (1. 174)
The bright-eyed mariner (11. 20, 40)
And he shone bright, and on the right (1. 27)
The Mariner, whose eye is bright .... (1. 618)

"Fall" is repeated twice, ominously, and later "falls" twice more. The dancers' feet and the beating heart are the only images of human life, both images of motion as much as of sight. The cards, "Smooth polished silent things", provide occasion for a complex reflecting image; the "great eyes of her rings" reflect in them:

And each one as it falls reflects
   In swift light-shadowings,
Blood-red and purple, green and blue,
   The great eyes of her rings. (st. 4)

The flashing colors resemble the glints of the coiling water-snakes in "The Rime", although these move in tracks of "shining white" and burn "blue, glossy green, and velvet black" (11. 279, 274). The light and shadow are conjoined and flash rapidly, "swift light-shadowings"; otherwise sensations are muted, "softly", "smooth", "silent". The woman is again described by gems, hand, and "secret brows", and the evaluations continue, "secret", "bless'd", "bann'd", "vain strange". "Bless'd" and "bann'd" imply at least the possibility of a blessed state from which one can be banished. The "vain strange land" image is especially significant; it is Rossetti's Waste Land, analogous with Willowwood,

Alas! the bitter banks in Willowwood, ...
Better all life forget her than this thing,
That Willowwood should hold her wandering!"
      ("The House of Life", Sonnet 51)

with Sister Helen's suspension "... between Hell and Heaven", with Lilith's condition of banishment from Eden, the lover's position in the "void" beneath heaven in "The Blessed Damozel", or the Ancient Mariner's punishment of perpetual life-in-death and repentance:

I pass, like night, from land to land;
I have strange powers of speech .... (11. 586-87)

It is a land which all men inhabit, not only the "bann'd", and over it hangs "darkness" and "the shadow of death":

A land without any order, –
   Day even as night, (one saith,) –
Where who lieth down ariseth not
   Nor the sleeper awakeneth;
A land of darkness as darkness itself
   And of the shadow of death. (st. 6)

"The shadow of death" appears throughout the Old Testament, often associated with darkness as in Psalm 107: 10 or Isaiah 9: 2 ("The people that walked in darkness have seen a great light: they that dwell in the land of the shadow of death, upon them hath the light shined"), the latter rendered famous by its inclusion in Handel's "Messiah". Again it appears in Jeremiah associated with a wasteland but not darkness:

Jeremiah 2: 6   ... that led us through the wilderness, through a land of deserts and of pits, through a land of drought, and of the shadow of death, through a land that no man passed through, and where no man dwelt?

William Rossetti lists Job and Ecclesiastes as perhaps the Old Testament books most impressive to his brother, and nine references to the "shadow of death" occur in Job alone, two associated with darkness. One contains the Rossettian description of a land "without order", and it could have been familiar to Rossetti as an excerpt from the chapter which began the Job readings of the older, unrevised burial liturgy.[7]

Job 10: 21, 22   Before I go whence I shall not return, even to the land of darkness and the shadow of death; A land of darkness, as darkness itself, and of the shadow of death into the morning, and maketh the day dark with night. . . . that

The land "without order" is death, or its verge. The "day even as night" phrase also suggests biblical passages, such as Amos 5: 8 or another from Job:

Amos 5: 8   Seek him that maketh the seven stars and Orion, and turneth the shadow of death into the morning, and maketh the day dark with night. . . . that maketh the morning darkness ....   (4: 13)

Job 3: 4, 5   Let that day be darkness; let not God regard it from above, neither let the light shine upon it. Let darkness and the shadow of death stain it; let a cloud dwell upon it; let the blackness of the day terrify it.

but it also resembles the "light is as darkness" phraseology of the passage from Job 10. The two lines, "Where who lieth down ariseth not/Nor the sleeper awakeneth" again are closest to a passage from Job,

Job 14: 2   So man lieth down, and riseth not: till the heavens be no more, they shall not awake, nor be raised out of their sleep.

This occurs in the chapter which begins, "Man that is born of a woman is of few days, and full of trouble. He cometh forth like a flower and is cut down: he fleeth also as a shadow and continueth not", a well-known meditation on death, though not formally part of the Episcopal service for the dead. The one who "saith", then, is Job, and the description of the land in which all men are doomed to exist is a description of death, which evokes phrases from Job lamenting death, darkness, and to a lesser extent, wasteland.

The last three stanzas refer to the card-game or fatality which the lady oversees. Rossetti once described what for him was the allegorical significance of *vingt-et-un*, which in the poem's early version had been the second title, "The Card-Dealer, or Vingt-et-un"; his explanation is at least as complex and moralizing as Hunt's much-criticized lengthy explanations of his pictures.[8] The speaker describes the game in absolute terms; it can be only "lost" or "won", the actions it causes are "base" not "brave", and it leads from apparent "Life" irrevocably to "Death". The combination of Coleridgean rhythm and the dance motif with the occurrence of secret murder and digging of a grave again suggests "The Ballad of Reading Gaol", where spectres dance in association with irrational murder and where the appearance and filling of the victim-murderer's grave is emphasized:

With yawning mouth the yellow hole
   Gaped for a living thing;
The very mud cried out for blood
   To the thirsty asphalt ring .... (st. 40)

The association of card-playing and dancing is especially Rossettian, however. The four suits seem to speak of crimes committed for the sake of money or insatiable passion:

   The heart, that doth but crave
More, having fed; the diamond,
   Skilled to make base seem brave;
The club, for smiting in the dark;
   The spade, to dig a grave. (st. 7)

Jewels, death, darkness, and the image of the intense heart ("As 'twere a heart that beat") have already appeared in the poem; the cards merely reproduce their images. In the last stanza the message of the cards is translated into words; the woman becomes an oracle of fatality, while her victim's death is literally the ebbing of his breath. "The Card

WINGED HUMAN-HEADED BULL. (N.W. Palace, Nimroud.)

Dealer" presents a single image, described only through a few brilliant colors, jewels, and simple details; the rest consists chiefly of indirect evidence of life — motions, breathings, speech — and the description of her deep effect upon others.

2. *"The Burden of Nineveh" (1850 and after)*: History as a Blind Beast

"The Burden of Nineveh" was begun in 1850 and in 1856 appeared in Morris' *Oxford and Cambridge Magazine*, where it attracted Ruskin's praise. A comparison of the 1856 and final versions reveals again that Rossetti's revisions were definite improvements. Although the final version has twenty stanzas and the 1856 version has twenty-one, only seventeen final stanzas are substantially present in the early poem. One stanza and two half-stanzas were omitted, parts of several rewritten, and others added.

Although Rossetti did not rework the theme as in "Sister Helen", his changes omit jocular or bombastic passages, and increase the poem's seriousness and consistency. From another point of view it can be argued that some of the excised stanzas were less inflated and indirect than their replacements. At any rate, it is interesting to see what Rossetti excluded. He revised the introductory stanza, excised five lines on the Museum and P.R.B., a neighboring stanza on the clergy, and a vague sentimental passage originally four stanzas from the end. The changes therefore affected all portions of the poem.

1856 Version:

Stanza 1:
I have no taste for polyglot:
At the Museum 'twas my lot,
Just once, to jot and blot and rot
In Babel for I know not what.
    I went at two, I left at three.
Round those still floors I tramp'd, to win
By the great porch the dirt and din;
And as I made the last door spin
And issued, they were hoisting in
    A winged beast from Nineveh.

Stanza 7b:
Here cold-pinch'd cheeks on yellow days
Shall stop and peer; and in sun-haze
Small clergy crimp their eyes to gaze
And misses titter in their stays,
    Just fresh from "Layard's Nineveh."

Stanza 8:
Here, while the Antique-students lunch,
Shall Art be slang'd o'er cheese and hunch,
Whether the great R.A.'s a bunch
Of gods or dogs, and whether Punch
   Is right about the P. R. B.

Stanza 17:
Then waking up, I turn'd, because
That day my spirits might not pause
O'er any dead thing's doleful laws;
That day all hope with glad applause
   Through miles of London beckon'd me:
And all the wealth of life's free choice,
Love's ardour, friendship's equipoise,
And Ellen's gaze and Philip's voice,
And all that evening's curtain joys,
   Struck pale my dream of Nineveh.[9]

The last three passages were deleted, never to reappear, while the introductory stanza is altered to pay tribute to Greece and the power of "art".

In our Museum galleries
To-day I lingered o'er the prize
Dead Greece vouchsafes to living eyes, –
Her Art for ever in fresh wise
   From hour to hour rejoicing me.
Sighing I turned at last to win
Once more the London dirt and din; .... (ll. 1-7)

This tribute is only indefinitely related to "The Burden"'s chief subject, the Assyrian bull, which although a work of dead art, produces no similar joy in the narrator. In the revised version Rossetti omits an 1850 note quoting the "dictionary" definition of "burden" as "Heavy calamity; the chorus of a song"; he does not say which dictionary,[10] but it could have been Dr. Johnson's or any of a number by his imitators.

There are three revisions within the poem which extend beyond individual lines and reveal Rossetti's concern with wording:

Stanza 3:
1856:   Some colour'd Arab straw-matting
           Half-ripp'd, was still upon the thing.
Works: The print of its first rush-wrapping,
           Wound ere it dried, still ribbed the thing.

Stanza 11:
1856:   A pilgrim. Nay, but even to some
            Of these thou wert antiquity!
Works: An alien. Nay, but were not some
            Of these thine own "antiquity"?

Stanza 15:
1856:   Delicate harlot, — eldest grown
            Of earthly queens! thou on thy throne ....
Works: Delicate harlot! On thy throne
            Thou with a world beneath thee prone....

The last two alterations increase the musicality of lines; the first exchanges description of a contemporary and mundane fact (a heavy object had been packaged to protect it while travelling) for an archaic and exotic one. The two half-stanzas which Rossetti inserts into the poem both elaborate on the decay and indignities of time:

Stanza 4a:
Oh when upon each sculptured court,
Where even the wind might not resort, —
O'er which Time passed, of like import
With the wild Arab boys at sport, —
    A living face looked in to see: —

Stanza 5b:
Lo thou! could all thy priests have shown
Such proof to make thy godhead known?
From their dead Past thou liv'st alone;
And still thy shadow is thine own,
    Even as of yore in Nineveh.

The "Burden"'s meter is iambic tetrameter, with only a few trochaic inversions, chiefly at the beginning of lines. The indented fifth and tenth lines are well set off; neither rimes with the preceding quatrain, but instead the fifth lines all rime with each other — "sea", "see", "be", "thee", "ecstasy", "porphyry" — and the tenth lines all conclude with "Nineveh". These variant lines cause the stanza seemingly to move outward at regular intervals, and contrast with the regular, relatively heavy stresses and internally binding rimes of the other lines, an accordion-like effect. It is not coincidence that many of the poem's most remembered and emphatic lines occur as the fifth and tenth of their stanza:

Its crown, a brow-contracting load;
Its planted feet which trust the sod: ...

>   (So grew the image as I trod:)
>   O Nineveh, was this thy God, —
>   Thine also, mighty Nineveh?   (st. 20, ll. 6-10)

Without such a device the ten-line tetrameter stanza could become even heavier and more concentrated, especially since Rossetti loads it with trisyllables. Often these are at the end of quintets; they create unusual rimes and add a weighty, sonorous swaying appropriate to this theme:

> With sardonyx and porphyry.   (st. 13)
> Fell into dust immediately.   (st. 12)
> From hour to hour rejoicing me.   (st. 1)
> When that was woven languidly?   (st. 3)

Also the fifth and tenth line rimes provide some of the refrain effect which Rossetti uses more overtly elsewhere, and they help to bind separate stanzas — the rime scheme continues aaaabccccd, eeeebffffd, ggggbhhhhd, and so forth. The four-successive-rimes pattern also adds conscious or unconscious humor, undercutting any heavy nostalgia or sensuous effect. One unusual rime — countenance/advance — occurred previously in Tennyson's "The Two Voices"; perhaps it remained in Rossetti's mind:

> I said: "The years with change advance;
> If I make dark my countenance,
> I shut my life from happier chance.
>   ("The Two Voices", st. 18)
> ... Showed all the kingdoms at a glance
> To Him before whose countenance
> The years recede, the years advance, ...
>   ("The Burden", st. 14)

The trod/sod/God rime is also a common one in Victorian poetry; it occurs in stanza twenty of "The Burden" and will occur later in Swinburne, Hopkins, and others; before Rossetti it had appeared in a hideous piece of doggerel by Patmore, in his 1844 *Poems*, a volume which Rossetti greatly admired:

> "Oh, hear me Lady Mabel!
>   You might animate a clod
> To speak. I have not spoken
>   But in true paths have I trod:

Ah! I have loved you, Mabel,
    And I also have loved God.
        ("Sir Hubert", XII, st. 14)

and it had occurred in Elizabeth Barrett, Tennyson, and elsewhere.

    The poem suffers from the lack of progression in idea, although each of the separate stanzas makes its ironic point well. The narrator's thoughts continue on much the same theme for fifteen stanzas; then comes the overt comparison of London to Nineveh. In the first stanza the narrator contrasts Grecian art with the mundane world outside the Museum; then he sees the statue of the winged bull being hoisted in — its significance not yet certain. The bull is described as the repositor of dark, dead secrets, its wings the "fossil cerements" of Nineveh's corpse. The "sic transit gloria mundi" theme is evident, but inconsistently seems to accompany both respectful interest in and contempt for past mysteries. Here the narrator evokes the beauty and mystery of this past:

What song did the brown maidens sing,
From purple mouths alternating,
    When that was woven languidly? (st. 3)

The stony silence of the bull's long existence is contrasted with the noise made by the British excavators, and the narrator asks mockingly whether this didn't cause Nineveh to seem once again full of life. But the statue casts a shadow over the London scene; perhaps, he continues, its continued possession of its dark shadow proves its immortality? Here Rossetti builds up a contrast between Nineveh and London — the spirit of Nineveh seems darker, the British have successfully appropriated Ninevan relics for their own ends — which will reverberate ironically when he perceives suddenly that his own civilization worships the same dark and blind god. His allusions to the story of Jonah compare oddly with the biblicalisms of "that zealous tract; Rome, Babylon and Nineveh"; despite Rossetti's satire, his own poem hinges on a prophetic contempt for lost and fallen kingdoms not too dissimilar from that which inspired Evangelical pamphleteers.[11] Suddenly he seems to shift the comparison; London becomes the city of darkness and Nineveh the city of beauty:

Now, thou poor god, within this hall
Where the blank windows blind the wall

> From pedestal to pedestal,
> The kind of light shall on thee fall
>   Which London takes the day to be:
> While school-foundations in the act
> Of holiday, three files compact,
> Shall learn to view thee as a fact
> Connected with that zealous tract:
>   "ROME, – Babylon and Nineveh."
> Deemed they of this, those worshippers,
> When, in some mythic chain of verse
> Which man shall not again rehearse,
> The faces of thy ministers.
>   Yearned pale with bitter ecstasy? (sts. 8, 9)

The rhetorical questions are Blakean, reminiscent of "The Tyger", "Ah, in what quarries lay the stone ...? Ah, what is here that does not lie...?" He suggests that some of the statues now housed with this may be from *its* antiquity, then returns to the "sic transit" theme, describing the city's past glory. The biblical allusions continue; first the description of Ninevan religious objects seems quasi-biblical (sardonyx occurs in Revelation as well as in Romantic poetry),[12] another allusion to Jonah follows, then the poet imagines Christ at his temptation looking down on the wrecked Nineveh, and Nineveh is described in biblical diction as a harlot. Suddenly the narrator shifts mentally to London, significantly noticing that during his abstraction the wind has risen and the "sunshine shivered off the day"; he imagines a future in which Britain may seem as undistinguished from Nineveh as the latter now seems from other ancient empires. This point prepares for his final comparison between the ethos of the two empires; the image of the great dark beast becomes the poem's last and climactic impression.

Significantly, although Rossetti's two admired fellow poets, Tennyson and Patmore, were at this time concerned with the theme of human evolutionary improvement,[13] Rossetti feels neither interest in nor optimism concerning the future:

> That future of the best or worst .... (st. 17)

Rossetti bypasses almost completely the great Victorian theme of evolution; he was unmoved by talk of earthly progress, and in his one poem briefly mentioning past evolution, "The Cloud Confines", he calls the future "a sealed seedplot". At the conclusion of "The Burden" he again refers to religion, inserting a respectful reference to Christ:

> Who, finding in this desert place
> This form, shall hold us for some race
> That walked not in Christ's lowly ways, ... (st. 19)

followed by an implicit condemnation of neglect of these "ways", "O Nineveh, was this thy God / Thine also, mighty Nineveh?" The contrast with Christian ethics is intended; both the Ninevites and British are being condemned. This is one of Rossetti's few poems which comments on the "condition of England", and the image of the bull is well selected to inspire loose meditation and oblique ironies; Rossetti would probably have seemed less skilled in more direct and particular indictment of his age. The points he does make are somewhat opaque and lack detail:

> That set gaze never on the sky; ...
> Its crown, a brow-contracting load;
> Its planted feet which trust the sod: ....

The images of the poem rise directly from the central image – light and dark, stone, gems and ritualistic accompaniments, biblical and ancient objects, trodding feet, buildings. As always in Rossetti, descriptions are not greatly particularized, and presences are known by portions or extensions of themselves, a face, a gaze, or a foot. The Assyrian bull is an image suited to this form of description – heavy and powerful of feature, simply chiselled, needing little detail in its description – a presence notable chiefly for its darkness, wings, and face. The idol is both ancient and exotic (unlike Arthurian antiquity which was already becoming tamed poetic territory through the incursions of Keats, Tennyson, and Patmore); it also expresses the dark side of biblicalism, the worship of "heathen" gods. The poem to me seems only inconsistent when it echoes a Blakean or Keatsian reverence for the unknown past (Ah! in what quarries lay the stone ...? What song did the brown maidens sing ...?), contradicting what in other passages seems an intended depreciation of the same civilization. One cannot both compare London unfavorably with Nineveh's "mystic" antiquity and then condemn Britain for its resemblance to Ninevan moral blindness, at least without careful definitions and distinctions. Rossetti's bull seems a form of compromise between Shelley's "Ozymandias" image and Keats' urn, simultaneously a sign of the transience of corrupt glory and an artifact inspiring meditation on past life. It looks forward to Wilde's sphinx, from which the moralistic connotations have been removed, and which incorporates a Keatsian tribute to an antique and beautiful object with something of a Rossettian imagination of what that object might have been; even some of the common allusions are similar:[14]

> Made proud with pillars of basalt,
>   With sardonyx and porphyry.
>   (st. 13, "The Burden")

> On pearl and porphyry pedestalled he was too bright to look upon ....
> ("The Sphinx", l. 95; unlabelled line nos. below also from "The Sphinx")

> ... whether bull or cow,
> Isis or Ibis, who or how,
>   Whether of Thebes or Nineveh?
>   (st. 11, "The Burden")

> When through the purple corridors the screaming scarlet Ibis flew ....   (1. 39)

> From *purple mouths* alternating,
>   When that was *woven* languidly?
>   (st. 3, "The Burden")

> ... stain with red fruits those pallid *lips*!
> *Weave purple* for his shrunken lips! ....   (11. 126-127)
>   (italics mine)

> The sunshine shivered off the day: ....
>   (st. 16, "The Burden")

> Your eyes are like fantastic moons that shiver in some stagnant lake ....   (1. 153)
> ... the dawn shivers ....   (1. 159)

> That set gaze never on the sky; ....   (st. 20, "The Burden")
> I weary of your steadfast gaze ....   (1. 150)

There are other evocations common to the two poems, of fire, songs, centuries, stones, and thrones; but whereas Rossetti eliminates from his meditation most of the happy evidences of love found in Keats' "Ode to a Grecian Urn", Wilde reinstates the theme of sensuality (distorted) in association with the antique monument:

> Did gilt-scaled dragons writhe and twist with passion as you passed them by?
>   (1. 50)

Wilde also moralizes at the conclusion of his poem, but he removes his attention from the oh-how-are-the-mighty-fallen! concerns of his predecessors, substituting the theme of the object as beautiful evil for the earlier themes of object as beautiful and object as evil. Whatever may be said of Rossetti's Assyrian bull, it is clearly a powerfully negative object, not an appealing or sensuous one, despite its sensual accompaniment in past times.

3. "On Mary's Portrait" (1847) and "The Portrait" (1870)

Rossetti wrote picture-poems at every period during which he wrote poetry at all. His brother lists three picture-poems begun or written in 1847 and two in 1848, and a sonnet on "Found" was composed in 1881, the year before his death. I count twenty-nine picture poems outside of "The House of Life", where several sonnets describe pictures. Many narrative or lyric poems present a single image or vaguely imagined painting (for example, in its first version "The Card Dealer" was subtitled "From a Picture"), and inversely, Rossetti frequently painted pictures to accompany poems.

"The Portrait" is a picture-poem which spans much of Rossetti's life. An early version was written in 1847, called "On Mary's Portrait", of which only nine and a half lines remain unchanged in the published form. The two versions are markedly divergent in emotion and manner, and form a case study in the contrast between Rossetti's earliest and later manner. The early "On Mary's Portrait" resembles other early Rossetti poems, especially "The Blessed Damozel" and "The Bride's Chamber". It contains four more stanzas and thirty-six more lines than the revised poem, although the stanza form is nearly identical in both.[15] Baum comments on what he feels is lacking in the first version, the "same acute sense of loss, the same troubled longing and regret, the same half-mystical vision, so familiar elsewhere in Rossetti's poetry written in the decade after his wife's death".[16] Although Baum's identification of Rossetti's love poems only with his wife and his resulting attempt to simplify the chronology of the poems of separation has been corrected by later writers, Baum has an accurate sense of the difference between the two versions.

Baum dismisses the early version's death of the beloved as "conventional romanticism", but it is a romantic mannerism consistently allied with several others which form poetic Pre-Raphaelitism. Pre-Raphaelitism may be mainly late romanticism carried into the Victorian period, but it has characteristics of its own which can be defined. Among these is the attempt to convey passion through literally presented and carefully separated sensations:

> It is not often I can read
>   When I sit here; for then her cheek
> Seems to lean on me, and her breath
>   To make my stooping forehead weak
> Again; and I can feel again
> Her hand on my hand quickly lain
>   Whenever I would turn the leaf,
>   Bidding me wait for her; and brief
> And light, her laugh comes to me then. (st. 3)

The separation of sensations can become merely a technique, very common in Patmore, of stopping abruptly at the end of lines, a trait which appears in "The Bride's Prelude" and here in descriptions of the lady:

> Scarcely a moment in the porch
>   Of that dim house of leaves she stood;
> Her face and shoulders, coming thence,
>   Shook off the shadows like a hood.
> Then, as she walked past through the noon,
> She saw where I was stretched; and down
>   From the broad bosom's slope, her eyes
>   Smiled to me in a kind surprise:
> She came near with her rustling gown. (st. 11)

The emphasis on the physical and literalistic in passion is applied even to the beloved's death:

> Where her friends read and think, is she
> In the dark always, choked with clay? (st. 2)

The later "The Portrait" presents a purposely undefined dream landscape with few distinguishing natural traits; while the landscape of "On Mary's Portrait" is also one of fantasy, the fantasy is more cheerful and elaborated:

> .... when Spring comes back
> Leaving, along the path it treads,
> Flowers, like a water-fowl's bright track, – (st. 6)
>
> The beauty of the heard and seen –
> The water-noise and the strong green; .... (st. 8)

"On Mary's Portrait" describes what the poet has already seen and experienced, and testifies to his ability, whatever the present, to take continuing delight in a joyous and specific past vision. "The Portrait", by contrast, is less an assertion of past truth than a hope for what has never yet been realized, a painful and uncertain prophecy which creates intense anxiety. In "On Mary's Portrait" Rossetti may refer to partial sources of the earlier, clearer, and more fulfilling vision when he associates it with his reading:

I mind the time I painted it.
    Drinking in Keats – or Hunt mayhap, –
Half down a yellow dell, warm, soft
    And hollowed, like a lady's lap,
(A golden cup of summer-heat
She called it once) I lay: .... (st. 5)

As in "The Blessed Damozel" the beloved not only approaches him suddenly and closely but bends down over him; here also she evokes associations of religion and heaven:

Then, as she walked past through the noon,
She saw where I was stretched; and down
    From the broad bosom's slope, her eyes
    Smiled to me in a kind surprise:
She came near with her rustling gown.
(So, along some grass-bank in Heaven,
    Mary the Virgin, going by,
Seeth her servant Rafael
    Laid in warm silence happily;
Being but a little lovelier
Since he hath reached the eternal year. (sts. 11, 12)

The scene suggests the painted version of "The Blessed Damozel", where she bends to where he lies from a surrounding cluster of leaves and woods. Again the literalism of describing only one aspect of physical proximity:

    There was no Time while we sat there.
But I remember that we found
    Very few words, and that our hair
Had to be untangled when we rose. (st. 13)

The line "And red-mouthed damsels meeting you" suggests the lines, quoted earlier, in "The Burden of Nineveh":

What song did the brown maidens sing,
    From purple mouths alternating ....

Not only the careful separation of slow sensations but the presence of heat, swooning, weariness, and thirst reminds us that we are in a familiar environ:

> But my soul tottered, being drunk
>   With the sunshine in which its thoughts
> Floated like atoms; and my feet
>   Stumbled along the mystic courts.
> So I waxed weary, ... (st. 7)
> The day was burning to its close:
>   This side and that, like molten walls
>   The skies stood round; at intervals
> Swept with long weary flights of crows. (st. 13)
>   Yea, Time weigheth like lead
> Upon my soul. Do you not think
> That where the world shelves to the brink
>   Of that long stream whose waters flow
>   Hence some strange whither, I may now
> Kneel, and stoop in my mouth, and drink? (st. 16)

It would be incorrect to view Rossetti's early poems as more occupied with nature and his later poems with sensual expression — here the young narrator feels a sensuous response, even a dizziness, at the mention of every object of his early world — the distinction is that in his later work this sensitive kinship between nature and emotion has ceased, and each stimulus is painful and gloomy; the happy face of nature has been withdrawn and he prefers shade over what now remains.

One of the most revealing traits of this poem, however, is its participation in the lady-tradition which was to so influence William Morris. As in Morris, the dignity, movements, attributes, and exotic expressions of the lady are emphasized:

> Her hands were lifted to put back
>   The branches from her path; her head,
> With its long tresses gathered up,
>   Looked cool and nymphlike in the shade
> That reached her waist; but the white dress
> Beneath was yellow with the press
>   Of sunshine; and her soundless feet
>   Seemed to move heavily for heat;
> And the low boughs fell round her face....
>   She marvelled with a kind of awe.
> And bending back her head to see
> The whole great figure perfectly,
>   Her sweet face fell into my breast,

> And remained, knowing its own rest,
> And with grave eyes looked up to me. (sts. 10, 15)

Each individual motion of the woman is praised separately, so that her movements seem almost mechanical embodiments of a mysterious and unknown whole surrounded with expressions of awe, wonder, ecstasy, surprise, and reverence. This conjoining of worship for the undefined with a minutely detailed happiness in periphera is the manner of Morris' "Priase of My Lady", and there are mild analogies between the two poems in the emphasis on dress, walk, hair, gravity. Even the see-perfectly-me rime suggests Morris' piled rimes on "ly"-adverbs:

> ... as for me,
> I choke and grow quite faint to see
> My lady moving graciously. (st. 22)

The impression of extreme exoticism and individuality is created without the mention of any of the lady's distinguishing traits of body or temperament; instead the acuteness of the viewer's response creates the illusion that she has been particularized; compare, for example, Amelotte in "The Bride's Prelude". "On Mary's Portrait" records within a frame the appearance of a fresh and happy vision, and is similar in this respect to a freer and less ambivalent version of "The Blessed Damozel"; of course it contains descriptions of discomfort and swooning along with postures of the lady which also suggest "The Bride's Prelude" and reveal perhaps the aspect of Rossetti's early temperament most akin to that of Morris. There are occasional suggestions of Keats; "red-mouthed" may be a Keatsianism, and the sunny-verdant-hilly world suggests that of early Keatsian-Huntian amorous fulfillment.

"The Portrait", published in 1870, contains twelve stanzas of nine lines each and is written in iambic tetrameter; the effect is different from that of the ten-line iambic tetrameter of "The Burden", however, with no syncopation and a looser quatrain-quintet division instead of the tight internally binding pattern of "The Burden". The poem is even less concerned with the portrait's ability to suggest what has now faded. In the final stanza the poet reiterates his purpose:

> Here with her face doth memory sit
>   Meanwhile, and wait the day's decline,
> Till other eyes shall look from it,
>   Eyes of the spirit's Palestine,
> Even than the old gaze tenderer:
> While hopes and aims long lost with her
>   Stand round her image side by side,

>   Like tombs of pilgrims that have died
>   About the Holy Sepulchre.

The middle line provides a quiet pause, not seeming to belong fully to either half. The stanza describes a kind of sensual mystical experience central to Rossetti's psychology, occurring most often in association with half-lights and half-presences, an image seen at "the day's decline", seeming "even than the old gaze tenderer".

A half-stated belief that only separation can render full knowledge and love possible seems to have inspired much of Rossetti's life and thought, and is implied here. An extended pensive figure of speech is developed, Memory sitting by the picture as tombs around the Holy Sepulchre; Memory is the pilgrim and has come to honor the dead. The religious imagery is heavy — the beloved is his Palestine, his Holy Land, her death the death of his divinity. Yet in both images there is hopefulness, for the pilgrim may reach Palestine and Christ has risen from the sepulchre. Many adverbs and conjunctions qualify and fill the stanza — "here", "Meanwhile", "Till", "Even", "While", "Like"; they provide a temporal and geographical penumbra to surround the vision, as embodied in "eyes", "spirit", "gaze", "image".

The portrait's eyes are especially emphasized, not because they speak of the beloved's identity but of "hopes and fears long lost with her", abstractions which he can only find again in her face. This is to some degree mystic narcissism, the seeing of one's spiritual self, and especially its past, in another. It is perhaps necessary that the portrait suggest few details to him, for greater specificity might destroy its function as evoker of reverie and auto-memory. The narrator is directly aware of his own psychology; his statements of the images of his responses are uninhibited and consistent:

>   This is her picture as she was:
>   It seems a thing to wonder on,
>   *As though mine image in the glass*
>   *Should tarry when myself am gone.*
>   I gaze until she seems to stir, —
>   Until mine eyes almost aver
>   That now, even now, the sweet lips part
>   To breathe the words of the sweet heart: —
>   And yet the earth is over her.
>   (italics mine)

There is a heavier painfulness to this version of the poem, a greater sense of the psychological as well as physical irreversibility of death. It too could be a reverie on "The Blessed Damozel", the face peering through a leafy background, but the background has become darker and the face less distinct than before. Expressions of time also cluster in this stanza — "that now", "even now", "yet", "when", "until"; since this experience concerns the near-merging of past and present, it requires continual statements about times and their qualifications. Words of partial doubt and hesitancy, "seems", "as though", "seems", "almost", further qualify the experience, until almost all that remains is "wondering". He conveys the uncertainty that comes with long gazing — he asserts not that her lips part or that they almost part, but that his eyes almost aver that they part, thus adding the qualification of his unreliable senses to what was already uncertain. The mirror, image, gaze, and breath words are familiar from "The House of Life", also the use of the indefinite "thing", and the emphasis on sweetness, stated not described:

That now, even now, the sweet lips part
To breathe the words of the sweet heart .... (st. 1)

The heart, lips, and their issue (words, breath) are again the central emblems of the female body.

The next stanza contains an almost metaphysical conceit; it expresses once more the sensation barely preserved from non-existence:

Alas! even such a thin-drawn ray
   That makes the prison-depths more rude, —
The drip of water night and day
   Giving a tongue to solitude. (st. 2)

The lover is alone and imprisoned; formerly he had sought an enigmatic and secret love, but in the absence of its object the secrecy and obscurity have become a prison. The thin light-ray and single water drop are good Rossettian comparisons, two elements reduced to their most confined manifestations, accessible to the most limited human perceptions.

Yet only this, of love's whole prize,
Remains, save what in mournful guise
   Takes counsel with my soul *alone*, —
   Save what is *secret* and *unknown*,
Below the earth, above the skies. (st. 2) (italics mine)

"Prize" and "guise" have vaguely archaic connotations, and "counsel" and "guise" can suggest secretiveness; the mystery is carefully posited as too distant and diffuse to be located, "below the earth, above the skies". It is associated with dimmed light:

> In painting her I shrined her face
>   'Mid mystic trees, where light falls in
> *Hardly at all*; a *covert* place
>   Where you might think to find a din
> Of *doubtful* talk, and a live flame
> *Wandering*, and many a shape whose name
>   *Not itself knoweth*, and old dew,
>   And your own footsteps meeting you,
> And all things going as they came. (st. 3)
>   (italics mine)

The religious nature of the experience is hinted in "shrined" and "mystic"; what is most significant in this dim and uncertain beatitude, however, is that the lover loses all consciousness of time, unravelling time backwards until he sees "all things going as they came". Not only does he meet his own footsteps in his journey, but even the images of his ideal wood lack an independent existence; he does not wish to return to past experience or extend his life but to discover a state in which time has not occurred, and from which nothing has been or can be lost. The shapes do not know their own names; they have been preserved from all restraints of definition and identity, freed from the necessity of creating "footsteps" at all. In Freudian terms the world of "all things going as they came" is of course a subconscious, with identity and progression withheld, and the self separated from its sources of impulse. Rossetti presents a nineteenth-century view of the artist, unhappy in the present and in society, seeking a return to youth and the timeless moments of the first individual experiences. The "live flame wandering" is an interesting Dantean image, a living being incorporated in one element, a burning passionate flame, wavering and unfixed; it is almost Rossetti's image of the self. Notice that these vague other selves are as central to the wood-vision as the beloved herself.

In the next stanza the woman is described through "the still movement of her hands"; he responds to "the pure line's gracious flow". The lady has become almost a series of motions, a well-balanced planar arrangement; the poet reiterates that neither she nor his dream-presence exist, only the portrait:

> And passing fair the type must seem,
> Unknown the presence and the dream.
>   'Tis she: though of herself, alas!
>   Less than her shadow in the grass
> Or than her image in the stream. (st. 4)

What he is observing becomes a "type", almost an abstract intellectual perception. Such a response is reminiscent of Rossetti's last paintings before his death, patterned in large angular designs, for example, the swirling upward motions of "A Sea Spell", so stylized that the subject's body could serve as a carpeting or wall-paper design.[17] Again the emphasis is ambivalent; the poet is perceiving that part of his beloved which he considers her "real" self – "'tis she" – but this real self is perceived in the absence of her physical body. It is not so much that in a literal sense the poet desires the return of his beloved; she is another of the presences that are most intensely perceived as they attenuate, vanish, or die, as her "shadow on the grass", her "image in the stream".

The mention of the stream heralds a lengthy series of water-images, beginning with spring-water and continuing until destructive rains appear.

>   And with her
> I stopped to drink the spring-water,
>   Athirst where other waters sprang:
>   And where the echo is, she sang, –
> My soul another echo there.
> But when that hour my soul won strength
>   For words whose silence wastes and kills,
> Dull raindrops smote us, and at length
>   Thundered the heat within the hills.
> That eve I spoke those words again
> Beside the pelted window-pane;
>   And there she hearkened what I said,
>   With under-glances that surveyed
> The empty pastures blind with rain. (sts. 5b, 6)

The poem presents an involved series of doublings – the portrait and the beloved, the portrait and the lover, the lover and his past self, the lover and the beloved – expressed in pictures, images, mirrors, reflections in the water, and here the echo of his soul to her song. Just as there are "woods" in the interior of the lover's psyche, so there are waters; he is "athirst" in his soul, a properly biblical conception. There are oxymorons; his (silent) soul "echoes" her song, he speaks words "whose silence wastes". For Rossetti an essential portion of the deepest experience was silence; perhaps this accounts for part of a slight tinge of anti-intellectualism in his opinions — to him one did not learn chiefly by many words or the amassing of data. All of the perceptions of the rain-stanza express unpleasantness, "wastes and kills", "dull", "smote", "thundered", "pelted", "empty", "blind". The rain is destructive; it begins as he first speaks to her of love and continues to affect her mental landscape as he speaks again indoors. The pastures now are "empty" and "blind"; at last mentioning they had contained her shadow. Also it seems symbolic that the lovers have been driven indoors, out of the wooded dim landscapes which the poet associated with the deepest and most secret love. The next day they attempt to capture indoors what they had known outdoors, but this is the foreshadowing of its loss. The imagery, ominously, is of a bird which has flown away and the now empty leaves;

> Next day the memories of these things,
>   Like leaves through which a bird has flown,
> Still vibrated with Love's warm wings;
> Till I must make them all my own
> And paint this picture. So, 'twixt ease
> Of talk and sweet long silences,
>   She stood among the plants in bloom
>   At windows of a summer room,
> To feign the shadow of the trees. (st. 7)

Perhaps the word "feign" is significant, also the contrast between "Love's warm wings" and his desire to capture the past experiences as "all his own". There may be an implied comparison between the blooming house plants in summer sunlight and the beloved, similarly bright and soon to fade. The nature of their companionship, easeful and sweet, is declared but not described. The evocations of nature here are simple — a bird, light, plants, trees.

Despite external tranquillity the poet feels "the sick burthen of my love"; appropriately premonition comes as a psychological weight, not a delineated image. To submerged sensations of sight and sound, the thin ray of light and the echo, is added "the fragrant air", again unspecific and located "all above and all around". One of his acute perceptions of sensation during tension follows:

> It seemed each sun-thrilled blossom there
> Beat like a heart among the leaves. (st. 8)

When blossoms are beating "like a heart" something is disturbed, overcharged. They are "thrilled" by the sun, as the leaves had "vibrated" previously; all nature throbs and pulses in accord with the poet's psychic sensations. The quatrain which follows is (like the concluding quatrain in every stanza) in the rime and meter of "In Memoriam", and it has a slightly Tennysonian sound:

O heart that never beats nor heaves,
   In that one darkness lying still,
   What now to thee my love's great will
Or the fine web the sunshine weaves? (st. 8b)
O heart, how fares it with thee now ....
      ("In Memoriam", iv)
   And dead calm in that noble breast
Which heaves but with the heaving deep.
      ("In Memoriam", xi)

The poet's perceptions are restricted again to half-realms, daylight comes no more, nothing is "left to see or hear", he only receives "solemn whispers" at "night-time" in "leaf-shadows", and even these shrink "at a breath"; all is retracting inward, withdrawing itself, curling up. Meadow, forest, water, and starlight, all the expressions of natural landscape previously seen, are conjoined in a single death image:

   ... and all the heath,
   Forest and water, far and wide,
   In limpid starlight glorified,
Lie like the mystery of death. (st. 9b)

The same image resurfaces again in variant form; the poet tells how he could have slept but wandered instead until dawn, when "unawares" and at the edge of sleep he sees again his desolate vision, once more vaguely Tennysonian:

   For unawares I came upon
Those glades where once she walked with me:
And as I stood there suddenly,
   All wan with traversing the night,
   Upon the desolate verge of light
Yearned loud the iron-bosomed sea. (st. 10b)
   And on the low dark verge of life
The twilight of eternal day.
      ("In Memoriam", L)

The chances of a bereaved lover coming "unawares" and "suddenly" to a place he associates particularly with his lost love are not great — compare Poe's "Ulalume — A Ballad" — and the entire experience is dreamlike, as is the vagueness of the "glades", her "walking", his "traversing". The lovers' weeping is the small image of the great sea's desolation, even as his own wanness resembles its pale "verge of light". The line "Yearned loud the iron-bosomed sea" merits a Cleanth Brooks explication; the sea's iron spirit and yearning bosom would seem to cancel each other oxymoronically; yet both sensations are conveyed together and are more painful from contrast.

In his final imaginings the lover evokes his heaven of love, where he is "rapt" and "awed"; it is "The Blessed Damozel" situation and the sensations are familiar, the beating heart, held breath, sense of secrecy, rest, wing, angels, the soul, music, and silence. The soul's "rapt" condition is a further expression of the vibrating, breathless, and tremulous emotions which have appeared previously in nature. One advantage of the hypothesized blessedness is that the soul does not hesitate or doubt but enters "at once" into its fullest perception:

When, by the new birth born abroad
   Throughout the music of the suns,
   It enters in her soul at once
And knows the silence there for God! (st. 11)

As in "The House of Life", God, the beloved, the soul, silence, music and even the idea of birth have merged. "The Portrait" is not so much a representation of the beloved as a meditation on the lover's associations with her image, and a recreation of his woods journey with her and into the inner self, his sense of loss and imaginary beatific reunion. Paradoxically the icon of the beloved can be worshipped only through separation; "integration" of the self seemed to Rossetti a form of psychic death, yet failure to meet his footsteps circling back caused him inexpressible anxiety.

4. Three Sonnets on Paintings

"For 'Our Lady of the Rocks' " is an early sonnet, although William Rossetti does not actually state when it was written but cites a Mr. Hardinge who dates it as written many years before 1869.[18] It is interesting to contrast it with later picture sonnets, "For 'The Wine of Circe'" and "Day Dream", written to describe pictures painted by his pupil Burne-Jones and himself. William Rossetti mentions that the poet has placed an "ulterior mystical interpretation"[19] on Da Vinci's painting, a form of "criticism" which very probably influenced the responses of Swinburne and more indirectly those of Pater. Before Dante Rossetti few perceived infinitudes of expression in Da Vinci's women, who were to be reduced to more ordinary stature again after the early twentieth century and passing of Bernard Berenson.

> Mother, is this the darkness of the end,
>   The Shadow of Death? and is that outer sea
>   Infinite imminent Eternity?
> And does the death-pang by man's seed sustained
> In Time's each instant cause thy face to bend
>   Its silent prayer upon the Son, while He
>   Blesses the dead with His hand silently
> To His long day which hours no more offend?

The choice of the "Madonna of the Rocks" is significant; it is a dark picture in which the Virgin is encased and bound in by rocks, much as Rossetti's painted women were compressed and flattened into small, heavily barricaded settings. The wall of rock in front, the elaborate, framing structure in front and above, the attendant angel, the near symbolic use of small flowers, the limited aperture extending outward in the background, are all features of Rossetti's work. A National Gallery guidebook comments of Leonardo's "Madonna", "In this picture at least, he is the first of the tenebrosi, the dark ones, the painters of shadow ... there are few pictures, even of the fifteenth century, in which the idea of form prevails so exclusively."[20] Of course it is the canonization of a particular sensibility that enables a modern art critic to identify as a matter of course this particular kind of painting with pure "form". The guidebook continues in words which could be equally applied to the painting and poetry of Rossetti, "It is in a world of solid form carved from his dark, scarcely human but still exquisite dreams".[21]

In the Leonardo "Madonna" the Virgin merely looks down at the earth, her hand held above her Son, who in turn is blessing (I think) St. John; at least I can see no indication that he is specifically blessing the dead or that she is concerned with death or the sea. Rossetti's mind is immediately preoccupied with the landscape as external expression of her psychology, and the small green river-sea becomes "Infinite, imminent Eternity". The words describing ultimate things are unspecific and frequently trisyllabic, as in "The House of Life". The quietude of the experience is emphasized, "silently", "silent"; religious and biblical allusions pervade, "death-pang by man's seed sustained", "Shadow of Death", "prayer", "blesses". The mother is described only by her "face", the Son by his "hands", and the pain of time contrasts with the Son's evocation of the timeless:

To His long day which hours no more offend?

Only the last word of the line is not a monosyllable; the single syllables have built to a mild climax. This octet differs from "The Portrait" in its ascription of emotions to the picture's personae and not merely to the viewer, and the relation between viewer and object is never stated, but contained in the projection of emotions onto the Madonna's psychology. Yet like "The Portrait" the sonnet presents a reverie in which the poet seeks to return to a world which time has never "offended" by its existence. It is the perfect moment of unself-conscious silence, attainable only partially and with difficulty.

> Mother of grace, the pass is difficult,
>   Keen as these rocks, and the bewildered souls
>   Throng it like echoes, blindly shuddering through.
>   Thy name, O Lord, each spirit's voice extols,
>   Whose peace abides in the dark avenue
> Amid the bitterness of things occult.

The words of uncertainty and hardship — "difficult", "blindly", "bewildered", "keen", "bitterness" — suggest also the frustrations of "The Portrait". Persons exist only as "souls" or "spirits", gathering loosely in "things"; God is known by his "name". For the silence of the octet are substituted "echoes" and the voices of spirits (although the latter could also be silent). The last two lines are a simple presentation of one of the essential paradoxes of Rossetti's mental experience, that both peace and bitterness are to be found (only) in the "dark" and the "occult". The occult regions are also the death-pangs mentioned before, and the narrow pass is death. The image is of a traveller passing through a narrow "avenue". Usually the journey images in his poetry are diffuse, but here less so. Just as the lover in "The Portrait" returned to the woods where he had been with his beloved, the soul struggles to return through a specific passageway to the secret regions of bitter selfhood and peace.

"For 'The Wine of Circe'" is one of Rossetti's few poems to illustrate the work of a contemporary painter besides himself.[22] He had intense respect for Edward Burne-Jones, first praising his early designs — "marvels of finish and imaginative detail, unequalled by anything unless perhaps Albert Dürer's finest works ...."[23] — then his paintings. In 1869 William Rossetti recorded in his diary his brother's opinion that two living Englishmen, Millais and Jones, showed "a higher executive power than himself".[24] (The omission of both Hunt and Brown from the list is noticeable; Rossetti did not exactly despair of his own powers.) The next year, 1870,[25] he wrote this sonnet on Burne-Jones' "The Wine of Circe"; on the sonnet he comments, "I have tried in the first lines to give some impression of the scope of the work, — the torn seaweed of the sea of pleasure."[26] It is a fully allegorical interpretation. There is no question as to what colors of the painting he is presenting:

Dusk-haired and *gold*-robed o'er the *golden* wine
   She stoops, wherein, distilled of death and shame,
   Sink the *black* drops; while, lit with fragrant *flame*,
Round her spread board the *golden sun*flowers shine.
Doth *Helios* here with *Hecaté* combine
   (O Circe, thou their votaress!) to proclaim
   For these thy guests all rapture in Love's name,
Till pitiless *Night* give *Day* the countersign?
       (italics mine)

Circe the temptress offers love, but unknown to its victims it is black as well as golden. The gold-yellow black-dark antithesis provides much of the octet's structure; otherwise Circe's psychology — unlike the Madonna's — is not described, only her allegorical significance and her elaborate garments and board. "Countersign" is a careful word for the end of the octet, trisyllabic, uncommon, and rather involved in meaning; Love as a deity is again known by his "name", and as in "The House of Life" the experience is defined for the reader — "death", "shame", "rapture", "Love", "pitiless". Ancient rites are suggested in "votaress", and the theme and diction — "countersign", "Helios", "Hecaté" — of course reinforce a vague archaism. Not only are sight and taste invoked but smell — "fragrant"; the distillation of the golden wine into its fundamental essence, the black drops, blends and reduces several previous images. Even more than in the sonnet "For 'Our Lady'", the octet is the description of a particular moment, "caught" before something else happens and extended temporally for poetic amplification. Rossetti is not a poet of motion but of arrested movement, rapid intense motion fixed incongruously in still life, the formalization of passionate gesture.

   The sestet plays on the dichotomy of dominance-submission. The open sea is always associated by Rossetti with desolation:

> Lords of their hour, they come. And by her knee
>   Those cowering beasts, their equals heretofore,
> Wait; who with them in new equality
>   To-night shall echo back the sea's dull roar
>   With a vain wail from passion's tide-strown shore
> Where the dishevelled seaweed hates the sea.

The only portion of Circe which appears is her knee, an emblem of authority. The victims have only their "hour" of lordship; in contrast is the infinitude and timelessness of the ocean. The sea's roar is "dull", the wail "vain", the seaweed "dishevelled" — all is tedious and dismal. The echo of the victims mirrors the echo of sea and shore, an uncertain allegory, since Rossetti also defines the sea as the "sea of pleasure", which presumably would not echo the wail of its victims. The small liquid of the cup has broadened to the unlimited destructive sea. Notice the many polysyllabic words which give an impeded sonority to this description of human wreckage. The theme of the evil seductress is of course no novelty in Rossetti; the year before writing this sonnet he had written "Eden Bower". Nonetheless it is interesting to compare the bitterness of the occult of the Leonardo sonnet: both poems present a pleasure-pain paradox, but the Circe-sonnet identifies the agent of both as woman. In Rossetti's poetry of this period the agent of evil has more and more shifted from an outside world restrictive of sexuality to the character of the sexual object herself.

"The Day-Dream" is one of Rossetti's last portraits of Jane Morris, completed in 1880.[27] In it she sits on a bench-like object almost completely surrounded by elaborately arranged leaves and branches, with the leaf patterns reflected in the folds of her sleeves. The background and foreground have merged until it is difficult to separate them; they have become a flat perspectiveless pattern resembling that of a tapestry. The sonnet "The Day-Dream" describes an instant of complete relaxation as the lady involuntarily drops a flower from her hand. It is a moment arch-expressive of reverie:

> The thronged boughs of the shadowy sycamore,
>   Still bear young leaflets half the summer through;
>   From when the robin 'gainst the unhidden blue
> Perched dark, till now, deep in the leafy core,
> The embowered throstle's urgent wood-notes soar
>   Through summer silence. Still the leaves come new;
>   Yet never rosy-sheathed as those which drew
> Their spiral tongues from spring buds heretofore.

The effect of the sonnet, as of the picture, is of closeness and crowding — the "thronged boughs", "shadowy" trees, the "dark" bird against the sky, the "embowered" throstle. Nature is young in bud and leaf, rosy-sheathed, and passionate — "urgent" notes soar — but also minute and hidden, in the leafy core of the forest, the bower, the sheathed buds. The bird and leaves are familiar Rossettian images, as in "The Portrait", but are presented with a finer detail than usual; even the sycamore was chosen for its variegated bark. The mention of budding "spiral tongues" is complementary to the emphasis on sheathed interiors, and the metaphorical "tongue" and the "wood notes" contrast with "summer silence"; once again to Rossetti the deepest of nature's sounds is silence or near silence. The preoccupation with branch, bud, and deep bower is now transferred to the image of the woman:

Within the branching shade of Reverie
Dreams even may spring till autumn; yet none be
    Like woman's budding day-dream spirit-fann'd.
Lo! tow'rd deep skies, not deeper than her look,
She dreams; till now on her forgotten book
    Drops the forgotten blossom from her hand.

The woman becomes an emblem of summer, her dreams budding and deep. The idea of dream or reverie is reinforced chiefly by repetition — "dreams", "day-dream", "spirit-fann'd", "deep", "look", "dreams", "forgotten" — and her reverie is reflected in her eyes and imaged in the blossom and the "deep skies". Again her look and hand are all that is described; she is barely given physical existence, the better to reflect lack of self-consciousness. The "spirit-fann'd" daydream is another Rossettian non-image, peculiarly non-visual since it is hard to define how a dream may be fanned — another breath and shadow projection. Much of the sestet consists of simple repeated words — "dreams" occurs twice, "dream" once, "deep" is followed by "deeper", "forgotten" appears twice. Although Rossetti's sonnets usually end quietly, this is an extreme example; the poem's effect depends on the reader's acceptance of sustained and crowded silence as an end in itself. One remembers ironically Rossetti's much quoted statement about the necessity of exitement and amusing incident in poetry:

    It seems to me that all poetry, to be really enduring, is bound to be as *amusing* (however trivial the word may sound) as any other class of literature; and I do not think that enough amusement to keep it alive can ever be got out of incidents not amounting to events ... however agreeably, observantly, or thoughtfully treated ...

eschew in writing all themes that are not so trenchantly individualized as to leave no room for discursiveness.[28]

Appreciation of Rossetti's sonnets depends to a large extent on the ability to ignore such a canon.

The three picture sonnets have all concerned a moment of painful knowledge, spell, or reverie, and have presented in varying degrees the psychology of object and viewer. In "The Day-Dream", for example, the poet intends to create suspension in the reader, yet this is also the psychological state of the poem's object, so that reader, poet, and object are united in trance. By contrast neither Circe nor the poet feel her spell completely; the emotions of the victims are described from without. In spite of these shifts in object-subject, Rossetti in general developed his mode of describing pictures early. He presented a single moment, extended it allegorically or rhetorically into 'timelessness', and dwelled upon the psychology of this suspended moment rather than upon the pictorial qualities of the scene or person being portrayed. For a man concerned almost exclusively with the psychology of inner states it is perhaps not surprising that painting came as a more frustrating labor than poetry.

The combination of painting-poem was nevertheless an excellent form of expression for Rossetti: the painting provided some of the frame he declined to represent in words, and the poem expressed his fundamental fascination with an inner, unimaged state. Neither is it surprising that Rossetti developed early and skillfully a type of poetry so native to his temperament, since the blessed-damozel and witch themes which were to determine much of his best work were also refined early in his writing. The sonnet form was further helpful in forcing Rossetti to concentrate his evaluations into a single idea or description, unlike the series of linked meditations in reverie poems such as "The Portrait".

B. PHILOSOPHICAL POEMS

An examination of Rossetti's poetry exclusive of narrative, sonnet, and ballad reveals much that resembles other Victorian contemplative, descriptive, and elegiac verse, both in the use of the lyric and in the sentiments and concerns expressed. One of the more unexpected and interesting of these forms of contemplative verse is the loosely philosophical poem. An early example is "The Sea-Limits", undated by William Rossetti but placed with the poems of 1849; during his late middle period Rossetti wrote "The Cloud Confines" (1871); and shortly before he died he composed his last directly philosophic poem, "Soothsay" (1880-81).

Carl Peterson points out the large number of Rossetti's poems organized around a triple expression of a theme; "The Sea-Limits", in loose conformity to this pattern, presents three stanzas on the trilogy "Earth, Sea, Man", and a concluding stanza on their synthesis. Rossetti's concern is with time and the "sea's speech", but also with the unhappiness and conflicts of man. Notice the use of language to reinforce theme, the use of words of subdued sound ("Murmurs", "murmur", "echo") and of thronging, pulsing, and surging, and suggestive phrases such as "secret continuance sublime" and "desire and mystery":

Con*si*der the *s*ea's listless chime:
   Time'*s s*elf it i*s*, made audible, –
   The murmur of the earth'*s* own *s*hell.
*S*ecret continuan*c*e *s*ublime
   I*s* the *s*ea'*s* end: our *s*ight may pa*ss*
   No furlong further. *S*ince time wa*s*,
Thi*s s*ound hath told the laps*e* of time. (italics mine)

Rossetti uses many sibilants; all substances and elements merge somewhat neutrally into one susurrant rhetorical mother-of-pearl. The sounds of man are analogous to those of nature (sea and woods), differing only in that they are not caused by natural forces but by the ill-natured and thronging tendencies of humanity.

"The Cloud Confines" also deals with human evil, time, the sea, and nature, but the increase in complexity of thought and manner is noticeable. Since "The Cloud Confines" was written after both "In Memoriam" and "Maud", it is possible to see Tennysonian influence in Rossetti's introduction of the theme of evolution, as well as in the refrain:

Still we say as we go, –
   "Strange to think by the way,
Whatever there is to know,
   That shall we know one day."

which may echo in its dropped syllables the rhythmic effect in "Maud":

Than let come what come may,
What matter if I go mad,
I shall have had my day. ...

> Then let come what come may
> To a life that has been so sad
> I shall have had my day.[29]

Rossetti, however, was so careful about possible Tennysonian borrowings that he must have felt there was little resemblance, or he would have altered the phrasing. The twelve-line stanza abbacccbdede of "The Cloud Confines", more elaborate than the eight-line stanza of "The Sea-Limits", provides for increased interweaving of rimes; there is also added variation in the shift within stanzas from iambic octet to trochaic quatrain. The rhythm is broken-backed throughout, with extra syllables in almost every line, causing an effect of irregular stumbling reminiscent of "Maud" and also appropriate to Rossetti's theme of doubt and curtailed hope.

In the first stanza universal mystery appears cloaked in the familiar and stereotyped "day", "night", "cloud", "morning", and "light", and true to Rossetti's usual immediate and indefinite mingling of nature and the human body, these phenomena have a "heart" and "lips". Man is characterized as "gazing"; the presences he evokes are vague and set forth by repetition, not description:

> To him wild shadows are shown,
>   Deep under deep unknown
> And height above unknown height.

Peterson comments on the prominence of the journey-road motif in Rossetti's imagination;[30] it appears here in the quatrain. The next stanza meditates on the nature of time much more complexly than the brief allusion to "ancient life" in "The Sea-Limits" had done, and the emphasis on cycles suggests "The Burden of Nineveh".

> The Past is over and fled;
>   Named new, we name it the old;
>   Thereof some tale hath been told
> But no word comes from the dead;
>   Whether at all they be,
>   Or whether as bond or free,
>   Or whether they too were we,
> Or by what spell they have sped.

William Rossetti felt that "The Cloud Confines" was one of his brother's more important efforts at philosophic verse, and quotes from a letter Rossetti wrote to him stating that it was "not meant to be a trifle";[31] probably these speculations were intended as serious hypotheses. We rename the past as old, he seems to say, but in actuality it contained its own originality and individual qualities just as our own present does, and for all that we hear "tales" of the past, we cannot reconstruct the experiences of those now dead. We don't know whether they exist after their corporeal life, whether they suffer or are blessed, or whether they are reincarnated in ourselves. I cannot see any specific added meaning in the line, "Or by what spell they have sped". The next stanza comments on the destructiveness inherent in "Time"; the poet makes no distinction between the discords of nature and those of human society, which together embody "Fate". Peace as well as war brings casualties; there is no use distinguishing the deaths resulting from violence and those of natural process; also he may be implying that peace brings petty dissensions and unhappiness as surely as war brings larger ones:

> What of the heart of hate
>   That beats in thy breast, O Time? —
>   Red strife from the furthest prime,
> And anguish of fierce debate;
>   War that shatters her slain,
>   And peace that grinds them as grain,
>   And eyes fixed ever in vain
> On the pitiless eyes of Fate.

The "red strife" and "prime" recall the "Nature, red in tooth and claw" and "dragons of the prime" of Tennyson's stanza fifty-six of "In Memoriam":

> Who trusted God was love indeed
>   And love Creation's final law —
>   Tho' Nature, red in tooth and claw
> With ravine, shriek'd against his creed —
>   ....
> No more? A monster then, a dream,
>   A discord. Dragons of the prime,
>   That tare each other in their slime,
> Were mellow music matched with him.
>   ("In Memoriam", LVI)

However Tennyson's poem describes the predation inherent in animal evolution, whereas Rossetti's "red strife from the furthest prime" is obviously more ambiguous and probably refers merely to human dissension and warfare. The "O Time" construction is also Tennysonian, although in "In Memoriam" he prefers to apostrophize Love and Sorrow in this manner. The "O ——— (abstract name)" formula had already become a terrible Victorian cliché. "Time" appears personified in Tennyson's "And Time, a maniac scattering dust" (L), an image difficult to forget, and of course it occurs frequently elsewhere in the elegy. "In Memoriam" contains statements of doubt/hope similar in tone to Rossetti's, as well as an analogous sense of life as progression to some future knowledge. Rossetti's next stanza compares the "heart of love" of man to Time's "heart of hate" of the previous stanza, so presumably man's impulses are superior to acts of blind nature. In both poets the thought of human love immediately suggests separation and death:

   Treasuring the look it cannot find,
The words that are not heard again. (XVIII)
Dear as remembered kisses after death ...
      ("Tears, Idle Tears", from "The Princess")
Thy hope that a breath dispels,
Thy bitter forlorn farewells
And the empty echoes thereof? (st. 4)

Rossetti's final stanza contains one of his most extreme examples of the mingling and shifting of auditory, visual, temporal, and tactile images, almost in Swinburnian manner. Certain key stereotyped words are considered automatically "poetic", and their rapid shifting and aggregation indicates increased emotion, a climax:

The sky leans dumb on the sea,
  Aweary with all its wings;
  And oh! the song the sea sings
Is dark everlastingly.

In their allusiveness and synesthesia the last two lines express all the message of "The Sea-Limits", in words more contrived and beautiful than anything in that poem. The final problem and climax is one central to Rossetti's psychology — the question of whether human identity can exist at all:

  Our past is clean forgot,
  Our present is and is not,
  Our future's a sealed seedplot,
And what betwixt them are we? —

That the nature of individuality was the central intellectual problem in

Rossetti's mind as he wrote this poem is apparent from William Rossetti's note:[32]

> ... he consulted me as to whether it might be better to leave the last four lines as they stand, or to substitute other lines "on the theory hardly of annihilation but of absorption". He also wrote to Mr. W. Bell Scott in the same connexion, saying: "I cannot suppose that any particle of life is 'extinguished', though its permanent individuality may be more than questionable. Absorption is not annihilation; and it is even a real retributive future for the special atom of life to be reembodied (if so it were) in a world which its own former identity had helped to fashion for pain or pleasure.[33]

This strange mixture of idealism and Lucretian atomism is a characteristic of all Rossetti's thought and forms part of the implied philosophic basis of his poetry — a hypothesis of the mingling of the undefined elements "body" and "soul".

Almost all Victorian poets were concerned in some way with atoms and the "spirit of things", an obvious reflection of both the naturalistic science and pietistic and evangelical religion of the age; here again Rossetti seems to write traditional Victorian philosophic poetry. Also, as Peterson, Miyoshi, and others have shown, Rossetti tried to exorcise through art a sense of the dividing and fragmenting of his identity. Here he seeks not to reverse this process or embody it in a single alter ego and beloved, but to postulate endless division and reabsorption as the basic law of nature, and take comfort from a complete renunciation of his former hope of individuality. Rossetti was fiercely (if sometimes inaccurately) proud of his own originality, and his sense of individuality and frustrated desire was as a result especially intense, yet one comfort resided in his reabsorption-philosophy: although our own selves will dissolve this may not constitute a lessening of identity, since we ourselves are merely combinations of former identities held in loose suspension, embodying and reliving unconsciously all that has ever existed in the past. It is almost a premonition of Oscar Wilde's theory of the self as a series of personae derived from the past, each one no more "true" an identity than any other. The endless cycle of life is in part one of stoicism and pain (appropriately the Stoic philosophers believed in reincarnation), the emotion expressed in Rossetti's final lines of "Soothsay":

Gaze onward without claim to hope,
Nor, gazing backward, court regret.

The cycle will recur, however, so that death's potentially most painful sting — annihilation — can be escaped.

"Soothsay" was written in 1871, 1880, and 1881, chiefly during the latter two years, and is therefore one of Rossetti's last carefully wrought philosophical poems. To one of Rossetti's best critics, Walter Pater, it seemed an exceptionally fine work:[34]

> One monumental lyrical piece, 'Soothsay', testifies — more clearly even than the 'Nineveh' — to the relative force, the dry reason, always at work behind his imaginative evocations, which at no time dispensed with a genuine intellectual structure.

I cannot understand why Pater's approbation alighted on this above other Rossetti poems; most of its ideas and images have appeared previously and there is no overabundance of either; the portions on friendship often degenerate into truisms, and the shift from one topic to another can seem as arbitrary as riming couplets on the alphabet. Although the title "Soothsay" is intended to suggest proverbial wisdom, its tone sometimes deteriorates into the didactic, always a dangerous stance for Rossetti. One of the main and recurrent themes, common to "The Sea-Limits" and "The Cloud Confines" and probably one which helped endear this poem to Pater, is that of the deep mystery at the heart of things, the impossibility of formal or definable knowledge:

> Let no man ask thee of anything
> Not yearborn between Spring and Spring.
> More of all worlds than he can know,
> Each day the single sun doth show.
> A trustier gloss than thou canst give
> From all wise scrolls demonstrative,
> The sea doth sigh and the wind sing.

As in "The Cloud Confines" the rhythm is irregular, lessening the effect of truism; for example the last line of the stanza is not specific in meaning, but the syncopation in the line's second half adds a certain complexity and undertow of unexpectedness, with the terminal double stresses providing a mild climax. The phrase "wind sing" seems a definite statement about the existence of something, however undefined that something may be. Of course the sense of indefiniteness created by the rhythm is appropriate to a statement of the limitations of knowledge. The mode of stringing together proverbs resembles Blake's "Auguries of Innocence" and his other strings of sententious sayings;

there is a vague similarity in thought between the openings of "Auguries" and of "Soothsay".

> To see a World in a Grain of Sand
> And Heaven in a Wild Flower,
> Hold Infinity in the palm of your hand
> And Eternity in an hour.
> ("Auguries", 11. 1-4)

> More of all worlds than he can know,
> Each day the single sun doth show.
> ("Soothsay")

Yet ironically Rossetti is making a point philosophically opposite to that of Blake; whereas Blake postulates eternity in every concrete or specific natural phenomenon, Rossetti is stating that these phenomena are all that can be known of existence, there are no experiences but these. Such a sudden shift to materialism would indeed be strange after all of Rossetti's poems of mystery and the occult, but the words which he uses to describe specific experience, "The sea doth sigh and the wind sing", in themselves suggest meanings beyond the material. Whereas to Blake all the spiritual world can be perceived in the physical one and to Rossetti none of it can be so perceived, both poets equally postulate or imply the existence of spiritual, eternal, or at least allusive meanings in nature.

Stanza twelve repeats and reinforces the poet's theory of the limits of philosophical knowledge; here what cannot be known is God, and he is unmeasurable. This is a common Victorian definition of God, and both Hopkins and Swinburne emphasized the unfathomable nature of their absolutes, as had Tennyson in a more strained and hesitant manner.

> Let lore of all Theology
> Be to thy soul what it *can* be:
> But know, – the Power that fashions man
> Measured not out thy little span
> For thee to take the meting-rod
> In turn, and so approve on God
> Thy science of Theometry.   (st. 12)

Theology, as a series of metaphysical postulates beyond the "yearborn between Spring and Spring", is an inherently inadequate and dubious mode of thought. A related statement in the next stanza is perhaps significant, in view of Rossetti's condemnation of Swinburne's parody of

Christ and comments on his own reluctance to expose Christianity to ridicule; this passage would indicate that he held such scruples at least until late in life;

> To God at best, to chance at worst,
> Give thanks for good things, last as first.
> But windstrown blossom is that good
> Whose apple is not gratitude.
> Even if no prayer uplift thy face,
> Let the sweet right to render grace
> As thy soul's cherished child be nurs'd.   (st. 13)

As in his youth he had assumed an aesthetic significance to religion in his "Songs of the Art Catholic", he still hoped that the formalisms of religion corresponded in some way to reality, although he feared they did not and that chance dominated all. The basic attitude of a man's spirit should be reverence and gratitude, the poet is saying, even if directed towards objects not approved by conventional theological systems. Swinburne would have agreed; his anti-religion was associated with reverence and submission towards what he considered more vital powers. Interestingly Blake's "Auguries" also contained tirades against those who would destroy childlike faith:

> He who mocks the Infant's Faith
> Shall be mock'd in Age and Death.
> He who shall teach the Child to Doubt
> The rotting Grave shall ne'er get out.
> He who respects the Infant's faith
> Triumphs over Hell and Death.   (11. 85-90)

Once again, though, the "Faith" he defends can be interpreted in more than one sense, while Rossetti is referring specifically to a belief in religious doctrine; Blake's statement is a philosophical assertion, Rossetti's a more circumscribed one of tolerance for something he cannot believe.

After opening the poem with meditations on the inacessibility of knowledge except through nature, Rossetti devotes stanza two to commenting that all men will be reduced to dust, certainly true, but a statement adorned only by an occasional sonorous or carefully monosyllabic line and his usual mingling of occurrences in the past and present.

> ... Of earthly kingship's mouldering might.
> The dust his heel holds meet for thy brow

Hath all of it been what both are now;
...
When none that is now knows sound or sight.

The next stanza is ambiguous; at first it seems to deny all earthly values, much after the manner of Rossetti's sister:

Crave thou no dower of earthly things
Unworthy Hope's imaginings.

Yet immediately he asserts the values of art, the communication of this art to others, and of love:

To have brought true birth of Song to be
And to have won hearts to Poesy,
Or any where in the sun or rain
To have loved and been beloved again,
Is loftiest reach of Hope's bright wings.

The reason for the transition from this to discussing the one and the many is unclear, but the next stanza returns to the problem of human identity, its division into diverse elements yet essential psychological integrity:

The wild waifs cast up by the sea
Are diverse ever seasonably.
Even so the soul-tides still may land
A different drift upon the sand.
But one the sea is overmore.
And one be still, 'twixt shore and shore,
As the sea's life, thy soul in thee.

It seems a strange point to argue, and the meaning of "soul-tides" and "drifts" is too vague to follow. Does he merely mean that atoms perpetually reassemble? Or that human identities actually change? The difference is crucial, and his resolution follows the non-statement of the problem. Peterson comments at length on Rossetti's tendency to create metaphors more emotionally powerful than the relationships or ideas they supposedly illustrate; the individual selves which unite in the sea of self become lost in the inevitable suggestion that the individual self merges into the sea of all identity. "As the sea's life, thy soul in thee", seems somewhat a comparison of the greater with the less. Notice again the use of trisyllabic and four-syllabled words accompanied by lines entirely of monosyllables, lines 1, 6, and 7.

The next stanzas, on friendship, are those in the poem which have chiefly attracted attention. Stanza five contains a psychological perception which may have been autobiographical as well as more generally accurate; he suspects that flattery may cause revulsion because it plays to a vaguely self-perceived weakness:

Be sure thy wrath is not because
It makes thee feel thou lovest it.

He comments on the supremacy of early friendships; later in life their own individualities divide men — a response especially interesting bebecause Rossetti found the search for a discrete and defensible self so essential:

As life wears on and finds no rest,
The individual in each breast
Is tyrannous to sunder them.

The next two stanzas seem to me to degenerate into melodramatic rant and moralism; it may not be coincidental that many of the rejected stanzas for "Soothsay" in Rossetti's notebook revolve around this preoccupation he was unable to exorcise:[35]

"I hate" says over and above
"This is a soul that I might love."
None lightly says "My friend": even so
Be jealous of that name "My foe".
An enemy for an enemy,
But dogs for what a dog can be.
Hold those at heart, and time shall prove.
—
Do still thy best, albeit the clue
Be snapt of that thou strovest to;
Do still thy best, though direful hate
Should toil to leave thee desolate.
Do still thy best, whom Fate would damn.
Say — such as I was made I am,
And did even such as I could do.
....
    The bitter stage of life
Where friend and foe are parts alternated.

That he omitted the two stanzas first quoted at least speaks favorably for his recognition of their poor quality. And in fairness four interesting lines from the omitted stanzas should be quoted, commenting on academicism and passion:

Anomalies against all rules
Acknowledge, though beyond the schools: —
Those passionate states when to know true
Some thing, and to believe, are two; ...

Belief can exist apart from scholarship or tradition. Another stanza, next in the poem, is often cited as exemplifying Rossetti's conscientiousness in revision; when his own works were bad he was tormented by guilt. Not surprisingly it forms one of the better portions of the poem; Rossetti was always sincere when expressing guilt:

Strive that thy works prove equal: lest
That work which thou hast done the best
Should come to be to thee at length
(Even as to envy seems the strength
Of others) hateful and abhorr'd, —
Thine own above thyself made lord, —
Of self-rebuke the bitterest.

A later stanza returns to almost the same theme:

How callous seems beyond revoke
The clock with its last listless stroke!
How much too late at length! — to trace
The hour on its forewarning face,
The thing thou hast not dared to do! ...
Behold, this *may* be thus! Ere true
It prove, arise and bear thy yoke.

The presentation of subjective guilt seems more honest in Rossetti when unaccompanied by the stiff-upper-lip and call-to-action approach; here again in dealing consciously with philosophy he seems to fall into the banalities of his age. There is another stanza which may be an attempt to describe something inherent in Rossetti's psychic configuration, but it is unclearly worded:

Unto the man of yearning thought
And aspiration, to do nought
Is in itself almost an act, —
Being chasm-fire and cataract
Of the soul's utter depths unseal'd.
Yet woe to thee if once thou yield
Unto the act of doing nought!

Rossetti seems to say that to an intense individual periods of rest or indolence are often the periods of deepest emotion and most allied to his sources of inspiration; they, not external actions, are the "chasm-fire and cataract" of his spirit. This is harmonious with Rossetti's comments on himself lying indolently and perceiving images,[36] or Keats' attraction to a state of intensity-in-suspension, a form of almost drugged concentration which seemed allied to sleep. Yet on the other hand Rossetti warns against "the act of doing nought"; he must here mean "doing nothing" in a strongly literal sense, perhaps an acedia to extreme that the artist cannot bring his images to paper or canvas. Once again, however, the imprecision and ambiguity which serve him reasonably well in lyric poetry, sonnets, and ballads, seem less "poetic" in his attempts at aphorism or philosophic statement.

Rossetti's last stanza returns to what had been another of his preoccupations in lyric poetry and sonnets — memory. Not surprisingly his two sonnets on the nature of the sonnet, the first of which speaks also of "monuments", were likewise written during this period:

Didst ever say, "Lo, I forget"?
Such thought was to remember yet.
As in a gravegarth, count to see
The monuments of memory.
Be this thy soul's appointed scope: —
Gaze onward without claim to hope,
Nor, gazing backward, court regret.

The last sentiment may be an increase in stoicism over "The Cloud Confines"; on the other hand, "Spheral Change", which concludes the "Miscellaneous Poems" section of the 1911 *Works*, was written a year later and ends once more in a tentative hope and yearning for an existence beyond the temporal and known. In my opinion "Soothsay" is no improvement in technique over the earlier "The Cloud Confines", though that was an advance over Rossetti's earliest philosophic poems. Any attempt to evaluate the poem beyond this would be arbitrarily subjective, and, as Pater's high praise of the poem demonstrates, extremes of opinion are possible. It is interesting that both here and in certain sonnets Rossetti had begun to codify and express his opinions on art and the creative process as he knew it, a pattern that may have been arbitrarily terminated by his death.

C. ROMANTIC AND PHILOSOPHIC LYRICS

The simple sad lyric is the Victorian genre of which Tennyson is justly the most noted practitioner, but it is fair also to credit Rossetti with good lyrics of this kind. Lang includes "Even So" (1859) in his anthology; Buckley "Sudden Light" (1854), "The Honeysuckle" (1853), "The Woodspurge" (1856), and "Even So". Others in this mode are "A Little While" (1859), "A New-Year's Burden" (1859), "Alas, So Long!" (1881), and there are several longer non-narrative love poems such as "The Stream's Secret" (1859-70) or "The Song of the Bower" (1860).[37] Notice that most of these lyrics were written in the 1850's, the period of the sonnets of regret and guilt for wasted opportunity. Their themes and devices are those encountered in other poems, but they indicate that in true Elizabethan tradition Rossetti was able to write songs as well as sonnets:

> The branches cross above our eyes,
>   The skies are in a net:
> And what's the thing beneath the skies
>   We two would most forget?
>   Not birth, my love, no, no, —
>   Not death, my love, no, no, —
> The love once ours, but ours long hours ago.
>   ("A New-Year's Burden")

Also a poem such as "Autumn Song", although severely ridiculed by Rossetti himself as a lachrymose imitation, "a howling canticle", "the assumption of false appearances",[38] reveals his ability to create a simple seasonal elegy, a form cherished by Patmore and perpetuated by Dixon and other later nineteenth — century poets until fluttering autumnal yellow leaves became one of the most blatant of elegiac cliches.[39] Appropriately for a self-conscious imitation, "Autumn Song" was an early poem, written in 1848:

> Know'st thou not at the fall of the leaf
> How the soul feels like a dried sheaf
>   Bound up at length for harvesting,
>   And how death seems a comely thing
> In Autumn at the fall of the leaf?[40]

Emotion has shifted considerably from that of Keats' "To Autumn", in which autumn, "season of mists and mellow fruitfulness", has its music also, with the diversity of bleating lambs, singing crickets, whistling red-breast, and twittering swallows.

In Rossetti's work there are a few poems which emphasize specific natural details as the expression of psychological states, and this type of poem has been much cited as Pre-Raphaelite. Most poems which exploit this technique are early, however; some are religious or quasi-religious narratives such as "Ave" and "My Sister's Sleep", while others are merely brief descriptions; the latter owe much to Patmore and slightly less to Tennyson's early poems. For example, Patmore's one contribution to *The Germ*, "The Seasons", is written in this mode:

> The winter comes: the frozen rut
>   Is bound with silver bars:
> The white drift heaps againt the hut;
>   And night is pierced with stars.
>   (st. 3; no. 2 "The Germ")

Tennyson creates many examples, some of which occur in the influential "Mariana":

> The sparrow's chirrup on the roof,
>   The slow clock ticking, and the sound
> Which to the wooing wind aloof
>   The poplar made, did all confound
> Her sense .... (st. 7)

Compare "A Half-Way Pause" (1849); like some of Patmore's poetry and "Mariana", this poem vaguely suggests the details-of-heat-and-stillness of "The Bride's Prelude", begun around the same time:

> The turn of noontide has begun.
>   In the weak breeze the sunshine yields.
>   There is a bell upon the fields.
> On the long hedgerow's tangled run
>   A low white cottage intervenes:
>   Against the wall a blind man leans,
> And sways his face to have the sun.
>
> Our horses' hoofs stir in the road,
>   Quiet and sharp. Light hath a song
>   Whose silence, being heard, seems long.
> The point of noon maketh abode,
>   And will not be at once gone through.
>   The sky's deep color saddens you,
> And the heat weighs a dreamy load.
>   ("A Half-Way Pause")

The somewhat later "Woodspurge" (1856), often cited for its symbolic detail, may also be vulnerable to Johnson's parody of the vacuous ballad narrative ("I put my hat upon my head / And walked into the Strand ...."), but its starkness and concentration on a single object are distinctive in Rossetti's poetry. The woodspurge is an emblem of sorrow:

From perfect grief there need not be
Wisdom or even memory:
One thing then learnt remains to me, –
The woodspurge has a cup of three.

... My eyes, wide open, had the run
Of some ten weeds to fix upon;
Among those few, out of the sun,
The woodspurge flowered, three cups in one.

From perfect grief there need not be
Wisdom or even memory:
One thing then learnt remains to me, –
The woodspurge has a cup of three.

Another Victorian mode which Rossetti used is the farewell poem of sentiment and hope: "Spheral Change" (1881), the last full poem printed in the *Works*, fulfills there a function similar to that of Tennyson's "Crossing the Bar". Both poems yearn for, then postulate, a continued existence, Rossetti more tentatively; but the simple, melancholic effect and the basic desire are similar. Rossetti includes the familiar patterns of death-images, passing shadows, and the evocation of the beloved. Compare the similar hesitant desire of "Insomnia" and "The One Hope" with that expressed in the first and last stanzas of "Spheral Change".

In this new shade of Death, the show
    Passes me still of form and face;
Some bent, some gazing as they go,
    Some swiftly, some at a dull pace,
    Not one that speaks in any case ....

O nearest, furthest! Can there be
    At length some hard-carved heart-won home
Where, – exile changed for sanctuary –
    Our lot may fill indeed its sum,
    And you may wait and I may come?

"Crossing the Bar" (1889) expresses Tennyson's wistful but confident anticipation of the "one clear call"; Spheral Change" is an affirmation of faith for Rossetti, but its return from exile occurs in a state of world-weariness ("Some bent, some gazing as they go") which approaches spiritual exhaustion.

D. POLITICAL SONNETS

Rossetti wrote nine "political" sonnets,[40] that is, sonnets which praise or condemn contemporary or recent events. Like his work in other small genres, they span his entire writing career — four of the sonnets were written in 1848 or 1849, two in the 1850's, one in 1871, and two at the end of Rossetti's life. Like his brother Rossetti was a nineteenth century liberal, but more erratic and intermittent both in his beliefs and in the extent of his interest, more tinged with the pessimism, aesthetic conservatism, and occasional royalist sentiment that would later be associated with Eliot, Yeats, or the younger Thomas Mann. His stance is that of moralist, one who opposes wicked aggression and praises virtue. Three of the sonnets, "Place de la Bastille", "On Wellington's Funeral", and "The Last Three From Trafalgar", comment generally on the significance of past historical events, although they are ostensibly occasional sonnets inspired by a particular commemoration or visit. He opposed (foreign) nationalist aggressions, particularly those of Russia, France, and Germany, looked back with pride at British achievements in the Napoleonic Wars, and expressed support of the nationalist revolutions of 1848.

The chronological sequence of the nine sonnets is as follows:

1840's:
1848 "At the Sun-Rise in 1848"
1849 "Vox Ecclesiae, Vox Christi"
1849 "Place de la Bastille, Paris"
1849 "On Refusal of Aid Between Nations"

1850's:
1852 "On Wellington's Funeral"
1859 "After the French Liberation of Italy"

1870's and 1881:
1871 "After the German Subjugation of France, 1871"
1878 "The Last Three From Trafalgar"
1881 "Czar Alexander the Second"

The early political sonnets are apocalyptic; like "'Retro me, Sathana!'" (1847), they anticipate an overthrow of the temporal order by an avenging God. The poet's imagination seems happiest when envisioning the climactic holocaust. In "At the Sun-Rise in 1848" the conflagration has already occurred (European revolutions, especially the Italian resistance to Austria), yet the poet shifts his concern to reproving undue human pride in these beneficial events. The final effect is that of Rossetti's other early "House of Life" sonnets which moralize on pride, vainglory, heedlessness, and God's transcendence:

> We saw priests fall together and turn white:
>   And covered in the dust from the sun's sight,
>   A king was spied, and yet another king ....
>   Still, Man, in thy just pride, remember this: —
>   Thou hadst not made that thy sons' sons shall ask
>   What the word *king* may mean in their day's task,
>   But for the light that led: and if light is,
> It is because God said, Let there be light.

The mild anticlericalism becomes more acute and ironic in the next year's "Vox Ecclesiae, Vox Christi". Rossetti alludes scathingly to the perversion and hypocrisies of which religious institutions and religiosity are capable:

>   Thence, (in hate of truth)
> O'er weapons blessed for carnage, to fierce youth
>   From evil age, the word hath hissed along: —
>   "Ye are the Lord's: go forth, destroy, be strong:
> Christ's Church absolves ye from Christ's law of ruth."
> Therefore the wine-cup at the altar is
>   As Christ's own blood indeed, and as the blood
>   Of Christ's elect, at divers seasons spilt
> On the altar-stone, that to man's church, for this,
>   Shall prove a stone of stumbling, — whence it stood
>   To be rent up ere the true Church be built.

Judgment and vengeance are emphasized; in the fullness of time this false structure will be destroyed.

Further biblical images of winepress, blood, smiting rod, and judgment occur in "On Refusal of Aid Between Nations". The world will bow beneath God's righteous decrees. If awkward in diction, the sestet contains one of Rossetti's more considered moral comments:

> ON REFUSAL OF AID BETWEEN NATIONS
>
> Not that the earth is changing, O my God!
>   Nor that the seasons totter in their walk, —
>   Not that the virulent ill of act and talk
> Seethes ever as a winepress ever trod, —
> Not therefore are we certain that the rod
>   Weighs in thine hand to smite thy world; though now
>   Beneath thine hand so many nations bow,
> So many kings: — not therefore, O my God! —

> But because Man is parcelled out in men
> To-day; because, for any wrongful blow
> No man not stricken asks, "I would be told
> Why thou dost thus;" but his heart whispers then,
> "He is he, I am I." By this we know
> That our earth falls asunder, being old.

Rossetti's chief weakness as a moralist is his disinterest in questions of relative justice and causation; this passage is a partial exception. The sonnet directly suggests Hopkins' much later "God's Grandeur"; both sonnets lament in quasi-biblical language the world's 'antiquity', weariness, and refusal to follow righteous paths:

> The world is charged with the grandeur of God.
> It will flame out, like shining from shook foil;
> It gathers to a greatness, like the ooze of oil
> Crushed. Why do men then now not reck his rod?
> Generations have trod, have trod, have trod;
> And all is seared with trade; bleared, smeared with toil;
> And wears man's smudge and shares man's smell: the soil
> Is bare now, nor can foot feel, being shod.

Notice again in both sonnets the familiar God-trod-rod rimes.

"Vox Ecclesiae" had celebrated the long-suffering saints and condemned their oppressors (compare "Dante at Verona"); the one remaining political sonnet of the 1840's, "Place de la Bastille", presents the noble sufferings, yearnings, and achievements of political saints. Again the decrees of God bring political freedom:

> How dear the sky has been above this place!
> Small treasures of this sky that we see here
> Seem weak through prison-bars from year to year;
> Eyed with a painful prayer upon God's grace
> To save, and tears that stayed along the face
> Lifted at sunset ....
> So was it, till one night the secret kept
> Safe in low vault and stealthy corridor
> Was blown abroad on gospel-tongues of flame.
> O ways of God, mysterious evermore!
> How many on this spot have cursed and wept
> That all might stand here now and own Thy Name.

These early sonnets respond to recent events with measured hopefulness as well as condemnation. Two of the later sonnets inveigh against oppression, one condemns an unjust regicide, and two celebrate a heroism securely embodied in fallen warriors. The political sonnets of the 1850's and 1870's use rather incongruous sexual metaphors for national upheavals. "After the French Liberation of Italy" (1859) contains Rossetti's most clearly recognizable description of copulation and its immediate aftermath, more literal than the frequently cited, slightly coy "Nuptial Sleep". It is a surprisingly early poem for this theme, but the accurate description of sexuality is conjoined with inevitable allegations of "whoredom". Only "paid joys of love" are describable. The strained and ponderously inexact metaphor creates an unpleasantly tumid effect; why is sexuality associated automatically with immoral lust, and how are these connected with the behavior of Italy and France? Presumably Rossetti is asserting that both Italy and the harlot perform abhorrent services for money; after the two evils are equated, all has been said. Even accepting his terms, it is rather snide to assume that Italy yearned for invasion, since clearly the case against France is that it had indulged in rapine and pillage; Italy was victim, not seductress.

AFTER THE FRENCH LIBERATION OF ITALY

As when the last of the paid joys of love
   Has come and gone; and with a single kiss
   At length, and with one laugh of satiate bliss,
The wearied man a minute rests above
The wearied woman, no more urged to move
   In those long throes of longing, till they glide,
   Now lightlier clasped, each to the other's side,
In joys past acting, not past dreaming of: –
So Europe now beneath this paramour
   Lies for a little out of use, – full oft
Submissive to his lust, a loveless whore.
   He wakes, she sleeps, the breath falls slow and soft.
Wait: the bought body holds a birth within,
An harlot's child, to scourge her for her sin.

A similar identification of national and personal disloyalty occurs with more grace in "A Last Confession" (1849, 1869-70), where the child-beloved-harlot figure leaves her Italian father to dally with the Austrian invader.

"After the German Subjugation of France, 1871" is another de-denunciation of political duplicity in the dubious personification of the 'faithless' woman. After the much heralded uprisings of 1871, the sonnet declares, France has now turned her favors to the outside aggressor, Germany; this German subjugation is also a birth, the child of former upheavals. Like the scourging harlot's child of the sonnet above, the poor infant is victimized by an appallingly clumsy metaphor — it is "out of the womb's rank furnace cast forlorn" — in order to extend the flames/Hell's Pentecost/destruction reference of the next line. In structure and imagery the sonnet somewhat suggests "Vain Virtues" of 1869.

> AFTER THE GERMAN SUBJUGATION OF FRANCE, 1871
>
> Lo the twelfth year — the wedding-feast come round
>   With years for months — and lo the babe new-born;
>   Out of the womb's rank furnace cast forlorn,
> And with contagious effluence seamed and crown'd.
> To hail this birth, what fiery tongues surround
>   Hell's Pentecost — what clamour of all cries
>   That swell, from Absalom's scoff to Shimei's,
> One scornful gamut of tumultuous sound!
>
> For now the harlot's heart on a new sleeve
>   Is prankt; and her heart's lord of yesterday
>   (Spurned from her bed, whose worm-spun silks o'erlay
> Such fretwork as that other worm can weave)
> Takes in his ears the vanished world's last yell,
> And in his flesh the closing teeth of Hell.

The chief weakness of these sexual-political sonnets is their inept personification — metaphorical arguments about power*lust* reduce to a literalistic absurdity: evil becomes Marianne performing unnatural acts with the Russian Bear, while the English lion waits his turn. Nations are incongruously blamed and commiserated for the evils they endure. Aggression and victimization become oddly mixed; the conquered nation is the seducing partner. In a context of economic want, opportunism, *nouveau-arrivé* corruption, and raw free-market capitalism, to lament the "unfaithfulness" of nations is simply silly. A consistent Rossetti might have approved of at least some wars and upheavals, since he had expressed a belief in "good" revolutions and "righteous" destruction.

Rossetti's last political sonnet, "Czar Alexander the Second", is one of the better. As in "Vox Ecclesiae" it attempts to express the irony of appearance-reality — this czar, killed by an anarchist in 1881, had according to Rossetti loved rather than oppressed his people.

> From him did forty million serfs, endow'd
>   Each with six feet of death-due soil, receive
>   Rich freeborn lifelong land, whereon to sheave
> Their country's harvest. These to-day aloud

>   Demand of Heaven a Father's blood, – sore bow'd
> >   With tears and thrilled with wrath; who, while they grieve,
> >   On every guilty head would fain achieve
> > All torment by his edicts disallow'd.
> > He stayed the knout's red-ravening fangs; and first
> >   Of Russian traitors, his own murderers go
> >   White to the tomb. While he, – laid foully low
> > With limbs red-rent, with festering brain which erst
> > Willed kingly freedom, – 'gainst the deed accurst
> >   To God bears witness of his people's woe.

Rossetti's Czar is another King James figure, a noble rejected ruler whose blood God will avenge on earth, who aided the poor, and whose pathetic corpse is described in some detail. As in other late poems the apocalyptic imagery has darkened and become more secularized, and human passions are disembodied in baroque palpitations and emanations.

The political sonnets are a mildly instructive if peripheral category of poem; although they reflect the stylistic shifts of his other poetry they are consistently moralistic and religious in tone. Rossetti had little to say on the evils of nations beyond declamations about "good" and "bad" rulers. His theme is consistently: The wicked merit the wrath of God! It is perhaps significant that whereas in the early sonnets he assumes or prophesies a final restitution and judgment, in the final sonnets there is no assurance that any moral world-order will be restored. The dead Czar has been temporally avenged and his corpse continues to bear witness to God of his people's woe, but there is no surety that this witness will result in their redemption or an ultimate progression in events. History remains "a sealed seed-plot"; all available auguries are dark.

E. CONCLUSION ON REFLECTIVE AND LYRIC POETRY

Rossetti's poetry revealed considerable variety; only a few poems are in the "Art Catholic" and Keatsian modes with which he has been sometimes linked in literary histories, and not all of his remaining poems are in the obscurely laden, sensual and guilt-ridden manner of "The House of Life". He wrote a great deal of occasionally moralistic verse resembling that of contemporary Victorians in sentiment and mode, and many of his techniques not only prepare for the decadents and symbolists but more immediately parallel those of Tennyson and Patmore, and influence those of Swinburne, Morris, and Hopkins. He was a sufficiently important figure to merit analysis as a member of several traditions. In general he tended towards two major forms of poetry, the contrived ballad and the sonnet or lyric containing a series of similar images suggestive of the beloved and the interior life (often fused). His ballads use imagery and landscape more arbitrarily and boldly, their stark mannerisms providing a cleanness and precision which the less theatrical poems lack. There are thematic and verbal overlappings between these categories, and a certain middle ground is tenanted by the longer narrative ballad, forced to expand simple balladic effects with some of the descriptions and less violent imagery characteristic of the non-balladic poems. The sonnets and lyrics repeat again and again an inner landscape of dim lights, woods, trees, waters, mirrors, birds, music, and certain aspects of the beloved (hair, eyes, gaze), and clearly show preoccupation with the experiences of shifting, changing, diminishing, and almost-ceasing-to-be. The Rossettian landscape is simpler and more self-absorbed than the Keatsian one, also less capable of delight and reflection of the external world. It contained several tendencies which endeared it to Rossetti's immediate successors; its preoccupation with sexual repression and guilt, its use of simple elemental imagery to convey the ultimate or fundamental powers of things, its elaborate baroque ornamentation, and its linguistic and philosophic tendencies towards simultaneous mingling and dissolution. It is no coincidence that in his sonnets and poetry *in propria persona* Rossetti was concerned equally with the beloved and with the annihilation of identity, with Love and with Death. Nevertheless, though these were types and figures deeply important to him, he seldom defined them in clear contrast, but blended them in the sombre and deliquescent ambiguity of his later works. At his best, Rossetti's poetry was stoically restrained in its evocation of images by which he managed to contain and express an acute sense of loss.

NOTES

1   It appears on October 23, 1852, 1147; see facing page. The number of alterations is noticeable; in general they are clear improvements in the interests of clarity, accuracy, and dramatic effect. For example, the biblical quotation is rendered more exact, and the sequence of victims clarified ("*him* ... *him* ... *him*" to "me ... thee ... him"). "Blood-red and purple" is more emphatically dramatic (or ominous) than "crimson and orange". As in the revision of "Jenny", there is a slight bowdlerization, in the deemphasis of the narrator's sensual response to the woman and the greater emphasis given to the poem's philosophical conclusion. The former occurs through omitting stanza 3 and line 4 of stanza 6, the latter through the clarification of the allegory in stanza 10. This slight tightening of diction and the personifications of the added stanza render the second version of the poem more serious and consciously weighty in tone.

THE CARD DEALER; or, VINGT-ET-UN.

FROM A PICTURE.*

> Ambition, Cupidité,
> Et délicieuse Volupté,
> Sont les sœurs de la Destinée,
> Après la vingt-première année.
> *Calendrier de la Vie,* 1630.

Could you not drink her gaze like wine?
 Yet, though their splendour swoon
Into the lamplight languidly
 As a tune into a tune,
Those eyes are wide and clear, as if
 They saw the stars at noon.

The gold that's heaped beside her hand,
 In truth, rich prize it were;
And rich the dreams that wreathe her brows
 With magic silence there;
And he were rich who should unwind
 That woven golden hair.

Some music surely fans the sense,
 A breath like closing plumes:
You know it by the spark called up
 From her eyes' purple glooms;
You almost feel the instant thrill
 Pulse through the lighted rooms.

And surely, where she sits, the dance
 Now pants its eager heat:
But not more lightly or more true
 Fall there the dancers' feet,
Than fall her cards upon the board
 As 'twere a heart that beat.

Her fingers let them softly through,—
 Smooth, polished, silent things;
And each one, as it falls, reflects,
 In swift light-shadowings,
Crimson and orange, green and blue,
 The great eyes of her rings.

Whom plays she with?—With thee: thou lov'st
 Those gems upon her hand.
With me: I search her secret will.
 All deem her bosom grand.
We play together, she and we,
 Within a vain strange land:—

A land without any order,
 Whose substance is as breath;
Where one lying down ariseth not
 Nor the sleeper awakeneth;
A land of darkness, as darkness itself,
 And of the shadow of death.

What be her cards, you ask? Even these:—
 The heart, that does but crave
More, being fed; the diamond,
 Skilled to make base seem brave;
The club, for smiting in the dark;
 The spade, to dig a grave.

And do you ask, what game she plays?
 With *him*, 'tis lost or won;
With *him* it is playing still; with *him*,
 It is not yet begun;
But 'tis a game she plays with all,
 The game of Twenty-One.

H. H. H.

---

* The picture is one painted by the late Theodore von Holst; and represents a beautiful woman, richly dressed, who is sitting at a lamp-lit table, dealing out cards, with a peculiar fixedness of expression.

2   Theodor von Holst, German romantic painter; Rossetti kept a reproduction of "The Card-Dealer" in his room.
3   *Letters*, I, 224, to Allingham, September 17, 1854: "I've been greatly interested in *Wuthering Heights*, the first novel I've read, and the best (as regards power and sound style) for two ages, except *Sidonia*."
J.R. Wahl adds the note, "William Morris and Edward Burne-Jones were introduced to *Sidonia* by D.G.R. and shared his enthusiasm for the book."
4   See Appendix, Part 9, for treatment of Rossetti and Wells.
5   Reproduced in Robin Ironside, *Pre-Raphaelite Painters* (London: Phaidon, 1948), and in Carl Peterson, *op. cit.*, 469. Other paintings also include stars and/or sun and moon — "Sancta Lilia" (1874), in which the woman wears a loose crown of stars, and "Astarte Syriaca", in which two globes which may be the sun and moon are behind the central female figure. Both these paintings are reproduced in *Masterpieces of Dante Gabriel Rossetti* (1829-1882) (London: Gowans and Gray, 1912).
6   William Rossetti, *Works*, xiv. "The Bible was deeply impressive to him, perhaps above all Job, Escclesiastes, and the Apocalypse."
7   The Episcopal burial service of Rossetti's time contained only verses 10:21 and 19:25-27 from Job. But a note to the latter in *The Book of Common Prayer: With Notes, Legal and Historical* by Archibald John Stephens, vol. 3 (London, 1854), p. 1726, reads in part, "The Book of Job ... hath been anciently esteemed of special use in this office; and the Western Church of old had nine several lessons at burial from hence, beginning at Job vii. 16." By "Western Church of old" I assume Stephens means the pre-Reformation Catholic Church. The modern Catholic "Matins of the Dead" contains Job 7:16-21 as a "First Lesson", with second and third lessons from Job 10 (*The Layman's Missal*, Baltimore: Helicon Press, 1962).
8   *Letters*, I, 46, to William Holman Hunt, September 1848:

"Vingt-et-un" is, as you of course know, the title of a game of cards, at which I have supposed the lady of the picture (personifying, according to me, intellectual enjoyment) to be playing, since twenty-one is the age at which the mind is most liable to be beguiled for a time from its proper purpose.

9   Walter K. Gordon, "A Critical Selected Edition of William Morris' *Oxford and Cambridge Magazine* (1856)", *DA*, 21 (1961), 3781-82, 451-459.
10 Samuel Johnson, LL. D., *A Dictionary of the English Language by Samuel Johnson, LL. D. in Four Volumes*. The Ninth Edition, Vol. 1 (London, 1805). The fourth meaning listed for "burden" is "the verse repeated in a song; the bob; the chorus". Dr. Johnson's phrases and meanings seem to have been freely borrowed by later dictionary-makers, however much his alleged demerits were attacked in their prefaces, and any of several dictionaries could have yielded Johnson's definition.
11 Carl Peterson, 291, suggests that "that zealous tract" may be "The Burden of Babylon: A Poem and Tract for the Times" (1850), "an intensely evangelical document". He feels "The Burden of Nineveh" could even be in part a response to that poem and reproduces some lines from it (292). Baum cites Layard's *A Popular Account of Discoveries at Nineveh*, an abridged version of Layard's *Nineveh and Its Remains*, as the source for Rossetti's note on the worship service held in the shadow of the great bulls, and states that a great many of the poem's details derived from Layard (*Dante Gabriel Rossetti: Poems, Ballads and Sonnets*. New York: Doubleday Doran, 1937), 114n.
Peterson cites the accounts of objects falling into dust and description of Assyrian reliefs as from Layard's *Nineveh* (London, 1849), pp. 326 and 332-333, respectively, but I have been unable to locate an edition which corresponds to his

numbering. The references to Christians kneeling in the trenches Rossetti himself footnoted.

12   See Revelation 21:20, "The fifth, sardonyx: the sixth, sardius, the seventh, chrysolyte, the eighth, beryl; the ninth, a topaz; the tenth, a chrysoprasus, the eleventh, a jacinth; the twelfth, an amethyst." The listing of jewels is a biblical mannerism; porphyry, however, is not a biblical stone. Browning uses "porphyry" nine times, including once in *Sordello*, but not "sardonyx"; Elizabeth Browning includes "porphyry" in her "Casa Guidi Windows" (1851). Keats surprisingly mentions neither, while Shelley refers to "porphyry" once and "sardonyx" never; Tennyson uses both, including a sardonyx in "The Palace of Art" and a porphyry in "The Princess" (both published before "The Burden") and in general is a frequent presenter of jewels. In "Columbus" occurs a biblically inspired list, "... jasper, sapphire, chalcedy, emerald, sardonyx, sardius, Chrysolite, beryl, topaz, chrysoprase, jacynth, and amethyst". He shared with Keats an occasional use of sapphires and a more frequent use of diamonds. One of Keats' diamond phrases, "Their glassy diamonding on Turkish floor" ("Fragment of 'The Castle Builder'") suggests Tennyson's similar identification of the Near-Eastern with the exotic. Keats discusses this preference in the same fragment:

Greek busts and statuary have ever been
Held, by the finest spirits, fitter far
Than vases grotesque and Siamesian jar;
Therefore 'tis sure a want of Attic taste
That I should rather love a Gothic waste
Of eyesight on cinque-coloured potter's clay
Than on the marble fairness of old Greece.   (11. 55-61)

When in the "diamond" passage of the poem he describes his imagined ideal room, the effect is vaguely pre-Raphaelite:

It should be rich and sombre, and the moon,
Just in its mid-life in the midst of June,
Should look thro' four large windows and display
Clear, but for gold-fish vases in the way,
Their glassy diamonding on Turkish floor;
The tapers keep aside, an hour and more,
To see what else the moon alone can show; ...
It is a gorgeous room, but somewhat sad ...   (11. 26-32, 48)

Further examination of Romantic and Victorian taste in jewel-allusions might reveal interesting shifts.

13   For an excellent discussion of Tennyson's interest in evolution in the early poems, see John Killham's *Tennyson and the Princess: Reflections of an Age* (London: Athlone, 1958), chapter XI, "The Princess and Evolution". Patmore reveals a similar interest in his *Poems* (1844). The mingling of patriotic and evolutionary themes is a generally spasmodic quality as well as a characteristic of the early Tennyson. However Patmore's concern with evolution is more vague, bombastic, and chauvinistic than Tennyson's.

14   See Appendix, part 14, "The French Symbolists and Wilde".

15   Paull F. Baum, ed., *An Analytical List of Manuscripts in the Duke University Library* ... (Durham, N.C.: Duke, 1937), 27. Baum compares the rime stanzas of the two versions, "The stanza is the same in both: two quatrains (abab and cdcd) connected with a c-rime, except that in A the first quatrain was somewhat looser, riming abcb."

For possible echoes of Wordsworth in "On Mary's Portrait", see Appendix, part 7.

16. *Ibid.*, 28.

17   Virginia Surtees, *The Paintings and Drawings of Dante Gabriel Rossetti...* (London: Oxford, 1971), vol. 2, plate 367.
18   *Works*, 663.
19   *Ibid.*
20   Philip Hendry, *The National Gallery London* (London: Thames and Hudson, 1960), 116.
21   *Ibid.* Consciously or not, Hendry is clearly a latter-day Paterian.
22   For a beautiful collection of Burne-Jones reproductions, see David Cecil, *Visionary and Dreamer Two Poetic Painters: Samuel Palmer and Edward Burne-Jones* (Princeton University Press, 1969). Plate 66 gives "The Wine of Circe", dated 1863-69.
23   *Letters*, I, 319. Later in II, 436, January 1862, he writes to Charles Eliot Norton of Burne-Jones, "I cannot convey to you in words any idea of the exquisite beauty of all he does. To me no art I know is so utterly delightful, except that of the best Venetians."
24   *Letters*, II, 745n, cited from *Rossetti Papers: 1862-1890*, ed. W.M. Rossetti (London: Sands, 1903), 407, 408. Whatever his melancholy concerning his own failures in painting, Rossetti was not without self-esteem.
25   W. Rossetti dates it 1869, but in a letter to Barbara Bodichon dated March 15, 1870, Rossetti encloses it as "a sonnet I have just written..." *Letters*, II, 816, 817.
26   *Letters*, II, 816.
27   Tennyson's "The Day-Dream" had appeared in Volume II of the 1842 *Poems*. The portrait is reproduced in *Masterpieces of D.G. Rossetti (1828-1882)* (London: Gowans and Gray, 1912), 62.
28   *Letters*, III, 1246, in a letter to Edmund Gosse, 1873.
29   "Maud", I, 11. 402-404, 409-411. Rossetti writes Allingham of his predominantly negative opinions on "Maud" in *Letters*, I, 266, 267, August 1855:

... much is surely artificial, and some very like rubbish .... The leading character is quite uncongenial and a person who, being made the medium of the social and other views, deprives them of all value in fact, though to be sure you know they're Tennyson's, or rather that T. has written so about them, for as for impressing one with sincerity, they read much more like a sort of thing the author thinks 'ought' to be written, but about which he feels lazy and thinks it (as some of his readers perhaps do) nothing but a bore. In style too these parts are generally quite overloaded and sometimes almost as bad as "Lady Geraldine's Courtship" .... The story throughout, from the 'flattened' father onwards, seems worthy rather of Alex. Smith than Tennyson.

Incidentally, Rossetti's comparison of "Maud" to Alexander Smith's poetry was not unique — "Maud", "Men and Women", and "Aurora Leigh", all published in 1855, suffered in reception from a pronounced critical revulsion from spasmody. See Mark Weinstein, *William Edmonstoune Aytoun and the Spasmodic Controversy* (New Haven: Yale, 1968), 172-191.
30   Peterson, 309.
31   *Works*, 669, and *Letters*, III, 1003, September 10th, 1871.
32   *Works*, 669.
33   The letter which William Rossetti cites is in *Letters*, III, 989, 990, August 1871. Elsewhere Rossetti speaks of his desire for religious belief (*Letters*, II, 582):

Its default in me does not arise from want of natural impulse to believe, nor of reflection whether what I should alone call belief in a full sense is possible to me. Thus I know that while discussion on such points with a believer is painful to me, it affords me no counterbalancing profit....

On the death of Alexander Gilchrist he writes to his widow concerning immortality (*Letters*, II, 439):

... what can be done except to trust to what is surely at least a natural instinct in all ... that such terrible partings from love and work must be, unless all things are a mere empty husk of nothing, – a guide to belief in a new field of effort and a second communion with those loved and lost?

34   Cited in *Works*, 669.
35   *Works*, 241, 242.
36   From Hastings Rossetti writes Ford Madox Brown a letter proclaiming his indolence in an off-hand way (*Letters*, I, 200, May 23rd, 1854):

There are most wonderful things to paint there, and here and everywhere; but I do not mean to paint a single one, as the pursuit of art is a bore, except when followed in the dozing style.

He comments on seeing images in a half-somnolent state (*ibid.*, 201):

Sometimes through the summer mists the sea and sky are one; and, if you half shut your eyes, as of course you do, there is no swearing to the distant sail as boat or bird, while just under one's feet the near boats stand together immovable, as if their shadows clogged them and they would not come in after all, but loved to see the land. So one may lie and symbolize till one goes to sleep, and that be a symbol too perhaps.

37   The most representative and well-arranged anthology of the poetry of Rossetti is that by Paull Baum, *Dante Gabriel Rossetti: Poems, Ballads and Sonnets* (New York: Doubleday Doran, 1937). His section "Lyrics" prints a substantial selection of brief poems of the kind to which I refer, including "Love-Lily", "First Love Remembered", and "A Young Fir Wood". See Appendix, part 13, "A Passage From Tennyson and Two Rossetti Lyrics".

38   *Letters*, I, 43, to Mrs. Gabriele Rossetti, dated "Towards September, 1848":

By the bye, I will transcribe you a howling canticle written by me yesterday – in what agony of tears let the style suggest. I hereby declare that if snobbishness consists in the assumption of false appearances, the most snobbish of all things is poetry.

He then quotes "The Fall of the Leaf".

39   Many later nineteenth-century poets create elegies illustrated by falling autumn leaves; the best is perhaps Hopkins' "To Margaret". Examples from Dixon include two songs, "The feathers of the willow / Are half of them grown yellow" and "Why fadeth thou in death, / Oh yellow waning tree?" See James Sambrook, *A Poet Hidden: The Life of Richard Warson Dixon 1833-1900* (London: Athlone Press, 1962), 50, 89.

Natural alterations frequently express decay and change – the shifts in sea and cloud, the presence of snow – and there are few nineteenth-century poets not in some way preoccupied with them. The elegiac tone becomes more automatic as the century progresses. The great ancestor of many autumnal elegiac poems must be Shelley's "Ode to the West Wind".

40   There could be debates concerning which sonnets are "political"; I have excluded those which celebrate historical events preceeding the French Revolution. Stephen Spector includes "The Staircase of Notre Dame, Paris" among the political sonnets. His is the only other discussion of political sonnets which I have seen, "The Centripetal Journey: The Poetry of Dante Gabriel Rossetti", unpublished dissertation, University of Pennsylvania, 1970, 49-52.

APPENDIX: SOURCES AND RESEMBLANCES

'Imitation is criticism'
(Blake, "Annotations to Reynolds")

Rossetti was extremely proud of what he considered his own originality in invention, guarding himself both from the appearance of having plagiarized and from what he believed to be the plagiarism of his work by others. Under the heading "Sentences and Notes" in his *Works* appears the assertion, "I was one of those whose little is their own" (p.607). Ford documents Rossetti's avoidance of Keatsianisms (*Keats and the Victorians*, pp. 123-126); one reason for his reluctance to print "My Sister's Sleep" was the resemblance of its stanza to that of the later "In Memoriam". He spoke of protecting his subject-matter from plagiarists:

I am now sending the printer seven new sonnets, of which four are for designs of mine – viz: two for "Cassandra", one for "Passover" and one for Magdalene. I think this may help me in defending the subjects against plagiarists. (*Letters*, ii, 740)

Several times throughout his life he commented on what he felt was his best trait:

... dwell particularly on the fact that my religious subjects have been entirely independent in treatment of any corresponding representation, and indeed altogether original in the inventions. (*Letters*, i, 104, August 1851, to William Rossetti)

... I painted in the style which I originated for years, when no works at all resembled mine except my own .... (*Letters*, ii, 504, April 1864, to Ernest Gambart)

If one could do something of this sort with one's inventions (much the best quality I have as a painter) one might really get one's brain into print before one died, ... like Albert Dürer, and moreover be freed perhaps from slavery to 'patrons' while one lived. (*Letters*, iii, 992, August 1871, to William Bell Scott)

Recent critics have frequently accepted Rossetti's self-evaluations, in part I believe because of an implicit bias toward the essentially romantic notion of the artist/poet as original genius. The practice of tracing sources has fallen into disrepute, and its adherents have been accused (sometimes with justice) of the assumption, corroborated by unconvincing and remote parallelisms, that poets literally 'copy' one another, and that literary history is some kind of endlessly extended echo chamber. This reaction may have obscured the extent to which Rossetti applied poetic inventiveness and imagination to the data of his wide reading and autodidactic erudition.

Study of poetic interrelationships can also lead to fairly general and complex problems in pattern-recognition, if one attempts to trace poetic mannerisms and techniques shared by many persons within a period. Several poets now considered minor may have significantly affected the style of someone now considered a very major figure – witness for example the influence of Elizabeth Barrett Browning on Rossetti, or that of Richard Watson Dixon on Hopkins. Study of resemblances and influences can also help one recognize that full blame for what later seem lapses in taste should seldom be placed on any one author – after reading Mrs. Browning, I am less revolted by Rossetti's practice of sending languishing, pious, youthful heroines to coyly erotic deaths. Ignorance of these interrelationships is ignorance of a worthy subgenre of the history of ideas, and neglect of a useful instrument for understanding poetry.

I have not written on several of the more substantial topics in the study of Rossetti's literary affinities, his resemblances for example to the Spasmodics, Coleridge, Browning, and Tennyson, and his influence on Wilde and Swinburne. The notes that follow are limited and partial, sketches that could be executed with greater thoroughness and attention to detail; I hope that they are convincing enough to suggest the outlines of several such larger designs.

1. *The Divine Comedy*

Despite the obviousness of the topic and frequent casual critical references, a detailed study of Rossetti's relation to the works of Dante has never been attempted. Most previous commentary has exhausted itself in vague platitudes or confined itself to parallels with the *Vita Nuova*, to the exclusion of *The Divine Comedy*. Peterson, for example, states that Rossetti used Dantean motifs chiefly between 1868 and 1871 (356), but by Dantean he refers to the Lady-love-worship motifs shared with other medieval romance poetry. He denies a relation between the journey imagery of Rossetti's early period and Dante's journey (371). I do not dispute Rossetti's different sensibilities and eroticized metaphysics, but the portions of "The House of Life" describing dim and weary journeys seem to me blurred and Blakean transmutations of the images of *The Divine Comedy*. Baum comments that "The Blessed Damozel" could be a compressed "Festus"; similarly, if an inattentive and untheologically minded reader were to skim *The Divine Comedy* looking for fine phrases and pictures, he or she would encounter numerous Rossettian expressions or landscapes. Many of these images of course are both common to all poetry and subject to the vagaries of translation, but it is my view that the extensive analogies to *The Divine Comedy* have never been adequately documented. I sketch only a few of these, since this is a substantial topic in itself.

Among the many common images are those of flames, mirrors, jewels, flashing lights, lamps, the lady's smiles, the sun and stars, angels, birds, snakes and monsters, boughs of trees, hills and pools of water, trances, swoonings, tears, spirits and presences. Rossetti's pauses throughout life's journey, like those of Dante, are often accompanied by notice of the positioning of the terrain and astronomical bodies. Dante's constant analogies suggest Rossetti's often cumbersome reliance on analogy throughout the journey sonnets of the early period.

Throughout his travels Dante experiences being lost, confusion, and a sense of overpowering drowsiness; he climbs pathways, turns back, hastens to the end, pauses, ascends and descends hills. Especially he is preoccupied with his own sloth, constantly admonishing himself to duty and expressing guilt. These suggest to me strongly both the moral and physical landscape of the early "House of Life" sonnets.

Inferno, Canto 13:

> ... when we for our part pushed on through
> a wood unmarked by any beaten track.
> Not green the leaves, but of a dusky hue;
>   not smooth the boughs, but gnarled and interwound;
>   not fruit-trees there, but poisonous brambles grew.
> Not rougher brakes or thicker could be found ....

Canto 15:

> 'Up there', I answered him, 'in the life lit
>   by sunshine, in a valley I went astray,
>   ere half my sum of days was yet complete.
> From it I turned at dawn but yesterday:

as to it I returned did he appear
and leads me home now by this narrow way.'
And he to me: 'And thou pursue thy star,
Thou canst not fail to reach the glorious port.

Compare the sestet of "The Landmark", sonnet 67, written in 1854:

But lo! the path is missed, I must go back,
    And thirst to drink when next I reach the spring
Which once I stained, which since may have grown black.
    Yet though no light be left nor bird now sing
    As here I turn, I'll thank God, hastening,
That the same goal is still on the same track.

The drowsy lingerer or sleeper occurs frequently in both poets:

Inferno, Canto 24:

'Henceforth thou thus must shake off sloth; for they
    who sit down or lie 'neath quilts will ne'er
    to fame,' the master said, 'find out the way; ....
Rise therefore: with thy spirit which, unless
    crushed by its body's weight, is conqueror
    in every fight, conquer thy weariness.
A longer stair must needs be mounted: nor
    is it enough to have left yon dismal throng:
    if learnt, now see thou profit by this lore.'

Purgatorio, Canto 1:

    ... and far away
    I recognized the shimmering of the sea.
We paced the lonely level, like as they
    who, the road lost, go seeking it anew
    and, till they find it, deem they vainly stray.

Compare "The Choice: III", Sonnet 73:

Think thou and act; tomorrow thou shalt die.
    Outstretched in the sun's warmth upon the shore,
    Thou say'st: "Man's measured path is all gone o'er:
Up all his years, steeply, with strain and sigh,
Man clomb until he reached the truth; and I,
    Even I, am he whom it was destined for."
    How should this be? Art thou then so much more
Than they who sowed, that thou shouldst reap thereby?

Nay, come up hither. From this wave-washed mound
    Unto the furthest flood-brim look with me;
Then reach on with thy thought till it be drown'd.
    Miles and miles distant though the last line be,
And though thy soul sail leagues and leagues beyond, –
    Still, leagues beyond those leagues, there is more sea.

Several of the stories used by Rossetti in paintings or for poems are recounted or alluded to in *The Divine Comedy*; for pictures he used Paolo and Francesca (*Inferno*, Canto 5), La Pia (*Purgatorio*, Canto 6), a description of an annunciation labelled "Ecce Ancilla Dei" (*Purgatorio*, Canto 10), and Proserpina (*Purgatorio*, Canto 28). There is a description of an Uzzah carving in *Purgatorio*, Canto 10, and Rossetti painted an Uzzah and the ark panel in the background of his 1854-58 "Hamlet and Ophelia". The description of Rachel and Leah in the meadow (*Purgatorio*, Canto 27) is unrelated to the Biblical version of their life; Rossetti used Dante's meadow version for his watercolor "Rachel and Leah". *The Divine Comedy* also contains brief references to Guinevere and the Sphinx, both used by Rossetti in paintings, and several classical allusions or stories which Rossetti was to use in sonnets – Helen of Troy, Circe, Ulysses and the Trojan horse, the Sirens, Apollo, Leander and Hero. Of course Rossetti chose unusually commonplace classical references, but it is perhaps worth noticing that he could have picked these particular allusions out of Dante as well as Homer or Virgil. All that Rossetti took from the *Aeneid*, including the underground terrain of Styx, Elysian Fields, Charon, and Lethe (the "sunk stream long unmet"), is of course present in Dante. Dante gave evidence of some slight interest in art; in *Purgatorio*, Canto 10, he admires greatly a series of carvings, and in *Purgatorio*, Canto 32, he alludes to the resemblances between painting and model, a favorite Rossettian motif.

Several of the innumerable Dantean descriptions of heavenly women suggest specific features of Rossetti's paintings or poems. For example, the description of seven queens surrounded by flowers in a meadow (*Purgatorio*, Canto 29) resembles Rossetti's Moxon engraving of Arthur and the seven queens in a meadow. Elaborate self-deprecations are undoubtedly common in medieval love poetry; Dante constructs his in *Paradiso*, Canto 5, 94-99, and Rossetti expresses a similar unworthiness complexly in "True Woman: Herself". Dante's heaven, like that of the Blessed Damozel, contains infinitudes of divinely paired lovers and saintly female companions with beautiful names (in *Purgatorio*, Canto 33, Lucy, Rachel, and Matilda, in *Paradiso*, Canto 32, Sarah, Rebecca, Judith, and Mary; in "The Blessed Damozel", Cecily, Gertrude, Magdalen, and Rosalys). As in "The Blessed Damozel", Dante's lady disappears into the heavenly circle, leaving a saddened lover below, and heaven and hell are described with literal attention to relative space and position:

Paradiso, Canto 22:

So, ere thou wend yet farther into it,
    look down once more, and the vast world survey,
        by me already placed, beneath thy feet ...
In vision I re-travelled, sphere by sphere,
    the seven heavens, and saw this globe of ours
        such, that I smiled, so mean did it appear ....

Canto 31:

Not from that heaven where highest the thunders sound
    is mortal eye so distant, though within
        what sea soever it lie deepest drown'd,
as there was mine from Beatrice, I ween;
    yet nought it mattered, for her image blest
        came down to me unblurred by aught between.

"The Blessed Damozel", stanzas 5 and 6:

It was the rampart of God's house
    That she was standing on;
By God built over the sheer depth
    The which is Space begun;
So high, that looking downward thence
    She scarce could see the sun.

It lies in Heaven, across the flood
    Of ether, as a bridge.
Beneath, the tides of day and night
    With flame and darkness ridge
The void, as low as where this earth
    Spins like a fretful midge.

Both poets use the motif of the lady who raises the lover up the Purgatorial stair:

Paradiso, Canto 26:

How long it is since God, thou fain wouldst hear,
    in the high garden placed me where yon dame
    rendered thee fit to climb so long a stair.

Compare Sonnet 3, "Love's Testament", sestet:

O what from thee the grace, to me the prize,
    And what to Love the glory, – when the whole
    Of the deep stair thou tread'st to the dim shoal
And weary water of the place of sighs,
And there dost work deliverance, as thine eyes
    Draw up my prisoned spirit to thy soul!

In Dante the lady's eyes are endlessly bright, blazing, and suggestive of mirror and reflective images, while Rossetti uses this symbology in a more muted fashion. Dante's natural descriptions are never very remote from their original Heraclitean components, and in this they suggest Rossetti's.

Inferno, Canto 14, 28-30:
O'er the whole sandy desert, falling slow,
 broad flakes of fires were being downward rain'd,
 as on a windless alp descendeth snow.

Canto 14, 88-90:
... nothing before thy eyes hath been displayed
 so worth thy notice as this present stream,
 which renders all fire-flakes above it dead.'

Sonnet 96, "Life the Beloved":
Though pale she lay when in the winter grove
 Her funeral flowers were snow-flakes shed on her
 And the red wings of frost-fire rent the sky.

Dante's massive and repetitive references to flames (disembodied spirits), tears, moving winged shadows, swoons, trances, dreams, and awakenings from sleep somewhat resemble the disembodied emanations and presences of Rossettian love. Dante's preoccupation with mirrors and reflective images is a well-known medieval scientific interest and iconographic cliché; Rossetti's interest in reflective surfaces is at least in part a conscious medievalism. Other common traits include emphasis on narrow passageways (see Rossetti's "For Our Lady of the Rocks"), much cloud, sun, and moon imagery, associations of love with music, harmony, and the fusion of sounds, and a belabored emphasis on the poet's inability to understand and transmit what he experiences. Rossetti, like Dante, images the soul as a little child (*Purgatorio*, Canto 16), and uses the sea almost solely in its classical contexts of destruction, ill-fated passion, and shipwreck. Dante's great emphasis on divine love as a fusion and harmony of elements accorded well with romantic concepts of synthesizing love and with Rossetti's emphasis on the fusing of sounds and presences, apparent in "The House of Life". Finally, Dante's relationship with his "beloved guide" who leads him to love and the lady provides a possible precedent for the strange mediating figure of "Love", which often confuses and obstructs relationships in "The House of Life".

(Citations of *The Divine Comedy* are from Geoffrey Bickersteth's translation, Oxford: Blackwell, 1965).

2. Poe

Rossetti illustrated Poe and told Hall Caine that Poe had been a source for "The Blessed Damozel"; his use of Poe's dead-woman and bird-messenger motifs is commented on in Paul Lauter, "The Narrator of 'The Blessed Damozel'", *MLN*, 73 (1958), 344-48. J. Runden, "Rossetti and a Poe Image", *NQ* (June 1958), 257-58, compares Poe's "To Helen" and Rossetti's "A Portrait", mentioning their common Psyche and Holy Land images, and Baum briefly comments on Poe's influence on Rossetti in his introduction to *The Blessed Damozel* ... (Chapel Hill: University of North Carolina Press, 1937).

There are similarities in Poe's and Rossetti's admiration for the Spasmodics, their view of the imagination, their use of archaisms, gothicisms, and polysyllables, their romantic distaste for science, and their melancholy preoccupation with the lost beloved; both associate her with heaven, the past, fair hair, music, dreams, death, their own souls, nebulous spectral shapes, celestial bodies, and a literal poetic cosmology. Rossetti shared several characteristics of Poe's early work: an emphasis on enclosures, rapturous trances and palpitating sensations, a frequent sense of noise pressing on the ears, and associations of silence, music, and awe. In "Ulalume" the lover, wandering at night and in dreams, imagines an encounter in the world of shades with his dead love and feels both intense hope and loss; essentially the same situation occurs to the wandering lover of Rossetti's "The Portrait" and "The Stream's Secret". Although Rossetti was not necessarily directly influenced by Poe in his emphasis of certain themes and psychic states – in his notes on Blake, Rossetti refers to Poe as "the weird American poet" (*Works*, 592) – he found confirmation of his own tastes in an earlier heir of the Romantic tradition.

3. Blake

This is a vast subject, generally avoided. The fullest treatment is Jakob Walter, *William Blakes Nachleben in der englischen Literatur des neunzehnten und zwanzigsten Jahrhunderts* (Schaffhausen, 1927). He devotes pp. 7-26 to "Der rein dichterische Enfluss auf Dante Gabriel Rossetti". See also B.J. Morse, "Dante Gabriel Rossetti and William Blake", *ES*, 66 (1932), 364-72, which presents some very tenuous parallels between the two poets, Kerrison Preston's *Blake and Rossetti* (London, 1944), and Deborah Dorfman, *Blake in the Nineteenth Century* (Yale,

1969). Rossetti's *Letters*, vol. ii, concerning his Blake editing are also instructive. Most important, however, is vol. ii of Gilchrist's *Life of William Blake, 'Pictor Ignotus'*, 2 vols. (London: Macmillan, 1863) (Rossetti's headnotes from the 1880 edition are reprinted in the *Works*), containing Rossetti's choices from Blake's designs and writings, the latter rephrased and revised by himself. His own "simplifications" are of course interpretations; his selections reveal which Blakean preoccupations he thought most important. Rossetti's Blake is an excellent poet in his own right, if neither Blake nor Rossetti, and should be reprinted. To skim this version is to see leap out from the page innumerable words, allusions, or motifs which suggest Rossetti's language and beliefs.

Both Rossetti and Blake disliked schools in art, especially Sir Joshua's, and resented perspective and realism in drawing, choosing instead an emphasis on outline, color, invention, idiosyncratic personality (Rossetti less so), nature, and imagination. Both disliked Rembrandt and recent models, admired Dürer, Raphael, earlier artists, Dante, and Chatterton, were angered by poverty, plagiarism, neglect, commercialism, and merchants in general. Both eschewed formal science, theologies, and measurements, and in religion were pious freethinkers. Blake was not interested in the Bible as history but as a series of examples and visions, and Rossetti was similarly unorthodox-but-respectful. Blake's dictum that "Imitation is Criticism" also suggests Rossetti's mixture of eclecticism and defiance.

Most significantly, both men hated sexual puritanism and restraints, also what they considered the deceits and tyranny of sexual attraction under present social regulations. In fact Rossetti might be said to have chosen from among Blake's writings the clearest expressions of artistic and sexual antiestablishmentarianism, and to have ignored Blake's political heterodoxy and simplified his irony and essential ambiguity.

For example, Rossetti preferred "Songs of Innocence" to "Songs of Experience" and gave his reasons:

The first series is incomparably the more beautiful of the two ... while in the second series, the five years intervening between the two had proved sufficient for obscurity and the darker mental phase of Blake's to set in and greatly mar its poetic value ... there can be no comparison between the first "Chimney Sweeper", which touches with such perfect simplicity the true pathetic chord of its subject, and the second, tinged somewhat with the commonplaces, if also with the truths, of social discontent. (*Works*, 596)

By contrast, Rossetti especially appreciated Blake's treatment of the fallen-woman theme. When the publisher suggested omitting "The Everlasting Gospel" from the volume of Blake's poems, Rossetti protested to Mrs. Gilchrist:

> Pray do make a stand for the passage from *The Everlasting Gospel* about the Woman taken in Adultery. It is one of the finest things Blake ever wrote, and if there is anything in it to shock ordinary readers it is merely in the opening, which could be omitted, and the poem made to begin with 'Jesus sat in Moses' chair' etc. (*Letters*, ii, 465, 466)

Of course such an omission would render the poem's context unintelligible. Possibly under pressure from the publisher (see *Letters*, ii, 471), Rossetti also excised passages in "The Everlasting Gospel" which speak directly of adultery. An excerpt of the foreshortened result:

> 'To be good only, is to be
> 'A God, or else a Pharisee.
> 'Thou Angel of the Presence Divine,
> 'That didst create this body of mine,
> 'Wherefore hast thou writ these laws
> 'And created Hell's dark jaws? ...
> 'What was thy love? Let me see't!
> 'Was it love, or dark deceit?'
>
> 'Love too long from me hath fled;
> 'Twas dark deceit, to earn my bread;
> 'Twas covet, or 'twas custom, or
> 'Some trifle not worth caring for.
> 'But these would call a shame and sin
> "Love's temple that God dwelleth in."
>
> (Rossetti's version of fragment from "The Everlasting Gospel")

In his discussion of Blake's prose style, Rossetti describes Blake's anger against plagiarists; he then lengthily digresses on the theme of the overshadowing of original genius by direct and indirect borrowings:

> In each style of the art of a period, and more especially in the poetic style, there is often some one central initiatory man, to whom personally, if not to the care of the world, it is important that his creative power should be held to be his own, and that his ideas and slowly perfected materials should not be caught up before he has them ready for his own use. Yet, consciously or unconsciously, such an one's treasure and possessions are, time after time, while he still lives and needs them, sent forth to the world by others in forms from which he cannot perhaps again clearly claim what is his own , but which render the material useless to him henceforward. Hardly wonderful, after all, if for once an impetuous man of this kind is found raising the hue and cry, careless whether people heed him or no. It

is no small provocation, be sure, when the gazers hoot you as outstripped in your race, and you know all the time that the man ahead, who they shout for, is only a flying thief. (*Works*, 599, 600)

The description parallels Rossetti's sentiments on his own work so closely as to seem virtual autobiography. As observed in the introduction to this Appendix, Rossetti resented artistic neglect, and in later years guarded his reputation jealously; he reproved what he considered to be plagiarism of his artistic designs and poetic manner, and believed his own conceptions of style had influenced numerous well-received imitators. He also regretted that Morris and Swinburne, who had both been strongly affected by his work, had published their poetry before he could complete a volume of his own. The suddenly personal and impassioned tone in an otherwise dry series of dutiful headnotes suggests a subject that concerned him deeply. Indeed throughout his life he never tired of pointing out the obscurity and lack of recognition suffered by a large number of his favorite poets and artists. A corollary of this resentment of the neglect suffered by genius was his enthusiasm in discovering and promoting the works of unknown predecessors and contemporaries. If Rossetti failed successfully to immortalize Ebenezer Jones and Charles Wells, he did aid in increasing the recognition accorded to several poets — Chatterton, Blake, Keats, Browning — who have since become firmly established in the canon of English poets.

4. *Lord Houghton's* The Life and Letters of John Keats

The parallels between a Houghtonized Keats and Pre-Raphaelite preoccupations is striking. These indicate, of course, not only the influence of Keats' preferences or of Houghton-as-critic, but the nature of what may have gradually become fashionable tastes within a small circle of artistic-literary intellectuals, self-identified with "rebellion" and feeling themselves the maligned guardians of art. Compare also my note on Rossetti and Leigh Hunt, number 8 below. Some resemblances between Houghton-Keats and the Pre-Raphaelites follow:

a. Houghton presented Keats as a rebel from the literary sanctions of his time, an original genius, one who wrote in a "spirit of outlawry" (57), a persecuted artist, a man of self-direction. Compare the self-images of Rossetti and Holman Hunt; both were preoccupied with the theme of unrewarded merit. Many of Rossetti's favorite literary figures were neglected in their lifetime or suffered early neglect — Poe, Blake, Wells, Jones, Chatterton, Patmore, Tennyson, Browning, Shelley.

b. Keats cultivated artistic friends, liked Raphael and painters earlier than Raphael. In 1819 he wrote his brother and sister-in-law:

> When I was last at Haydon's, I looked over a book of prints, taken from the fresco of the church at Milan, the name of which I forget. In it were comprised specimins of the first and second age in Art in Italy. I do not think I ever had a greater treat, out of Shakespeare; full of romance and the most tender feeling ... even finer to me than more accomplished works, as there was left so much room for imagination. (152)

According to Houghton, Keats had some talent in both music and painting. Compare Rossetti's interest in several arts and his excitement over medieval models in art, poetry, and draperies. Hunt was also at this time an amateur poet and something of a decorator and designer as well as painter.

c. Keats depreciated science, considered Newton inferior to poets, and believed sequential reasoning valueless and irrelevant, preferences which pleased Rossetti. Like Rossetti he disliked his everyday work, although for different reasons.

d. Keats was tolerant and detached in religious matters; in a letter to Bailey, he commented, "You know my ideas about Religion. I do not think myself more in the right than other people, and that nothing in this world is probable" (132). But also, to Brown, "Is there another life? ... There must be, we cannot be created for this sort of suffering" (212). Both attitudes were expressed with some consistency by Rossetti all of his life (*cf.* "The One Hope", "Soothsay", "Spheral Change", letters to Mrs. Gilchrist).

e. Keats admired old books, the gothic, archaisms and arcane rimes; compare Rossetti's word lists, use of interesting archaisms and rimes. Houghton comments on the inappropriateness of some archaisms in their new context (119-120), an opinion with which Holman Hunt probably agreed.

f. Keats championed Chatterton and the unphilosophical Coleridge, and contemned didacticism in poetry; Rossetti greatly admired Chatterton, disdained Coleridge as philosopher (see his poems on each), disliked overt moralizing.

g. Keats was subject to passive trances; he describes himself as overcome by the identity of those around him (134), and as experiencing periods of suspended activity. Compare Rossetti's frequent descriptions of swooning, of indolence or dozing, and of a feeling of suspension between places, acts, or perceptions.

h. Keats divided women into two categories: To his sister-in-law he wrote of his admiration for "a rich Eastern look" (137) in women, declaring "As a man of the world, I love the rich talk of a Charmian; as an eternal being, I love the thought of you. I should like her to ruin me, and I should like you to save me" (138); Rossetti's similar dual sterotypes of feminine character are discussed in David Sonstroem's *Rossetti and the Fair Lady*.

i. Keats concluded a letter to Haydon, "So now in the name of Shakespeare, Raphael, and all our Saints, I commend you to the care of Heaven" (33); compare the Brotherhood's list of Immortals and use of religious terminology to describe themselves and those they admired.

j. The Brotherhood's (especially Hunt and Millais') concern with natural models was amusingly foreshadowed by Keats' claim that he and Brown would introduce an elephant into their play

but have not historical reference within reach to determine us as to Otho's menagerie. When Brown first mentioned this I took it for a joke; however, he brings such plausible reasons ... that I am giving it a serious consideration. (174)

k. Keats' interest in a British Museum sphinx — "there is a sphinx there of a giant size, and most voluptuous Egyptian expression ...." (155) — suggests Rossetti's watching of the Assyrian Bull of Nineveh being carried to its location there.

l. Throughout the *Life* Keats wrote descriptions of what he saw, composed poems at specific scenes; Rossetti was to do both throughout his first trip to Belgium and France.

m. Keats was very interested in the Paolo and Francesca episode from *The Divine Comedy*, admittedly and often admired Dantean setpiece in the early nineteenth century. Like Rossetti he was attracted by its sexuality rather than its theology:

The fifth canto of Dante pleases me more and more; it is that one in which he meets with Paulo and Francesca. I had passed many days in rather a low state of mind, and in the midst of them I dreamt of being in that region of Hell. The dream was one of the most delightful enjoyments I ever had in my life; I floated about the wheeling atmosphere, as it is described, with a beautiful figure, to whose lips mine were joined, it seemed for an age; and in the midst of all this cold and darkness I was warm; ever-flowery tree-tops sprung up, and we rested on them, sometimes with the lightness of a cloud, till the wind blew us away again." (160)

Compare Rossetti's painting of this story.

n. Keats appreciated the melancholy and macabre in art. Houghton compares Keats' "Ode to Melancholy" with Blake and Fuseli's paintings, which Rossetti admired. See also my note on Rossetti, Keats, jewels, and the gothic, Chapter 3, note 11.

o. Rossetti was unusually attracted to the theme of the lost beloved in his own work, a motif which also preoccupied Keats more than other Romantic poets, for obvious reasons. Compare Keats' "I feel the flowers growing over me" (225) with Rossetti's "And yet the earth is over her" ("On Mary's Portrait").

p. In Keats' art beauty, transience, and melancholy were associated to an unusual degree. Houghton concludes his *Life* with the melancholy moral:

The world of thought must remain apart from the world of action, for, if they once coincided, the problem of Life would be solved, and the hope, which we call heaven, would be realized on earth. And therefore men
    Are cradled into poetry by wrong:
    They learn in suffering what they teach in song ... (231)

That is, the message of poetry is sorrowful. Experience and sadness are likewise associated throughout Rossetti's work.

I would like to emphasize that these are not direct comparisons of Keats and Rossetti but of Keats' life and works, as interpreted by Houghton, with the ideas and practices of Rossetti.

5. "No Ship Came Near": A Rejected Echo of Coleridge?

A possible indication of remote Coleridgean influence on "The Bride's Prelude" occurs in "No Ship Came Near", apparently a rejected stanza for "The Bride's Prelude". It is written in the appropriate form and William Rossetti annotates it as such·

No ship came near: aloof with heed
    They tacked, as still as death;
For round our walls the sea was dense
With reefs whose sharp circumference
Was the great stronghold's sure defense.

If so, the stanza could refer to the bride's original castle before it burned, or to the stronghold to which the burned-out family fled. Rossetti may have eliminated the stanza because of its too obvious suggestion of "The Rime of the Ancient Mariner".

6. The Nineteenth-Century Literary Ballad: "The Rime" and "The Ballad of Reading Gaol"

"The Rime of the Ancient Mariner" and "The Ballad of Reading Gaol" seem to me closely related in theme and language, more so than the few specific verbal parallels which can be found suggest; Wilde's skill is shown in his ability to rework Coleridge's preoccupations in a simple stanza and meter without any suggestion of direct mimicry. Both poems concern a man who has sinned against the natural order through murder and who must suffer a prolonged repentance. Both men are separated from society and ultimately forgiven by God. In both poems certain psychological states are emphasized – heat, thirst, hallucinations, feverishness, the pain expressed in perceptions of dancing evil spirits and lurid colors. Wilde does not repeat phrases so much as single words and psychological responses, but some of these are sufficiently parallel to be listed. There are important contrasts as well – whereas the social and religious bonds of Coleridge's poem represented community and forgiveness, in Wilde's poem society builds an inhuman prison and religion ordains an unforgiving and unheeding chaplain. In "Reading Gaol" the murderer's fellow prisoners stare upon and watch him with sympathy; in "The Rime" the eyes of the dead men follow the Mariner with a curse.

"Ancient Mariner":
A speck, a mist, a shape, I wist!
And still it neared and neared:
As if it dodged a water-sprite,
It plunged and tacked and veered.   (11. 153-56)

"Reading Gaol":
They glided past, they glided fast
   Like travellers through a mist:
They mocked the moon in a rigadoon
   Of delicate turn and twist.   (III: st. 20)

"Ancient Mariner":
With throats unslaked, with black lips baked,
Agape they heard me call: ....   (11. 162-163)

"Reading Gaol":
We waited for the stroke of eight
   Each tongue was thick with thirst ....   (III: st. 33)

"Ancient Mariner":
And straight the Sun was flecked with bars, ...
As if through a dungeon-grate he peered
With broad and burning face.   (11. 177, 179-80)

"Reading Gaol":
And through the bars that hide the stars
White faces seemed to peer.   (III: st. 13)

"Ancient Mariner":
The loud wind never reached the ship,
   Yet now the ship moved on! (11. 327-328)

"Reading Gaol":
The morning wind began to moan,
   But still the night went on .... (III: st. 26)

"Ancient Mariner":
The charmed water burnt alway
A still and awful red. (11. 270-271)

"Reading Gaol":
And I knew that somewhere in the world
   God's dreadful dawn was red. (III: st. 28)

"Ancient Mariner":
Till noon we quietly sailed on,
Yet never a breeze did breathe:
Slowly and smoothly went the ship,
Moved onward from beneath. (11. 354-357, 373-376)

"Reading Gaol":
Silently we went round and round
   The slippery asphalt yard;
Silently we went round and round,
   And no man spoke a word. (IV: st. 7)

"Ancient Mariner":
For the dear God who loveth us,
He made and loveth all. (11.616-17)

"Reading Gaol":
But God's eternal Laws are kind
   And break the heart of stone. (V: st. 12)

There is incidentally an echo of "Christabel" in II: st. 4: "Nor did he peek and pine" ("Christabel", 1. 295: "Off wandering mother! Peak and pine! ...."),

7. Resemblances to Wordsworth in "On Mary's Portrait"

Since "On Mary's Portrait" is an early poem, it is interesting to see two possible resemblances to Wordsworth, in stanzas 4 and 7. "For while the world moves, she knows how", suggests the Lucy poem, "A Slumber did My Spirit Seal":

> No motion has she now, no force;
>   She neither hears nor sees;
> Rolled round in earth's diurnal course,
>   With rocks, and stones, and trees.

Also compare Rossetti's

> Sometimes the mind receives
> At such a moment that deep lore
> Which wise men have toiled vainly for ....

with Wordworth's several poems on the same theme, especially

> One moment now may give us more
> Than years of toiling reason.
>
>   ("To My Sister")

8. Leigh Hunt

Leigh Hunt may possibly have been another influence on Rossetti. Like Rossetti, Hunt was instrumental in introducing Italian literature into England through his translations, and like the early Rossetti, is conventionally considered a poet of word-painting and bright colors. Virtually identical comments have been made attempting to link Rossetti's and Hunt's ancestry with their artistic temperament, sense of color, *et cetera*. Leigh Hunt was also, like Rossetti, a poet of sensual and sexual themes. Significantly, one of his chief concerns was the relation of the visual arts to poetry. In his *Reflector* (published 1810-1811) he comments at length on painting and sculpture, since the fine arts "are in their first infancy and must be handled tenderly" (Ian Jack, *English Literature: 1815-1832*, Oxford, 1963, 321). The idea suggests Rossetti's belief that after Keats, the next 'poet' should be a painter. Leigh Hunt was of course an ardent and consistent advocate and publisher of Keats' poetry. Rossetti was given to tracing early appearances of Keats' works and looked up "La Belle Dame Sans Merci" in Hunt's *Indicator*.

In *Imagination and Fancy* (1844), Hunt expressed several poetical preferences which were to become Rossetti's – for Dante, for Renaissance and Romantic poetry above that of other periods, and for Coleridge and Keats among the Romantics. Shelley's poetry was admired, but its philosophical speculations dismissed as unpoetic, a view shared by Rossetti. Like Rossetti, Hunt considered Coleridge's philosophy irrelevant, his poetry supremely imaginative; he reprinted several passages and poems later admired and used by Rossetti (*e.g.*, "A damsel with a dulcimer" from "Kubla Khan"), and he discussed Coleridge's meter at length in his introduction. Leigh Hunt's list of his five favorites is exactly the same as Rossetti's — not only "Christabel", "The Ancient Mariner", and "Kubla Khan", but also "Love; or Genevieve" and "Youth and Age". Both men believed poetry to be an artistic category superior to and more inclusive than painting.

There were many reasons, then, why Rossetti could have been drawn to the interests and opinions, if not the poetry, of Leigh Hunt. In 1848 he sent copies of his early poems and translations to Hunt asking his advice on whether he should choose poetry or painting as a career; doubtless he directed his question to Hunt because of the latter's known interest in both arts. Hunt answered that poetry "is not a thing for a man to live upon while he is in the flesh", of which Doughty dourly comments, "Nothing could have more certainly damped Rossetti's poetic ardour" (*A Victorian Romantic*, Oxford, 1960, 62). An interesting study could describe the relation of Leigh Hunt's thought and poetry to Rossetti's, as well as the nature of early Victorian views on the relationship of literature and visual arts.

9. Charles Wells

Throughout his life Rossetti consistently eulogized the works of Charles Wells (*Stories After Nature, Joseph and His Brethren*). His first mention of Wells in a letter occurs in August, 1848 (*Letters*, i, 40), and upon Wells' death in 1879 he wrote:

Alas the mighty Wells! What has it profited him to have been born the greatest English poet since Shakespeare! ...
In my belief, Wells had fuller dramatic genius than any Englishman at all except Shakespeare; and if he had done what he might, would have stood — we may not dream of saying by the side of that unapproachable man — but in as distinct and solitary a place between him and all others. Wells had a firmer hold on the human heart and a more piercing gaze into the springs of human action than belonged to any predecessor, contemporary, or successor. (*Letters*, iv, 1626, 1627)

For Rossetti's critical evaluation of Wells, see his *Works*, 593.

In his long introduction to Charles Wells' *Joseph and His Brethren: A Dramatic Poem* (London, 1908), Theodore Watts-Dunton describes Rossetti's introduction of the book to many friends. In two conversations which Watts-Dunton had with Rossetti concerning Joseph, they discussed chiefly the description of Potiphar's wife; he quotes Rossetti as claiming that Wells "had given us a portrait of a lecherous woman, perfectly astounding for vigour — you will find that she makes a pretty successful villainess" (xxiv). The two men then discuss a Persian sexual tale which minimizes the guilt of the woman involved. In 1860 Rossetti drew a pen and ink sketch of "Joseph Accused Before Potiphar" (see *The Paintings and Drawings of Dante Gabriel Rossetti (1828-1882): A Catalogue Raisonné*, Virginia Surtees, Oxford, 1971, vol. ii, plate 194).

The title of Wells' other volume, *Stories After Nature*, suggests the Pre-Raphaelites' frequent use of "nature" as a slogan. In Wells the "nature" invoked seems to be romantic passion, destined to be thwarted by a series of cruel fathers, rivals, extreme misfortunes, and intricately Boccaccian plots. The associations of frustrated sexuality, early death, detailed descriptions of bloodshed and pain, conflict of love and friendship, the passive noble maiden, and powerful cruel father suggest the German *Sturm und Drang*, but also the world of "The Bride's Prelude" or of R.W. Dixon's narratives. Precious adolescent melodrama is played against medieval decor, Palamon and Arcite rendered even more artificial and ahistorical. In Pre-Raphaelite usage the term "nature" could in some cases mean something like "delineation of intense, rarified emotions", assumed to occur most frequently as concomitants of romantic frustration or deferred gratification. In Wells they found a precedent for this association.

10. "Jenny" and W.B. Scott's "Rosabell"

"Jenny" bears interesting resemblance in manner and point of view to W.B.Scott's much earlier "Rosabell". At the age of nineteen Rossetti had written Scott appreciatively:

A few years ago I met for the first time (in a publication called the *Story-Teller*) with your two poems, 'Rosabell' and 'A Dream of Love'. So beautiful, so original did they appear to me, that I assure you I could think of little else for several days.... (*Letters*, i., 33)

In 1855, eight years later, Rossetti wrote Allingham concerning Scott:

I think myself that *Maryanne* [the altered title of 'Rosabell']with all its faults, is better worth writing than the *Angel in the House*. As exemplified in this poem, as well as in other respects, Scott is a man something of Browning's order, as regards his place among poets, though with less range and even much greater incompleteness, but also, on the other hand, quite without affectation ever to be found among his faults, and I think, too, with more of that commonly appreciable sort of melody in his best moments. (*Letters*, i., 247, 248)

"Jenny" and "Rosabell" are noticeably similar in sentiment and opinion. Both poems describe the prostitute's idyllic rural past or days in the country, an alternate respectable life which could have been hers, her miserable future, her love of finery, the responses of children to her; both poets are sympathetic with her fate although repelled by her choices. Scott's poem, though wearisomely prolix, does make an attempt to reproduce the woman's consciousness, and as a result achieves some verisimilitude, but Scott is also more melodramatic and evasive in presenting stereotyped "rakes" and coarse women who socialize the victim to her trade, and unlike Rossetti, does not consider the possibility that the seducers may be men of background and tastes similar to his own. Both poets see the prostitute's problem as essentially one of sin; neither considers, for example, the scarcity of occupations by which women could support themselves, or the possibility that a woman might lack opportunities for marriage.

11. David Scott

Rossetti thought highly of the paintings of David Scott, W.B. Scott's brother who had died young. "[His paintings] ... with all their executive shortcomings, are amongst the noblest of our time ..." he wrote Alexander Gilchrist (*Letters*, ii, 412, see also *Letters*, ii, 453), and he managed to insert several paragraphs on David Scott in his comments on Blake's artistic influence on later painters, asserting that:

David Scott will one day be acknowledged as the painter most nearly fulfilling the highest requirements for historic art, both as a thinker and a colourist (in spite of the great claims in many respects of Etty and Maclise), who had come among us from the time of Hogarth to his own .... it is not only or even chiefly on his intellectual eminence that this statement is based, but also on the great qualities of colour and powers of solid execution displayed in his finest works, which are to be found among those deriving their subjects from history. (*Works*, 591, 592)

One such historical painting by David Scott, "The Traitor's Gate", persistently suggests to me the ambience and motif of Rossetti's poem "The King's Tragedy" (the only one of Rossetti's few historial poems to use Scottish materials, which was written while visiting W.B. Scott and Alice Boyd at Penkill Castle). "The Traitor's Gate", originally entitled "Thomas Duke of Gloucester, having been secretly carried off from England at the command of King Richard II, taken into Calais, where he was murdered", depicts a boat with several crowded, dark figures surrounding the aloof, passively suffering Duke; the bodies and boat are outlined ominously against the sky as they enter the dark tunnel; grim, pointed masonry closes in behind them. The elongated, medievally draped forms with staring eyes and bent shoulders suggest some of Rossetti's early 'medieval' paintings, and the use of a heavy frame to enclose a small space strikingly resembles the claustrophobia of many of Rossetti's own compositions. Like Thomas of Gloucester, James of Scotland is a virtuous man betrayed and about to be immured and murdered. "The Traitor's Gate" was painted in 1841 and exhibited in 1842; it is reproduced in *The Scottish School of Painting* (London: Duckworth and Co., 1906, facing p. 240). See also the reproduction of "Russians Burying Their Dead" (1831-32) in *Three Centuries of Scottish Painting: An Exhibition Arranged by the National Gallery of Canada Ottawa 1968*, plate 31, p. 25.

12. Elizabeth Barrett Browning

A. *Critical commentary*: The best treatment of Elizabeth Barrett Browning's influence on the Pre-Raphaelites is in Alethea Hayter, *Mrs. Browning: A Poet's Work and its Setting* (London: Faber, 1962), 231-232. She indicates Elizabeth Barrett Browning's influence on Rossetti, Morris, and Meredith, and mentions the embarrassed prejudice of critics and biographers who minimize Mrs. Browning's importance to their subjects. Her comments on Elizabeth Barrett Browning and Rossetti follow:

> The influence of "The Poet's Vow" is plainly visible in "The Blessed Damozel", written when Dante Gabriel Rossetti was in his nineteenth year — visible in the theme, in the metre, in the imagery of pulse and flame and seraph flight, in the archaisms, even in the use of brackets ....
>
> In emotional content, nothing could be less like the "Sonnets from the Portuguese" than the "House of Life" sequence, but the tone of voice used to express such different sentiments is often disconcertingly the same .... Rossetti too builds sonnets round first kisses and love letters, meditates on equal troth, on love and death, on love's sacrament, makes poetry out of love's repetitions; like the first draft of the "Sonnets from the Portuguese", his sonnets have a string of titles embodying the word 'love' — "Love's Redemption", "Love's Baubles", "Parted Love"; his imagery, like hers, is of flames and wings and pulses.

John Hobbs, "The Poetry of D.G. Rossetti", Diss. Yale, 1968, cites resemblances with Elizabeth Barrett Browning in footnotes *passim*; he does not commit himself on whether these indicate influence, cross-influence, or fortuitous verbal patterns.

B. *Parallels with 1844* Poems: It seems probable that the 1844 *Poems* were the greatest influence; William Rossetti comments that Mrs.

Browning and old ballads took the place of Shelley in Rossetti's affections when he was sixteen or seventeen (*Works*, xiv), and this would have been just after the 1844 *Poems* were published.

Since *Festus* is seriously considered a source for "The Blessed Damozel", the 1844 volume's "A Drama of Exile", complete with sinning Adam, virtuous Eve, angels, and a literal imagery ("There is a sound through the silence, as of the falling tears of an angel") should be credited also. Among other things, it contains the assumption that the male lover is in some way unworthy of the female beloved; Baum finds this assumption in "The Blessed Damozel" mystifying and ascribes it to a vestigal influence of the *Festus* plot. Rossetti felt this emotion in his identification with Beatrice's suitor, and in life about his dead wife; (see his remarks to Mrs.Gilchrist). Elizabeth Barrett Browning alters the Adam myth to make woman man's aid and redeptress; Eve is also passionately verbal, conscientious and expressive. Other common images and qualities in the heavenly visions of both poems: robes, stars, zodiac, flames, chanting, trees, healing, learning of new speech, exotic plants, ultimate vision of Christ, new consecration, movement of angels, sudden disappearance of vision, use of polysyllables and quasi-religious archaisms which attempt simplicity. Several expressions from Elizabeth Barrett Browning's "A Drama of Exile" suggest the language of "The Blessed Damozel":

"and float it up the ether"
"Beneath the leaning stars"
"zodiac ... curls"

Compare "across the flood of ether" (stanza 6), with "... the curled moon / Was like a little feather / Fluttering far down the gulf ... ("The Blessed Damozel", stanza 10). Rossetti's "The Blessed Damozel" seems to suggest the sort of geographical terrain more specifically described in "A Drama". As indicated previously, Rossetti carefully avoided direct borrowings but was able to use tone and effects of his predecessors with great skill.

The piously-accepting-mother, dying-daughter situation of "My Sister's Sleep" (later embarrassing to Rossetti) appears in a prolix version in Elizabeth Barrett Browning's "Isobel's Child". "Bertha in the Lane", like Aloÿse in "The Bride's Prelude", is a religious older sister, languishing in the noon heat, who confesses her sexual sin to a younger sister; she prepares a wedding dress for her sister's marriage to her own faithless ex-lover, announces her own approaching death (self-induced), and the poem ends (!). Compare the abrupt halt of Rossetti's poem after the confession has ended and the contrast in the character of the two sisters. Also the choruses of "Isobel's Child" are suggestive of "Rose Mary". Like Rossetti, Mrs. Browning preferred Keats to Shelley, and in her "A Vision of Poets" she mentions Coleridge while pointedly ignoring Wordsworth.

Another parallel is between "A Portrait" by Mrs. Browning and Rossetti's first version of his "The Portrait", called "On Mary's Portrait". Both write of a young woman's death, heaven, the painting of her portrait by a lover, her hair, books, forehead and light walk.

> A PORTRAIT
> "One name is Elizabeth." — Ben Jonson
>
> I will paint her as I see her.
>   Ten times have the lilies blown
>   Since she looked upon the sun.
> ... Moving light, as all young things,
>   As young bird, or early wheat
>   When the wind blows over it.
> ... And her voice, it murmurs lowly,
>   As a silver stream may run,
>   Which yet feels (you feel) the sun.
> ... And a stranger, when he sees her
>   In the street even, smileth stilly,
>   Just as you would at a lily.

Also, like the Blessed Damozel, she's been dead ten years; notice lilies, bowers, stillness, grain, water, birds. The situation in which lover envisions dead beloved as though she were a portrait not only occurs in Rossetti's two poems, "The Portrait" and "On Mary's Portrait", but also in his paintings of "The Blessed Damozel".

C. *Parallels with "Sonnets From the Portuguese"*: Mrs. Browning's use of personification frequently resembles that of "The House of Life", for example, in the first sonnet's personified Love and Death figures. She accompanies her personifications with solemn, formalizing polysyllables, and like Rossetti, shifts effects so rapidly that personification and abstraction do not serve their usual categorizing and explanatory purpose; rather they contribute to the merging and changing of essences and images.

More specific parallels between Mrs. Browning and 'Rossetti could be cited, but what is significant are the similarities in tone and manner. They are a surprising testimony to the influence of Elizabeth Barrett

D. *Note on Mrs. Browning as Source for Poe, Tennyson*: In view of Poe's great admiration for Mrs. Browning (he dedicated his 1845 *Poems* to her) it is interesting to see the following rimes in "A Drama of Exile" (1844):

Fare ye well, farewell!
The sylvan sounds, no longer audible,
Expire at Eden's door.
   Each footstep of your treading
Treads out some murmur which ye heard before.
Farewell! the trees of Eden
Ye shall hear nevermore.

      (repeated with minor variants *4 times* in a long chorus; compare "The Raven")

Poe frequently resembles her in his use of odd rimes on polysyllabic words.

Also, although elsewhere she imitates Tennyson, Mrs. Browning's "The Soul's Travelling" seems a possible source for his *Maud*.

13. A Passage from Tennyson and Two Rossetti Lyrics

Notice the analogies in mood and phrasing between Tennyson's 1842 lyric from "The Miller's Daughter" and Rossetti's "Even So" and "A New Year's Burden":

Love that hath us in the net,
Can we pass, and we forget?
Many suns arise and set.
Many a chance the years beget.
Love the gift is Love the debt.
   Even so.
Love is hurt with jar and fret.
Love is made a vague regret.
Eyes with idle tears are wet.
Idle habit links us yet.
What is love? for we forget:
   Ah, no! no!

      ("The Miller's Daughter")

The branches cross above our eyes,
   The skies are in a net:
And what's the thing beneath the skies
   We two would most forget?
     Not birth, my love, no, no, –
     Not death, my love, no, no, –
The love once ours, but ours long hours ago.

      ("A New Year's Burden")

14. "The House of Life" and "Modern Love"

Parallels with Meredith occur chiefly between the sonnet sequences, "Modern Love" and "The House of Life", but these are not trivial; especially compare the iconoclasm/idealism of the two retrospective, autobiographical presentations of what love is not. Meredith uses personifications somewhat in Rossetti's manner — Love, Death, Memory, Passion, child, marriage; he also relies on Rossettian images of hair, coins, fire, whirling winds, dead years, prison, slow dancing.

Meredith, "Modern Love":

I

... Then, as midnight makes
Her giant heart of Memory and Tears
Drink the pale drug of silence, and so beat
Sleep's heavy measure, they from head to feet
Were moveless, looking through their dead black years,
By vain regret scrawled over the blank wall.
Like sculptured effigies, they might be seen
Upon their marriage-tomb, the sword between;
Each wishing for the sword that severs all.

Rossetti, "The House of Life", 101, 99, 39, 97:

When vain desire at last and vain regret ....

    What time with thee indeed I reach the strand
Of the pale wave which knows thee what thou art,
    And drink it in the hollow of thy hand?

    And why does Sleep, waved back by Joy and Ruth,
Tread softly round and gaze at me from far? ....
O lonely night! art thou not known to me,
A thicket hung with masks of mockery
    And watered with the wasteful warmth of tears?

A SUPERSCRIPTION

Look in my face; my name is Might-have-been;
    I am also called No-more, Too late, Farewell; ...
Unto thine eyes the glass where that is seen
    Which had Life's form and Love's, but by my spell
    Is now a shaken shadow intolerable,
Of ultimate things unuttered the frail screen.

Mark me, how still I am! But should there dart
    One moment through thy soul the soft surprise
    Of what winged Peace which lulls the breath of sighs —
Then shalt thou see me smile, and turn apart
Thy visage to mine ambush at thy heart
    Sleepless with cold commemorative eyes.

Meredith, "Modern Love":

IV

... Whom self-caged Passion, from its prison-bars,
Is always watching with a wondering hate ....
Oh, wisdom never comes when it is gold,
And the great price we pay for it full worth:
We have it only when we are half earth.
Little avails that coinage to the old!

VII   The gold-eyed serpent dwelling in rich hair ....

XIII   ... When the renewed for ever of a kiss
          Whirls life within the shower of loosened hair!

Compare "The House of Life", 1, 92, 78, 71, 33, 2, 11:

A Sonnet is a coin ...
In Charon's palm it pay the toll to Death.

Or gold, whose master therewith buys his bane; ....

      That, ere the snake's, her sweet tongue could deceive,
And her enchanted hair was the first gold.

     Then loose me, love, and hold
Thy sultry hair up from my face; that I
May pour for thee this golden wine, brim-high,
    Till round the glass thy fingers glow like gold.

... when thou bend'st with soul-stilled face
O'er poet's page gold-shadowed in thy hair?

Now, shadowed by his wings, our faces yearn ...

    ... when Death's nuptial change
Leaves us for light the halo of his hair.

Warmed by her hand and shadowed by her hair
    As close she leaned and poured her heart through thee ....

Other Meredith passages which seem to echo Rossetti:

... our souls were in our names.
      ("Love in the Valley")

Life said, As thou has carved, such am I.
Then memory, like the nightjar on the pine,
And sightless hope, a woodlark in night sky,
Joined notes of Death and Life till night's decline:
Of Death, of Life, those inwound notes are mine.

      ("A Ballad of Past Meridian")

Compare "The House of Life", 31, 33, 101, 86:

Breathe low her name, my soul; for that means more.

Then Love breathes low the sweetest of thy names; ....

Ah! let none other alien spell soe'er
But only the one Hope's one name be there, –
    Not less nor more, but even that word alone.

LOST DAYS

The lost days of my life until to-day,
    What were they, could I see them on the street
    Lie as they fell? ....
I do not see them here; but after death
    God knows I know the faces I shall see,
Each one a murdered self, with low last breath.
    "I am thyself, – what hast thou done to me?"
"And I – and I – thyself," (lo! each one saith,)
    "And thou thyself to all eternity!"

15. *The French Symbolists and Wilde*

A. There are several fundamental if coincidental similarities between Rossetti and French symbolist poetry; the reputation of each in England doubtless furthered that of the other. Verlaine's translator (C.F. MacIntyre, *Selected Poems* by Paul Verlaine, Berkeley: University of California Press, 1970), 204, even mentions a correspondence with Rossetti as remote as that of their common use of the mistress-as-sister concept. The following passages, at least, seem to me suggestive of Rossettian Pre-Raphaelitism or of "The House of Life":

Nerval, "Fantaisie":

Puis un château de brique à coins de pierre,
Aux vitraux teints de rougeâtres couleurs,
Ceint de grands parcs, avec une rivière
Baignant ses pieds, qui coule entre des fleurs;

Puis une dame, à sa haute fenêtre,
Blonde aux yeux noirs, en ses habits anciens ...
Que, dans une autre existence peut-être,
J'ai déjà vue – et dont je me souviens!

"Fantasy":

then an old brick chateau with stone corners,
and the leaded glass of the windows, color of rose,
begirt by great parks, where a river flows,
bathing the stones as it glides among the flowers;

then a lady, at the tall window of her chamber,
a blond with dark eyes, in an old-time gown ...
whom I have seen before, perhaps, and known
in another existence – and whom I remember!

Verlaine, "Mélancholia, VI. Mon Rêve Familier"

Son nom? Je me souviens qu'il est doux et sonore,
Comme ceux des aimés que la Vie exila.

Son regard est pareil au regard des statues,
Et, pour sa voix, lointaine, et calme, et grave, ella a
L'inflexion des voix chères que se sont tues.

"Melancholia, VI. My Familiar Dream"

Her name? I remember it sonorous
and sweet as the names of those loved long ago,

exiled by Life, and like a statue's wide
gaze is hers. Serene and grave, her voice
has the tone of those dear voices that have died.

The translations are by C.F. MacIntyre, in *Selected Poems* by Paul Verlaine and *French Symbolist Poetry* (Berkeley: University of California Press, 1970 and 1966).

B. Wilde's "Sphinx" contains a passage on the deserted desert god somewhat parallel in theme to "The Burden of Nineveh". It reveals a clearly changed sensibility, however, partly the result of French influences; there is more directness in presenting the bitter and the ironic:

Ten hundred shaven priests did bow to Ammon's altar day and night,
Ten hundred lamps did wave their light through Ammon's carven house – and now

Foul snake and speckled adder with their young ones crawl from stone to stone
For ruined is the house and prone the great rose-marble monolith!

Wild ass or trotting jackal comes and couches in the mouldering gates:
Wild satyrs call unto their mates across the fallen fluted drums.

And on the summit of the pile the blue-faced ape of Horus sits
And gibbers while the fig-tree splits the pillars of the peristyle.

The God is scattered here and there: deep hidden in the windy sand
I saw his giant granite hand still clenched in impotent despair. (11. 107-116)

"The Sphinx" also contains the Styx and Charon image used in the introductory sonnet of "The House of Life":

False Sphinx! False Sphinx! By reedy Styx old Charon, leaning on his oar,
Waits for my coin .... (11. 171-72)

"The Sphinx" doubtless owes its most direct debts to French poetry, which contains the languid jewelled boredom, sexual distaste, arcane Eastern references, and imagery of the sphinx, pyramid, and cat also present in Wilde's poem. Rossetti's Assyrian bull has little of the complex sensuality and attractiveness of Wilde's sphinx. Passages of similar sensibility, however, occur in Nerval, Baudelaire, Corbière, and Verlaine.

SELECTED BIBLIOGRAPHY

This is not intended to be an exhaustive bibliography for the study of Rossetti's poetry, since one is contained in William Fredeman's *Pre-Raphaelitism: A Bibliocritical Study* (Cambridge: Harvard, 1965). I have placed asterisks in front of items published after 1964, the year in which Fredeman's entries end. For convenience, also, I have subdivided the bibliography into several sections: A. Earlier Drafts and Versions of Rossetti's Poems; B. Works by Rossetti; C. Biographical Materials on Rossetti; D. Works on Rossetti's Poetry and Translations; E. Sources and Influences; F. Related Works. Some duplication of listings in the different categories seemed appropriate.

A. EARLIER DRAFTS AND VERSIONS OF ROSSETTI'S POEMS

Studying Rossetti's revisions is not difficult because of the careful work of Paull Baum and others in printing early manuscript versions. The following list is intended only as a guide to the most important versions and does not include each of several appearances of the same manuscript, or discussions of Rossetti's revisions. The list does not claim thoroughness, but may save others from discovering some of these versions more slowly than is necessary.

Baum, Paull Franklin, "The Bancroft Manuscripts of Dante Gabriel Rossetti", *Modern Philology*, 39 (1941), 47-68.
    Contains the early "Jenny", eighteen "The House of Life" sonnets, and other poems.
——, *Dante Gabriel Rossetti: An Analytical List of Manuscripts in the Duke University Library with Hitherto Unpublished Verse and Prose* (Durham: Duke University Press, 1931).
——, *Dante Gabriel Rossetti: "The Blessed Damozel". The Unpublished Manuscript, Texts, and Collation* (Chapel Hill: University of North Carolina Press, 1937).
    In connection with this see John Sanford's article below.
——, "Rossetti, 'The White Ship', Duke University Library", *Duke University Library Notes*, 20 (1948), 2-6.
"The Card Dealer; or Vingt-et-Un", *Athenaeum* (October 23, 1853), 1147.
Gordon, Walter Kelley, *A Critical Selected Edition of William Morris' 'Oxford and Cambridge Magazine' (1856)*. Diss. Pennsylvania, 1960 (Ann Arbor: University Microfilms, 1961).
    Reprints all 17 poems and 6 book reviews, with 6 of 21 tales and 36 of 82 essays. The three Rossetti poems included are "The Staff and Scrip", "The

Blessed Damozel", and "The Burden of Nineveh". Gordon used the Rutgers University Library set of the original 12 numbers.

Howe, Merrill L., "Some Unpublished Stanzas by Dante Gabriel Rossetti", *MLN*, 48 (1933), 176-79.

Metzdorf, R.F., "The Full Text of Rossetti's Sonnet on Sordello", *Harvard Library Bulletin*, 7 (1953), 239-43.

The version in the 1911 *Works* was a partial reconstruction by William Michael Rossetti; an autograph of the entire sonnet has been found.

Rossetti, Dante Gabriel, "Of Life, Love, and Death: Sixteen Sonnets", *Fortnightly Review*. 11 n. s. 5 (March, 1869), 266-73.

*———, *Poems and Translations 1850-1870 Together with the Prose Story 'Hand and Soul'* (London: Oxford University Press, 1965).

Rossetti, William, ed., *The Germ ... Being a Facsimile Reprint of the Literary Organ of the Pre-Raphaelite Brotherhood, Published in 1850: With an Introduction* (London: Stock, 1901).

*(Also a reprint *The Germ Thoughts Towards Nature in Poetry, Literature, and Art*, with an intro. by William Michael Rossetti, New York: AMS Press, 1965).

Sanford, John Albert, "The Morgan Manuscript of Rossetti's 'The Blessed Damozel'", *Studies in Philology*, 35 (1938), 471-86.

Symons, Arthur, "Notes on Two Manuscripts", *English Review*, 54 (1932), 514-20.

Notes alterations in "Eden Bower".

Troxell, Janet Camp, ed., *Rossetti's Sister Helen* (New Haven: Yale, 1939).

———, "The 'Trial Books' of D.G. Rossetti", *Colophon*, n.s. vol. 3, no. 2 (Spring, 1938), 243-58.

Wahl, John Robert, ed., *Dante Gabriel Rossetti: Jan Van Hunks* (*Arents Tobacco Collection Publications*, No. 3) (New York: New York Public Library, 1952).

Records variants in successive manuscripts.

Wallerstein, Ruth, "The Bancroft Manuscripts of Rossetti's Sonnets, with the Text of Two Hitherto Unpublished Sonnets", *MLN*, 44 (1929), 279-84.

Wise, Thomas, J., *The Ashley Library: A Catalogue*..., 11 vols. (London: Privately printed, 1922-36). See vol. 8: 169-83; vol. 9: 112-19; vol. 10: 169-70.

B. WORKS BY ROSSETTI

POETRY

Dante Gabriel Rossetti: 'The Blessed Damozel': The Unpublished Manuscript, Texts, and Collation. Edited with an introduction by Paull Franklin Baum (Chapel Hill: University of North Carolina Press, 1937).

Dante Gabriel Rossetti: Jan Van Hunks (*Arents Tobacco Collection Publications*, No. 3). Edited from the original manuscripts by John Robert Wahl (New York: New York Public Library, 1952).

Dante Gabriel Rossetti: Poems, Ballads and Sonnets. Selections from the Posthumous Poems and from His Translations. Hand and Soul. Selected with an introduction by Paull Franklin Baum (New York: Doubleday Doran, 1937).

**Dante Gabriel Rossetti Poems and Translations 1850-1870 Together with the Prose Story 'Hand and Soul'* (London: Oxford University Press, 1965).

The House of Life: A Sonnet Sequence by Dante Gabriel Rossetti. With an introduction and notes by Paull Franklin Baum (Cambridge, Mass.: Harvard University Press, 1928).
Rossetti's Sister Helen. Edited by Janet Camp Troxell (New Haven: Yale University Press, 1939).
The Works of Dante Gabriel Rossetti. Edited with preface and notes by William M. Rossetti. 2 vols. (London: Ellis, 1911).

LETTERS

*Doughty, Oswald and J.R. Wahl, eds., *The Letters of Dante Gabriel Rossetti*, 4 vols. (London: Oxford University Press, 1965-67).
Rossetti, William M., ed., *Preraphaelite Diaries and Letters* (London: Hurst and Blackett, 1900).
——, ed., *Ruskin: Rossetti: Pre-Raphaelitism. Papers 1854 to 1862* (London: Allen, 1899).

PAINTINGS

*Surtees, Virginia, ed., *Dante Gabriel Rossetti: 1828-82. The Paintings and Drawings*. 2 vols. (London: Oxford University Press, 1971).
Masterpieces of D.G. Rossetti (1928-1882): Sixty Reproductions from the Original Oil Paintings (London: Owens and Gray, 1912).

C. BIOGRAPHICAL MATERIALS ON ROSSETTI

Adrian, Arthur, "The Browning-Rossetti Friendship: Some Unpublished Letters", *PMLA*, 73 (1958), 538-44.
Baum, Paull F., "Two Victorian Poets", *Yale Review*, 39 (March, 1950), 570-72. Includes critical review of Doughty's *A Victorian Romantic*.
Benson, Arthur C., *Rossetti* (*English Men of Letters*) (London: Macmillan. 1904).
Caine, Hall, *Recollections of Rossetti* (London: Cassell, 1928).
Cassidy, John A., "Robert Buchanan and the Fleshly Controversy", *PMLA*, 67 (1952), 65-93.
Doughty, Oswald, *A Victorian Romantic: Dante Gabriel Rossetti* (London: Oxford University Press, 1960).
*Fleming, Gordon H., *Rossetti and the Pre-Raphaelite Brotherhood* (London: Hart-Davis, 1967).
*——, *That Ne'er Shall Meet Again* (London: Michael Joseph, 1971).
*Fredeman, William E., *Prelude to the Last Decade* (Manchester: John Rylands Library, 1971).
Marillier, H.C., *Dante Gabriel Rossetti: An Illustrated Memorial of His Art and Life* (London: Bell, 1899).
* Sonstroem, David, Review of four recent books on Rossetti, two biographies (Fredeman's *Prelude to the Last Decade* and Fleming's *That Ne'er Shall Meet Again*) and two critical works (Howard's *The Dark Glass* and Vogel's *Dante Gabriel Rossetti's Versecraft*), *VS*, 16 (1972), 235-37.
Vincent, E.R., *Gabriele Rossetti in England* (Oxford University Press, 1936).

Waller, R.D., ed., *The Rossetti Family 1824-54* (Manchester University Press, 1932).

D. WORKS ON ROSSETTI'S POETRY AND TRANSLATIONS

*Baker, Houston A., "The Poet's Progress: Rossetti's 'The House of Life'", *VP*, 8 (1970), 1-14.
Bartlett, Phyllis, *Poems in Process* (New York: Oxford University Press, 1951). Discusses Rossetti's revisions.
Baum, Paull F., "*Dante Gabriel Rossetti: Poems*, edited by Oswald Doughty", review, *VS*, 1 (1957), 203-204.
Bracker, Jon, "Notes on the Texts of Two Poems by Dante Gabriel Rossetti", *LCUT*, 7 (1963), 14-16.
Broers, Bernarda C., *Mysticism and the Neo-Romanticists* (New York: Haskell, 1966; rpt. Amsterdam: Paris, 1923).
*Brown, Thomas H., "The Quest of Dante Gabriel Rossetti in 'The Blessed Damozel'", *VP*, 10 (1972), 273-277.
Buchanan, Robert, *The Fleshly School of Poetry and Other Phenomena of the Day* (London: Strahan, 1872).
*Christensen, Trilby, *Theme and Image: The Structure of D.G. Rossetti's 'House of Life'*. Diss. Ohio, 1972 (Ann Arbor: University Microfilms, 1972).
*Cooper, Robert M., *Lost on Both Sides: Dante Gabriel Rossetti: Critic and Poet* (Athens: Ohio University Press, 1970).
*Culler, A. Dwight, "'The Windy Stair': An Aspect of Rossetti's Poetic Symbolism", *Ventures*, 9 (1969), 65-75.
Doughty, Oswald, "Rossetti's Conception of the 'Poetic' in Poetry and Painting", *Essays by Divers Hands (Transactions of the Royal Society of Literature*, n.s. 26) (London, 1953).
*Eldredge, Harrison, "On an Error in a Sonnet of Rossetti's", *VP*, 5 (1967), 302-303.
Evans, B. Ifor, *English Poetry in the Later Nineteenth Century* (London: Methuen, 1933).
*Fisher, Benjamin Franklin, IV, "Rossetti's 'William and Marie': Hints of the Future", *ELN*, 9 (1971), 121-129.
*Fox, Steven, *Art and Personality: Browning, Rossetti, Pater, Wilde and Yeats.* Diss. Yale, 1972 (Ann Arbor: University Microfilms, 1972).
Fredeman, William, *Pre-Raphaelitism: A Bibliocritical Study* (Cambridge, Mass.: Harvard University Press, 1965).
——, *The Pre-Raphaelites and Their Critics: A Tentative Approach Towards the Aesthetic of Pre-Raphaelitism*. Diss. Oklahoma, 1956 (Ann Arbor: University Microfilms, 1956).
——, "Rossetti's 'In Memoriam': An Elegiac Reading of the 'House of Life'", *JRLB*, 47 (1964-1965), 298-340.
Ghose, S.N., *Dante Gabriel Rossetti and Contemporary Criticism (1849-1882)* (Dijon: Imprimerie Darantière, 1929).
*Going, William T., "The Brothers Rossetti and Youth and Love", *PLL*, 4 (1968), 81-104.
*Gordon, Jan B., "A Portrait of 'Jenny': Rossetti's Aesthetics of Communion", *Hartford Studies in Literature*, 1 (1969), 89-106.
*——, "The Imaginary Portrait: Fin-de-Siècle Icon", *University of Windsor*, 5 (1969), 81-104.

*Golden, Arline Hersh, *Victorian Renascence: The Amatory Sonnet Sequence in the Late Nineteenth Century*. Diss. Indiana, 1970 (Ann Arbor: University Microfilms, 1970).
*Greene, Michael, *A Study of D.G. Rossetti's Poetry and Aesthetic*. Diss. Indiana, 1969 (Ann Arbor: University Microfilms, 1970).
*Hammond, Lewis Kenneth, *The Treatment of Sexuality in the Poetry of Dante Gabriel Rossetti*. Diss. Wisconsin, 1972 (Ann Arbor: University Microfilms, 1972).
*Harris, Ronald L., *Interior Action in Rossetti's 'The House of Life'*. Diss. U.C.L.A., 1970 (Ann Arbor: University Microfilms, 1971).
*Harris, Wendell V., "A Reading of Rossetti's Lyrics", *VP*, 7 (1969), 299-308.
*Hayward, Ralph M., III, *Dante Gabriel Rossetti's 'The Early Italian Poets': A Study in the Art of Translation*. Diss. Tulane, 1971 (Ann Arbor: University Microfilms, 1971).
Heath-Stubbs, John, *The Darkling Plain: A Study of the Later Fortunes of Romantic Poetry from George Darley to W.B. Yeats* (London: Eyre and Spottiswood, 1950).
*Hobbs, John Nelson, *The Poetry of Dante Gabriel Rossetti*. Diss. Yale, 1968 (Ann Arbor: University Microfilms, 1968).
Holberg, Stanley M., *Image and Symbol in the Poetry and Prose of Dante Gabriel Rossetti*. Diss. Maryland, 1959 (Ann Arbor: University Microfilms, 1959).
*——, "Rossetti and the Trance", *VP*, 8 (1970), 299-314.
*Howard, Ronnalie Roper, *The Dark Glass: Vision and Technique in the Poetry of Dante Gabriel Rossetti* (Athens: Ohio University Press, 1972).
*——, *The Poetic Development of Dante Gabriel Rossetti, 1847-72*. Diss. Pennsylvania State, 1969 (Ann Arbor: University Microfilms, 1969).
*——, "Rossetti's 'A Last Confession': A Dramatic Monologue", *VP*, 5 (1967), 21-29.
*Hume, Robert D., "Inorganic Structure in 'The House of Life'", *PLL*, 5 (1969), 282-95.
*Hunt, John Dixon, *The Pre-Raphaelite Imagination 1848-1900* (London: Routledge and Kegan Paul, 1968).
Hyder, Clyde K., "Rossetti's 'Rose Mary': A Study in the Occult", *VP*, 1 (1963), 197-207.
Jackson, Elizabeth, "Notes on the Stanza of Rossetti's 'The Blessed Damozel'", *PMLA*, 58 (1943), 1050-56.
*Johnson, Wendell Stacy, "D.G. Rossetti as Painter and Poet", *VP*, 3 (1965), 9-18.
*Johnston, Robert D., *Dante Gabriel Rossetti* (New York: Twayne, 1969).
*Kendall, J.L., "The Concept of the Infinite Moment in 'The House of Life'", *VN*, 28 (Fall, 1965), 4-8.
Knickerbocker, K.L., "Rossetti's 'The Blessed Damozel'", *Studies in Philology*, 29 (1932), 485-504.
Lang, Cecil, "The French Originals of Rossetti's 'John of Tours' and 'My Father's Close'", *PMLA*, 64 (1949), 1219-22.
——, *Studies in Pre-Raphaelitism*. Diss. Harvard, 1949.
*Langford, Thomas A., "Rossetti's 'The Blessed Damozel, 71'", *Ex* 30 (1971): Item 5.
Lauter, Paul, "The Narrator of 'The Blessed Damozel'", *MLN*, 73 (1958), 344-48.
*Lewis, Rodger C., *The Poetic Integrity of D.G. Rossetti's Sonnet Sequence, 'The House of Life'*. Diss. Toronto, 1969.
Lindberg, John, "Rossetti's Cumaean Oracle", *VN*, 22 (Fall, 1962), 20-21.

*McGann, Jerome J., "Rossetti's Significant Details", *VP*, 7 (1969), 41-54.
Mégroz, R.L., *Dante Gabriel Rossetti: Painter Poet of Heaven and Earth* (London: Faber, 1928).
*Miyoshi, Masao, *The Divided Self: A Perspective on the Literature of the Victorians* (New York University Press, 1969).
*Nelson, James, "Aesthetic Experience and Rossetti's 'My Sister's Sleep'", *VP*, 7 (1969), 154-58.
*——, "The Rejected Harlot: A Reading of Rossetti's 'A Last Confession' and 'Jenny'", *VP*, 10 (1972), 123-129.
Omans, Glen Allen, *Medieval French Poetic Form in Victorian Poetry*. Diss. Minnesota, 1963 (Ann Arbor: University Microfilms, 1963).
Paolucci, Ann, "Ezra Pound and Dante Gabriel Rossetti as Translators of Guido Cavalcanti", *Romanic Review*, 51 (1960), 256-67.
Pater, Walter, *Appreciations* (London: Macmillan, 1889).
Peterson, Carl, *The Poetry and Painting of Dante Gabriel Rossetti*. Diss. Wisconsin, 1961 (Ann Arbor: University Microfilms, 1961).
Robillard, Douglas, "Rossetti's 'Willowwood' Sonnets and the Structure of 'The House of Life'", *VN*, 22 (Fall, 1962), 5-9.
Robson, W.W., "Pre-Raphaelite Poetry", *British Victorian Literature: Recent Revaluations*, edited by Shiv Kumar (New York University Press, 1969), 172-191.
*Ryals, Clyde de L., "The Narrative Unity of 'The House of Life'", *JEGP*, 69 (1970), 241-57.
*Seigel, Jules Paul, "Jenny: The Divided Sensibility of a Young and Thoughtful Man of the World", *SEL*, 9 (1969), 677-93.
*Sonstroem, David, *Rossetti and the Fair Lady* (Middleton, Conn.: Wesleyan University Press, 1970).
*Spector, Stephen, *The Centripetal Journey: The Poetry of Dante Gabriel Rossetti*. Diss. University of Pennsylvania, 1969 (Ann Arbor: University Microfilms, 1970).
*——, "Love, Unity, and Desire in the Poetry of Dante Gabriel Rossetti", *ELH*, 38 (1971), 432-458.
*Stein, Richard L., "Dante Gabriel Rossetti: Painting and the Problem of Poetic Form", *SEL*, 10 (1970), 775-792.
Storey, George, "Robert Buchanan's Critical Principles", *PMLA*, 68 (1953), 1228-32.
*Stevenson, Lionel, *The Pre-Raphaelite Poets* (Charlotte: University of North Carolina Press, 1972).
Symons, Arthur, "Notes on Two Manuscripts", *English Review*, 54 (1932), 514-20.
——, *Studies in Strange Souls* (London: Sawyer, 1929).
Tietz, Eva, "Das Malerische in Rossettis Dichtung", *Anglia*, 51 (1927), 278-306.
*Tobias, R.C., "The Year's Work in Victorian Poetry: 1969", *VP*, 8 (1970), 219-260. (Comments on "Jenny", 252).
Todd, William B., "D.G. Rossetti's Early Italian Poets, 1861", *BC*, 9 (1960), 329-31.
Troxell, Janet C., "The 'Trial Books' of D.G. Rossetti", *Colophon* n.s., vol. 3, no. 2 (1938), 243-58.
*Vogel, Joseph F., *Dante Gabriel Rossetti's Versecraft* (*University of Florida Humanities Monograph*, no. 34) (Gainesville: University of Florida Press, 1971).
——, "'White Rose' or 'White Robe' in 'The Blessed Damozel'", *ELN*, 1 (1963), 121-23.

Wallerstein, Ruth, "Personal Experience in Rossetti's 'House of Life'", *PMLA*, 42 (1927), 492-504.
Weatherby, Harold L., "Problems of Form and Content in the Poetry of Dante Gabriel Rossetti", *VP*, 2 (1964), 11-19.
Welby, T. Earle, *The Victorian Romantics: The Early Work of Dante Gabriel Rossetti, William Morris, Burne-Jones, Swinburne, Simeon Solomon and Their Associates* (London: Howe, 1929).

E. SOURCES AND INFLUENCES

Cramer, Maurice, "What Browning's Literary Reputation Owed to the Pre-Raphaelites", *ELH*, 8 (1941).
——, "Browning's Literary Reputation at Oxford 1855-1859", *PMLA*, 57 (1942), 232-40.
Culler, Dwight and Helen, "The Sources of 'The King's Tragedy'", *Studies in Philology*, 41 (1944), 427-41.
Culler, Helen, *Studies in Rossetti's Reading*. Diss. Yale, 1944 (Ann Arbor: University Microfilms, 1944).
DeVane, William, "The Harlot and the Thoughtful Young Man", *SP*, 29 (1932), 463-484.
*Dorfman, Deborah, *Blake in the Nineteenth Century* (New Haven: Yale University Press, 1969).
*Duerksen, Roland A., *Shelleyan Ideas in Victorian Literature* (The Hague: Mouton, 1966).
Fehr, Bernhard, *Studien zu Oscar Wilde's Gedichten* (Berlin: Mayer und Muler, 1918).
*Fike, Francis, "Gerard Manley Hopkins' Interest in Painting After 1868: Two Notes", *VP*, 8 (1970), 315-334.
Ford, George H., *Keats and the Victorians: A Study of His Influence and Rise to Fame, 1821-1895 (Yale Studies in English*, vol. 101) (New Haven: Yale University Press, 1944).
*Gordon, Walter Kelley, "Pre-Raphaelitism and 'The Oxford and Cambridge Magazine'", *JRULB*, 29 (1966), 42-51.
Gray, Mrs. Nicolette, *Rossetti, Dante, and Ourselves* (London: Faber, 1947).
Holthausen, Ferdinand, "D.G. Rossetti und die Bibel", *Germanisch-Romanische Monatsschrift*, 13 (July-August 1925), 310-12; 14 (January-February 1926), 73-76.
*Hosmon, Robert S., "*The Germ* (1850) and *The Oxford and Cambridge Magazine* (1956)", *VPN*, 4 (1969), 36-47.
McKillop, Alan D., "*Festus* and 'The Blessed Damozel'", *MLN*, 34 (1919), 93-97.
*Laurent, Martha Long, *Tennyson and the Poetry of "The Germ": A Study in the Early Pre-Raphaelite Poets' Relation to Tennyson*. Diss. Georgia, 1965 (Ann Arbor: University Microfilms, 1965).
Morse, B.J., "Dante Gabriel Rossetti and Dante Alighieri", *Englische Studien*, 68 (1933), 227-48.
——, "Dante Gabriel Rossetti and William Blake", *Englische Studien*, 66 (1932), 364-72.
Preston, Kerrison, *Blake and Rossetti* (London: Moring, 1944).
Routh, James, "Parallels in Coleridge, Keats, and Rossetti", *MLN*, 25 (1910), 33-37.
Runden, J., "Rossetti and a Poe Image", *Notes and Queries*, 203 (June, 1958), 257-58.

Shine, Wesley, "The Influence of Keats Upon Rossetti", *Englische Studien*, 61 (1927), 183-219.
Short, Clarice, "Ozymandius and Nineveh", *Notes and Queries*, 201 (October, 1956), 440-41.
Turner, Albert Morton, "Rossetti's Reading and Critical Opinions", *PMLA*, 42 (1927), 465-91.
Unwin, Rayner, "Keats and Pre-Raphaelitism", *English*, 9 (1951), 229-35.
Villard, Leonie, *The Influence of Keats on Tennyson and Rossetti* (Saint-Etienne: Mulcey, 1914).
Walter, Jakob, *William Blakes Nachleben in der englischen Literatur des neunzehnten und zwanzigsten Jahrhunderts* (Schaffhausen, 1925 and 1927).
Willoughby, L.A., *Dante Gabriel Rossetti and German Literature* (London: Oxford University Press, 1912).

F. RELATED WORKS

*Alighieri, Dante, *The Divine Comedy*: Text with translation in the metre of the original by Geoffry L. Bickersteth (Oxford: Blackwell, 1965).
——, *The Vision*, trans. R.H.F. Cary (London: William Smith, 1844).
*Antippas, Andy P., "Tennyson's Sinful Soul: Poetic Tradition and Keats Turned Imbecile", *Tulane Studies in English*, 17 (1969), 113-34.
Bailey, Philip, *Festus, a Poem*. 17th American edition (Boston: Sanborn, Carter, and Bazin, 1856).
Banks, J.A. and Olive, *Feminism and Family Planning in Victorian England* (New York: Schocken, 1964).
Basler, Roy, *Sex, Symbolism, and Psychology in Literature* (New Brunswick: Rutgers University Press, 1948).
Bate, Walter Jackson, *The Stylistic Development of John Keats* (New York: Humanities Press, 1958).
Baum, Paull F., "Coventry Patmore's Literary Criticism", *University of California Chronicle*, 25 (1923), 244-60.
Blunden, Edmund, *Leigh Hunt: A Biography* (London: Cobden-Sanderson, 1930).
Broers, Bernarda C., *Mysticism and the Neo-Romanticists* (New York: Haskell, 1966; rpt. Amsterdam: Paris, 1923).
Browning, Elizabeth Barrett, *The Complete Poetical Works of Elizabeth Barrett Browning* (Boston: Houghton Mifflin, 1900).
Browning, Robert, *The Works of Robert Browning*, ed. F.G. Kenyon. 10 vols. (London: Ernest Benn, 1966; rpt. 1912 ed.).
*——, *Poetical Works 1833-1864*, ed. Ian Jack (London: Oxford, 1970).
*Bryant, H.B., *The Spasmodic School: A Study of a Victorian Literary Phenomenon*. Diss. Vanderbilt, 1968 (Ann Arbor: University Microfilms, 1968).
Buchanan, Robert, *The Fleshly School of Poetry and Other Phenomena of the Day* (London: Strahan, 1872).
*Buckley, Jerome, ed. and intro., *The Pre-Raphaelites* (New York: Random, 1968).
——, *Tennyson: The Growth of a Poet* (Boston: Houghton Mifflin, 1960).
*——, *The Triumph of Time: A Study of the Victorian Concepts of Time, History, Progress, and Decadence* (Cambridge, Mass.: Harvard University Press, 1966).
Bush, Douglas, *Mythology and the Romantic Tradition in English Poetry* (Cambridge, Mass.: Harvard University Press, 1937).

Carr, J. Comyns, *Some Eminent Victorians. Personal Recollections in the World of Art and Letters* (London: Duckworth, 1908).
Cassidy, John A., "Robert Buchanan and the Fleshly Controversy", *PMLA*, 67 (1952), 65-93.
*Charlesworth, Barbara, *Dark Passages: The Decadent Consciousness in Victorian Literature* (Madison and Milwaukee: University of Wisconsin Press, 1965).
Church of England, *The Book of Common Prayer and Administration of the Sacraments* with notes by Archibald John Stephens (London: Harrison and Son, 1849-54).
——, *The Book of Common Prayer and Administration of the Sacraments, and Other Rites and Ceremonies of the Church* (London: Oxford University Press, 1843).
Coleridge, Samuel T., *The Poems of Samuel Taylor Coleridge*, ed. Ernest Hartley Coleridge (London: Oxford University Press, 1912).
Collins, John Churton, *Illustrations of Tennyson* (London: Chatto and Windus, 1891).
*Cunningham, Gilbert F., *The Divine Comedy in English: A Critical Bibliography: 1782-1900* (New York: Barnes and Noble, 1965).
De Sua, William J., *Dante Into English* (Chapel Hill: University of North Carolina Press, 1964).
*Enscoe, Gerald E., *Eros and the Romantics: Sexual Love as a Theme in Coleridge, Shelley, and Keats* (The Hague, Paris: Mouton, 1967).
*Engelberg, Edward, *The Symbolist Poem: The Development of the English Tradition* (New York: E.P. Dutton, 1967).
Evans, B.Ifor, *English Poetry in the Later Nineteenth Century* (London: Methuen, 1933).
*Faverty, Frederic E., ed., *The Victorian Poets: A Guide to Research* (Cambridge, Mass.: Harvard University Press, 1968).
*Fox, Steven, *Art and Personality: Browning, Rossetti, Pater, Wilde, and Yeats*, Diss. Yale, 1972 (Ann Arbor: University Microfilms, 1972).
*Fredeman, William E., *Pre-Raphaelitism: A Bibliocritical Study* (Cambridge, Mass.: Harvard University Press, 1965).
*Gent, Margaret, *Theme and Symbol in the Poetry of William Morris*. Diss. Leeds, 1970.
Ghose, S.N., *Dante Gabriel Rossetti and Contemporary Criticism (1849-1882)* (Dijon: Imprimerie Darantière, 1929).
Gilchrist, Alexander, *Life of William Blake, "Pictor Ignotus"*. 2 vols. (London: Macmillan, 1863).
Groom, Bernard, *The Diction of Poetry from Spenser to Bridges* (University of Toronto Press, 1955).
Hamilton, Walter, *The Aesthetic Movement in England* (London: Reeves and Turner, 1882).
Hayter, Alethea, *Mrs. Browning, A Poet's Work and Its Setting* (London: Faber and Faber, 1962).
*——, *Opium and the Romantic Imagination* (Berkeley and Los Angeles: University of California Press, 1970).
Heath-Stubbs, John, *The Darkling Plain: A Study of the Later Fortunes of Romantic Poetry from George Darley to W.B. Yeats* (London: Eyre and Spottiswood, 1950).
*Hirsch, Gordon D., "Tennyson's Commedia", *VP*, 8 (1970), 93-106.
Hough, Graham, *The Last Romantics* (London: Methuen, 1947).
Houghton, Lord (Richard Monckton Milnes), *The Life and Letters of John Keats* (London: J.M. Dent, 1927).

*Hunt, John Dixon, *The Pre-Raphaelite Imagination 1848-1900* (London: Routledge and Kegan Paul, 1968).
Hunt, Leigh, *The Poetical Works of Leigh Hunt*, ed. H.S. Milford (London: Oxford University Press, 1923).
——, *Selected Essays* (London: J.M. Dent, 1929).
Hunt, William Holman, *Pre-Raphaelitism and the Pre-Raphaelite Brotherhood*. 2 vols. (London: Macmillan, 1905-1906).
Johnson, Wendell Stacy, "The Bride of Literature: Ruskin, the Eastlakes, and Mid-Victorian Theories of Art", *VN*, 26 (Fall, 1964), 23-28.
*——, *Gerard Manley Hopkins: The Poet as Victorian* (Ithaca: Cornell University Press, 1968).
*Keats, John, *The Poems of John Keats*, ed. H.W.Garrod (London: Oxford University Press, 1966).
*Lang, Cecil, ed. and intro., *The Pre-Raphaelites and Their Circle* (Boston: Houghton Mifflin, 1968).
Layard, Austen H., *Discoveries among the Ruins of Nineveh and Babylon; with Travels in Armenia, Kurdistan, and the Desert* .... (New York: G.P. Putnam, 1853).
——, *Nineveh and Its Remains: With an Account of a Visit to the Chaldaean Christians of Kurdistan, and the Yezidis, or Devil-Worshippers; and an Inquiry into the Manners and Arts of the Ancient Assyrians*. 2 vols (London: John Murray, 1849).
Killham, John, *Tennyson and The Princess: Reflections of an Age* (London: Athlone, 1958).
MacGillivray, James R., *Keats: A Bibliographical and Reference Guide with an Essay on Keats' Reputation* (University of Toronto Press, 1949).
*MacIntyre, C.F., trans., *French Symbolist Poetry* (Berkeley: University of California Press, 1966).
McKillop, Alan D., "A Victorian Faust", *PMLA*, 40 (1925), 743-68.
*Maturin, Charles, *Melmoth the Wanderer* (Lincoln: University of Nebraska Press, 1968).
Meinhold, Wilhelm, *Sidonia the Sorceress, the Supposed Destroyer of the Whole Reigning Ducal House of Pomerania*, trans. by Lady Wilde; Mary Schweidler, *The Amber Witch* (London: Reeves and Turner, 1894).
*Merritt, James D., ed., *The Pre-Raphaelite Poem*. With an introduction (New York: Dutton, 1966).
Miles, Alfred H., *The Poets and Poetry of the Nineteenth Century*. 11 vols. (London: Routledge, 1905-1907).
(Vol. 5, Charles Kingsley – James Thomson, includes selections from Ebenezer Jones, Dobell, Woolner, Alexander Smith, Joseph Skipsey, R.W. Dixon.)
*Miyoshi, Masao, *The Divided Self: A Perspective on the Literature of the Victorians* (New York University Press, 1969).
Omans, Glen Allen, *Medieval French Poetic Form in Victorian Poetry*. Diss. Minnesota, 1963 (Ann Arbor: University Microfilms, 1963).
*Ostriker, Alicia, *Vision and Verse in William Blake* (Madison and Milwaukee: University of Wisconsin Press, 1965).
Packer, Lona Mosk., "William Michael Rossetti and the Quilter Controversy: 'The Gospel of Intensity'", *VS*, 7 (1963), 170-83.
Paden, W.D., *Tennyson in Egypt: A Study of the Imagery in his Earlier Work* (Lawrence: University of Kansas Press, 1942).
Patmore, Coventry. *Courage in Politics and Other Essays 1885-1896* (London: Oxford University Press, 1921).
——, *The Poems of Coventry Patmore*, ed. with an intro. by Frederick Page (London: Oxford University Press, 1949).

——, *Principle in Art, Etc.* (London: G. Bell and Sons, 1912).
*Patterson, Charles I., *The Daemonic in the Poetry of John Keats* (Urbana: University of Illinois Press, 1970).
*Pearsall, Ronald, *The Worm in the Bud: The World of Victorian Sexuality* (London: Weidenfeld and Nicholson, 1969).
*Peckham, Morse, *Victorian Revolutionaries: Speculations on Some Heroes of a Culture Crisis* (New York: George Braziller, 1970).
Praz, Mario, *The Romantic Agony*. Second edition (London: Oxford University Press, 1951).
Pyre, J.F.A., *The Formation of Tennyson's Style* (Madison and Milwaukee: University of Wisconsin Press, 1921).
Saintsbury, George, *A Historical Manual of English Prosody* (1910 edition; rpt. New York: Schocken, 1966).
*Sampson, Ronald V., *The Psychology of Power* (New York: Random, 1965).
Shell, Ada, "The Meter of Christabel", *The Fred Newton Scott Anniversary Papers*, ed. C. De Witt Thorpe and Charles Whitman (University of Chicago Press, 1929).
Schmutzler, Robert, *Art Nouveau* (London: Thames and Hudson, 1964).
*Schneider, Elizabeth W., *The Dragon in the Gate: Studies in the Poetry of G.M. Hopkins* (Berkeley and Los Angeles: University of California Press, 1968).
*Stevenson, Lionel, *The Pre-Raphaelite Poets* (Charlotte: University of North Carolina Press, 1972).
Swinburne, Algernon Charles, *Essays and Studies* (London: Chatto and Windus, 1875).
——, *Selected Poetry and Prose*, ed. and intro. John D. Rosenberg (New York: Random, 1968).
Temple, Ruth Z., *The Critic's Alchemy: A Study of the Introduction of French Symbolism into England* (New York: Twayne, 1953).
Tennyson, Alfred, *Poems* (London: Moxon, 1859).
——, *Poems of 1842*, ed. Christopher Ricks (London: Collins, 1968).
——, *The Poems of Tennyson*, ed. Christopher Ricks (London: Longmans, 1969).
*Verlaine, Paul, *Selected Poems*, trans. C.F. MacIntyre (Berkeley: University of California Press, 1970).
*Wasserman, Earl, *The Finer Tone: Keats' Major Poems* (Baltimore: John Hopkins, 1967).
Wells, Charles, *Joseph and His Brethren: A Dramatic Poem*. With an introduction by Algernon Charles Swinburne and a note on Rossetti and Charles Wells by Theodore Watts-Dunton (London: Oxford University Press, 1908).
——, *Stories After Nature*. With a Preface by W.J. Linton (London: Lawrence and Bullen, 1891).
*Wilde, Oscar, *The Artist as Critic: Critical Writings of Oscar Wilde*, ed. Richard Ellmann (New York: Random House, 1968).
——, *Essays and Lectures* (London: Methuen, 1909).
——, *The First Collected Edition of the Works of Oscar Wilde 1908-1922*, ed. Robert Ross. Vol. 4, *Poems* (Rpt. London: Methuen, 1969).
Williams, Charles, ed., *A Book of Victorian Narrative Verse* (London: Oxford University Press, 1927).
*Weinstein, Mark A., *William Edmonstoune Aytoun and the Spasmodic Controversy* (New Haven: Yale University Press, 1968).
Welby, T. Earle, *The Victorian Romantics: The Early Work of Dante Gabriel Rossetti, William Morris, Burne-Jones, Swinburne, Simeon Solomon and Their Associates* (London: Howe, 1929).

INDEX

Abstraction, abstract nouns, 33, 36-37, 46, 52, 72, 75, 84, 87, 91, 94, 96, 99, 101, 154, 172, 174, 281
Afterlife, 8
  lovers reunited in, 102, 130, 133, 140
Allingham, William H., 158, 255, 277
Alliteration, 34, 36-37, 40, 53-54, 85, 181
Ambition, work, 9, 18, 23-24, 26-27, 31-32, 36, 41, 92, 94
Ambiguity, 76, 78, 88, 184, 244
Ambivalence, doubt, 22, 25, 47, 73, 78, 90, 118, 129, 219, 236
Anxiety, fear, 2, 7, 20, 26, 35, 41, 78, 87, 109-10, 217, 226
  sex viewed in terror, 142
  woman figure viewed in terror, 171
Apocalypse, the, see the *Bible*.
Apollo, 38-39
Archaisms, see Medievalisms.
Arnold, Matthew, 8, 12, 57, 90
  "Dover Beach", 89
  "Empedocles on Etna", 27, 90
  "The Forsaken Merman", 63
  "To Marguerite", 90
  "Sohrab and Rustum", 90
  "The Strayed Reveller", 90
  "A Summer Night", 90
Art, 8-9, moral content of art 23-24, 27, art in "House of Life" sonnets
  40, woman as art object
  42-43, art in "Michelangelo's Kiss"
  89-91, art in Victorian poetry

257, art of Burne-Jones
258, dozing pursuit of art
270, medieval models in art
3, 18, 39, 62, 241, 244, 263
See also Painting and poetry.
Arthur (King), engraving of, 263
Athenaeum, The, 200
Augustine, St.
  Confessions, 94
Bailey, Philip, 3, 14, 197, 270
  Festus, 14, 261, 280
Banks, J.A. and Olive, 11, 101
Baker, Houston, 18, 92
Barrett, Elizabeth, see Browning, Elizabeth Barrett.
Baudelaire, Charles, 193, 286
Baum, Paull, 1, 14, 44, 47, 52-53, 91, 134, 157, 195, 215, 256, 258, 261, 266
Beatrice, see Dante.
Beloved, Rossetti's relation to;
  11, death of female beloved
  31, silent communion with beloved
  60, beloved indirectly evoked
  89, beloved suggests death
  95, life desolate without beloved
  134, beloved known in unconscious
  266, lost beloved in Poe and Rossetti
  272, lost beloved in Keats and Rossetti
  280, unworthy of female beloved
  2, 9, 19, 37, 39, 41, 81, 87-88, 92, 215-17, 220, 223-24, 226, 228, 237, 251, 254, 281

Berenson, Bernard, 227
Bible, the, Preface, i, 22, 154, 255
  quotations, 24, 29, 32, 175-76, 198, 202-3, 205, 211-12, 256
  See also Biblical diction, Religion.
Biblical diction, 22-24, 26, 36, 38, 212-13, 223, 227, 250, 256, 263
Bickersteth, Geoffrey, 265
Binding devices, 20, 31, 36, 47, 52, 71, 166, 209
Blake, William, 2-5, 11, 62, 198, 212-13, 261, 266-70, 272, 278
  "Annotations to Reynolds", 259
  "Auguries of Innocence", 238-40
  "Book of Thel", 71
Blurring, blending, 24, 46, 48-49, 51-52, 57-59, 61-62, 64-65, 67, 71, 76-89, 113, 173
Boccaccio, Giovanni, 128, 277
Bodichon, Barbara, 257
Boyd, Alice, 278
Brawne, Fanny, 6
Brontë, Emily,
  Wuthering Heights, 255
Brooks, Cleanth, 226
Brown, Ford Madox, 197, 229, 258, 270
Browning, Elizabeth Barrett, Preface, i, 3, 4, 12, 94, 96, 98-99, 159, 191, 194, 202, 257, 260, 279-82
  "Bertha in the Lane", 110
  "Casa Guidi Windows", 286
  "Isobel's Child", 281
  "Lady Geraldine's Courtship", 16
  "A Portrait", 281
  "The Seraphim", 198
  "Sonnets from the Portuguese", 100, 281-82
  "A Vision of Poets", 281
Browning, Robert, 1, 3, 5, 12, 49, 53, 149, 159, 257, 260, 269-70
  "The Ring and the Book", 27
  "Sordello", 256
Bryant, H.B., 12
Buchanan, Robert, 2, 16, 64
Buckley, Jerome, 12, 14, 101, 245
Bunyan, John, 24, 94
"The Burden of Babylon", 255

Burne-Jones, Edward, 131, 226, 229, 255, 257
Burne-Jones, Georgiana, 11
Butler, Josephine, 196
Caine, Hall, 11, 96, 101, 266
Can Grande della Scala, 137
Carlyle, Thomas,
  On Heroes and Hero Worship, 139
Cavalcanti, Guido, 196
Caverley, Charles,
  "Ballad", 196
Charlesworth, Barbara, 8-9, 101
Charon, 78, 86, 263, 286
Chatterton, Thomas, 269-70
Christ, 11, 24, 126, 139, 145, 212, 220, 227, 240, 280
Chronology, Preface, i, 19-20, 22, 43, 94-95, 98, 100, 103, 131, 135, 174, 187, 200, 215, 238
Circe, 263, see also "For 'The Wine of Circe' ".
Claustrophobia, 6, 108, 279, see also Imprisonment.
Coleridge, Samuel, T., Preface, i, 3-5, 39, 50, 71, 160, 178, 180, 185, 188-89, 193, 196, 199, 202-3, 260, 270, 272-74, 281
  "Christabel", 15, 155, 167-71, 276
  "The Eolian Harp", 61
  "Kubla Khan", 15, 168, 275-76
  "Love", 15, 276
  "Rime of the Ancient Mariner", 5, 15, 62, 108, 114, 132, 149-50, 156, 160, 167-68, 171, 177, 180, 182-83, 186-87, 201, 204, 276
  "Youth and Age", 15, 276
  Mystery poems and "Rose Mary", 167-74, 192
Colonna, Vittoria, 42
Color, use of, 1, 3, 5-6, 21, 57, 66-67, 81, 104, 131, 148-50, 155, 172, 174, 176, 181, 188, 202-4, 229, 275
Composition, see Methods of composition.
Compound words, hyphenates, 21, 28, 49-52, 99, 148, 172
Cooper, R.D., 27, 96

Corbière, Tristan, 286
Cornforth, Fanny, 10, 197
Courtly love, 78, 81, 122-30
Crashaw, Richard, 38, 65
Culler, A.D., 10
Cupid, 101
Dante Alighieri, 4, 11, 29-30, 41, 93, 101, 134-40, 160, 195, 220, 275
   Beatrice, as figure, 8, 135-36
   Divine Comedy, the, 137, 260-65, 271
   Vita Nuova, 12, 93, 196, 260
da Polenta, Count Guido, 137
Da Vinci, Leonardo, 227, 230
   "Madonna of the Rocks", 227
Death,
   41, fear of death in early sonnets
   58-59, death in Keats
   99, Tennyson's use of "Death"
   160, death in later narratives
   277, early death in Wells
   280-81, death of E.B.B. heroines
   19, 21, 37, 43, 63, 68, 72, 76-77, 84-90, 94-95, 110, 116, 130-31, 180, 182-85, 187-88, 202, 204-6, 223, 225, 227-28, 235-36, 238, 244, 254-55, 266, 273, 276
Decadents, Preface, i, 8-9, 66, 92, 160, 192, 253
Description(s), descriptive,
   4, descriptions of early Rossetti and Keats
   40, 50, 52, 57, 66, 185, natural description
   77, 80, subjective, evaluative descriptions
   94, 100, landscape descriptions
   105, 137, repetitive descriptions in "The Bride's Prelude"
   115, reluctance to use descriptive adjectives
   116, 120-22, 172, description in Keats and Rossetti
   198, Wilde's description
   251, description of copulation
   263, 265, description in Dante
   1, 28, 72, 82, 84, 99, 128, 149, 173, 175-76, 192, 203, 213, 229, 232, 234, 246
Development, Preface, i, ii, 1, 3-4, 20, 36, 43, 96, 102, 141, 199
Dixon, Richard W., 3, 122, 193, 215, 258, 260, 277
Dobell, Sydney, 3, 4, 16
   "Keith of Ravelston", 16
   The Roman, 16
Dorfman, Deborah, 266
Doubt, see Ambivalence.
Doughty, Oswald, 4, 10-11, 27, 93, 276
Dream, reverie, 79, 192, 200, 203, 220-22, 226-27, 231-32
Dunn, Henry, 11
Durant, Will, 195
Dürer, Albert, 229
Düsseldorf's Artists' Album, 142-45
Elegy, 94, 97, 236, 245, 258
Emanation, 57, 71, 113, 162, 265
Engelberg, Edward, 98
Enscoe, G.E., 195
Evans, B. Ifor, 74
Evolution (scientific), 212-13, 235
Failure, 24, 27, see also Loss.
Fate, fatality,
   189, fatalism of last narratives
   200, 206, female figure as fatality
   11, 84, 87, 100, 141, 166, 174, 177, 185, 190, 235
Fear, see Anxiety.
Female, feminine,
   166, 124, female passitivy
   141, sexually aggressive female
   145, feminine fidelity
   37, 87, 89, 109, 124, 140, 143, 169, 201
   See also Woman, woman image, Lady.
Ford, George, 1, 4-8, 15, 120, 196, 259
Fortnightly Review, The, 100
Fredeman, William, 1, 18, 92, 95, 98, 100
Freud, Sigmund, 90, 141, 222
Froissart, Jean, 190
   Chronicles, 129
Fuseli, Henry, 272

Gambart, Ernest, 259
Germ, The, 12, 114, 246
Gilchrist, Alexander, 258, 278
Gilchrist, Anne (wife of Alexander Gilchrist), 11, 268, 270, 280
Greene, Michael, 12
Guilt,
   9, preoccupation with guilt
   88-91, guilt in "House of Life" and Victorian poetry
   109-11, 113, 115, 129, guilt in "The Bride's Prelude"
   120, lack of guilt in Keats' protagonists
   253, guilt-ridden manner of "House of Life"
   254, sexual repression and guilt
   261, guilt in "House of Life" and Dante
   11, 25, 27, 36, 74, 85, 277
Guinevere,
   in the *Divine Comedy*, 263
   See also Morris, William, "The Defense of Guenevere".
Hake, Gordon, 11
Händel, George Frideric,
   Messiah, 205
Hardinge, Mr., 226
Haydon, Benjamin, 271
Hayter, Alethea, 12, 279, 281
Helen of Troy,
   in the *Divine Comedy*, 263
Hendry, Philip, 257
Henry VI, of Germany, 137
Heraclitus, Heraclitean, 57, 67, 173-74, 265
Hero,
   in the *Divine Comedy*, 263
Hobbs, John, 12, 93, 279
Holberg, Stanley, 98
Hopkins, Gerard M., Preface, i, 1, 2, 47, 52, 53-54, 68, 77, 84, 148, 151, 171, 210, 239, 254, 260
   "God's Grandeur", 48, 250
   "Henry Purcell", 98
   "Hurrahing in Harvest", 52
   "I Wake and Feel the Fell of Dark", 36, 48

   "Loss of Euridyce", 98
   "Pied Beauty", 52
   "The Sea and the Skylark", 49
   "Spelt from Sibyl's Leaves", 99
   "The Wreck of the Deutschland", 2, 12, 18, 52, 56, 73
   "To Margaret", 258
Hough, Graham, 1
Lord Houghton, see Milnes, Richard Monckton.
Howard, Ronnalie, Preface, ii, 12, 93, 197
Hunt, Diana Holman, 15
Hunt, Leight, Preface, i, 3-4, 15, 50, 217, 219, 269-70, 275-76
   "The Fish, the Man, and the Spirit", 50
   "On a Lock of Milton's Hair", 45
   Imagination and Fancy, Indicator, Reflector, 275
Hunt, William Holman, 6-7, 23, 105, 119, 127, 194, 197, 229, 255, 269-71
Hyder, Clyde, 166-67
Identity,
   13, preoccupation with identity
   28, 32, 89, confusion of identity
   39, divisions within identity
   43, dissociation of identity
   236, 241, existence of human identity
   270, overcome by others' identity
   59, 88, 220, 222, 237
Imagery, image(s),
   22, swooning
   57, 60, nature fading
   62, merging
   64, kiss
   65, tears
   66-68, richness
   66-67, 78, 83-84, metals
   66-67, 256, jewels
   68-69. sea
   69-71, fire
   76-77, marmoreal
   77, living creatures
   82, synaesthetic
   97, hermaphrodite

155, coiling serpent
164, 172, beryl
166, elemental
169, snake
171, moon
249, biblical
254, in Rossetti's poetry
261-65, in Dante
16, 21, 23, 26, 29, 33, 36, 38-41, 43, 52, 60, 72, 74-78, 80, 83-84, 87, 114, 118, 132-33, 135, 147-48, 150, 155, 160, 172-78, 181, 183-84, 189, 192, 202-6, 213-14, 222-26, 231, 238, 244, 258
See also listings for individual poems, and for Biblical diction, Female, Journey, Light, Monument, Personification, Reflection, and Woman.
Immortality, 2, 211, see also Afterlife.
Imprisonment, 83-85, 108, 113, 183, 221
Influence, Rossetti's on successors, 3-4, 178, 192-93, 254
Ironside, Robin, 255
Isolation, 8, 89, 108
Israelites, 80
Jack, Ian, 275
Jackson, Elizabeth, 196
Jeffrey, Francis (Lord), 6
Joan of Arc,
  as Rossetti heroine, 191
Johnson, Samuel, 208, 247, 255
Johnson, W.S., 12, 14
Johnston, R., 18, 145
Jones, Ebenezer, 269-70
Jones, Howard, 1
Journey(s), as metaphor, 24, 29-30, 32-33, 36, 38, 234
  See also Dante, the *Divine Comedy*.
Keats, John, Preface, i. 1-6, 8-9, 11, 15, 49, 58-59, 61, 64, 71, 123, 130, 133, 169, 172, 186, 193-99, 213-14, 217, 219, 244, 253-54, 256, 259, 269-72, 281
  "The Castle Builder", fragment, 256
  "Endymion", 6

"The Eve of St. Agnes", 7, 15, 58, 62, 65, 116-22
  "How Many Bards", 45
  "Isabella", 116-22
  "La Belle Dame Sans Merci", 16, 275
  "Lamia", 120, 155, 195
  "Ode on a Grecian Urn", 62, 76, 213-14
  "Ode to a Nightingale", 58-59
  "On Seeing the Elgin Marbles", 49
  "The Poet", 45
  "To Autumn", 245
  "When I Have Fears", 49
  Narratives compared with Rossetti's, 103-22
Kendall, J.L., 18, 92
Killham, John, 256
Kranach, Louis, 201
Lady, Pre-Raphaelite, see Woman.
Lang, Cecil, 4, 12, 120, 186, 195, 245
Landscapes, Rossetti's portrayal of, 13, 33, 86, 172, 224-25, 227, 254, 261
  See also Description.
Laurent, Martha, 12
Lauter, Paul, 266
Layard, Austen H., 255
Layman's Missal, The, 255
Leander,
  in the *Divine Comedy*, 263
Leigh-Smith, Barbara, 11
Lewis, C.S., 193
Light, 5, 18, 21, 28-29, 59, 67, 71, 77, 121, 185, 222, 225
Loss,
  27, loss in later sonnets
  25, 82, 215, 226, 254, sense of loss
  19, 21, 31, 34-36, 75, 182, 224
Lucretius, Lucretian, 237
  See also Tennyson, "Lucretius".
Luke, St., 23
McGann, Jerome, 14
McKillop, Alan, 14
Malory, Sir Thomas, 123, 190
  Morte d'Arthur, 129
Mary (Virgin), 191, 217, 227, 229
MacIntyre, C.F., 285-86
Medievalism, archaisms,

5, medievalism in Keats and Coleridge
21, few archaic words in later sonnets
129, medievalisms in Morris and Rossetti
139, medievalized Toryism
1, 3, 4, 23, 26, 36, 64, 78, 81-82, 86-87, 97, 105, 123, 168, 172, 178, 181, 185, 190, 195, 209, 222, 229, 261, 265-66, 270, 277, 279, 280
Meditation, see Dream, reverie.
Meinhold, Wilhelm,
Sidonia the Sorceress, 15, 141, 195, 200-1, 255
Memory, 77, 79, 88, 90, 94, in "House of Life"
101. 105, 118, 120, 129, 220, 224
Meredith, George, 3, 279, 283-85
"A Ballad of Past Meridian", 284
"Love in the Valley", 284
"Modern Love", 283-85
Merritt, James, 12
Meter, 46, 48, 54-55, 57, 62, 78, 84, 101, 133, 135, 146, 151, 168, 197, 209, 225, 273
Michelangelo Buonarroti, 198
Methods of composition, 18, 94, 190
Miles, Josephine, 194
Mill, John Stuart, 194
Millais, Effie Ruskin, 12
Millais, John E., 229, 271
Miller, Annie, 197
Milnes, Richard Monckton (Lord Houghton), 6-7, 9, 15, 269-72
Milton, John, 192
Miyoshi, Maseo, 12, 32, 91, 97, 101, 237
Monosyllables, monosyllabic words, 21, 30, 34, 36, 39, 42, 44, 46-49, 52, 98, 132, 182, 202, 228, 240, 242
Monuments, monumental, 48, 76-78, 85-86, 101, 214, 244
See also stasis.
Moral(s), morality, moralize, 6-9, 15, Keats' morality
15, moral content of art
16, conventional morality of Spasmodics
25-27, moral decision in "The Choice"
27, 135, 141, moralistic manner of early sonnets
43, moral bases of art
75, morality of Swinburne and others
104, moral attitude in later ballads
119, 206, moralistic terminology of Hunt
138-40, morality in "Dante at Verona"
213-14, moralizing in Wilde
248, 250, 253, morality in political sonnets
272, moral of Houghton's *Life*
4, 23, 41-42, 96, 101, 103, 120, 122, 133, 138-40, 157-59, 163-65, 180, 183, 188-89, 192-93, 213, 261
Morality, Victorian, 11, 75, 88-91, 103, 111, 158, 165-66, 242
Morris, Jane Burden, 31, 93
in "Pandora", 40
in "Astarte Syriaca", 40
in "The Day-Dream", 230
Morris, William, Preface, i, 9, 74, 87, 93, 96, 122-31, 140, 149, 171, 178, 181, 190-91, 195-96, 218-19, 254-55, 269, 279
Morris and Pre-Raphaelite woman, 122-30
Defense of Guenevere, 122-30, 171, 182, 193
Oxford and Cambridge Magazine, The, 131, 207
Moses, 80
Mystery, 160, 182, 239, mystery poems
165, 174, 203, 222
Mystical, mysticism, 4, 80, 172, 174, 177, 220, 227
Nature, natural descriptions,
28, darkening perception of nature
60, nature falling off
82, nature known indirectly
86, approaching artifice

105-8, nature in "The Bride's Prelude"
118-19, 121-22, nature in Keats and Rossetti
173-74, nature in "Rose Mary"
194, nature in Hunt
233-35, 239, nature in philosophic poems
277, nature as a slogan
Preface, i, 29, 52, 57, 78, 83, 149, 187, 216, 218, 224, 226, 230, 237, 245, 277
Nerval, Gérard de, 285-86
"Fantaisie", 285
Newton, Sir Isaac, 270
Norton, Charles Eliot, 257
Omans, Glen A., 178, 195
Originality, Rossetti's emphasis on, 4, 15, 150, 237, 260-61, 268-69, 272
Orpheus, 101
Oxford and Cambridge Magazine, The, 131, 207
Oxymorons, 73, 223, 226
Painting and poetry, relation of, 4, 28, 40, 66-67, 74, 87, 101, 104-5, 112, 127, 190, 215, 226, 270, 276, 278-79
Paradox, 5, 38, 40, 73, 76-78, 84, 165, 202, 228
Parody, 37, 81, 86, 97, 150, 177, 192-93, 239
188, of Rossetti by himself
196, of Rossetti by others
Pater, Walter, 2, 4, 8, 9, 66, 88, 198, 227, 244
Marius the Epicurean, 9
Patmore, Coventry, 2, 3, 12-13, 50, 65, 110, 159, 193, 202, 212-13, 216, 245-46, 253, 256, 270
"Lilian", 50
"The River", 51
"The Seasons", 114
"Sir Hubert", 210-11
Poems, 210, 256
Peckham, Morse, 12
Personifcation, 20, 29-30, 32, 36-37, 52, 56, 72, 99-101, 144, 185, 187, 220, 252, 254, 281

Peterson, Carl, 18, 20, 29, 92, 94, 101, 197, 233-34, 237, 241, 255
Philomel, 40
Poe, Edgar A., Preface, i, 3, 5, 96, 198, 266, 270
"Ulalume", 226, 266
Poems, 282
Politics, political beliefs, 4, 8, 104, 128, 134-40, 179, 191-92, 200, 248, 250, 258
Polysyllables, polysyllabic words, 21, 30, 34-37, 42, 44-47, 49, 56, 80, 98, 162, 227, 230, 240, 266, 280-82
Pre-Raphaelitism, Pre-Raphaelite Brotherhood,
Preface, i, 3, 7, 11-12, 15-16, 66, 105, 113, 115, 178, 194, 197-98, 200, 207, 215, 246, 256, 269, 271, 277, 285
122-30, Pre-Raphaelite woman
Preston, Kerrison, 266
Progress, 26, 212
Prostitution, 158, 196-97, 277-78
Raphael (Raffaello Santi or Raffaello Sanzio), 270-71
Reflection, 33, 63, 160, 162, 189, 204, 223, 265
Religion, religious
9, guilt a religious emotion
22, 27, religion in early sonnets
74, imagery not religious
165, 177, religion and sorcery
172, religious and mystical references
239, definition of God
249, 253, religion in political sonnets
257, Rossetti's desire for religious belief
270, Keats detached in religious matters
271, P.R.B.'s use of religious language
1, 18, 23, 29-30, 38, 77, 87, 90, 126, 139-140, 145, 171, 174-75, 190, 212, 220, 222, 227, 240, 246, 273, 280

Remorse, 9, 25, 33, 36
Revenge, 103, 141-56, 159, 192, sexual revenge poems
  160, revenge in later ballads
  185, insistence on revenge
  253, God as avenger
Reverie, see Dream.
Revisions, Preface, i, 18, 25, 54, 57, 100, 103, 131, 142-45, 157, 187, 189, 195, 207-9, 215-19, 242-43, 254
Rhythm, Preface, i, 3, 26, 31, 36-39, 43-44, 47, 56-57, 81-82, 98-99, 145, 150-52, 160, 166-67, 170-71, 186-87, 189, 192, 201, 206, 233-34, 238
Rimes, 44, 47, 54, 98, 132, 146-47, 152, 171, 181-82, 202, 209-10, 270
Robillard, D., 18, 92
Robson, W.W., 14
Romantics, traits of
  1, medievalized description
  3, tendency toward palpitating diction
  45, polysyllabic phrases
  49, monosyllables
  61, "silent song"
  71, 86, synaesthesia
  77, images of living creatures
  79, past
  99, abstractions
  116, emphases in theme
  134, motif of beloved known in unconscious
  155, serpent maiden
  256, taste in jewel-allusions
  260, notion of artist/poet
  265, concept of synthesizing love
  272, lost beloved
  94, 102, 130, 149, 215, 266, 275
  See also separate listings for Keats, Coleridge, Wordsworth, Shelley, and Leigh Hunt.
Rossetti, Christina, 3, 11, 211
Rossetti, Dante G.
  Paintings and Drawings:
    Arthur (King), engraving of, 263
    "Astarte Syriaca", 255
    "The Dancing Girl", 100
    "Dantis Amor", 202
    "The Day-Dream", 2, 39
    "Found", 215
    "Joli Coeur", 100
    "Joseph Accused Before Potiphar", sketch, 277
    "Lady Lilith", 112
    "Rachel and Leah", 263
    "Regina Cordium", 100
    "Sancta Lilia", 255
    "A Sea Spell", 223
    "Unfinished Replica of Giotto Painting of Dante", frontispiece
  Poetry
    Poems, 160
    Works, 244, 259
    Individual poems,
    "After the French Liberation of Italy", 248, 251
    "After the German Subjugation of France", 248, 251-52
    "Alas, So Long", 245
    "Autumn Song", 97, 101, 245, 258
    "Ave", 23, 246
    "The Blessed Damozel", 1, 5, 14, 23, 102, 131, 133, 135-36, 140-41, 143, 150, 154, 162, 164-60, 188, 193, 204, 215, 217, 219, 226, 261, 263-64, 266, 279, 280-81; blessed-damozel themes, 232
    "The Bride's Prelude", 1, 5, 12, 23, 102-37, 143, 160-72, 174, 181, 194, 197, 216, 219, 246, 272, 277, 280
    "The Bride's Chamber" (early title for "The Bride's Prelude"), 215
    "The Burden of Nineveh", 5, 139, 177, 207-15, 217, 219, 234, 255, 286
    "The Card Dealer", 5, 22, 25, 157, 188, 194, 200-207, 215
    "The Cloud Confines", 212, 233, 244
    "Czar Alexander the Second", 248, 252
    "Dante at Verona", 5, 22, 103-4,

131, 134-41, 166, 181, 187, 190-91, 250
"The Day-Dream", 226, 230-32
"Eden-Bower", 21, 103, 131, 141, 145, 150-56, 159, 169, 182, 184, 204, 230
"Even So", 97, 245, 282
"The Fall of the Leaf", see "Autumn Song".
"For a Venetian Pastoral by Giorgione", 30
"For 'Our Lady of the Rocks' ", 226-28
"For 'The Wine of Circe' ", 226, 228-30, 232
"God's Graal", fragment, 103, 190-92
"A Half-way Pause", 246
"Henry the Leper", 195
"The Honeysuckle", 98, 245
"The House of Life", 2, 6, 18-101, 103, 109, 113, 150, 160, 162, 172, 174, 185, 202, 215, 226-27, 249, 253, 261, 265, 279, 281, 283, 285-86
Pt. 1, "Youth and Change", 18, 95
Pt. 2, "Change and Fate", 18
"Introductory Sonnet", 32, 67, 76, 81
Sonnet 1, "Love Enthroned", 46, 69
Sonnet 2, "Bridal Birth", 19, 53
Sonnet 3, "Love's Testament", 19, 29, 46, 264
Sonnet 4, "Lovesight", 19, 29, 54, 57-58, 64, 74
Sonnet 5, "Heart's Hope", 41, 44, 58, 79 (quoted), 126
Sonnet 6, "The Kiss", 53-54, 69, 95
Sonnet 6a, "Nuptial Sleep", 53, 60, 64, 251
Sonnet 7, "Supreme Surrender", 19
Sonnet 8, "Love's Lovers", 64
Sonnet 9, "Passion and Worship", 29, 44, 49, 53, 69
Sonnet 10, "The Portrait", 47, 69
Sonnet 11, "The Love-letter", 61
Sonnet 12, "The Lovers' Walk", 44, 49, 69, 72
Sonnet 13, "Youth's Antiphony", 53
Sonnet 14, "Youth's Spring-tribute", 44, 46-47, 51
Sonnet 15, "The Birth-Bond", 31, 63, 75, 134
Sonnet 16, "A Day of Love", 46, 69
Sonnet 17, "Beauty's Progress", 47, 81
Sonnet 18, "Genius in Beauty", 19, 46-47
Sonnet 19, "Silent Noon", 30, 51, 65-66
Sonnet 20, "Gracious Moonlight", 51, 66
Sonnet 21, "Love-sweetness", 63
Sonnet 23, "Love's Baubles", 279
Sonnet 24, "Pride of Youth", 66, 95, 98
Sonnet 25, "Winged Hours", 99
Sonnet 26, "Mid-rapture", 64, 66
Sonnet 28, "Soul-light", 52
Sonnet 31, "Her Gifts", 51
Sonnet 33, "Venus Victrix", 68
Sonnet 34, "The Dark Glass", 52, 68, 95
Sonnet 35, "The Lamp's Shrine", 95
Sonnet 36, "Life-in-love", 68
Sonnet 39, "Sleepless Dream", 65, 67
Sonnet 40, "Severed Selves", 60, 67-68, 70
Sonnet 41, "Through Death to Love", 72
Sonnet 43, "Love and Hope", 69
Sonnet 44, "Death-in-love", 48, 68
Sonnet 45, "Secret Parting", 64

Sonnet 46, "Parted Love", 279
Sonnet 47, "Broken Music", 65, 73, 98
Sonnets 49-52, "Willowwood", 58, 60, 65, 204
Sonnet 54, "Love's Fatality", 83 (quoted)
Sonnet 56, "True Woman: Herself", 39, 58, 66, 73, 263
Sonnet 57, "True Woman: Her Love", 40, 69
Sonnet 58, "True Woman: Her Heaven", 58, 64
Sonnet 61, "The Song-Throe", 37, 39, 42, 65, 72, 76 (quoted)
Sonnet 62, "The Soul's Sphere", 45, 58, 68, 70
Sonnet 63, "Inclusiveness", 73
Sonnet 64, "Ardour and Memory", 39, 66, 70
Sonnet 65, "Known in Vain", 28, 30-31, 72
Sonnet 67, "The Landmark", 33, 262
Sonnet 68, "A Dark Day", 34
Sonnet 69, "Autumn Idleness", 5, 28-29, 58, 69
Sonnet 70, "The Hill Summit", 28-30, 33
Sonnets 71-73, "The Choice", 25-26, 28-29, 95, 100, 138
Sonnet 71, "Eat Thou and Drink", ("The Choice", no. 1), 64, 67
Sonnet 72, "Watch Thou and Fear", ("The Choice", no. 2), 25, 58, 70
Sonnet 73, "Think Thou and Act", ("The Choice", no. 3), 26, 262
Sonnets 74-76, "Old and New Art", 23, 138
Sonnet 78, "Body's Beauty", 70-71
Sonnet 79, "The Monochord", 52, 73
Sonnet 83, "Barren Spring", 60, 70
Sonnet 85, "Vain Virtues", 45, 58
Sonnet 86, "Lost Days", 35, 68, 285
Sonnet 88, "Hero's Lamp", 70
Sonnet 89, "The Trees of the Garden", 21
Sonnet 90, "Retro Me Sathana", 21, 72, 138
Sonnet 91,"Lost on Both Sides", 31-32
Sonnets 92, 93, "The Sun's Shame", 22, 70
Sonnet 94, "Michelangelo's Kiss", 42
Sonnet 95, "The Vase of Life", 27
Sonnet 96, "Life the Beloved", 70, 73
Sonnet 97, "A Superscription", 27, 45, 85, 283
Sonnets 99-100, "Newborn Death", 27, 64
Sonnet 101, "The One Hope", 60, 88, 270
"Jan van Hunks", 103, 183, 187-90, 192, 196
"Jenny", 22, 25, 102, 139, 141, 150, 156-59, 193, 277-78
"Joan of Arc", fragment, 103, 190-92
"The King's Tragedy", 5, 102-4, 128, 130-31, 134-35, 139, 160, 179, 182-87, 194, 253, 278-79
"A Last Confession", 16, 150, 158, 251
"A Little While", 245
"Love's Nocturne", 27, 96-97
"The Mirror", 98
"My Sister's Sleep", 1, 5, 95, 246, 259, 280
"A New Year's Burden", 245, 282
"No Ship Came Near", fragment, 272-74
"On Mary's Portrait", 215-26, 272, 274-75, 281
"On Refusal of Aid Between Nations", 248-49
"The Orchard-Pit", 21
"Place de la Bastille, Paris", 248,

250
"The Portrait", 136, 194, 215-26, 228, 266
"Rose Mary", 5, 21, 103-4, 130, 143, 145, 160-78, 184, 191-93, 197, 281
"The Sea-Limits", 232, 236, 238
"Sister Helen", 101-103, 130-31, 141-50, 152-54, 156, 159, 164, 187-88, 191-92, 204, 207
"The Song of the Bower", 245
"Songs of the Art Catholic" (early title for Rossetti's poems), 240, 253
"Soothsay", 233-39, 242, 244
"Spheral Change", 244, 247, 270
"The Staircase of Notre Dame, Paris", 258
"The Stream's Secret", 245, 266
"Words on the Window-pane", 98
"The Woodspurge", 1, 245, 247
"The Staff and Scrip", 103-4, 128, 130-35, 140, 160, 181, 190
"Sudden Light", 134
"Troy Town", 103, 141, 152, 191
"Vox Ecclesiae, Vox Christi", 248-50, 252
"The White Ship", 15, 103-4, 160, 178-84, 192
Rossetti, Elizabeth Siddal ("Lizzie"), 10-11, 93, 100, 197
Rossetti, Frances (wife of Gabriele Rossetti), 11, 196, 258
Rossetti, Lucy Brown, 12, 274
Rossetti, William, 4, 7, 10-11, 95-98, 100, 116, 131, 135, 142, 203, 205, 215, 226, 229, 232, 234, 237, 255, 257, 259, 272
Routh, James, 196
Runden, J., 266
Ruskin, John, 3, 123, 197
Sampson, Ronald, 194
Schneider, Elizabeth, 12
Scott, David, 278-79
Scott, William Bell, 3, 237, 259
    "The Witch's Ballad", 183
    "Rosabell", 277-78
    "A Dream of Love", 277

Sensuality, sensual,
    104. 109, sensuality in "The Bride's Prelude"
    105, 108, sensuality in "The House of Life"
    114, sensual qualities in Patmore
    119, 121, sensuality of Keats and Rossetti
    214-5, 286, sensuality of Wilde's sphinx
    218, sensual response in early Rossetti
    4, 8, 25, 130, 153-54, 220
    See also Sexuality, erotic and sexual love
Sexism, 11, 158
Sexuality, erotic and sexual love,
    2, eroticism of Rossetti's themes
    11, studies of sexual patterns
    18, "House of Life" as meditation on erotic love
    64-65, sexuality in sonnets
    88-91, sexuality in Victorian poetry
    93, sexually authoritarian society
    101, sexual idealism
    108-10, 116, sexuality in "The Bride's Prelude"
    118-20, sexuality in Keats and Rossetti contrasted
    122, 128-30, sexual idealizations of early poems
    125, sexuality in Morris and Rossetti contrasted
    139, Rossetti a sexual moralist
    141-60, ballads of sexual revenge and "Jenny"
    201, sexually agressive woman
    9, 21, 27, 35, 75, 84, 87, 102-4, 139-40, 160, 166, 168, 190, 192, 200, 230, 251, 260, 271, 275, 277, 280, 286
Shakespeare, William, 33, 271
Sharp, William, 96
Shaw, Bernard, 94
Shell, Ada, 167
Shelley, P.B., 7, 61, 96, 256, 270, 275, 280-81
    "Sonnet: England in 1819", 45

"Alastor", 62
"Prometheus Unbound", 65
"The Cloud", 71
"Ozymandias", 213
Shine, Wesley, 120
Silence, 31, 41, 60-63, 75, 106, 202, 224, 226-28, 266
Smith, Alexander, 16
Sonstroem, David, 10, 93, 101, 271
Spasmodics, 12, 15-17, 256-57, 260, 266
Spector, Stephen, 12, 258
Stasis, 87, 105
Stein, Richard, 101
Stevenson, Lionel, Preface, ii
Stoics, stoicism, 237
Surtees, Virginia, 277
Swinburne, Algernon C., 1, 3-4, 9, 14, 16, 49, 53, 56, 68, 77, 84, 91, 96, 116, 123, 141, 192-93, 210, 227, 236, 239-40, 254, 260, 269
  "After Death", 14
  "Laus Veneris", 48
  "Ave Atque Vale", 74
Symbolism,
  Rossetti as early symbolist, 39, 98, 160, 193, 197, 253, 285-86
Symons, Arthur, 3, 8-9
Synaesthesia, 71, 82, 86
Tennyson, Alfred, Preface, i. 1-6, 8-9, 12, 14, 49-50, 52, 62, 65, 72, 90, 99, 114, 119, 123, 149, 159, 193, 195, 202, 211-13, 234, 239, 245-46, 253, 260, 270, 282
  "Adeline", 90
  "The Ballad of Oriana", 90
  "Columbus", 256
  "Crossing the Bar", 247
  "The Day-Dream", 2, 257
  "Eleänore", 90
  Idylls, 90, 190
  "In Memoriam", 2, 18, 53, 76, 89, 94, 99, 225, 233, 235-36, 259
  "Kate", 90
  "The Kraken", 45, 160
  "Lilian", 90
  "Lucretius", 27
  "Margaret", 63, 69
  "Mariana", 246
  Maud, 16, 233-34, 257, 282
  "The Miller's Daughter", 282
  "The Palace of Art", 256
  The Princess, 79-80, 256
  "Tears, Idle Tears", 80
  "Recollections of the Arabian Nights", 50
  "Rosalind", 90
  "Sonnet to J. M. K.", 50
  "Tithonus", 41
  "The Two Voices", 210
  "Ulysses", 26-27
  "A Vision of Sin", 90
Thompson, James, 160
Time, 26-27, 36-37, 41, 85, 89-90, 101, 145, 209, 221-22, 233-34
Tolkien, J.R., 193
Trollope, Anthony, 11
Ulysses, 263
Verlaine, Paul, 285-86
  "Mélancholia", 285
Victorianizing, of Keats and others, 7, 80, 116, 122
Villard, Leonie, 120
Violet the Danseuse, 15
Vogel, Joseph, Preface, ii, 197
von Holst, Theodor
  painting as source for "The Card Dealer", 200, 202, 255
Wahl, J.R., 255
Walter, Jakob, 266
Watts, George, 11
Watts-Dunton, Theodore, 96, 201
Weatherby, Harold, 14, 91
Weinstein, Mark, 12, 14, 16, 257
Wells, Charles, 5, 269-70, 276-77
  Stories After Nature, 15, 134, 276-77
  Joseph and His Brethren, 201, 276-77
Wilde, Oscar, 3-4, 8, 160, 192-93, 213, 237, 260, 273-74, 285-86
  "The Ballad of Reading Gaol", 177-78, 183, 187, 206, 273-74
  "Charmides", 73
  The English Renaissance of Art, 178, 198
  "In the Golden Room", 73
  "The Sphinx", 214, 286

Williams, Charles, 193
Woman, woman image, Lady
  13, woman-like beasts
  23, pious women in early writings
  25-26, seductress in "The Choice: I"
  39-40, woman in 1881 sonnets
  46, elegant qualities in women
  74, 82, 87, 96, Lady in "House of Life"
  104, "Fallen" woman in early work
  122-31, women in "The Bride's Prelude" and *The Defense of Guenevere*
  141-5, 150, 159, women in ballads of sexual revenge, "Sister Helen", "Eden Bower", "Jenny"
  160, "sinning" woman
  170-71, women in "Rose Mary" and Coleridge
  194, 196, women in Victorian period
  227, Rossetti's paintings of women
  251, harlot, 'faithless' woman
  260-61, 263, 265, women in Dante and Rossetti
  266, Poe's dead-woman motif
  268, Blake and fallen woman
  271, Keats and women
  281, women in E.B.B. and Rossetti
  Preface, i, 4-5, 11, 31, 37, 61, 91, 101, 103, 110, 135, 139, 200-4, 206, 218-19, 222
Woolner, Thomas, 122
Wordsworth, William, 7, 50, 76, 192, 274-75, 281
  Sonnets, 45
  "A Slumber Did My Spirit Seal", 274
Work, see Ambition.
Yeats, W.B., 43, 193
  Byzantium, 160, 197